Acknowledgements

Many thanks to all those who contributed their valuable time and effort to the publication of this edition:

Sara Abraham
Kimberly Alazard
Tania Ambridge
Dana Anagnostou
Miiko Anderson
Brahim Aoumaich
Cat Beurnier
Allison Bush
Shannon Byrne
Kathleen Casoli
Annie Cefalu
Sallie Chaballier
Rowena de Clermont-Tonnerre
Amanda Collins
Niki Cook
Heather Coombs
Isabel Cooney Gogibu
Bridget Corbani
Meg Cutts
Kim Dancey
Christopher D'Arcy
Karena D'Arcy
Cathy Delattre
Jennifer Diamant Foulon
Rebecca Dinari
Rhona Dumonthier-Finch
Sara Dupoux
Claire Fitzpatrick
Caronine Garbutt
J. Shay Graydon
Kerry Gregory
Mary Rose Guiné
Josh Hakim
Ming Henderson-Vu Thi
Emily James
Ross James

Myriam Kiperman-Amar
Francesca Lahiguera
Taina Lance
Kirsty Lepage
Andrea Lipieta
Dr. Jocelyn McGinnis
Orianne Morin
Rachel Moss
Heather Nevin
Carina Okula
Laurent Parent Berteau
Caroline Peletengeas
Carole Pelletier
Lyndsay Peters Saussol
Mat Pritchard
Anne-Lise Puget
Diana Ripple
Joanne Robinson
Alison Ryan
Dr. Nancy Salzman
Miriam Sander ten Have
Sophie Schindler
Shui Shakir-Khalil
Lousie Shanks
Lou Simpson
Lara Stancich
Samantha Steed
Amy Terdjman
Stephanie Thom
Lynna Tsou
Stephanie Vannucchi-Bombrun
Claire Varnica
Vicky di Vittorio
Brendi Waks
Alexandra Wood
Pat Zraidi

"Appreciation is a wonderful thing. It makes what is excellent in others belong to us as well." **Voltaire**

Contents

ABCs of Parenting in Paris

5th edition

_____

The essential guide to survive – and thrive – with children in the French capital.

_____

messagEA

A mother support group publication

Project Manager: Dana Anagnostou
Managing Editor: Emily James
Production Manager: Christopher D'Arcy
Business Manager: Lara Stancich

Cover Design and Photo Editor: Rachel Moss
Book Design: J. Shay Graydon

A mother support group publication

The prior editions of this book were published as the *ABCs of Motherhood in Paris*.

ABCs of Motherhood in Paris, 1st edition, 1989/90
Compiled and edited by Lynne Williams Chaillat

ABCs of Motherhood in Paris, 2nd edition, 1992
Edited by Anne Belkind

ABCs of Motherhood in Paris, 3rd edition, 1995
Compiled and edited by Fiona King and Fiona Plucknett

ABCs of Motherhood in Paris, 4th edition, 2001
Project Manager Jessica Paffenbarger
Edited by Josh O'Donovan and Kathleen Rochester

ABCs of Parenting in Paris, 5th edition
Copyright © 2006 by MESSAGE Mother Support Group
ISBN 10 : 2-9505099-4-0
ISBN 13: 978-2-9505099-4-9
Dépôt légal mai 2006

Printed in France by:
RGP
75, division Général Lelerc
92160 Antony

Foreword to 5th Edition of "ABCs of Parenting in Paris"
by Polly Platt

I'm sitting here with the 5th edition of "ABCs of Parenting in Paris" open on my lap, in an ecstasy of envy just looking at in the index: Baby Sitters! Bilingualism! Dentists! Driving in France! and imagining the thrill of moving to Paris with this treasure. No desperation! No staggering around in a bewildered fog!

This book is packed full of everything a foreign mother in Paris needs to know or even possibly might need to know, whether it's prenatal or postnatal, up through the French school system and French bureaucracy. Furthermore, it is clearly, appealingly presented, clearly, concisely written, sensible and sensitive. Bravo to Kay Roudaut, the founder of MESSAGE and Lynne Chaillat, the editor of the first guide in 1984, and the team who put this new 5th edition together.

There was no MESSAGE, no book like this -- other mothers had a husband with a company or an embassy to help -- when I arrived in Paris from Vienna in 1967 with my three half-Austrian, German-speaking daughters, ages 7, 9 and 11. Before rushing back to Vienna, Ande, my new Serbian husband, presented us to his two little French sons, Pierre and Stéphane, ages 3 and 5. Since the Caesarian death of their mother they had been living in Paris with their Roumanian grandparents.

Now, except for the grandparents, we would all be living together. Without Ande. He couldn't give up his job there with a UNESCO branch until he figured out what he might do in Paris to pay the rent.

What language he expected us to communicate in he didn't say. My daughters didn't speak French or even English, though they understood it, sort of. The little French boys spoke only French. In fact, Pierre, the 3 year old, didn't speak anything. For that matter, he could hardly walk. He was autistic, but we didn't know that then. The grandparents said he was a little slow.

The first thing I needed to do was find an au pair, or at least a baby sitter. How should I do that? I'd be driving a lot, what were the things I should know in France -- with its reputation for competing with Spain for the most road accidents in Europe? I needed to find a doctor for Pierre. After a few days it was clear that he wasn't just "a little slow" but practically comatose. He just lay there all day. What kind of a doctor?

I had assumed that the Roumanian grandparents would be helpful. But they had no answers for any of this. It wouldn't have helped much if they did, for my schoolgirl French was Greek to them and their French (they had no other language but Roumanian) was a waterfall for me.

This was the beautiful romantic city everyone raved about? Being stranded alone in the Gobi desert couldn't have been much worse. Besides, my daughters were miserable. They wanted their garden in Vienna.

I finally made my way to the American Cathedral. The then Dean had no time to see anyone who proposed giving less than one million dollars to the Cathedral, but a member of the Junior Guild took pity on me and got me started until Ande got back. She initiated me to the fine points of driving in France (otherwise known as horrors). I found an au pair -- an American who spoke French -- and a dentist for the children who spoke English. I didn't find a doctor for Pierre, that would have to wait until I could convince Ande that this was serious. Meanwhile, the G.P. I did find weighed him, measured his height, and said he was a little slow.

All of this is beautifully indicated and explained in "ABCs of Parenting in Paris". Even facilities for a child like Pierre are tactfully suggested in the Health and Medicine, Childcare and Education chapters. Everything else imaginable is also indicated, even an alert about lead poisoning and advice about breast pumps.

The only thing missing is Trilingualism. Not that this is a pressing concern for anyone else. I didn't realize it was for me, either, until a luncheon one Sunday at a country auberge. Ande was visiting from Vienna, and we had mostly gotten through lunch with our usual language mix: Ande speaking French to the boys, German to the girls and English to me, the girls speaking German to him and to me and trying hard to get a few words in French out to the boys. Stéphane, a great talker, rattled along in fast-forward French I didn't understand a word of.

Towards dessert, the father at the table next to us leaned over to me and said in careful, slow French:
"*Madame*, I think I have understood that you are speaking three languages in your family?"
"*Oui, Monsieur*," I said.
"*Eh bien, Madame*, I'm a doctor, and I must tell you that this is very bad for the children."
To which I longed to say, "Very bad for me too, *Monsieur*!"

Polly Platt is the author of "French or Foe?: Getting the Most Out of Visiting, Living and Working in France" (Distribooks) and "Savoir-Flair: 211 tips for Enjoying France and the French" (Culture Crossings Limited).

Introduction to the 5th Edition of "ABCs of Parenting in Paris"
By *Petite Anglaise*

Living in Paris as an expat is one thing, living in Paris as an expat mother, or mother-to-be, is another kettle of fish entirely.

There I was, feeling as Parisian as the next person, having lived in the city of light for eight long years, when I became pregnant. The little I knew about pregnancy, childbirth and parenthood came from observing friends and their experiences in the UK. At the end of the day, I thought, naïvely, how different could things really be in France? Aside, of course, from the fact that I would obviously need to familiarise myself with a whole new area of vocabulary, so as to be able to hold forth at length about the status of my cervix, as pregnant women have a tendency to do.

A birth plan? "Never heard of one of those!" the French midwife replied, dismissively. "Anyhow, the only say you are likely to get in the matter is at what stage in the proceedings you would like to have an epidural."

Gas and air? "If you are having problems with flatulence, we can have a chat about making some changes to your diet," the gynaecologist said, sympathetically.

This was going to be more complicated that I had thought.

With the benefit of hindsight, I wonder if it might not be a good idea to set up a master class for expat expectant mothers. Modules on surviving Paris: which pushchairs fit through metro turn-stiles when tipped backwards at a 60° angle, the (few) *métro* stations without (many) stairs, the handful of restaurants with genuine no-smoking sections, high chairs and/or changing facilities. Also featuring the "Pushchair Proficiency Test", a diploma designed to teach new mums the skills needed to negotiate the pavements of Paris without any mishaps.

Other optional subjects might include how to speak assertively and obtain that precious "reserved" seat on the bus/*métro*, and how to embark on salary negotiations with a North African nanny who is an expert in the art of bartering.

And of course, last but not least, how to work the system in your favour via judicious use of your offspring. Did you know, for example, that having an under 4 with you entitles you to jump to the front of the queue at the taxi ranks at Paris railway stations? Or that a carte enfant+ entitles up to four people accompanying the child to a 50% discount on trains? Or that supermarkets will deliver your shopping for free if you are visibly pregnant??

In the absence of such a master class, the "ABCs of Parenting in Paris" makes indispensable reading.

Petite Anglaise is the author of a blog about life in Paris, which can be found at www.petiteanglaise.com

Editors' Preface to the 5th Edition

When we first began the editing process for the 5th edition of this book, it was hard to see how we would be able improve on the prior, highly praised edition (then known as the *ABCs of Motherhood in Paris*).

We started by changing the title to *ABCs of Parenting in Paris*, in an effort to reflect the ever-increasing involvement of fathers in the life of their children — a trend we want only to encourage!

We then thought about our own use of the 4th edition, and how impressed we always have been to find information on so many topics. We wanted to underscore the helpfulness of the guide, so we decided to organise the topics into **11 main chapters**:

Activities	Health & Medicine	Shopping
Administration	Living	Travel
Childcare	Organisations & Charities	Work
Education	Pregnancy, Birth & Newborn	

We think the chapter topics are self-explanatory, but to ensure that you can find the information you need we have expanded the **index** and **table of contents**. Also, to help you find your way around the book, we have included **cross-references** throughout – when referring you to another chapter, this will be preceded by ☞, otherwise you can assume that the reference is to another section in the same chapter.

We hope that this will enable you to navigate your way through the guide easily and find easily the topic you need information on. Each chapter has its own **chapter introduction** and a short **chapter table of contents** as well, so by turning to the first page of a chapter you can know quickly whether or not you are looking in the right place.

We also updated and revised the contents of the book, keeping in mind the double focus of living, and being a parent, in Paris. As a result, we have pruned topics that included general parenting or "Paris life" information, and instead added an **Other Resources** section at the end of each chapter, directing you to more general information.

This gave us room to add **brand new sections**, such as an entire chapter on being a working parent in France, focussed guidance on how to choose a maternity facility in Ile de France, extended sections on childcare options and the French education system and lots of additional information on family holidays in France.

We were also able to give readers personal recommendations, tips and practical advice from members of MESSAGE (a network of over 1300 English-speaking families in the Paris area), mainly taken from comments posted on the members-only website, or offered by MESSAGE members in response to our specific requests. You will know you are reading the *opinion of a MESSAGE member* by the bold font that the text is in, and the first name of the member following the quote.

Further, to reflect the huge increase in Internet use since the 4th edition, for almost every topic or resource listed we also give you a **web address** – denoted with 🖳 — to go to for further details. And to help you with your Google searches (not to mention conversing in French!) we've expanded the on-topic **Vocabulary** sections, which are now found at the end of almost every chapter.

What has not changed is that the book is still chock-full of resources and information, and has been researched, complied, written and reviewed by an extensive team of MESSAGE members. In addition a number of chapters have been reviewed by professionals. Whilst every care has been taken to ensure the accuracy of the information in the book, please consult a medical, legal or other practitioner for professional advice relevant to your personal circumstances. Of course, all information though correct to the best of the Editors' knowledge at the time of publication, is subject to change.

If you think we have missed something, you spot something that needs updating, or you know of new information for the next edition, please let us know on abcs@messageparis.org.

Finally, a few pointers:
- we have chosen to use **UK English**, so North American readers should keep this in mind if they find themselves scratching their heads (as one of us often did during our editing meetings) at a particular term, such as nappies, pushchairs, lifts....
- for most addresses we have provided the nearest **métro** stop and one or more **bus** lines that run by the address.
- if it is generally more convenient to drive to a particular location, we have indicated this with 🚗 followed by basic driving instructions,
- for getting to a location by train, you'll see **SNCF** followed by the train station.

Nevertheless, it is a good idea to call ahead or check on the web for the best route from your address . . . especially if you are travelling with a bag full of nappies and a pushchair, since there is often no lift.

We hope that the *ABCs of Parenting in Paris* will be a valuable source of information to you if you have just arrived, and that it will open up new horizons to those of you who have been here a while.

Dana Anagnostou   Emily James
Project Manager   Managing Editor

Activities

Compiled and edited by Heather Coombs, with contributions from Meg Cutts and Caronine Garbutt

In Paris there is so much to do and see that you might not know where to start! This chapter is intended to give you an idea of what is out there and how to find out more. Hopefully you will find it a useful starting point for your explorations. The chapter is divided into the following sections:

A note on getting around: where applicable, we have indicated the closest *métro* station, driving directions, SNCF train stop or bus line that will take you to the activities listed in this section. To ensure that you're taking the quickest route from your home, look up itineraries on 🖳 www.ratp.fr (for public transport), 🖳 www.mappy.fr (if driving), or check out *Le Bus Répertoire des 80 lignes* (available from newsagents) for detailed bus maps (including each stop). ☞Living for information on the French public transport system.

ANIMALS

Here are some ideas for animal-related days out. It is also worth remembering that many parks in Paris and the suburbs have duck ponds and farm zoos (see Parks and Play, below). Do double-check opening times and prices before setting out.

Zoos

Ménagerie du Jardin des Plantes
Jardin des Plantes, 57, rue Cuvier, 75005 Paris
M° Austerlitz or Jussieu, bus 24, 63, 89
Apr - Sep 09h00 - 17h00, Sat 09h00 - 18h00, Sun & public holidays 09h00 - 18h30
Oct - Mar 09h00 - 17h00, Sun & public holidays 09h00 - 17h30
01.40.79.37.94
www.mnhn.fr
Entrance: Adult €6, child €3.50
Founded in 1794 after the French Revolution, this is the oldest zoo in the world still open to visitors. The zoo, aviary and reptile house have 350 mammals, 480 birds and 70 reptiles. And all this in the heart of Paris. It is a great place for little children to run around. Restaurant/snack bar and several picnic tables. Easy pushchair access. No dogs allowed.

Parc Zoologique de Paris
Bois de Vincennes, 53, avenue de St. Maurice, 75012 Paris
M° Porte Dorée, bus 46, 86, 325
Feb - Oct 09h00 - 18h00, Sundays and holidays 09h00 - 18h30.
Nov - Jan 09h00 - 17h00
01.44.75.20.10
Entrance: €5
Large (1,200 animals) and attractive zoo in the Bois de Vincennes. Sandpit/play area, also a train ride around the zoo (charged separately).
Restaurant/snack bar, picnic area near giraffes. Changing table in toilets near the rhino enclosure.

Château de Thoiry
78770 Thoiry-en-Yvelines
40km west of Paris, A13 direction Versailles, A12, N12 direction Dreux, D11 direction Thoiry.
Oct - Apr 10h00 - 17h00
Apr - Sep 10h00 - 18h00
01.34.87.53.76
www.thoiry.tm.fr
Entrance: Adult €26, children €18.50 for all parts of the château, including the safari park. Cheaper entrance for certain parts of the park, see website. A "safari park" with wild animals roaming free. Arrive at opening time as it gets overcrowded on holiday weekends. Miniature tourist trains do a circuit of the zoo and botanical gardens.
Separate entrance fees for gardens (with some zoo animals, reptile house and playground) and château. Tea room, picnic areas and playground for older children.

"Château de Thoiry is a great idea for young kids. There are two parts including a drive-through safari (with herd animals, hippos, rhinos, elephants, giraffes, buffalo, bear, lions and zebras). You drive straight in and pay, then enter the safari park at reduced speed. Allow an hour to complete this part.

After that there is the zoo, so you should park your car as close to the château as you can. There is a fair amount of walking so bring a stroller and bring some change - there is a little train that can drop you at the playground and monkey house for €2. They have otters, wolves, tigers, birds, giant hamsters, monkeys and flamingos, and there is a great playground!!"
Wendy F., American mother of two

Activities

Espace Rambouillet
Office National des Forêts, 3, rue Groussay,
78520 Rambouillet
🚗 50km south-west of Paris, A13, N10 exit
Chevreuse, Cernay-la-Ville. Or from Porte d'Italie,
A10, exit Dourdan.
Jan - Apr 10h00 - 17h00, closed Mon
May - Nov 09h30 - 18h00 daily, 18h30 weekends
and holidays.
Closed Dec.
01.34.83.05.00
💻 www.onf.fr/espaceramb
A wild park stretching over 250 hectares and divided into three "forests". The "Eagle Forest" has over
120 birds of prey in aviaries. There are birds of prey
shows daily, check website for times. The "Deer
Forest" has a discovery path with observation
points. The "Wild Forest" is self-explanatory. Picnic
area with fast food restaurant (in summertime only).
No pets.

L'Ile aux Oiseaux
Chemin d'Arpajon à Lardy, 91630 Cheptainville
🚗 N20, D19, D449 and A6
Open daily 10h00 - 19h00
01.64.56.15.81
💻 www.ileauxoiseaux.com
Entrance: Adult €6.70, child €4.60
Bird watching in a beautiful garden setting.

Aquariums

Centre de la mer, Institut Océanographique
195, rue Saint-Jacques, 75005 Paris
RER B Luxembourg, bus 38, 82, 85, 89, 21, 27
Tue - Fri 10h00 - 12h30, 13h30 - 17h30. Sat, Sun
10h00 - 17h30
01.44.32.10.70
💻 www.oceano.org/cme
Entrance: Adult €4.60, child (under 11) €2
Traditional aquarium with tropical fish. Short educational films on fish. Nice for older children.
Workshops organised. No baby changing facilities.

**Aquarium du Musée National des Arts d'Afrique
et d'Océanie**
293, avenue Daumesnil, 75012 Paris
M° Porte Dorée, bus 46, PC
10h00 - 17h15, closed Tue
01.44.74.84.80
💻 www.musee-afriqueoceanie.fr
Entrance: Adult €4, child €2.60, family ticket (adult
with up to two children under 12) €5
Beautiful aquarium with brightly coloured sea fish
and fresh-water fish, turtles and crocodiles. No
baby changing facilities.

Butterflies (Papillons)

Serre aux papillons
Jardinerie Poullain, 78940 Queue-les-Yvelines
🚗 A13, A12 direction Rambouillet, then N12
direction Dreux, exit La Queue les Yvelines
SNCF from Gare de Montparnasse to Garancières
La Queue les Yvelines
Open daily from late Mar - early Nov 09h30 -
12h00, 14h30 - 18h00
01.34.86.42.99
Entrance: Adult €6, child €4.50
In the atmosphere of an equatorial jungle, over 700
species of butterflies fly around you among orchids
and rare plants. From 10h00 to 15h00, you can see
butterflies emerging from their cocoons. There is
also a butterfly house at the Parc Floral de Paris
(see Parks and Play for details).

Farms

There are many open farms where children can
spend the day and help feed the animals. These
tend to be on the outskirts of Paris, and are often
located in parks.

Ferme de Paris George-Ville
Route du Pesage (behind the Hippodrome de
Vincennes), Bois de Vincennes, 75012 Paris.
M° Château de Vincennes, bus 112
Oct - Mar weekends 13h30 - 17h00
Apr - Sep 13h30 - 19h00
Jul and Aug, Tue - Sun 13h30 - 19h00
01.43.28.47.63

Entrance: €2
A working farm with cows, sheep, goats, donkeys, etc., which children can pet. There are fields of crops, vegetable gardens and fruit trees. You can see how butter is made and how wool becomes yarn. The Bois de Vincennes offers ideal picnic areas, but no other facilities. Guided tours possible.

Ferme Pédagogique du Hameau de la Reine

Hameau de la Reine, Petit Trianon, Château de Versailles, 78000 Versailles
Wed, Sat 14h00 - 16h00 and every afternoon during Zone C school holidays (☞Education)
01.40.67.10.04
Entrance: Adult €5, under 18s free.
Like a little country village set in the grounds of the Château de Versailles, Marie Antoinette herself oversaw the building of this farm. Cows, goats, sheep, swans and ducks, all in an historical setting. There is a special entrance to get to this; you do not have to go through the main Versailles entrance, rather, you can drive straight into the grounds and park, and visit the village.

Ferme Pédagogique d'Ecancourt

95280 Jouy-le-Moutier
🚗 A15 exit 12
RER A Cergy-Préfecture, then bus 48c, stop "Ecancourt"
Mon - Fri 9h00 - 12h00, 13h30 - 18h00.
Sat, Sun and holidays 9h30 - 12h00, 17h00 - 18h00
01.34.21.17.91
🖥 www.villecampagne.org

Ferme du Piqueur

Parc de St Cloud, 92210 St Cloud
Open to public on Wednesdays, weekends and public holidays.
01.46.02.24.53
🖥 www.lafermedupiqueur.com
Opened in 1998 for children aged 4 to 12 years. Workshops (*ateliers*) on Wednesdays and during school holidays with themes related to animals and gardening, etc. Phone in advance to book. Children can pet the animals. Some workshops for parents and children on Sundays.

Ferme Ouverte de Gally

Route de Saint-Cyr to Bailly
78210 Saint-Cyr-l'Écoxe
🚗 25km southwest of Paris, A13, to exit 6 direction Versailles, then D307 direction Bailly, exit Bailly/Noisy-le-Roi, then D7 direction St-Cyr-l'Ecole
Wed, Sat, Sun, public and school holidays 10h00 - 12h30, 14h00 - 18h00
01.30.14.60.60
🖥 www.gally.com
Entrance: Adult €3.30. Child €2.50
A range of animals such as horses, cows, donkeys, goats, sheep, fowl and rabbits. Playground with swings and slide. Picnic tables near the car parks, and a large gardening and plant shop.
Open day in March with attractions suitable for young children, such as blacksmiths, milking of cows, and sheep-shearing. Special activities on Wednesdays and weekends, and special events linked to the major holidays.

ARTS

Arts and Crafts

The arts and crafts stores and associations listed below offer children's courses in painting, drawing, craft jewellery with beads, sculpting with modelling clay, mosaics, collage, scrapbooking, card making, candle decorating and many more. Most of them also offer special workshops during the school holidays, and can supply you with a calendar of events. The courses are held in French.

Loisirs et Création
Carousel du Louvre
99 rue de Rivoli, 75001 Paris
01.58.62.53.95
www.loisirsetcreation.com
The best chain store for children's craft activities and arts and crafts supplies. With branches in Paris and the suburbs, they offer workshops and demonstrations on various craft hobbies (scrapbooking, card-making, jewellery making with beads, ideas for working with modelling clay etc.). The courses are for children of all ages and adults.

BHV
14, rue du Temple, 75004 Paris
Tél : 01 42 74 90 00
www.bhv.fr.
Their fantastic arts and craft department often hosts demonstrations for children and adults. Further information on their website.

Créa - Rougier et Plé
0 825 160 560.
www.crea-tm.fr
Nationwide arts and crafts supplies store offering regular workshops and demonstrations for children and adults. Further information on their website.

La Ferme de Gally
www.gally.com
This is a garden nursery store with a number of branches in the suburbs. They also have a very good crafts department inside the stores. They offer a great variety of craft hobby workshops (mosaïque, scrapbooking, candle decorating, sculpting with modelling clay) for children on Wednesday and Saturday afternoons. For more information you can visit their website (click on *ateliers* et *animations*) or contact them at:
Saint-Cyr-L'Ecole 01.30.14.60.60
Claye-Souilly 01.60.27.26.36
Gometz le Chatel 01.60.12.75.75
Saulx-les-Chartreux 01.69.34.34.44
Sartrouville 01.61.04.64.64

La Maison des Enfants
6, rue du Général de Gaulle
78430 Louveciennes
01.39.69.78.16
This association organises various arts and craft courses to children aged between 5 - 12 years. The courses available are painting, drawing, pottery and ceramics and many more.

Workshops (ateliers)

Creative activities, even for very young children, are usually held on Wednesdays when French schools are closed. Ask at your local *mairie* or *ADAC (Association pour le Développement de l'Animation Culturelle)*. Paris also has over 40 *Centres d'Animation et Espaces Jeunes*, that are run through the *mairies*. In the suburbs, try the community centres (*Maison des Associations, Centres de Loisirs* or *MJC, Maisons des Jeunes et de la Culture*).

ADAC de la Ville de Paris hosts a huge range of courses for children of all ages and for adults as well. The courses available range from painting (all media), drawing, sculpting, pottery & ceramics, *bandes dessinées* (comic strips and how to create your own comic book), engraving on lino cuts, music, drama and many more. The courses take place in studios all over central Paris and are open to anyone living in Paris or in Ile de France.

ADAC Ville de Paris
Maison des Ateliers
Les Halles, 75001 Paris
Mon - Fri 14h00 - 18h00
01.42.33.45.54
🖥 www.adacparis.com
To request a brochure on all the courses available, you can send an e-mail to info@adacparis.com

Many museums and larger toyshops organise workshops with a theme, as do some theme parks such as the Jardin d'Acclimatation (see Theme Parks, below).

Frimousse magazine and *Le Paris des Tout-Petits* are both excellent sources of information on workshops.

Arts and Crafts in English

Pottery

Atelier du Soleil in Louveciennes offer pottery courses for both children and adults. For more information contact Sandra on 01.39.18.55.74

Scrapbooking in English

Both children and adults can take scapbooking classes and participate in regular workshops and crop groups by contacting Caronine Garbutt on 06.10.98.43.05.

Circuses

Touring circuses put up posters advertising their visits, both in Paris and the suburbs. Performances are usually on weekends and Wednesday afternoon. Below are some of the best permanent circuses in Paris.

Cirque Alexandra Bouglione
Jardin d'Acclimatation, Bois de Boulogne, 75016 Paris
M° Les Sablons

Performances all year, Wed, Sat, Sun
01.45.00.87.00

Cirque du Grande-Celeste
22 rue Paul Meurice, 75020 Paris
M° Porte-des-Lilas
Performances Sat, Sun, school holidays. Closed May - August.
01.53.19.99.13
🖥 www.grandceleste.com

Cirque d'Hiver Bouglione
110, rue Amelot, 75011 Paris
M° Filles du Calvaire, Oberkampf, Saint Sébastien Froissart
End Oct - end Jan
01.47.00.12.25
Rumoured to be the best in Paris, this is one of the rare traditional circuses with an orchestra.

Or why not try getting in the ring?

Cirqu'Aouette - Centre d'initiation aux arts et techniques du cirque
25, rue Auguste Lançon, 75013 Paris
M° Corvisart
01.45.80.29.75
🖥 www.cirquaouette.org
A circus school for children aged 3 to 12.

Film in English

Many cinemas in and around Paris show films in their original English version. When looking for a film, be sure the showing you want is in *Version Originale (V.O.)*. Many films for children are dubbed into French (*Version Française*, or *V.F.*), so always check first to avoid disappointment! If you are keen on seeing a children's film in English during the day, it is advisable to plan on going immediately after the film is released. After the first week or so, many cinemas then only show the English version in the evenings, at the showings (*séances*) after 19h00 or 20h00. The bigger cinemas usually have a screen showing *V.O.*, at a wider range of times and the UGC *Ciné Cités* at Forum des Halles, Bercy and la

Défense show films in *V.O.* during the day.

Forum des Images
Forum des Halles, Porte St. Eustache, 75001 Paris
01.44.76.62.00
💻 www.forumdesimages.net
The *Forum des Images* in Les Halles occasionally shows English-language films in their children's program. Showings are at 15h00 Wednesdays and Saturdays, with a discussion and snack afterwards.

Music

Cité de la Musique
Daily 12h00 - 18h00, closed Mon
01.44.84.44.84
💻 www.cite-musique.fr
Located in the Parc de la Villette (see Parks and Play) this museum is a treasure trove of musical instruments. It also runs activities for children from age 8 (sign up for between 16 and 30 sessions), on weekends for families, and concerts for children from age 3.

Opéra de Paris-Bastille
Place de la Bastille, 75012 Paris
M° Bastille
0 892 89 90 90, ask for the brochure "*Jeune public*"
💻 www.operadeparis.fr
The *Opéra National de Paris* runs a programme of shows designed for children from age 3, featuring both music and dance (*spectacles pour enfants*).

La Mi-Pierrot
72 rue des Grands-Champs, 75020 Paris
M° Nation
01.43.56.32.45
This association offers music classes for children from birth to age 7, featuring action songs and rhymes and listening activities.

Musical Activities in English
American Church. (☞Organisations and Charities) The American Church runs a youth music pro-gramme which takes place on Wednesdays and offers activities for ages 3 - 18. Activities include a "cherub choir" for the pre-school age group, a prep choir for 7 - 8 year olds, and a children's choir and handbells for ages 8 - 11. There is also a youth choir and handbells for teenagers. For more infor-mation about the groups, contact Bonnie Woolley on bw@respirando.net.

Music Together
💻 www.musictogether.com
A music and movement approach to early childhood music development for babies, toddlers, and young children. Groups meet weekly at members' homes. For information about current locations, or setting up a new group, email cmMusicTogether@wanadoo.fr.

Puppet Shows

Le Guignol, also known as *les Marionnettes*, is a traditional French entertainment for children. They are interactive puppet shows, performed in small theatres located in parks all over Paris. Most stories feature the servant Guignol whose adventures inevitably require him to address the audience directly. Children love shouting responses and become active participants.

Outdoor *Guignol* theatres present short, Punch-and-Judy style shows which run for about 20 min-utes. They are rather flexible regarding starting times as they may wait until enough children are present. Some will only perform if the weather is nice enough. They are usually open from April until October.

Indoor theatres generally feature longer versions (about 45 minutes, including an intermission) of familiar children's stories, with large casts of hand puppets and lavish sets.

Most puppet theatres are open on Saturday, Sunday and Wednesday afternoons starting at about 15h00, plus every day during school holi-days. Very few have morning performances.

The ideal age range is 3 to 7 years, but younger children are welcome too. Some theatres can be reserved for birthday parties. Performances usually cost around €3.

Always check *Pariscope* and *Frimousse* for times, prices and current attractions.

Theatre

Paris is a great place for children's theatre, although there is a lot of talking on stage. Most performances are on Wednesday, Saturday and Sunday afternoons. Check *Pariscope* or *Frimousse* for current listings.

Theatre in English:
International Players
9 rue Claude Liard, 92380 Garches
01.47.01.01.91
🖳 www.internationalplayers.info
Amateur Anglophone theatre group, based in Le Pecq and St-Germain-en-Laye, puts on two shows a year. There are over 60 members of all ages and various nationalities and they welcome new members every year from Paris.

The Kiosque jeunes

Kiosque jeunes are cultural information points for young people under 28. As well as distributing guides and brochures, their ticket offices (*billetteries*) offer cheap or free tickets for shows, films, the theatre, exhibitions or sporting events.

Kiosque jeunes Bastille
14, rue François Miron, 75004 Paris
M° Bastille
01.42.76.22.60
Mon - Fri 10h00 - 19h00

Kiosque jeunes Champ de Mars
101, quai Branly, 75015 Paris
M° Bir-Hakeim
01.43.06.15.38
Mon - Fri (closed Thurs morning) 10h00 - 18h00

Theatre Classes

For theatre, dance and music classes you can check at your *mairie* in September: - over 40 *centres d'animations* offer classes in all kinds of disciplines for 4 to 13 year olds. There are also the workshops (almost 400) of the ADAC (*Association pour le Développement et l'Action Culturelle*) for 3 to 14 year olds in a wide range of subjects, including music and drama.

Association du Théâtre pour l'Enfance et la Jeunesse (ATEJ)
99-103 rue de Sèvres, 75006 Paris
01.44.18.44.86
🖳 www.atej.net
Publishes an annual guide entitled *Théâtre en France pour les Jeunes Spectateurs*, with 600 useful addresses. Order on their website.

Children's Theatre in French
Abricadabra Théâtre - Péniche Antipode
Opposite 69, quai de la Seine, 75019 Paris
M° Riquet, Jaurès, bus 60
01.40.03.03.84
🖳 http://abricadabra.nerim.net
Performances Wed, Sun and school holidays, mid Jun - end Sept
Entrance: €6
For children from one year

Activities

Antre Magique
50, rue Saint Georges, 75009 Paris
M° Saint Georges
01.39.68.20.20
Magic theatre accessible to 1 year olds and up.
Children participate, but you need to phone and
reserve.

Théâtre Astral
Parc Floral (East side), route de la Pyramide,
75012 Paris
M° Château de Vincennes, RER A Vincennes, bus
46, 112
01.43.71.31.10
Indoor theatre for 3 to 8 year olds near playgrounds. Wednesday and Sunday afternoons, and
during school holidays. Separate entrance fee.

BOOKS

Many libraries and bookshops offer activities to get children interested in reading, normally in the form of
storytime (*heures de conte*), or themed and author events. These are often held on Wednesday afternoons or weekends.

Libraries

Libraries (*bibliothèques*) in France are state-run,
and generally very well-equipped. They are also
sometimes called *mediathèques*, which means that
they include CD, DVD and video sections and,
sometimes, a cinema.

Larger libraries often stock a small selection of
books in English, both for adults and children, and it
is always worth asking.

Municipal libraries in Paris are open all year round
from Tuesday to Saturday. The children's sections
are open all day on Wednesdays and Saturdays,
and after school (normally from 16h30) on
Tuesdays, Thursdays and Fridays.

Reading of books, newspapers and magazines is
free, but to borrow you need to join. Membership is
not limited to residents of Paris - those in the suburbs can also join a Paris library. Books can be borrowed for free, but CDs, videos and audiocassettes
require an annual subscription fee. To join, you
need to present a form of identification, and a proof
of address (*justificatif de domicile*) such as a utility
bill (*facture EDF/GDF, France Telecom*) or a rent
receipt (*quittance de loyer*) less than three months

old. For minors, parental authorisation is required.
This means you must go along with the child, show
your identification, leave a photocopy of the child's
identification, and present either a utility bill or rent
receipt.

Envue jeunesse, a quarterly programme of children's events at Paris libraries, is downloadable
from www.paris-bibliotheques.org. The website
also has a list of libraries by *arrondissement*.

Municipal libraries in the suburbs may charge a
membership fee, though child membership is often
free. Opening times will also be different from those
of Paris libraries, so it is best to call for details. For
library activities in the suburbs, contact your local
mairie.

Children's Libraries with Books in English
American Library in Paris
10, rue du Général-Camou, 75007 Paris
Tue - Sat 10h00 - 19h00
01.53.59.12.60
www.americanlibraryinparis.org
The best English language lending library in the
Paris region - its children's and young adult collection contains over 8,000 volumes. It is open to all

nationalities, with a range of membership options.

The library offers numerous activities for children from age one. The Mother Goose Lap Sit, featuring English rhymes, songs and stories, is for toddlers aged 1 to 3. All toddlers must have an adult lap to sit on. It takes place twice a month and lasts 30 minutes. Sign up in advance.

For 3 to 5 year olds, there is a weekly story hour held on Wednesdays, with both a morning and an afternoon session. The programme often features filmstrips, puppets, or feltboard stories. No sign-up is necessary.

Examples of events for 6 to 12 year olds include visits from professional story tellers and authors, introductions to Shakespeare, and weekly creative expression events.

There are also events aimed at teenagers.

MESSAGE Library

An English language library launched in 2003 run by, and for the use of, MESSAGE members. It currently opens for one Wednesday morning per month 10h00 - 12h00 at St George's Church in the 16th *arrondissement* (☞Organisations and Charities), and has a growing stock of books for children, plus tapes and educational CDs. The adults' section includes books and videos about parenting and life in France. Book donations welcome. For further details contact: library@messageparis.org

Municipal Libraries

The following are Paris municipal libraries that specialise in children's books, and that also have books in English:

Bibliothèque Isle Saint-Louis
21, rue St Louis en l'Isle, 75004 Paris
M° Pont Marie
01.43.25.58.21

Bibliothèque l'Heure Joyeuse
6/12, rue des Prêtres Saint Séverin, 75005 Paris
M° St-Michel
01.43.25.83.24
Oldest children's library in Paris; has beautiful old books.

Bibliothèque Courcelles
17 ter, avenue Beaucour, 75008 Paris
M° Ternes
01.47.63.22.81

Bibliothèque Brochant
6, rue Fourneyron, 75017 Paris
M° Brochant
01.42.28.69.94

Bibliothèque Lancry
11, rue de Lancry, 75010 Paris
M° Jacques Bonsergent, République
01.42.03.25.98

Bibliothèque Diderot
42, avenue Daumesnil, 75012 Paris
M° Gare de Lyon
01.43.40.69.94

Bibliothèque Gutenberg
8, rue de la Montagne d'Aulas, 75015 Paris
M° Lourmel, Balard
01.45.54.69.76

Bibliothèque Benjamin-Rabier
141, rue de Flandre, 75019 Paris
M° Crimée
01.42.09.31.24

Bibliothèque Orteaux
40, rue des Orteaux, 75020 Paris
M° Alexandre Dumas
01.43.72.88.79

Here are some libraries in the suburbs that stock English books:

Bibliothèque Municipale
20, rue Maurice Labrousse, 92160 Antony
01.40.96.17.17

Bibilothèque de la Mairie
1, avenue Jean-Jaurès, 92140 Clamart
01.46.62.36.52

Bibliothèque-discothèque Jacques Prévert
6, passage Jacques Prévert, 92700 Colombes
Bus 164, 167, 176, 304: Eglise de Colombes
01.47.84.85.46

Mediathèque Meaux,
4, rue Cornillon, 77100 Meaux
01.64.36.40.59

Espace Landowski
28, avenue André Morizet, 92100 Boulogne
Billancourt
M° Marcel Sembat
01.55.18.46.10

Bookshop Activities in English

For bookshop addresses and tips on where to buy children's books in English (☞Shopping).

Finding reading activities in English is a priority for many parents. Here is a list of options:

Brentano's Kids' Bookworm Club
🖥 www.brentanos.fr/pages/clubs/kidsclub
For children aged 3 to 9 years old. Activities take place on average once a month at the bookshop in the 2nd *arrondissement*, and are mostly oriented around American holidays. They include story reading and arts and craft activities, such as making Valentine's cards, Easter eggs, Halloween trick-or-treat bags, and snowflakes. Many activities take place downstairs in the children's department (spiral staircase, no lift).

Club members receive a bimonthly Kids' Newsletter announcing the events, which must be reserved in advance. Annual membership is €15.

WH Smith Kids' Club
🖥 www.whsmith.fr
Reading sessions, activities and treats, once a month on a Wednesday afternoon at 15h30. It is free and lasts about three quarters of an hour. Children's department on first floor, no lift.

The Red Wheelbarrow Bookstore
🖥 www.theredwheelbarrow.com
Hosts events with children's illustrators and writers. Send an email to red.wheelbarrow@wanadoo.fr to be added to the mailing list.

MESSAGE Events

For MESSAGE members, many meetings are organised around a book theme. In addition to the regular library meetings (see above), these range from storytime sessions and "lap sits" to book swapping meetings and monthly read-alongs for school-age kids at Shakespeare & Co. If you are a MESSAGE member, see your latest MESSAGE Magazine for a list of current activities in your area.

INDOOR PLAY AND RAINY DAYS

Getting out and about in bad weather can be a challenge... Here are some ideas for places to play indoors, other than the bedroom or the living room. For more ideas, see Meeting Places below.

Ludothèques

The beauty of *ludothèques*, which are essentially toy and board game lending libraries, is that they are open to all ages and provide a free space to sit and play. They are great places to visit when you want to get out of the house, especially if you have children of different ages to entertain. Parents or carers must stay with children under 8.

Ludothèques are fairly cheap to join (they are state-run), normally requiring a modest annual subscription. To become a member you will be expected to provide a proof of address such as a utilities bill (*facture EDF/GDF* or *France Télécom*) or rent receipt (*quittance de loyer*) and proof of identity. Often membership is limited to local residents. Toys and board games can be borrowed in the same way as books from libraries. *Ludothèques* also organise children's events based around toys.

To find your local *ludothèque*, and there will almost certainly be one in your town or *arrondissement*, contact:

Association des Ludothèques Françaises
01.43.26.84.62
🖳 www.alf-ludotheques.org

Indoor Play Areas

Antrebloc
5-7, rue Henri Barbusse, 94800 Villejuif
01.47.26.52.44
🖳 www.antrebloc.com
Walls, blocks and various shapes for those who love to climb. Suitable for children over 7 accompanied by an adult. Lessons and holiday courses available.

JumpFun
2, avenue de Bures (Chemin de Melan), 78540 Marsinval, Vernouillet
🚗 A14 or A13 exit Poissy-Orgeval.
Wed, Sat, Sun from 14h30
🖳 www.jumpfun78.com
Entrance fee €6
A multi-level adventure play area for ages 2 to 12. A good birthday party venue (reserve in advance).

Ludimax
ZAC du Trianon, rue de la Pépinière, 78450 Villepreux
01.72.33.90.90
🖳 www.ludimax.fr
10h00 - 18h00 every day.
Closed Tue during school term.
Entrance fee €7 for children 2 and up on weekends and Wed, €6 on schooldays, €2.50 for 1 year olds. Adults and babies free.
An indoor amusement area with huge structures for the children to climb on and explore. Organises birthdays and has a snack counter and tables where parents can sit while the children play. A great place to meet other Anglophone parents and kids.

Activities

Playmobil Funpark
22-24, rue de Jachères, Parc Silic Fresnes
94260 Fresnes
RER B to Antony, then bus 396 to La Cerisaie
A86 exit Fresnes or A6 exit Rungis-Delta,
then N186 direction Versailles and first exit.
10h00 - 19h00 every day. Closed Mon during
school term.
01.49.84.94.44
www.playmobil.com
Entrance fee: €1.50 (free for under 3)
A large play centre which is well-stocked with the
Playmobil range of toys. The large room is divided
into themes - pirate ships, jungle, cowboys and indi-
ans, train, zoo/farm, doll houses, and there are several games set-up in each area with bins full of
fencing, animals, figurines, etc, related to each
theme. Cafeteria with light lunch available. Baby
changing facilities, bottle-warmer, high chairs. Be
warned: the exit is via the boutique.

Ideas for Indoor Play for under Three's

It is often hard to know what to do with this age group on a rainy day. Here are some ideas and some suggestions from MESSAGE members:

- **Musée Antoine Bourdelle** - lots of room to run around and all the sculptures are out of reach!
- **La Villette, Cité des Sciences** – free entry to the area with fish tanks downstairs.
- **Musée d'Oceanie et Arts Africains** – large aquarium in the basement, with plenty of room for chil-
  dren to let off steam!
- In the **Fnac Eveil et Jeux** shops, there is usually a children's play area.

*"I have even taken the PC bus 45 minutes in one direction, then stopped for a snack, and got back
on the other way to come home. Other ideas: we live near a bus station (Porte d'Auteuil) We used
to go and watch the buses come and go! And the bus drivers would let him climb on before the timer
rang for them to go!" Ami S., American mother of three.*

*"I was really impressed by the offerings at Ludimax for the under 2 set - a mini play area that has
several activity tables and assorted toys. There is also an isolated "play kitchen" area that you can
sit in while your child plays. The great thing about Ludimax is that you as a parent have access to
every area of the facility so if you want to walk, climb, roll, etc. and stay with your child while he/she
plays, it's no problem and they do encourage that - it's all cushioned and very adult-friendly as
well!" Cat B., American mother of one.*

MEETING PLACES

Feeling isolated is one of the most common complaints among parents of young children, and loneliness is an especially easy trap to fall into when you're living in a foreign country with little family support and few established friendships.

If you do not speak French, a good starting point for newcomers are the churches and associations, including MESSAGE, linked to the large expatriate community in and around Paris. They offer many routes to make friends and get involved in community life (☞Organisations and Charities).

The following ideas and addresses are aimed mostly at families with children under six.

Parent and Child Drop-in Centres (Accueil parents-enfants)

These French-speaking centres are usually open to children up to ages 3 or 4 (though some welcome children up to 6), accompanied by an adult. Some ask for a small financial contribution. They are especially useful if you are unable to find a place in an *halte-garderie* (☞Childcare), but would like your child to be in a group with other children. However, in these centres you must remain with the child. There are a variety of toys and books for the children, and some also have a special area for playing with water where little ones can pour and splash to their hearts' content without soaking your home! (For other play areas see Indoor Play and Rainy Days, and Parks and Play).

La Maison Verte

Most of the drop-in centres listed below were inspired by the concept of the *Maison Verte*, the brainchild of the French psychoanalyst Françoise Dolto.

In Dolto's own words, the *Maison Verte* is "a place where tiny children can play and interact with their parents. A place to develop an interactive social life right from birth, for parents who sometimes feel very alone with the everyday problems they are having with their children. Neither a day-care centre nor a play group, much less a clinic, this is a home where mothers, fathers, and little children come to meet friends."

Every *Maison Verte*, or affiliated institution, is autonomous. They are organised as independent non-profit associations. During opening times, visitors can just drop in, without making an appointment and may stay for just a few minutes or for an entire afternoon. Visitors may be asked to make a small contribution to the running of the *Maison Verte*, usually €1 or €2.

For addresses and information on the *Maison Verte* (in English) consult 💻www.francoise-dolto.com.

PMI Centres

The *Centres de Protection Maternelle and Infantile (PMI)*, are first and foremost state-funded medical centres for children aged up to 6 and their parent. (☞Health and Medicine).

But *PMI* centres often organise weekly playgroups (*accueils jeunes*), aimed at supporting parents and providing little ones with a place to play. There are often health professionals on hand to answer parents' questions. Above all, the meetings are a good way to meet other local parents.

For a list of *PMI* centres in Paris, visit 💻 www.paris.fr and for addresses in the suburbs, contact your local *mairie*.

Le café de l'école des parents
164, boulevard Voltaire, 75011 Paris

Social Activities in English for Older Children

As your children grow up, keeping up their English and helping them feel 'connected' with other English speakers will be far easier if they have English-speaking friends and social contact.

Here are some ideas for where to find them!

British Scouts

There are British Scout Association groups in Chantilly, Maisons Laffitte and Bougival for age 6 and over. Here is an overview of the activities of the Chantilly group:

The Scouts in Chantilly boast about 50 members including beavers, cubs and scouts. All the sections are mixed, boys and girls aged 6 to 15. Each group meets twice a month in the scout hall at St Peter's Church (☞Organisations and Charities). Many of the meetings, especially in the summer, are outdoor including camps, hikes, bike rides or other adventure activities in the nearby forests. The materials and award programmes from the British Scout Association are used, and all meetings are conducted in English (except for venture activities with French qualified instructors).

For further information on these scout groups, contact Gill Barratt (District Commissioner) on 01.45.33.92.87

USA Girl Scouts

There are over 250 Girl Scouts in the USA Girl Scouts Overseas Paris neighbourhood from ages 4 to 17. Membership is open to American girls living overseas and girls of all nationalities attending an American or International school. There are Daisy troops for four and five year olds; Brownie troops for girls 6 - 8; Junior troops for girls from 8 - 11, and a "Studio 2B program" for the 11 - 17 year old crowd.

Some troops are organized at schools; others meet in members' homes. Meetings are either monthly or every other week, depending on the needs of the girls in the troop. Trained Girl Scout adults advise and assist the girls during all meetings and activities.

See 🖥www.parisgirlscouts.org for further information.

Boarding School Children

The British and Commonwealth Women's Association (☞Organisations and Charities) run a group during school holidays for children at boarding schools outside France.

From the BCWA website: "The aim of the boarding school group within the BCWA is to provide a support network both for the young people who are away at school, and for their mothers. We meet regularly over coffee to exchange news and plan holiday activities for the 9 - 18 year olds. We find that as the older children become more independent they begin to develop friendships, and contact each other when they are at home to plan outings or parties for themselves."

M° Charonne
Tue 10h00 - 22h00, Wed - Sat 10h00 - 19h00
01.43.67.54.00
www.cafe-des-parents.com
A café where parents can meet, chat, and use the Internet. Their programme of workshops and debates is available on the website.

English Language Playgroups

The parent-organised playgroup is a rare beast in France, where professionally-run drop-in centres and state-run childcare are a speciality. However, the English-speaking community has more than filled the gap. Playgroups differ from childcare in that parents are expected to stay with their children, or at least stay on a rota basis to help with the organisation.

Many churches and associations that serve the English-speaking community have regular playgroups that use their premises. At the time of going to press, regular playgroups were being held at St George's Church in the 16th *arrondissement*, St Michael's Church in the 8th *arrondissement*, the American Church in the 7th *arrondissement*, the Holy Trinity Church in Maisons Lafitte and St Peter's Church in Chantilly (☞Organisations and Charities).

Another way of finding a local playgroup is to join MESSAGE, whose members organise social events, including regular playgroups or park meetings throughout Paris and the surrounding areas. And if there is no regular playgroup near you, belonging to MESSAGE makes it easy to start one up yourself.

Activities

MUSEUMS

Paris is, of course, teeming with many excellent museums, from the world-famous Louvre, Musée d'Orsay and Centre Pompidou, to the offbeat Musée de la Contrefaçon - and everything in between . Most of the large, and many of the smaller, museums have lots to interest children and the guidebooks listed in the Other Resources section at the end of this chapter are a great source of ideas and information for a cultural or educational outing.

Art

Here are some MESSAGE members' favourite museums on an arty theme for children:

Musée en Herbe
Jardin d'Acclimatation, Bois de Boulogne
75016 Paris
M° Les Sablons
Mon - Fri 10h00 - 18h00, Sat 14h00 - 18h00 (Sat during school holidays 10h00 - 18h00)
01.40.67.97.66
www.musee-en-herbe.com
Entrance: €3
Suitable for children from age 3, this museum aims to introduce children to artistic activities, and encourage an interest in the world around them, thanks to many interactive exhibits. Runs children's workshops.

Musée Dali Espace Montmartre
11, rue Poulbot, 75018 Paris
M° Abbesses
Open daily 10h00 - 18h30
Jul - Aug 10h00 - 21h30
01.42.64.40.10
www.daliparis.com
Entrance : Adult €7, child (age 8 - 26) €5
Great fun for both children and adults, the voice of Salvador Dali himself guides you around this collection of sculptures and other art works. Also runs workshops for children.

Musée de l'Union Centrale des Arts Décoratifs
107, rue de Rivoli, 75001 Paris
M° Palais Royale-musée du Louvre
01.44.55.57.50

www.ucad.fr
Entrance : Adult €6, child (under 18) free
A huge selection of applied and decorative art from the Middle Ages to the present day. The exhibits illustrate different artistic techniques involving wood, metal, ceramics and glass. Also runs workshops for children.

Musée Marmottan-Monet
2, rue Louis-Boilly, 75016 Paris
M° La Muette
10h00 - 18h00, closed Mon
01.44.96.50.33
www.marmottan.com
Entrance: Adult €6.50
Opposite the Jardin de Ranelagh in beautiful buildings, this museum has many impressionist works by Monet, Pissarro and Renoir.

Musée Rodin
77, rue de Varenne, 75007 Paris
M° Varenne
Open all year, closed Mon
Gardens only 09h30 - 16h45 (summer),
09h30 - 17h00 (winter)
Museum and gardens Apr - Sept 09h30 - 17h45,
Oct - Mar 09h30 - 16h45
01.44.18.61.24
Entrance: €5 (€1 gardens only), free 1st Sunday of the month.
Lovely gardens with sculptures for children to run around in. There is a cafeteria in the museum. Entrance to the gardens is free if you have a pushchair with you - and there are two sandpits situated right at the far end of the gardens, behind the high hedges.

Science Museums

Whether your child is into biology or paleontology or just likes interactive science museums, Paris and the suburbs have a lot to offer.

Musée National d'Histoire Naturelle
36, rue Geoffroy Saint Hilaire, 75005 Paris
M° Jussieu, Gare d'Austerlitz, bus 24, 63, 67, 89
01.40.79.36.00
🖳 www.mnhn.fr
This is a group of natural history museums in Paris and throughout France. Its Paris address is next to the Jardin des Plantes. Once inside the park, the museums are spread out among various galleries, each with separate opening times and entrance fees:

Grande Galerie de l'Evolution
Open daily 10h00 - 18h00 except Tue
Entrance: Adult €8, child (4 - 18) €6
Opened in 1994 to great reviews. Displays on evolution covering all living creatures, including an exhibit of extinct and endangered species.

Galerie d'Anatomie Comparée et de Paléontologie
Open daily 10h00 - 17h00 except Tue
Entrance: Adult €6, child (4 - 18) €4
Skeletons of all the vertebrates in the world, fossils, large crystals.

Galerie de Minéralogie and Salle au Trésor
Open daily 10h00 - 17h00 except Tue
Entrance: Adult €6, child (4 - 18) €4
Giant crystals and precious stones.

Galerie Paléobotanique
Open daily 10h00 - 17h00 except Tue
Entrance: Adult €6, child (4 - 18) €4
A cross section of a 2,000 year old tree with arrows marking events in history, exhibits on the history of the plant world.

Galerie d'Entomologie
Weekdays 13h00 - 18h00 except Tue, weekends 10h00 - 18h00
Entrance: Adult €6, child (4 - 18) €4
The world of insects in 1,500 specimens.

Serres (Great Greenhouses)
Weekdays 13h00 - 18h00 except Tue, weekends 10h00 - 18h00
Entrance: Adult €6, child (4 - 18) €4
Tropical plants from around the world.

Musée de l'Homme
17, place du Trocadéro, 75116 Paris
01.40.79.36.00
M° Trocadéro, bus 22, 30, 32, 63, 72, 82
Weekdays 09h45 - 17h15 except Tue, weekends 10h00 - 18h30
Entrance: Adult €7, child (4 - 13) €5
A small, approachable museum that you can get round in a couple of hours.
Do not miss the skeleton of Lucy, an anthropoid from Ethiopia which dates back 3.2 million years. The museum originally consisted of a mixture of objects from the Royal Cabinet, curiosity cabinets dating back to the 16th century and anthropological exhibits. It is undergoing major renovations to cover the history of man in the context of natural history and culture, starting with the origin of man as a species.

Cité des Sciences et de l'Industrie
30, avenue Corentin-Cariou, 75930 Paris
M° Porte de la Villette, bus 75, 139, 150, 152, PC1 and PC2
Parking between the quai de la Charente and Boulevard Macdonald
Tue - Sun 10h00 - 18h00
01.40.05.70.00 / 01.40.05.80.00
🖳 www.cite-sciences.fr
Entrance: Permanent exhibits: Adult €7.50, child (7 - 18) €5 Planetarium : €3 supplement
Cité des enfants : €5
The Cité des Sciences et de l'Industrie is well worth going to the edge of Paris to visit. The exhibits in the main part of the museum cover all aspects of science and industry and include interactive exhibits.

However, the highlight of the museum for families is undoubtedly the Cité des Enfants. This section is split into two separate areas: one for 3 - 5 year olds and one for 5 - 12 year olds, but kids of any age can enter either side.

The section for younger children includes a "construction" site where they can help build a house out of cardboard bricks, using wheelbarrows and mechanical cranes. It also has an exhibit where they can play with boats in canals (waterproof smocks provided).

The 6 - 12 section includes an ant farm tunnel made of plexiglass that the children can crawl through, a butterfly room, TV cameras they can use to film each other and a fountain with four pumps demonstrating four different pump techniques.

The complex also includes the Géode IMAX cinema in the round, a submarine, an aquarium and it is attached to the Parc de la Villette, a large modern park with a great dragon slide (on the side of the main building) and various "follies" (see Parks and Play).

The museum is extremely popular and it is a good idea to phone on the morning of your visit to reserve tickets or buy them in advance on-line. The tickets are valid for a specific two hour period. If you try to buy them on arrival at the museum you may end up with tickets for several hours later.

Palais de la Découverte
avenue Franklin D. Roosevelt, 75008 Paris
M° Champs-Elysées Clémenceau, Franklin D. Roosevelt, RER Invalides, bus 28, 42, 52, 63, 72, 73, 80, 83, 93
Tue - Sat 09h30 - 18h00, Sun, public holidays 10h00 - 19h00
01.56.43.20.20
🖳 www.palais-decouverte.fr
Entrance: Adults €6.50, child (under 18) €4.
The Palais de la Découverte is an interactive children's science museum covering chemistry, physics, maths, geophysics, life sciences, astrono-

my and astrophysics. Centrally located just off the Champs Elysées, it is a big favorite with French children and has fun exhibits for kids such as an electric globe that makes their hair stand on end, a planetarium (for a supplement), a rat laboratory, the Pi room and an acoustics room.

Exploradome
Bois de Boulogne, Jardin d'Acclimatation, Neuilly entrance, 75116 Paris
M° Pont de Neuilly, bus 93, 43
Open daily 10h00 - 18h00. Closed first two weeks of August and major holidays.
01.53.64.90.40
🖳 www.exploradome.com
Entrance: Adult €5, child €3.50
Some 40 hands-on exhibits in this small children's science museum. The motto of the Exploradome is "it is strictly forbidden NOT to touch", which accurately sums up the spirit of the place. Children can make ring shaped clouds out of fog, play with optical illusions, see the effects of wind on sand or play with a square wheel. It is a small museum, but worth a visit if you are in the Jardin d'Acclimatation (It also has the benefit of being indoors in case of a sudden change in weather!).

Extra Activities at the Exploradome

Workshops
The Exploradome also has scientific and multimedia workshops for children aged 5 and up. If you sign your child up for a workshop, you can purchase a combined visit/workshop ticket for €8, which is cheaper than the individual tickets.

Parties
The Exploradome can be rented for children's birthday parties for a fee of €22, or €25 including brunch, per child.

Musée des Arts et Métiers
60 rue Réaumur, 75003 Paris
M° Arts et Métiers, Réaumur-Sébastopol, bus 20, 38, 39, 47
Tue - Sun 10h00 - 18h00, Thu 10h00 - 21h30
01.53.01.82.00
💻 www.arts-et-metiers.net
Entrance: Adult €6.50, child (under 18) free
The deceptively titled Arts and Crafts Museum is actually dedicated to technical innovations from the 16th century to modern day. Exhibits include the plane used by Louis Blériot for the first-ever channel crossing and the first movie cameras. There are daily thematic tours (45 minutes), general tours (90 minutes) and demonstrations (25 minutes). See website for timetables.

Musée de la Curiosité et de la Magie
École de Magie, 11, rue St-Paul, 75004 Paris
M° Saint Paul , bus 67, 69, 76, 96
Wed, Sat, Sun 14h00 - 19h00
01.42.72.13.26
Interactive games and magic shows for children. On Saturdays, the École de Magie runs magic workshops for over 12's.

Parc aux Étoiles
2, rue de la Chapelle, 78510 Triel-sur-Seine
01.39.74.75.10
💻 www.parcauxetoiles.fr
Situated to the west of Paris in the grounds of the Château de la Tour, this park has a large telescope that the public can go and see. The entry hall houses temporary exhibits on astrophysics and astronomy.

Maison de l'Environnement
Parc de l'île Saint-Germain
92130 Issy-les-Moulineaux
Mon - Fri 09h00 - 12h30 and 14h00 - 18h00, Sun 14h00 - 18h00. Closes 17h00 Nov - Jan
01.55.95.80.70
💻 www.maisonenvironnement92.net
Permanent exhibition "If I were water...", as well as a library of 13,000 books, videos and CD-ROMs. Occasional presentations to groups and to the public. Gardens open to the public.

Musée de l'air et de l'espace
Aéroport de Paris-Le Bourget
M° La Courneuve, then 152 bus. Bus 350 (from M° Gare de l'Est, Gare du Nord or Porte de la Chapelle), 152 (from M° Porte de la Villette)
🚗 A1 from Porte de la Chapelle, exit 5 Aéroport du Bourget
April - Sept 10h00 - 18h00 (closed Mon all year), Oct - Mar 10h00 - 17h00
01.49.92.70.58
💻 www.mae.org
Entrance: Adult €7, child (under 18) free
The museum charges a supplement for visits to the Concorde plane, Boeing plane and planetarium; consult the list of prices on arrival for the various packages including several options. Free parking, shop, cafeteria, handicap access and picnic room.

OUTDOOR ACTIVITIES

Specialised Parks and Outdoor Centres

There are some great facilities for outdoor sports in the Paris area, offering a wide variety of sporting disciplines grouped together in one location. The majority of these places are most easily accessible by car:

Parcs Interdépartementaux des Sports

These specialised sports parks are situated within striking distance of Paris. They are also open to walkers and casual visitors.

Parc de Puteaux

Ile de Puteaux, 92800 Puteaux
🚗 Near La Défense, via the Pont de Puteaux
Early Oct - end Mar 8h30 - 17h30
Early Apr - end Sept 8h00 - 20h00
01.41.38.34.12
Tennis fans will find a training wall and 20 tennis courts for hire. Also football grounds.

Parc du Tremblay

11, boulevard des Alliés,
94500 Champigny-sur-Marne
RER A Champigny, then bus 116 stop Parc-du-Tremblay
Mid Oct - mid Apr 09h00 - 21h00
Mid Apr - mid Oct 08h00 - 22h00
01.48.81.11.12
On 73 hectares, football, rugby, tennis, table tennis, children's play area, mini-golf, mini-tennis, archery, remote control car circuit.

Parc de Choisy-le-Roi

Plaine Sud, Chemin des Bœufs, 94000 Créteil
RER D from Gare de Lyon, Villeneuve-Prairie
Early Oct - end Mar 08h00 - 20h00
Early Apr - end Sep 08h00 - 22h00
01.48.53.85.77
In addition to offering tennis, archery, hockey, foot-ball and athletics, this park is also a *base nautique* (watersports base) with 30 hectares of water, used for windsurfing, sailing and canoeing.

Aventure Land

Route d'Artheuil, 95420 Magny-en-Vexin
🚗 A86, then A15 direction Cergy, then N14 direction Rouen.
Open daily Apr - early Nov
0 820 099 629
💻 www.aventureland.fr
Prices from adult €9, child €7
The themed park Parc Naturel du Vexin specialises in sports, with activities suitable for children from 3 years and up. Mini-golf, mazes, inflatables, pony rides, trampoline, go-karting, quad bikes, educational trails and play areas.

(For details of more theme parks see Parks and Play).

Bases de plein air et de loisirs

These are larger centres further from Paris offering a range of outdoor and water sports.

Base de plein air et de loisirs de Buthiers

Rue des Roches, 77760 Buthiers
🚗 A6, then RN152 exit URY, then direction Malesherbes
RER D Malesherbes
01.64.24.12.87
💻 www.base-de-buthiers.com
Set in the Fontainebleau forest. From June to August, you will find an outdoor pool, slides and a paddling pool. All year round there are climbing activities, hiking, mountain biking, tennis, orientation, nature trails and archery.

Base de plein air et de loisirs de Saint-Quentin-en-Yvelines

Route Départemental (RD) 912, 78190 Trappes
🚗 A13, then A12 exit Trappes

RER C Saint Quentin-en-Yvelines
Open daily 07h30 - 22h30
01.30.16.44.40
💻 www.aileconcept.com/bpalsqy
Nature reserve with 200 hectares of water and 400 hectares of green space. Sailing, windsurfing, kayaking, horse riding, golf, children's farm. In the summer you will also find a swimming pool with waves, fishing, mini-golf and bike hire.

Base de plein air et de loisirs Le Port Aux Cerises
Rue Port aux Cerises, 91210 Draveil
🚗 RN7 or RN6
RER C or D, Juvisny-sur-Orge
Open from February school holidays to November school holidays
01.69.83.46.00
💻 www.portauxcerises.fr
Leisure activities for all the family. Tennis, football, pony rides, mini-train, mini-golf, merry-go-round, fishing. In the summer, you will find a swimming pool with waves, pedal boats and canoeing.

River Trips

There are many companies offering a variety of trips on the rivers and canals in and around Paris. A few are listed here. For more detailed information see *L'Officiel des Spectacles* and *Pariscope* magazines and most travel guides.

Bateaux Mouches
Pont de l'Alma, right bank, 75008 Paris
M° Alma-Marceau, RER C Pont de l'Alma
01.40.76.99.99 (information)
01.42.25.96.10 (reservations)
💻 www.bateaux-mouches.fr
Departures every 30 - 45 minutes. One hour trip. Dinner cruises.

Bateaux Parisiens Tour Eiffel
Port de la Bourdonnais, 75007 Paris
Just below the Eiffel Tower (can also board from Notre Dame and Saint Germain des Prés).
M° Trocadéro

0 825 010 101
💻 www.bateauxparisiens.com
Trips weekdays, every hour; weekends and holidays, every half hour. Lunch and dinner cruises.

Bateaux Vedettes de Paris
Port de Suffren, 75007 Paris
M° Bir-Hakeim
Free parking at foot of Eiffel Tower
01.44.18.19.50
💻 www.vedettesdeparis.com
Regular departures every day. Dinner trips, receptions.

Bateaux Vedettes du Pont-Neuf
Square du Vert Galant, 75001 Paris
M° Pont-Neuf, parking Quai des Orfèvres.
01.46.33.98.38
💻 www.vedettesdupontneuf.com
Regular daily departures.

Compagnie des Batobus
Port de la Bourdonnais, 75007 Paris
0 825 050 101
💻 www.batobus.com
Day pass €11 adults, €5 under 16's. Hop-on hop-off service, runs all year round, but less frequently in the winter. Eight stops along the Seine.

Paris Canal
19-21 quai de la Loire, 75019 Paris
01.42.40.96.97
💻 www.pariscanal.com
Trips along the Canal Saint-Martin and the Seine.

Canauxrama
13, quai de la Loire, 75019 Paris
01.42.39.15.00
💻 www.canauxrama.com
Trips on the Canal Saint-Martin, the Canal Saint Denis, the Seine and the Marne.

PARKS AND PLAY

Come rain or shine, children need to play, and you need to get out of the apartment... This section aims to ensure you will not be stuck for ideas, or stuck at home.

Parks

At the smallest end of the scale are playgrounds (*aires de jeux* and *squares*), which are generally fenced areas with gardens, park benches and some play equipment for younger children. Gardens (*jardins*) have more green space, and although playing on the grass is not always permitted, they often have play equipment for children. *Parcs* are bigger green areas with activities for children, such as merry-go-rounds (*manèges*), puppet shows, boating, and elaborate play equipment. Park opening hours are seasonal and are usually posted at the entrance. Most are open from 09h00 to 17h00 in winter, with later closing in the summer months. They can get crowded with older children on school days from 16h30. Dogs are usually not allowed in the *squares* and smaller fenced gardens.

If you like more space, try the Bois de Vincennes and the Bois de Boulogne to the east and west of Paris respectively, and the bigger suburban parks, which often have sports facilities (see Sport for details). Parc des Sceaux, Parc de Saint Cloud and the many forests (*fôrets*) outside of Paris (including Chantilly to the north, St. Germain to the west and Meudon to the south-west) are also well worth a visit.

For information on local parks and playgrounds, contact your local *mairie*, and for updates on events (*animations*) in the main parks in Paris, including children's activities, consult 💻www.paris.fr.

Parks in Paris

Here are some of the capital's best parks.

Jardin des Tuileries
75001 Paris
rue de Rivoli
M° Tuileries, Concorde, Palais Royal, bus 21, 72, 73, 76, 95
Elegant park stretching between the Louvre and Place de la Concorde. There is a free, fenced-off play area with unusual play equipment and swings for older children. Paid activities include a boat pond, with boats for hire, in-ground trampolines, an antique merry-go-round and pony rides.

Jardin des Plantes
75005 Paris
M° Austerlitz, Jussieu, bus 24, 63, 67, 89
01.40.79.30.00
This park has something for everyone. Featuring a botanic garden and an "Alpine" garden, there are three play areas (one fenced off), a zoo, a greenhouse and a maze. Wonderfully quiet on weekdays. Children are not allowed on the grass, but the wide walkways between the rows of flowers are great for riding tricycles provided it is not too crowded. There are two (small) restaurants in the park and McDonald's (with a fun play structure and ball pit upstairs) is right across the street. The Museum of Natural History (see Science Museums for details),

Activities

bordering the park, makes it a full day's trip, even if it rains.

Jardin du Luxembourg

75006 Paris
boulevard St Michel, rue de Médicis, rue de Vaugirard
M° Notre Dame des Champs, RER B Luxembourg, bus 21, 27, 38, 58, 82, 83, 84, 85, 89
Classical gardens and a fenced adventure playground filled with unusual play equipment, slides, and climbing structures (small charge for children and parents), a carrousel, pony rides and puppet show. During the summer, there is a drop-in childcare centre located near the other children's activities, and live music in the bandstand. Several eateries. One lawn, close to the Port Royal entrance, is open to sit on in the summer.

"The Jardin du Luxembourg has everything - the sail boats, the donkeys, a great enclosed play area with seats conveniently nearby for tired parents, and for older kids and adults there is basketball, tennis, jogging, lounging in the sun and beekeeping lessons." Meg C., American mother of one.

"The other GREAT thing about the Jardin du Luxembourg is that, except for a very small area at one end, no dogs are allowed!" Caroline P., Canadian mother of one.

Parc Monceau

75008 Paris
boulevard de Courcelles, avenue Velasquez,
M° Monceau, Villiers, bus 30, 84, 94

01.42.27.08.64
Large green area, beautifully tended, fenced-off area with play equipment, sandpit and a swan pond. Roller skating and biking possible.

Bois de Vincennes

75012 Paris
avenue Daumesnil
M° Porte Dorée, bus PC, 46, 86
Divided into several areas, these 995 hectares of green space include the major Parisian zoo, a lake for boating, bike rentals for adults with child seats attached, and several play areas with a wide assortment of children's games and equipment for all ages. The Château de Vincennes, at one side of the bois, makes an interesting visit for older children.

Parc Floral de Paris

75012 Paris
esplanade du Château de Vincennes, or route de la Pyramide (opposite *château*)
M° Château de Vincennes, RER A Vincennes, bus 46, 112
Mar - Sep 09h30 - 20h00, Oct - Feb 09h30 - 17h00

Let's go for a Walk!

Here are some ideas for getting out and about in Paris with the pushchair:

The Promenade Plantée (🚶 www.promenade-plantee.org) in the 12th arrondissement (M° Bastille, Gare de Lyon): an old railway turned into a long green promenade where roller skating and biking are prohibited. The area beneath, at street level, is called Le Viaduc des Arts, and has some interesting shops to browse. Large green lawns for playing and sunbathing, and there is a cafeteria and children's play area too.

Le Guide Vert lists 30 child-friendly itineraries for walks through Paris, complete with historical background, museums to visit, places to eat and ideas on what to do if it rains!

01.43.43.92.95

💻 www.parcfloraldeparis.com

Entry fee: €1 for adults and children over six. This park has flower, bonsai and rose displays, as well as nature-related exhibitions for children and a botanical greenhouse. It also has pedal cars, a lake, one of the best-equipped play areas in Paris, a train ride and even wandering peacocks. Cafés and a large picnic area. Easy pushchair access although some paths are gravelled. It can get crowded at weekends. There are concerts for children - visit the website to check their programme.

Parc de Montsouris

75014 Paris

boulevard Jourdan, rue Gazan, avenue Reille, RER B Cité Universitaire, bus 21, PC

"Parc Montsouris has a big pond with lots of turtles, ducks, and even a "wild" (I guess) blue heron who makes frequent appearances. There's a merry-go-round and pony rides (both require tickets) in season, and best of all, lots and lots of beautiful, accessible grass and HUGE beautiful trees. Not for nothing was it designed as a 19th century "jardin anglais."

The park stays open quite late in summer so it's perfect for evening picnics. There's a big play area "down below" (near the pond/lake) for older kids (roughly 6 to 12, though little ones like it too), and a nice area "up above" for the little ones with a sandpit, see-saws, climbing frames, and so forth. Concerts in the band stand are fairly frequent on summer weekends, and everything is pushchair accessible. There are stairs in the park, but always a way to circumvent them." Ruth H., American mother of two.

Parc André Citroën

75015 Paris

quai André Citroën, rue Leblanc M° Lourmel, Javel, Balard, RER C Boulevard Victor, bus PC, 42 01.45.57.13.35

Beautiful park with large lawns, fountains and small canals (used for water play in summer), immense greenhouses, fun for running and playing ball. Small areas with play equipment.

Parc Georges Brassens

75015 Paris

rue des Morillons, rue Périchaux M° Porte de Vanves, bus 89, 48, 95 Beautiful park with play area with sandpits, climbing structures, slides, puppet show, pony rides, swings (small charge). Some of the large stones from the buildings that used to be there have been left deliberately to provide a great place for children to climb. Old books fair every weekend.

Bois de Boulogne

75016 Paris

M° Les Sablons, Porte Maillot, Porte Dauphine, Porte d'Auteuil, bus 82, 73 A huge wooded area on the western boundary of Paris. There are bike and boat rentals, lots of green areas for picnicking and several lakes. It is one of the most "untamed" parks in Paris, but one special large section, the Jardin d'Acclimatation, is set aside just for children (see Theme Parks for details).

Jardin des Serres d'Auteuil

75016 Paris
avenue de la porte d'Auteuil
M° Porte d'Auteuil
01.40.71.76.07
Beautiful 19th century greenhouse with exotic plants.

Parc de La Villette

75019 Paris
avenue Jean Jaurès, avenue Corentin Cariou, boulvevard Macdonald
M° Porte de la Villette, bus 75, 139, 150, 152, 250A, PC
01.40.03.75.75
🖥 www.villette.com
This is a huge, modern space of open fields where children can play football and families can picnic.

There are half-submerged sculptures and wide paths through experimental gardens (bamboo garden, music garden, cloud maker). There is also a

Get Away for the Day!

Here are some ideas for parks outside Paris, recommended by MESSAGE members.

"I like Etangs du Val d'Or, Guyancourt (92) because, though it is right off the A86, you feel as if you're out in the country. And what it has is water. Good for the soul. There are two ponds with paths and forest all around, picnic tables here and there, beautiful views abound. This is the place to bring your older kids on bikes, and easy to pass a whole afternoon picnicking and biking. There are no playgrounds, but there is a snack truck that arrives every nice afternoon around 3pm." Wendy F., American mother of two.

"In Suresnes, the Parc du Château is very pretty, more an "English-style" park with a bit of woodland, a large grassy area that you are allowed to sit and play on, a duckpond, playgrounds, a huge geyser fountain the kids can play in when it's hot, and a little aviary where there are partridges, pheasants and peacocks. It's not a huge park, but it's beautifully landscaped and very pleasant." Andrea U., American mother of one.

"In Boulogne Billancourt, the Square Leon Blum is lovely: lots of grass and huge trees for shade, and climbing stuff for both big and little kids." Ami S., American mother of three.

"For the Antony area, Parc Heller has an animal petting area and a ponyland. Parc de Sceaux is gorgeous and a great place to take a walk." Karena D., Singaporean mother of one.

"The Ile Marante in Colombes has a pool, skating rink, great climbing structures, slides, swings, a toddler play area, large open grassy areas for soccer/picnics, bike riding/jogging paths for adults and kids, merry-go-round, and looks onto the Seine." Yvonne L., American mother of one.

large outdoor space just for children filled with unusual post-modern jumping and climbing toys and a guard at the gate. For older kids there is the space-age dragon slide across the canal, the Cité de Science (see Science Museums for more information), the Géode Dome with IMAX films (for ages 3 and up) and the Cité de la Musique. There are toilets for small children.

"Parc de la Villette is my kids' favourite - they love the bouncy place, and the big dragon, and for me the best part is there is plenty to do inside if it starts raining - planetarium, the Cité des Enfants - plus places to eat. For families with more than one child, it's great because there is something for all ages, and a €60 annual membership gets you unlimited access to the Cité des Enfants, planetarium and exhibitions for the whole family - you still have to get tickets, but can skip the long lines and use a members-only line." Dana A., American mother of five.

Parc des Buttes Chaumont
75019 Paris
rue Manin, rue Botzaris
M° Buttes Chaumont, Botzaris, bus 60, 75
A beautiful park for a walk or for older children to run up and down the steep hills, under the waterfall and across the drawbridges. There is also a beauti-

---

When it Feels Too Hot to Go Anywhere, Try the Following Places for Summer Water Play:

- The water jets in Parc André Citroen (15th)
- The huge geyser fountain kids can play in at Parc du Château in Suresnes
- The enormous sprinkler in the Jardin d'Acclimatation (16th)
- The lake and the water play area in Parc de Chantereines in Villeneuve
- The wading pool in Parc André Malraux in Nanterre

---

ful view of Montmartre. There are two puppet show locations, as well as live entertainment around the lake on fine days. Two small, but attractive play areas with climbing structures, slides and elaborate sandpit. Rain shelter adjacent to largest play area.

Theme Parks
The Paris area has a number of theme parks catering to children from toddlers to teenagers. With the possible exception of Disneyland Paris, the parks outside Paris are most easily accessible by car. Check websites for up-to-date opening times and entrance fees.

Jardin d'Acclimatation
Bois de Boulogne, 75016 Paris
Main entrance at Carrefour des Sablons.
M° Les Sablons (10 minute walk), M° Porte Maillot (return train ride to park €3 for children, €5 for adults), bus 43, 73, 82, PC, 174
Jun - Sep 10h00 -19h00
Oct - May 10h00 - 18h00
01.40.67.90.82
🖳 www.jardindacclimatation.fr
Entrance: €2.50, free for under 3s. Book (*carnet*) of 14 entries for €25. Annual subscription (*abonnement annuel*) €80.00. Rides €2.50 each, reduction if buying a carnet.
This park is part of the Bois de Boulogne and covers 18 hectares with over 50 activities: roundabouts, petting zoo/farm, puppet show, trampolines, pony rides, miniature golf, elaborate outdoor and small indoor playgrounds, animals, and an enchanted river trip. Includes a good roller coaster ride suitable for children 6 to 8 years old. A vegetable garden on site runs gardening workshops for children. Restaurants, snack bars and picnic area. Changing table in WC near pony club.

Money saving tip from a MESSAGE member:
"The Jardin is divided so that you need not encounter a pay ride if you do not wish to do so (this is what we usually do). As for free activities, if you keep left after the entry from the Sablons side, there is a wonderful play area with great

climbing equipment for older children as well as for younger children, a splash area in summer, the puppet show, the sand pit as well as the farm area. Although to get to the farm area, you pass a carrousel (paying) and the pony rides (paying)." Kim D., South African mother of two.

Château de Breteuil

78460 Choisel
35km west of Paris in the Chevreuse valley.
🚗 leave Paris by Pont de Sèvres, direction Chartres-Bordeaux, exit Saclay, then Route de Chevreuse, exit St Rémy les Chevreuse and follow signs.
SNCF to Saint-Rémy-lès-Chevreuse
Sundays and holidays only, May - Oct, a "Baladobus" runs from the train station to the château.
01.30.52.09.09 for schedules
Gardens open at 10h00 and the château at 14h30 (11h00 Sundays and public holidays).
🖥 www.breteuil.fr
Entry €11.50 for adults, free for children under 6. Château surrounded by 75 hectares of parkland with recreation areas, rides, Little Red Riding Hood's House (*maison de Chaperon Rouge*) and various other fairy tale-based attractions, storyteller in the summer. The *château* has 40 wax figures depicting the life of the nobility. *Crêperie*, picnic area and changing facilities.

France Miniature

25, Route du Mesnil, 78990 Elancourt
🚗 25 km west of Paris via A13/12 or A86, exit Elancourt, follow signs. Free parking.
SNCF from la Défense or Montparnasse to La Verrière, then bus 411 to France Miniature stop. Combined train/bus/entry ticket available at train stations.
Open daily 10h00 - 18h00 (spring and autumn), 10h00 - 19h00 (summer).
Closed November to March
01.30.16.16.30
🖥 www.franceminiature.com
Entry €14.50 adult, €9.50 child (4 - 14), reduction for large families.

Five hectares with 150 model French monuments, town squares, villages, working model trains and landscapes, etc. Fascinating indoor museum with 50 realistic miniature scenes, including lovely scenes of Christmas around Europe and the world of Santa's elves. Restaurant with regional specialties, snack bar, picnic area, playground, trampolines. Changing tables in disabled toilets. Easy pushchair access. No animals allowed.

Parc Astérix

60128 Plailly
🚗 30km north of Paris, A1 direction Lille, exit for Parc Astérix between exits 7 and 8. Parking €5.
RER B to Roissy Charles de Gaulle Terminal 1, then Park Astérix bus shuttle every 30 minutes (09h30 - 18h00). Return shuttles every 30 minutes from 16h30.
Apr, Sep, Oct 10h00 - 18h00 weekends. Jul, Aug daily 10h00 - 19h00
03.44.62.31.31
🖥 www.parcasterix.fr (French version of the website allows you to buy tickets online.)
Entry €33 adult, €23 child (3 - 11). (two day passes €62 and €42)
Rides and attractions for children from three years up, including mini-roller coaster, bumper cars, boat rides, dolphin shows, magic shows, face painting, plus some of Europe's best roller coasters for older children. Children do not need to be familiar with the Astérix comic books to enjoy the park. The number of water rides makes it a great summer

Activities

Here are Some Tips for Making the Most of Your Trip to Disneyland:

- **Invest in the Proximity Passport:** for €89 per year it gives access to both parks 325 days of the year. For €19 extra, you can buy a pass which includes free parking

- **Make use of the FastPass system:** this allows you to jump the queue for rides, by coming at a pre-arranged time and using the special "FastPass" queue. The main attractions all have FastPass machines near the entrance and, once you have inserted your pass, they print a slip of paper telling you when to come back

- **Remember the Baby Switch option:** this allows one parent to stand at the head of the queue with the baby while the other goes on the ride. Then they swap over, so the other parent gets a go without having to queue again

- **If you want to go to a restaurant that includes a show,** take the time to stop and reserve a table a few hours before

- **If you are taking a picnic,** the picnic area is outside the parks, near the moving walkways to the car park

destination. Restaurants (fast food and table service), picnic areas (some covered). Relais Bébé facilities (areas for preparing meals, feeding and changing babies), pushchair hire and good pushchair access.

La Mer de Sable
60950 Ermenonville
🚗 A1 exit 7 direction Ermenonville.
Free parking.
RER B to Roissy Charles de Gaulle Terminal 1, CIF bus (one bus daily each way at 10h30 to and 18h10 from the park, taking about 40 minutes). Combined ticket including transport and park entry available. Open daily June - Aug 10h00 - 18h00. April, May and Sept open weekends, Wed, public and school holidays.
01.48.62.38.33
💻 www.merdesable.fr
Entry adult €16.50, child (3 - 11) €14.00.
Wild west shows, Indian train attack, equestrian displays, ranch, puppet shows, animated jungle, shooting the rapids, North African bazaar, Chinese pagoda, miniature train, fun fair, play areas, etc.
Restaurants, picnic area. Changing facilities at first aid post.

Disneyland Paris Parks
77777 Marne la Vallée
🚗 A4, exit 14, past Gare de Lyon, Bercy exit.
Parking €8
RER A to Marne la Vallée/Chessy.
Open daily 09h00 - 20h00 (winter), 09h00 - 23h00 (summer).
A range of ticket options. Entry for adults from €41 for one park/one day to €109 for a three-day pass for both parks. Entry for children (3 - 11) from €33 to €89 for three-day pass to both parks.
💻 www.disneylandparis.com
The two parks together (Disneyland and Walt Disney Studios) make up more than a long day so if

you plan on visiting both thoroughly it might be better to purchase a two-day pass or Proximity passport. Tickets can be purchased online and at *métro* stations.

The Disney Village outside the parks is free and has a variety of restaurants and shops, including a Hard Rock Café and American diner themed

restaurant. In the winter the New York hotel has a skating rink and skate rental. *Relais Bébé* facilities are found on Main Street in Disneyland and behind the Studio Services in Walt Disney Studios. Most toilets are found near eating establishments and include changing tables. Disney rents pushchairs and wagons and also has lockers near the main entrance.

SEASONAL ACTIVITIES

The French love their routines and rituals and, of course, their holidays! This shows in the amount of events and festivals that come around on an annual basis. In this chapter, we provide just a small selection of the best ones to take your children to.

Salons (Exhibitions)

Whatever your family's pet interest is, there is bound to be an annual *Salon* that caters for it. *Salons* are themed exhibitions with many stands and events, usually held in large exhibition centres (*parcs des expositions*), such as the *Paris Expo* centres at the Porte de Versailles (15th *arrondissement*) and the Porte de Champerret (17th *arrondissement*). Each *Salon* is normally held at around the same time each year. The biggest *Salons*, such as the *Foire de Paris* (Paris Fair) can last for up to a week and attract thousands of visitors. Pushchair access and changing facilities are generally good, and there are places to eat. Expect to pay an entrance fee.

Holidays from Back Home

Just because you are in France does not mean you and your children have to miss out on May Day, summer *fêtes*, Halloween, Guy Fawkes, Thanksgiving or Christmas the way you remember it: it is all out there, it is just a matter of knowing where to look.

A good starting point if you are looking for a place to celebrate is to contact the churches and associations, including MESSAGE, linked to the expatriate community (☞Organisations and Charities).

The quarterly MESSAGE magazine and members' website has a schedule of events organised by its members, many of which are linked to national holidays.

Seasonal Calendar

January

Festival International de la Géode, Parc de la Villette, 19th *arrondissement*.
Film festival on the Géode's giant screen.
01.40.05.79.99
🖥 www.lageode.com

Nouvel an chinois (Chinese New Year). Spectacular street parades in the 3rd and the 13th *arrondissements*.

Fête des Tuileries. Traditional fun fair with a big wheel in the Jardin des Tuileries, 1st *arrondissement*.

February

Salon de l'agriculture at the Parc des expositions, Porte de Versailles, 15th *arrondissement*.
🖥 www.salonagriculture.com

March

Journées des nouveau-nés at the Ferme de Paris,

Bois de Vincennes, 12th *arrondissement*. Visit the newborn calves, kids and lambs. Similar events held at other farms, for addresses see the section on Animals, above.

Chorus des enfants Hauts-de-Seine
Festival of music and song in towns throughout the Hauts-de-Seine department.
01.47.74.64.64

Salon du Livre (Book Salon) at the Parc des expositions, Porte de Versailles, 15th *arrondissement*.
💻 www.salondulivreparis.com

April

Grandes eaux musicales. Fountain displays set to music at the Château de Versailles, until October.
💻 www.chateauversailles.fr

Le Printemps des musées. Free entrance to museums throughout France (held on a Sunday). It is worth choosing a smaller museum to explore, as the big-name museums are always heaving.
💻 www.printempsdesmusees.culture.fr

May

Le Printemps des rues. Street theatre and performances, with a different theme each year. Throughout Paris, and free.
💻 www.leprintempsdesrues.com

◁)) TIP

Keep an eye on *métro* and street billboards to keep up to date. Some towns have electronic billboards advertising up-coming cultural events organised by the *mairie*.

Les 24 Heures du cerf-volant. Annual kite and balloon festival held in Brie-Comte-Robert (77) in mid May.
01.60.62.64.00

Summer

Look out for free open-air concerts on summer weekends. Call 0 820 007 575 for events in Paris. In the suburbs, check with your *mairie*.

Your local fire-station may hold an open day (*journée portes ouvertes*) during the summer, with hose-pipe demonstrations, first-aid refreshers, and the chance for the kids to get in a fire-engine.

June

La journée des enfants de la Foire Saint-Germain. Free art workshops, games and activities for children held on a Sunday in mid-June. Place St Sulpice, 6th *arrondissement*.
💻 www.foiresaintgermain.org
Fête de la Musique. 21st June. On Midsummer's eve, concerts abound in the streets of Paris…
💻 www.fetedelamusique.culture.fr

Jazz à La Villette. Free open-air concerts in the Parc de la Villette, from late June to early July.
💻 www.cite-musique.fr

July

Fête Nationale. The 13th and 14th July sees parties (*bals de pompiers*) at fire stations and firework displays throughout France. Military parade and fly-over on the Champs Elysées on the morning of the 14.th.

Do not miss the end of the *Tour de France* on the Champs-Elysées. End of July (on a Sunday). Free.

August

Paris Plage. If you cannot get away from the capital like everyone else, do not despair! From the end of the July to the end of August, the beach comes to the banks of the Seine in central Paris. Go in the morning to avoid the crush. Highlights of previous years have included a children's swimming pool opposite the Île de St Louis, concerts by the Pont de Sully, children's art workshops at the Pont Marie and various sporting activities.

Autumn

Dominated by *la rentrée* (back to school), autumn has plenty of cultural events to welcome families back from their summer breaks.

September

Journées du patrimoine. Cultural events held throughout France on the third weekend of September, with a different theme each year. Many houses opened up to the public for this event only.
💻 www.journeesdupatrimoine.culture.fr

Journées Portes Ouvertes de la Garde Républicaine
See the French cavalry at first hand, with horse-manship and motorbike displays, music from the military band, and activities for children including wall-climbing. Held at the Quartier des Célestins in the 4th *arrondissement*

October

Fête des Vendanges. Traditional street celebrations held in Montmartre to celebrate the harvesting of grapes from its vineyard. Held on a Saturday in early October.
💻 www.fetedesvendangesdemontmartre.com

Mondial de l'automobile (even-numbered years) at the Porte de Versailles. For car-lovers of all ages!
💻 www.mondial-automobile.com

Festival de Marne. Annual cultural festival held in the Val-de-Marne department.
01.55.09.16.20
💻 www.tourisme-valdemarne.com

Salon du Chocolat in late October. Mum, you deserve it!
💻 www.chocoland.com

November

Salon du livre de la jeunesse. Organised by the *mairie* in Montreuil (93).
01.55.86.86.55

Winter

Look out for open-air ice-rinks opposite the *Hôtel de Ville*, the Gare Montparnasse, on the Eiffel Tower and in front of the Grande Arche de la Défense from December to February. There is a small charge for skate hire.

December

Salon du cheval, du poney et de l'âne. A must for horse lovers. Early December
💻 www.salon-cheval.com

Do not miss the Christmas window displays at Galeries Lafayette and other department stores in central Paris. Can get crowded on Wednesdays and weekends; go early in the day if you can.

Open air *marchés de Noël* (Christmas markets) are generally widespread in France. These marchés are great place to stock up on unusual gifts. The *marché* at La Defense has some great places to eat. Look out for one near you.

Activities

SPORT

Sport for Pre-schoolers

Baby Swimming (Bébé nageurs)

Many pools run *bébé-nageur* sessions for children from three months up to the age of 6. The term *bébé-nageur* (swimming baby) is misleading in that the aim is not to teach children to swim, but to create a warm, secure environment in which they can become at ease in the water. Parents accompany their children, and swim nappies must be worn if your child is not potty trained. The sessions usually last between 30 minutes and an hour.

To register, the child's health booklet (*carnet de santé*) is required to show that the child's vaccinations are up to date (☞Health and Medicine). A letter from the doctor certifying that the child is in good health may also be requested. Payment is generally in the form of an annual fee, but if you join the class after one or two terms the fee is often reduced.

To find a *bébé-nageur* class near you, contact your *mairie*.

FAEL (Fédération des Activités Aquatiques d'Eveil et de Loisir)
01.43.55.98.76
🖳 www.fael.asso.fr
This is a national association that sets standards for *bébé-nageur* classes, and it is worth inquiring if your local pool is accredited by them. The FAEL website has a list of accredited centres that have been deemed to meet rigorous safety and hygiene standards (including a minimum water temperature of 32°C) and have specially qualified instructors.

For information on pools and water parks see Swimming, below.

Baby Gym
Great fun for little ones and parents alike, these sessions can also be a good opportunity for social contact. For other ideas for getting out and about with under three's, see Meeting Places.

Gymborée
Aquaboulevard de Paris, 4, rue Louis-Armand, 75015 Paris
M° Balard
Centre commercial "Elysée Village"
18, avenue de la Jonchère
78170 La Celle Saint Cloud
01.40.71.61.60
🖳 www.gymboree-france.com
This baby-gym encourages parental participation and classes are organised into seven different age groups, from three months to 6 years. There are gym activities with music and songs, colourful padded play areas, ropes, ramps, ladders, tunnels, and more. Sessions last 45 minutes. Call or consult the website for details of times and prices. Free trial session.

Vitamôme
14, boulevard Raspail, 75007 Paris
M° Sèvres-Babylone
01.40.23.93.66
Classes for children aged 2 to 6 years.

Bébé Gym
21, rue de l'Amiral Roussin, 75015 Paris
M° Cambronne
88-90, rue de l'Assomption, 75016 Paris

 TIP

If you live in Paris, you can get information on municipal *bébé-nageurs* and baby gym classes by calling *Paris Info Mairie* (an enquiry service for sports and cultural activities) on 0 820 007 575.

M° Ranelagh
17, avenue du Docteur Arnold Netter, 75012 Paris
M° Bel-Air
Gymnase des Radiguelles, 1, rue des
Tourneroches, 92150 Suresnes
01.46.97.93.57
These classes teach physical co-ordination, with
lots of laughter and music and are aimed at ages
three months to 6 years. You will find games to
develop motor skills, lots of music, bubbles, and
fun. The youngest children do the classes with their
parents.

Sport for School-age Children

Team and individual sports classes are open to children from around age 6, sometimes earlier. The
options are too numerous to list in this guide, so the
first point of call for information on classes (which
normally take place on Wednesdays and
Saturdays, but occasionally after school) should be
your local *mairie*.

In early summer, the *mairie* should send all residents a programme of municipal classes due to
begin in September. There are forms to fill in and a
dossier to put together, usually including proof of
address, passport-size photos and a medical certificate. The standard of instruction and facilities in
state-run classes is high and prices are reasonable,
as activities are subsidised for local residents. It is
usually possible, if spaces are available, to attend
classes in another town for a slightly higher fee. It is
also possible to join a class halfway through an
academic year.

If your *mairie* does not offer the sport you are looking for, or if you would like your child to join a competitive club, the best lines of enquiry are the local
and national sporting federations. A list of these can
be found in the guide *Parisports: Le Guide du Sport
à Paris* (see the Other Resources section at the
end of this chapter).

Also consult 🖳 www.paris.fr under *sport*, where
you can book tennis courts online and get up-to-

date information on what sports activities are available in Paris.

Sporting activities in English for children are available at the Standard Athletic Club in Meudon, a
sports and social club serving the English-speaking
community. For information on joining the club, contact:

Standard Athletic Club
Au Clos Obeuf
Route Forestière du Pavé de Meudon
92360 Meudon
01.46.26.16.09
🖳 www.standac.com

Cycling

Paris is great for cycling. It has about 150km of bike
paths and there are plenty of places where you can
buy or rent bikes or have repairs done.

Every Sunday and bank holiday between March
and November (09h00 - 17h00), a large part of *la
voie rapide* along the Seine is closed off for biking,
walking or roller-skating. On the left bank, the section is closed between the Musée d'Orsay and the
Eiffel Tower and on the right bank, from the Louvre
to Bastille. Also on Sundays and bank holidays (all
year round) the following areas are closed off:

• the banks of the canal Saint Martin in the 10th *arrondissement*
• the *quais* de Valmy and Jemmapes, between rue Louis Blanc and rue de la Grange-aux-Belles in the 10th *arrondissement*
• the roads around the rue Nationale in the 13th *arrondissement*
• the grounds of the *mairie* in the 14th *arrondissement* (14h00 - 18h00)
• the banks of the Loire and the Marne
• the Bassin de la Villette and the Canal de l'Ourcq in the 19th *arrondissement*
• the main road through the Bois de Boulogne

Activities

Bicycle Hire

Maison Roue Libre is an organisation owned by the RATP which hires bikes (together with safety helmets and babyseats), provides cycle maps and a repair service and organises cycling tours. They can be found at the following locations:

Maison Roue Libre Les Halles
Forum des Halles
1, passage Mondétour, 75001 Paris
Opposite 120 rue Rambuteau
M° Chatelet les Halles
Open daily 09h00 - 19h00
0 810 441 534
🖳 www.rouelibre.fr

Maison Roue Libre Bastille
37, boulevard Bourdon, 75004 Paris.
M° Bastille
Open daily 09h00 - 19h00
01.44.54.19.29
🖳 www.rouelibre.fr
There are further rental points at place de la Concorde, boulevard Vincent Auriol, Bois de Boulogne (outside the Sablons entrance to the Jardin d'Acclimatation), Bois de Vincennes, Boulogne-Billancourt and St Germain-en-Laye. You can hire your bike at one location and bring it back to another.

You can also hire bikes from the following places:

Bicloune
93, boulevard de Beaumarchais, 75003 Paris
01.42.77.58.00

Glisse Attitude
59, boulevard Beaumarchais, 75003 Paris
01.44.61.74.67

Au réparateur de Bicyclettes
44, boulevard de Sébastopol, 75003 Paris
01.48.04.51.19

Paris Vélo
2, rue de la Fer-à-Moulin, 75005 Paris
01.43.37.59.22

La Maison du Vélo
11, rue Fénelon, 75010 Paris
01.42.81.24.72

Cycles Laurent
9, boulevard Voltaire, 75011 Paris
01.47.00.27.47

Bicyclub de France
8, place de la porte de Champerret, 75017 Paris
01.47.66.55.92
Hire of bicycles weekends and holidays at Bois de Boulogne, Bois de Vincennes, Canal de l'Ourcq, Vallée de Chevreuse (Saint-Rémy), St Germain-en-Laye forest and Rambouillet forest.

For more addresses, check the *Pages Jaunes* (🖳 www.pagesjaunes.fr) under *Location de cycles*.

Cycling Tours

Several associations organise cycling tours through the capital, which is a nice way to get acquainted with the city. Some run tours in English.

Paris à vélo, c'est sympa!
37, boulevard Bourdon, 75004 Paris
M° Bastille
01.48.87.60.01
🖳 www.parisvelosympa.com

Paris-Vélo
2, rue du Fer-à-Moulin, 75005 Paris
M° Censier-Daubenton
01.43.37.59.22
Tours only for groups

Fat Tire Bike Tours
24, rue Edgar Faure, 75015 Paris
01.56.58.10.54
🖳 www.fattirebiketoursparis.com
Child bikes, child seats, child tandems and trailers available.

La Maison Roue Libre
(details as above)

Mountain Biking (VTT - vélo tout terrain)
Guide books (*VTT Evasion*) are available covering itineraries through the most picturesque forests around Paris. Published by the French Forestry Commission, they are available from bookshops, sport shops and tourist offices.

Fédération Française de Cyclotourisme FFCT
8 rue Jean Marie Jego, 75013 Paris
01.44.16.88.88
Information on cycling routes, best areas to cycle, maps, etc.

Horse Riding

Fédération Française d'Equitation (FFE)
9, boulevard Macdonald, 75019 Paris
01.53.26.15.50
Fax 01.53.26.15.51
🖳 www.ffe.com
General information on places to ride and take lessons in Paris and the suburbs.

Le Club Hippique du Jardin
Jardin d'Acclimatation, Bois de Boulogne, 75016 Paris
01.45.01.97.97
🖳 www.jardindacclimatation.fr
Lessons available to adults and to children from the age of 3.

Ice Rinks

Look out for the temporary rinks that are installed by local *mairies* in the winter - the children will love open air skating! You can find them in front of the Hôtel de Ville, on the first floor of the Eiffel Tower and at La Défense, to name but a few.

There is a permanent ice rink at *Disneyland Paris*. For other permanent rinks, consult 🖳www.page-jaunes or 🖳www.paris.fr and search under *patinoire*.

Martial Arts

Aiki and Judo school
American Church in Paris
65, Quai d'Orsay, 75007 Paris
01.34.17.73.67
🖳 http://eastwardho.free.fr

or:
70, rue de Montreuil
au fond de la cour, 94300 Vincennes
01.43.74.83.57
🖳 http://eastwardho.free.fr
A martial arts association open to children from age 4 and adults.

Roller-Skating/ Roller-Blading

Roller-skating is very popular in Paris and there are many parks and walkways where it is possible to skate. Roller-skating on the pavements is allowed, but it is forbidden on the *métro* and in cycle lanes. A good time and place to roller-skate is in the areas that are closed to traffic on Sundays (see Cycling, above).

Rinks (patinoires à roulette or Rollers parcs)
If you want to meet other roller fanatics, then a roller-skating rink is the place to go. But beware: the level of skating may be high! Here are a few addresses:

Le stade Boutroux
1, avenue Boutroux 75013 Paris
M° Porte d'Ivry

Rollerparc Avenue
Z.I. Les Ardoines, 94400 Vitry sur Seine (Entrance 100 Rue léon Geoffroy)
RER C Les Ardoines
01.47.18.19.19
🖳 www.rollerparc.com
For skating of all kinds, with 6,000 square metres of indoor and outdoor skating facilities.

Boulevard Vincent-Auriol
Opposite 61, boulevard Vincent Auriol, 75013 Paris
M° Chevaleret

Parc Suzanne Lenglen
5, rue Camille Desmoulins, 75015 Paris
M° Balard
Undercover rink for all weather skating.

Boulevard de la Chapelle

American Sports

Yes, they exist in France! Here are some pointers...

Baseball

Stade Pershing
Route du Bosquet Mortemart, Bois de Vincennes, 75012 Paris
M° Château-de-Vincennes, bus 112
01.43.28.28.93
The Stade Pershing is the capital of baseball in Paris. Most Saturdays, there are kids of all ages playing on the Mortemart field and on Sundays there are adult games on the Pershing or Mortemart fields.

A good Paris-based club is the PUC (💻 www.pucbaseball.com), which has teams of all ages and skill, and softball, too.

Fédération Française de Baseball Softball & Cricket
41, rue de Fécamp, 75012 Paris
01.44.68.89.30
💻 www.ffbsc.org
Numerous teams in and around Paris for *minis* (6 years old and above), *cadets*, juniors, and seniors.

Fédération de Football Americain
79, rue Rateau, 93120 La Courneuve
01.43.11.14.70
💻 www.fffa.org
Football teams for ages 11 - 18 and older in and around Paris.

Opposite 22, boulevard de la Chapelle, 75018 Paris
M° La Chapelle

Boulevard Davout
134, boulevard Davout, 75020 Paris
M° Porte de Montreuil

Le Paris des Tout-Petits has other addresses (see the Other Resources section at the end of this chapter).

Clubs and Organised Skates
Pari Roller
01.43.36.89.81
💻 www.pari-roller.com
This club organises a Friday night skate, which begins at 22h00 at Place Raoul Dautry in the 14th *arrondissement*. The ride last three hours and is cancelled when it rains or when the streets are wet.

Rollers & Coquillages
💻 www.rollers-coquillages.org
This club organises a Sunday afternoon skate from Bastille.

Roller Squad Institute
01.56.61.99.61
A roller-skating school which runs beginners' outings. It meets at *l'Espace Roller* at Les Invalides every Saturday at 14h00.

To discover other clubs and associations, contact the *Federation Française de Roller-Skating* which has a complete list of clubs and associations:

FFRS
05.56.33.65.65
💻 www.ffrs.asso.fr

Hiring Roller Skates
If you do not own skates or blades, then you can hire them from Go Sport or Decathlon (☞Shopping).

Swimming

For up-to-date information on timetables and prices for the 35 municipal pools in the capital, consult www.paris.fr and click on *sport* and *piscines*. If you live in the suburbs, contact your *mairie* or official town website. You can also consult *Parisports: Le Guide du Sport à Paris.*

If you would like to find a swimming team for your child to join, try:

Fédération Française de Natation
148 Avenue Gambetta, 75020 Paris
01.40.31.17.70
🖥 www.ffnatation.fr

Water Theme Parks
Aquaboulevard de Paris
4, rue Louis Armand, 75015 Paris
M° Balard
01.40.60.10.00
🖥 www.aquaboulevard.com
Wave pool, against-the-current river, spas and Jacuzzis, whirlpool, geysers, water cannons, walls of water, waterbed with bubbles, waterfall, water mushroom, swimming and aqua-gym pool. Seven giant slides, with different levels of difficult. Best to get there at opening time as it gets very crowded. Expensive. Please note that children under 3 are not allowed due to insurance restrictions.

Outdoor Pools
Piscine Roger le Gall
34, boulevard Carnot, 75012 Paris
M° Porte de Vincennes
01.44.73.81.12
50m indoor pool, 25m outdoor pool. Paddling pool for toddlers. Cafeteria.

Buttes aux Cailles
5, place Paul Verlaine, 75013 Paris
M° Place d'Italie
01.45.89.60.05
33m indoor pool, 25m outdoor pool and toddler pool with sunbathing area.

◀» TIP

Strictness varies from pool to pool, but bear in mind that small nylon racing trunks are required at most pools for boys and men - no shorts-style swimming trunks are permitted. Many pools also require swimming caps, so it is worth bringing them along just in case (available from sports shops like Go Sport or Decathlon).

MESSAGE Members Nominate their Favourite Pools:

"The pool that I love taking my kids to is Piscine des Buttes aux Cailles in the 13th not far from Place d'Italie. There are large outdoor and indoor pools AND most especially an outdoor shallow kiddie pool that was a lifesaver last summer. There is lots of room to sunbathe and some interesting architecture." Janet H., American mother of two.

"The Standard Athletic Club in Meudon is my favourite but you have to be a member or be invited by a member to go there! It's a small outdoor pool in the middle of the Meudon forest and it's just so nice to sit in the grass and feel like cars are a million miles away!" Meg C., American mother of one.

"The pool at Bois Colombes is our favourite pool. There is a small wading pool for babies/toddlers with toys, and there is another pool with a slide, water waves, mushroom shower and tubes that spout water. Then there's the adult pool. There's also a jacuzzi, sauna, hammam and a gym upstairs." Yvonne L., American mother of one.

Activities

Piscine d'Auteuil
Hippodrome d'Auteuil, 75016 Paris
M° Ranelagh, La Muette
01.42.24.07.59
25m indoor pool, toddler pool. Roof opens in summer. Closes at 13h00 on race days at the Hippodrome d'Auteuil.

Piscine Georges-Herment
15, rue David d'Angers, 75019 Paris
M° Danube
01.42.02.45.10
50m indoor pool, paddling pool for toddlers. Diving boards. Roof opens in summer. Grass area for picnics.

Piscine de l'Ile de Puteaux
voie Georges Hassoux, Ile de Puteaux near the Pont de Puteaux.
M° Pont de Neuilly, bus 43 to Neuilly Bagatelle.
01.46.92.93.34
New sports centre with indoor, outdoor pools and toddler pools.

Piscine des Closeaux
boulevard Marcel Pourtout, 92500 Rueil-Malmaison
01.47.51.71.11
Indoor and outdoor pools. Cafeteria and sunbathing area.

Centre Aquatique de Bois Colombes
30/42, rue Jean-Jaurès, 92270 Bois-Colombes
01.46.49.87.70

Centre Aquatique de Neuilly-sur-Seine
27/31, boulevard Inkermann, 92200 Neuilly-sur-Seine
01.41.92.02.20
4 pools : Indoor 25m, children's pool, toboggan, outdoor pool. Cafeteria. Public parking available.

Piscine de Plein Air La Grenouillère
Parc de Sceaux
148, avenue du Général de Gaulle, 92160 Antony
Open from early June for the summer season.
01.46.60.75.30
Large main pool with shallow end and toddler paddling pool. Outdoor café, grass for picnics.

For parks with paddling pools and water play, see Parks and Play, above

OTHER RESOURCES

Hopefully, this chapter will have given you plenty of ideas - now here are some of the best references to take them further, and keep up-to-date with the latest events.

Books
Around Paris with Kids: 68 Great Things to Do Together
(Fodor's Guides)
Aimed at visitors to Paris, this is a child-friendly approach to the main tourist sites, parks and museums, with good practical tips and advice on where to eat afterwards.

Le Paris des tout-petits: 6000 adresses et conseils
(Mango)
A must-have for every aspect of family life, this directory-style guide includes sections on workshops, outings and sport for children under 6. See also Le Paris des juniors (Mango) for children aged 6 to 14.

Découvrir Paris est un Jeu d'Enfant 2005
(Parigramme)
This guide is very easy to use even if you do not speak French. Helpful for exploring the capital and the suburbs with children aged 3 to 12.

Le Guide Vert: Paris Enfants
(Michelin)
Ideas for walks through Paris, with detailed sections on museums, parks and activities.

The following free guides are published by the *Mairie de Paris*, and available from the *mairies* of each *arrondissement* or the reception (*bureau d'accueil*) of the *Hôtel de Ville* in the 4th *arrondissement*:

Le guide des loisirs et du temps libre pour les enfants et adolescents
Information on extra-curricular activities organised by the Mairie de Paris in schools, sports establishments and other associations, and how to access them. Also available for consultation on
🖥 www.paris.fr/fr/la_mairie/publications

Parisports: Le Guide du Sport à Paris
A comprehensive 500 page guide with full details of pools and watersports facilities in Paris.

Tout-petit à Paris
A practical guide for parents of children under three, including ideas for activities and outings. Also at
🖥 www.paris.fr/fr/la_mairie/publications.

If you live outside Paris, it is worth contacting the *mairie* of your town, which usually publishes its own guide (*guide pratique*) for residents, including provisions for children's activities.

Press

The monthly *Frimousse*, available from newsagents, comes out in a format similar to *Pariscope*, with details of hundreds of activities for children in the Paris region. It has a good workshop (*atelier*) section, plus reviews, features, and day-by-day diary listings of shows, exhibitions, music, cine-

ma and family outings. An annual subscription costs around €25.

Paris-Mômes is a free magazine on children's activities published every two months with the national newspaper *Libération*.

Pariscope comes out on Wednesdays. It is the main weekly listings magazine for the Paris region, with a separate section for children's events. Available from kiosks and newsagents.

If you belong to MESSAGE, the quarterly magazine includes the full schedule of MESSAGE get-togethers organised by MESSAGE members, ranging from coffee mornings and regular playgroups at members' homes, to museum and park visits. The schedule is also available on the members-only section of the website.

Internet

Here are some of the best "what's on" websites for children's activities:

🖥www.cityjunior.com is an excellent website in French that offers cultural news and events for 0 - 14s in Paris and Ile de France.

🖥www.pidf.com is the official tourist website for Paris and the Ile de France, and has an English language version.

🖥www.commeundimanche.com has a search engine that trawls for activities based on your child's age.

🖥www.maman.fr is a great all-round website - see the *où sortir* (where to go out) section for tips from French mums.

The MESSAGE website 🖥www.messageparis.org has a great discussion forum for members which is invaluable if you are looking for ideas or information on things to do. Examples of topic threads have ranged from where to find music classes in English to which *métro* stations have lifts down to the platform for strollers.

Addresses

Got visitors? If there is something we have missed, you are bound to find it at the main tourist office.

Office de Tourisme
127 avenue des Champs Elysées, 75008 Paris
RER Charles-de-Gaulle-Etoile, M° George V
0 836 683 112
Fax. 01.49.52.53.00
info@paris-touristoffice.com

VOCABULARY

Art gallery....................................... *la galerie d'art*
Bus station.................................... *la gare routière*
Cathedral..................................... *la cathédrale*
Church... *l'église*
Garden... *le jardin*
Ice rink... *la patinoire*
Library... *la bibliothèque*
Museum.. *la musée*
Park... *le parc*
Puppet show .... *un spectacle de marionnettes*
Railway station.............................. *la gare (SNCF)*
Swimming pool............................... *la piscine*
Theatre.. *le théâtre*
Tourist information office .... *le syndicat d'initiative*

What are your opening times?..................... *Quelles sont les heures d'ouverture?*
How much is the entrance fee?.................... *Quel est le droit d'entrée?*
I would like to buy (two) tickets .... *(Deux) billets s'il vous plaît.*
I would like to reserve (two) places .... *Je voudrais réserver (deux) places.*
Is it free for children?........................... *Est-ce c'est gratuit pour les enfants?*
I would like to buy a monthly/annual ticket .... *Je voudrais un forfait mensuel/annuel.*
What age do you have to be? .... *C'est à partir de quel age?*
How can I get to (the swimming pool)?.............. *Pour aller à (la piscine) s'il vous plaît?*

Administration

Compiled and edited by Shui Shakir-Khalil

When you first move a new country you find yourself confronted by what seems like an insurmountable list of administrative tasks to deal with. Every country works differently and this chapter aims to give you an idea of what you need to do in France, and what to expect when dealing with the French administrative system.

BUREAUCRACY

Ask anyone about the trials and tribulations of French bureaucracy and you are sure to be in for a few good stories. As foreigners, we can feel unduly put upon by seemingly endless requirements and ambiguous instructions - and there is always that one missing document you did not include with your application! But rest assured that French citizens have to go through the same convoluted processes and have their own interesting tales to tell. These experiences all reflect the fact that French law relies more heavily on written forms of proof than the British or American traditions.

Help with Administrative Matters

The *Mairie de Paris* website at ⌨ www.paris.fr is a useful source of information with details on which documents are required for various procedures. This is a good way of double-checking that your file is complete.

The print version of the *Pages Jaunes* has a section on *Les Infos Administratives*. This handy reference tells you which departments to approach and lists the relevant *Pages Jaunes* heading for each.

Items Commonly Requested

Photographs

For photographs, try photo developers or photo booths with video systems that allow you to stop the image when you feel happy with the results. This is particularly useful when photographing young or highly mobile children. These booths are found in large *métro* or *RER* stations and at some branches of Fnac Service.

Proof of Residence (Justificatif de domicile)

This generally means *EDF/GDF* (*Electricité de France/Gaz de France*), water or *France Telecom* bills bearing your name and address. It is worth writing to the utility companies to request bills in both spouses' names. Bills should be recent (i.e., under three months old) or they may not be accepted. Some departments accept a recent rent receipt

(*quittance de loyer*), your home insurance certificate or your tax bill (*avis d'imposition*) as proof of residence. If your utility bills are not in your name or the name of your spouse, you will need the bill itself, an *attestation d'hébergement* from the person named on the bill, and a copy of that person's identification (*carte d'identité, carte de séjour* or passport). An *attestation d'hébergement* is simply a letter signed by the person concerned, certifying that you live at this address and giving the date of your arrival.

It is common to be asked for originals and photocopies of two different proofs of residence.

Translated Documents

Documents in another language must be translated for official purposes by a court sworn translator (*traducteur assermenté*). Your home country embassy or your *mairie* will have a list of approved translators.

Timbre fiscal

Many administrative services are paid for using a special stamp (*timbre fiscal*) which is a form of tax levied by the French government. You may have to present the *timbre fiscal* as part of your application, or when collecting the finished document. It can be purchased from the *préfecture* where you are making your application, from your local *Trésor Public* or tax office (*Hôtel des Impôts*) or from a *tabac*. Make sure you know exactly what value of *timbre fiscal* you need.

Administration

Administration

Copie certifiée conforme

This is a stamp from the *mairie* certifying that the official concerned has seen an original document (provided it is in French) and that the copy presented is a true copy of the original. Any *mairie* can provide this service. Bring the original document and the copies.

Extrait de casier judiciaire

This is your police record in France, which you may be asked to produce by a new employer, for example. To obtain it, write to: *Casier Judiciaire* National, 107, rue Landreaux, 44317 Nantes Cedex 03, asking for your *extrait de casier judiciaire bulletin n° 3* (*bulletins n° 1* and *2* are versions reserved for legal authorities and administrative departments) and giving your surname, maiden name if applicable, first names, sex, date and place of birth and full address. Your letter must be signed and dated, and include a photocopy of proof of identification. You can print an application form from the website of the *Ministère de la Justice* at
🖳 www.justice.gouv.fr.

Voter Registration (Inscription sur la liste electorale)

European Union citizens aged 18 and over can now register to vote in France for European and municipal elections. Only French citizens can vote in general and presidential elections. Register at your local *mairie*, with your passport and a proof of residence (see above).

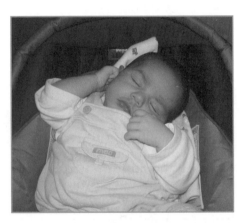

MAIRIES

Each *arrondissement* in Paris, and *commune* outside of Paris, has its own *mairie* (town hall). The opening hours in Paris are Mon - Fri 09h00 - 18h00 and Sat 09h00 - 12h30, though most services are unavailable on Saturday. All *mairies* offer the same services, though the organisation and staff vary considerably from one *mairie* to another. To make the most of the numerous services available, you will need to be relatively fluent in French and have a good feel for French culture. If your French is basic, it might be worth going along with someone who can help you. This is French administration at its best (or worst), so if you are trying to get some kind of paperwork sorted out, make sure you write down everything you are told and ask for the civil servant's name. Try not to arrive 20 minutes before the *mairie* closes, as staff will be starting to leave their offices and will have other things on their minds.

What Can Your *Mairie* Do for You?

Mairies handle a variety of administrative services, including:

- registration of birth (*déclaration de naissance*). The father (or midwife/doctor) must register the birth within three days at the local *mairie*. Some hospitals also provide this service
- processing of birth, marriage and death certificates (*extraits d'actes de naissance, mariage, décès*)
- processing of family register (*livret de famille*)
- civil marriages
- school enrolment (*inscription scolaire*) for *crèches*, nursery schools and primary schools
- elections: European Community citizens can register to vote in European and municipal elections

Administration

Administration

CARTE DE SEJOUR

The (in)famous *carte de séjour* is your official identification and you are required to carry it with you at all times. You can be required to present it to the police during a spot identification check, or it can be used as identification when writing a cheque for your groceries, when collecting parcels from the post office, etc.

Note that since November 2003, European Union citizens are no longer required to hold a *carte de séjour*. This dispensation does not apply to citizens of the Czech Republic, Estonia, Hungary, Latvia, Lithuania, Poland, Slovakia, and Slovenia.

Cartes de séjour are issued by your local *préfecture*. Usually, two or three visits are needed for your application. For your first visit, take a proof of residence, your passport and long-term visa (*visa de long séjour*) to your *préfecture*. At the section *Règlementation des Etrangers*, arrange for an appointment (*rendez-vous*) to make your formal application. At this first visit, you will be given a set of instructions as to which documents are needed at your appointment, usually six weeks to two months later.

At the appointment, your file (*dossier*) will be reviewed and, if everything is in order, your application is accepted for processing. You will receive a temporary permit (*récipissé*) that will serve as an interim document for identification. Keep it with you until such time as your permanent *carte* is ready (usually two and a half months). When the card is ready, you will have to return to the *préfecture* to collect it.

And when you get your *carte de séjour*, give yourself a well-deserved pat on the back!

Change of Address

You must go to your local *préfecture*, *sous-préfecture*, *mairie* or *commissariat de police* (according to local procedure) to change the address on your *carte de séjour*. You will need your *carte* and two proofs of change of residence (*justificatif de domicile*). The change may be made immediately, or a replacement *carte de séjour* may need to be issued.

Loss of Carte de Séjour

You must declare the theft of your *carte de séjour* to the *commissariat de Police*, or a loss to your local *préfecture* or *sous-préfecture*. You will need to fill out a declaration of loss (*déclaration de vol/perte des papiers*) and then wait for one month before applying for a new card, just in case your old one is recovered.

BIRTH REGISTRATION

All births in France must be declared at the local *mairie*, within three days following the birth. You will need:

- proof of identity for the parent making the declaration
- a document from the hospital or clinic (*acte de naissance*) where the child was born stating time of birth
- a certified translation of your marriage certificate, OR the passports of both parents, OR your *livret de famille* (if your spouse is French or you were married in France).

If you are not married, you might want to register your child at the *mairie* before the birth. This procedure (*reconnaissance d'un enfant*) formally establishes who the legal parents of the child are.

The child will automatically take the name of the father if the parents are married or, if unmarried, both parents have "recognised" the child. However, parents can choose for their child to take the surname of the mother, or a combination of both surnames. In order to do this, go to any *mairie* (before the birth) with your identification and the staff will prepare a document that both parents sign. Present this document later when registering the birth. If there is no agreement between unmarried parents, the child will have the surname of the parent that registers the birth first.

Many hospitals and clinics take care of the birth registration for you. Check in advance of the birth, however, as the first three days go by very quickly!

You may also need to register the birth at your home embassy within the year following the date of birth to avoid penalty or loss of citizenship. Call your embassy for further details. (☞ Living for a list of embassies).

Administration

ADOPTION

If you are considering adoption while in France there are two options open to you. The first option is to adopt a ward of the French state; in this case you may have to wait approximately five years and should be aware that the youngest wards of state are aged three months. Alternatively, you can try to adopt outside France, which generally involves a far shorter wait.

Conditions for Adoption

You will first undergo psychological and educational evaluations and receive an assessment of your family situation. Once you have received approval (*agrément*), you are allowed to adopt. This approval is valid for five years, and you will need to confirm in writing each year that you still seek to adopt a child (specifying any changes in your family situation during the year). In addition, both partners should be over 28, or have been married for at least 2 years. If you are unmarried, you should be over 28, and the child should be at least 15 years younger than you. Having children already does not prevent you from adopting.

Adoption plenière

This type of adoption means that the child loses all ties with his or her original family, and becomes a legitimate child of your family, taking your family name. *Adoption plenière* is irrevocable, and the adoptive parents hold parental authority.

Adoption simple

With this type of adoption, the child retains some links to his or her original family, for example the right of inheritance. The family name of the adoptive parents can be added to the original name, or can replace it. *Adoption simple* can be revoked by the courts, though only in serious circumstances.

Background Information

Before you even begin to make any official enquiries, contact an association to discuss your situation, and consult some websites or books for background information.

Enfance et familles d'adoption
221, rue Lafayette, 75010 Paris
M° Louis Blanc
Thu 14h00 - 17h00. Closed during school holidays.
01.40.05.57.70
Fax 01.40.05.57.79
www.adoptionefa.org
A group of over 90 associations (in each *département*) of 8,000 adoptive families able to help and inform adoptive or prospective adoptive parents, before and after an adoption. The website has a wealth of useful information for those looking into adoption for the first time. They also publish a review, *Accueil*, and booklets about the practical and legal aspects of adoption.

Circle of Friends
01.45.51.26.93
An English-speaking women's support group offering information, counselling and fellowship to those concerned with adoption, infertility or pregnancy loss.

Official Enquiries

DDASS, Direction départementale des affaires sanitaires et sociales
94-96, quai de la Rapée, 75012 Paris
M° Gare de Lyon, Bercy
01.43.47.77.77
This is the French social services department, part of which handles adoptions, in particular family assessments (*étude de foyer*), which is one of the first steps French residents must go through when

initiating an adoption. It has been noted that the *DDASS* favours French families, and this, together with the fact that there are extremely few children available for adoption, means that non-French couples have a very slim chance of adopting within France.

The following department offers information on adopting abroad:

Mission de l'adoption international au ministère des affaires étrangères
224, boulevard St Germain, 75303 Paris cedex 07
M° Rue du Bac

Mon - Fri 09h30 - 12h30 and 14h30 - 17h30
01.43.17.90.90 (switchboard)
Fax 01.43.17.93.44
💻 www.france.diplomatie.fr
This is a government office which, on written request, will supply fact sheets on official foreign adoption agencies. Their website also supplies information about approved agencies working on international adoption in various countries.

If you are in France on a temporary basis, contact your embassy to check your home country's regulations regarding adoption.

THE SOCIAL SECURITY SYSTEM

Payment into the French Social Security system (*la Sécurité Sociale* or *la Sécu*) is compulsory for every person working in France (including those working part-time) and entitles the contributor and his/her dependants to a range of health and social security benefits, e.g., medical insurance, maternity benefits, sick pay and family allowances. (In certain cases, an exception may apply to seconded employees who may be entitled to remain affiliated to a social security scheme in their country of origin.)

Registering for Social Security

Your employer is responsible for registering you with Social Security, but you may have to make the first move. You should go to your nearest Social Security office, *Caisse Primaire d'Assurance Maladie* or *CPAM* (you will find the address in the Pages Jaunes (💻 www.pagesjaunes.fr)), where you will be given the necessary forms to be completed by your employer. Once registered, your file is allocated to a specific office in your area and you will be given a number (*numéro d'immatriculation*) on a small card called the *carte vitale*.

This number is yours for life: should you leave France and return 20 years later, you still retain the same number.

Carte Vitale

This is an electronic card the size of a credit card on which your Social Security details are recorded.

You need to produce it every time you go to a hospital or visit a health professional so that you will be automatically reimbursed by Social Security. The *carte vitale* has only recently been introduced, so not all health professionals are equipped to deal with it yet. From time to time, you will still be given a form, called a *feuille de soins*, which you must complete and send to your local Social Security office (*CPAM*) for reimbursement.

In order to update the information contained on your *carte vitale* (e.g., to declare a pregnancy or record a dependent child), you must send the relevant paperwork to your local *CPAM* office. You can then either give your *carte vitale* to the *CPAM* for updating, or update it yourself using one of the computer terminals (*bornes*) provided in hospitals, pharmacies and Social Security offices. You can locate a terminal in your area at 💻 www.sesam-vitale.fr.

Administration

Caisse Primaire d'Assurance Maladie (CPAM)

The *CPAM* is the department within Social Security that reimburses a percentage of the costs of medical treatment. Many people also choose to take out a private medical insurance policy (*mutuelle*) to cover the difference between the amount reimbursed by Social Security and the cost of treatment. Social Security will pay 100% of the cost of treatment only in specific cases; e.g., some antenatal and maternity care (see below). The *CPAM* publishes a list of the rates at which medicines and services are reimbursed. In theory, doctors are free to charge whatever they like; however, if you use the services of a doctor or hospital/clinic *conventionné* it means that the treatment undertaken should not cost more than the limits set by Social Security (☞Health and Medicine).

Claiming for Costs of Treatment and Medicines

Healthcare professionals are paid directly at the time of appointments. All medical professionals, institutions, laboratories and pharmacies should eventually be equipped with *carte vitale* readers, making the whole process of obtaining reimbursement for medical expenses more efficient. If your healthcare professional is equipped with a card reader, he can produce the *feuille de soins* on the computer and forward it electronically to the *CPAM*, which will then process the reimbursement. But use of the card does not in itself constitute payment, so you still need to pay directly at the appointment.

A percentage of the costs of medicines may also be reimbursed by the *CPAM*. To claim, you must buy your medicines from a pharmacy with a prescription (*ordonnance*) given to you by your doctor.

Most pharmacies now accept the *carte vitale* and thereby receive payment directly from the *CPAM*. Simply hand over your *ordonnance* and your *carte vitale*. If you have a French *mutuelle* and your local pharmacy accepts the *carte vitale*, you can provide

the pharmacy with details. The benefit in doing this is that the pharmacy then receives payment directly from both the *CPAM* and your *mutuelle*, and you need only pay for the difference between the cost of the medicines and the amount covered by Social Security and your *mutuelle*.

If you do not have a *carte vitale*, or the pharmacy does not accept it, the pharmacist will either complete the *feuille de soins* given to you by the doctor, or will provide a completed *volet de facturation*. All medicines have stickers (*vignettes*) on the packaging that pharmacists peel off and attach to the *feuille de soins* or *volet de facturation*. You will not be reimbursed if these *vignettes* are missing. You must send the *feuille de soins* or *volet de facturation* to the *CPAM* together with a copy of your prescription.

Note that doctors may prescribe items that are not reimbursed at all.

Medecin Traitant

As a consumer of French medical services and facilities, you are free to choose your family doctor, clinic, hospital and laboratory. However, when visiting a specialist you will be reimbursed at a lower rate (60% instead of 70% of the base rate) unless you have been referred by your *medecin traitant*. This doctor is a general practitioner that you will have chosen by filing a *Déclaration de Choix du Médecin Traitant* form, signed by the doctor of your choice, with your *CPAM* office. The form can be downloaded at 🖳 www.ameli.fr.

This referral requirement does not apply, however, in the case of emergencies (provided the specialist ticks the correct box on the *feuille de soins*), or if you are too far away from home to see your *medecin traitant*.

It also does not apply to visits to the gynæcologist or ophthalmologists, both of whom may be consulted without a referral from your *medecin traitant*. However note that in both cases you will only be reimbursed at the higher rate if you have a *medecin traitant*, as these specialists must note the *medecin traitant* on the reimbursement form.

You can also visit the dentist without a referral, but if the dentist suggests that you see a mouth surgeon (e.g. for removal of wisdom teeth), you must obtain a referral from your *medecin traitant* in order to be reimbursed at the higher rate.

Children up to age 16 can see any doctor, including specialists, without a referral (☞Health and Medicine).

Reimbursement of Medical Costs or Benefits during Pregnancy

To be eligible for full benefits, you must have been registered with Social Security for more than a month before the beginning of the pregnancy. In addition, your pregnancy must be officially confirmed before the 14th week by your doctor, gynæcologist or obstetrician, who will certify your pregnancy on a form called *Vous Attendez un Enfant*. After completion, one section is sent to the *CPAM* and another section to the *CAF* (*Caisse d'Allocations Familiales*). The *CAF* is the department within Social Security that provides maternity, child and housing benefits for low-income families.

If you arrive pregnant in France from another EU country after the 14th week, or did not realise you are pregnant until after this time, consult your doctor, gynæcologist or obstetrician who can write a letter explaining your situation to the *CAF*. Your benefits may be suspended initially but, if the explanation is accepted by the *CAF*, they will be paid retroactively.

You should receive a booklet from the *CPAM* entitled *Guide de surveillance médicale de la mère et du nourrisson*. It includes a personalised diary of compulsory examinations with your doctor, ultrasound specialist, laboratory, etc. You will also receive a set of stickers that correspond to each of these appointments. Place the appropriate sticker

on the *feuille de soins* before sending it to the *CPAM* as they entitle you to 100% reimbursement of all medical examinations and cover you and the baby until 12 months after the birth.

If you do not have the compulsory examinations and laboratory tests by the dates specified, or do not return your forms promptly, your benefits will automatically be stopped. The baby must also have compulsory medical check-ups at 8 days, 9 months and 24 months of age (☞Health and Medicine).

The *CAF* will send you a document entitled *Demande de Prestations Familiales*, which is an application to receive benefits to which you may be entitled. This can look rather daunting if you do not speak French, but it is straightforward and requires details of your marital status, family situation, employer, previous records, etc. Once completed, you return it to the *CAF*.

The *CAF* will also send a form called *Déclaration de Ressources de l'Année*, which establishes whether you are eligible to receive benefits above the basic entitlements. It asks you for details of household income, professional status, etc. After completion, you return it to the *CAF*.

Once you are fully registered, you will find the *CAF* extremely efficient. They will send you details of your benefits and keep you informed of any changes. For example, you are entitled to further monthly benefits on the birth of your second and subsequent child/ren. The monthly payments are made directly into your bank account with a statement forwarded to your address.

For further information consult 🖳 www.caf.fr and 🖳 www.ameli.fr.

Administration

FAMILY BENEFITS

CAF Benefits

If you are registered with the French Social Security system, you may be entitled to a number of child benefits from the CAF (*Caisse d'Allocations Familiales*, 🖳 www.caf.fr). These include:

Prestation d'accueil pour Jeune Enfant (PAJE)

This is the umbrella term for four separate benefits: *Prime à la naissance*, *Allocation de base*, *Complément de libre choix de mode de garde*, *Complément de libre choix d'activité*. These benefits replace all previous child benefits for children born since 1st January 2004. They are all subject to income restrictions and are paid only to women who have officially declared their pregnancy by the 14th week, and who complete the compulsory medical visits during their pregnancy and the compulsory check-ups for the baby.

- *Prime à la naissance*: this is a one-off benefit paid in the seventh month of pregnancy. Subject to income restrictions.

- *Allocation de base*: this is a monthly benefit paid for each child under three years old. Subject to income restrictions. In 2006, the *allocation de base* was €168.20.

- *Complément de libre choix de mode de garde*: this is a monthly benefit to help with childcare expenses. The amount depends on your income, the number of children you have, their age and the kind of childcare you use.

- *Complément de libre choix d'activité*: this benefit was previously called *Allocation parentale d'éducation*. If you have two or more children and have worked for a minimum of two of the last five years (in France or an EU country, periods of compensated

unemployment count), and you give up work (taking parental leave: *congé parental*) or switch from full-time to part-time work to take care of your children, you are entitled to this benefit until your youngest child's third birthday. The full amount in 2006 was €521.85 paid monthly (tax free). The amount of the benefit changes annually, and there are other benefits if you have a disabled child.

Other Benefits

- *Allocations Familiales*: this tax free benefit is paid if you have two or more children, regardless of your income, as long as the children are under 20 (children over 16 are included if they are full-time students or earn less than the amount fixed by the CAF and continue to be your dependants). Contact your CAF for the current amounts (🖳 www.caf.fr).

- *Allocation de rentrée scolaire*: this helps with costs incurred at the beginning of the school year for families with children aged 6 to 18. Payments depend on income.

- *Bon de vacances*: this provides funding for holidays. Again payments depend on income.

- *Complément familial*: this is granted to families with three or more children, and depends on income.

- *Prime de démenagement*: you can receive this bonus payment if you need to move house because of the birth of your third child (or fourth) and are also eligible for certain housing benefits.

- *Aide au logement de familles nombreuses*: this provides assistance with housing costs, payments depend on income.

- *Avantages EDF*: this provides assistance with fuel costs, payments depend on income.

Carte Famille Nombreuse

Families with three or more children are considered a *famille nombreuse*, and may apply to the French National Railways (*SNCF*) for a carte *famille nombreuse*. This card entitles the holder to reduced rates at swimming pools, museums, cinemas etc. as well as half price *métro* travel and a substantial discount on trains (☞Travel ☞Pregnancy, Birth and Newborn).

Paris Pass Familles and Paris Forfait Familles

You qualify for the *Paris Pass Familles* (regardless of income) if you have three or more children, or if you have a disabled child, and you have been a resident of Paris for at least three years (or three out of the last five years). You also qualify after one year if you have been transferred to Paris by a company. It entitles you to free access to municipal services, e.g., museums, parks, swimming pools, etc.

The *Paris Forfait Familles* is an annual credit of €200 - €305 (in 2005), depending on income, to be used for expenses such as school supplies, school lunches, childcare, cultural activities for younger children. If you have a disabled child, instead of the annual credit, you will receive a monthly allowance of €153 (in 2005.) The *Paris Forfait Familles,* has the same qualifying criteria as the *Paris Pass Familles* except that there is a fixed upper income limit.

Apply for both these services from the *Bureau d'Aide Sociale*, your local *mairie* or *CASVP* (*Centre d'Action Sociale de la Ville de Paris*). More information can be found at:

Bureau d'Aide Sociale
5, boulevard Diderot, 75012 Paris
01.53.26.83.00

Tax Advantages

In France, you are given tax reduction for each child – the more children you have, the less tax you pay. This applies not only to general income tax (*impôt sur le revenu*) but also to your local tax (*taxe d'habitation*).

Allocation pour Naissances Multiples (Multiple Births)

Conditions for obtaining this card are the same as those for the *Paris Pass Familles*. Apply at the *Bureau d'Aide Sociale* or *CASVP* within six months of giving birth to multiples (☞ Pregnancy, Birth and Newborn).

Further Information

The *CAF* has a booklet detailing its benefits or you can visit 💻www.caf.fr. *Allô Social* is a telephone service run by the *Mairie de Paris* which gives advice and information about matters of social benefit (01.40.27.98.00). See also the *Mairie de Paris* website at 💻www.paris.fr.

SEPARATION AND DIVORCE

Regardless of your nationality or the country in which you married, you can get a divorce in France if you are a French resident. This is not a simple paperwork procedure, but a legal process requiring one or two lawyers which takes at least six months to complete.

Marriage Counselling

You may wish to consult a marriage counsellor (*conseiller conjugal*), who can help to clarify issues and facilitate communication between the spouses. Marriage counsellors can be found by contacting the *AFCCC* (see below), or using the *Pages Jaunes* (💻 www.pagesjaunes.fr).

If you are a MESSAGE member, the Medical Practitioners Directory or the Support Directory can assist with names of English-speaking marriage counsellors. For more information contact: info@messageparis.org.

Alternatively, you can consult the classifieds section of the Fusac magazine.

Separation

There are two ways in which couples can negotiate a temporary separation. One way is to apply for a court decision (*séparation de corps*). This process involves hiring a lawyer (*avocat*). See Finding a Lawyer or Notary, below.

A couple can also separate privately, without an official decision (*la séparation de fait*). The problem here is that under French law you could be financially responsible for the debts incurred by your spouse. An unofficial separation agreement cannot be legally enforced, but if it has been put in writing and signed by both parties, then you can use it once you start divorce proceedings. While the agreement will not protect your rights in respect of third parties, it will be valid between you and is a big help when it comes to sorting out visitation rights with children.

Your lawyer will contact a judge (*juge*) to organise a legal separation. A judge will issue a separation decision, which deals with the questions of custody, visiting and maintenance payments. It can also deal with the financial situation of the spouses – typically, the wealthier spouse is asked to make a contribution. This is required under the terms of *la contribution obligatoire aux charges du mariage*, or mandatory contribution to the expenses of the couple.

If you wish to leave the country quickly, it is a good idea to get a separation organised beforehand, in order to provide legal protection for yourself should any unforeseen circumstances occur during your absence.

Legal separation can end in either divorce proceedings or annulment. Annulment of legal separations is fairly easy and can be performed either by a notary (*acte notarié*), or by a declaration at the *mairie* (*déclaration devant la mairie*). A legal separation may sound frighteningly final to a couple going through a "bad patch", but it is the best way to stay on the right side of French law and help you avoid a heart-rending tug-of-war later over your children.

Divorce

Divorce proceedings take several months, in part due to the overloaded French judicial system, but also because of delays during which you are given time to change your mind.

There are four types of divorce in France: mutual

consent (*requête conjointe*), request by one spouse accepted by the other (*demande acceptée*), due to the "fault" of one partner (*pour faute*), or long term separation (*rupture de la vie commune*). In each case, decisions need to be taken on the division of assets and liabilities, the custody of children, visiting rights and maintenance payments. For a full discussion of the requirements and implications of each type of divorce, consult "Vital Issues", an AAWE publication listed in the Other Resources section at the end of this chapter.

It may be necessary for one spouse to leave the family home, and possibly to leave France. In this case there are two options:

- The spouse moves out and reports the move at the local police station giving his or her reasons, which are logged in the police report book (*main courante*).
- A request for an emergency hearing can be made. The judge can then organise the separation and might allow the spouse and children to leave France if necessary.

Useful Telephone Numbers

Association Française des Centres de Consultation Conjugale (AFCCC)
Galerie des Demoiselles
44, rue Danton, 94270 Kremlin-Bicêtre
Mon - Fri 9h00 - 17h00
01.46.70.88.44
Marriage counsellors and lawyers help you choose the solution that best suits your situation.

Comité National des Services de Médiation Familiale
Le Mesnil de Louvigny, 14111 Louvigny
02.31.73.67.97
To facilitate dialogue and prepare separations.

Divorcés de France
8, rue Albert-Bayet, 75013 Paris
01.45.86.29.61

01.45.85.60.00
🖥 www.ddf.asso.fr
Information about divorce: finding a lawyer, dealing with children, helping to prepare the divorce, etc.

CNIDFF (Centre National d'Information sur les Droits des Femmes)
7, rue du Jura, 75013 Paris
01.42.17.12.34
01.42.17.12.00
🖥 www.infofemmes.com
This association has a useful website, offers an advice and family mediation service, and also sells a guide entitled *Le divorce: vos droits*.

Administration

RENTING OR BUYING A HOME

Whether you decide to rent or buy your home, the French procedures and rules will vary from what you may be used to back home. This section summarises certain major points, but is by no means exhaustive; the books listed on the Other Resources section at the end of this chapter will direct you to other sources for more detailed information.

Renting

Here are some of the major points of the tenancy law of July 6th, 1989 (*loi 6 juillet 1989*) and later modified by the laws of July 21, 1994 (*loi 21 juillet 1994*) for unfurnished (*non-meublé*) flats. If you rent a furnished (*meublé*) flat, your rights as a tenant are not regulated by these laws and are only those stipulated in your lease agreement.

If you rent an unfurnished flat, the minimum legal period for the lease (*bail de location*) is three years. If you rent a furnished flat the minimum period is only one year. Your landlord cannot ask for a security deposit (*caution*) of more than two months rent, not including maintenance and service charges (*hors charges*). If you use an agency, there will also be agency fees which are normally about one month's rent. The security deposit will be returned within two months of handing over the keys when you leave. The reimbursement of your security deposit can be held up for a longer period of time if the annual service and maintenance charge report (*décompte des charges*) has not been written up. It is normal to be asked to present pay slips (*fiches de paie*) showing that the rent represents no more than a third of your total income and, for foreigners, a financial guarantee (*garantie de caution*) is also needed.

Before moving in, an inspection of the premises (*état des lieux*) must take place between the tenant and the landlord. Sometimes a bailiff (*huissier*) must be called in to do the inspection, in which case his fees are split between tenant and landlord. When you vacate your lodging it must be reinspected (*état des lieux de sortie*). All repairs must be made and the place must be cleaned. If the flat needs repairs other than those due to what is considered normal usage, the owner can deduct the costs from your security deposit.

Breaking a Lease

This can be done at anytime as long as you give three months notice (*congé*). This period of notice can be shortened to one month if you have been fired, laid off or are required to make a job transfer; the one-month-notice also applies to unemployed people who need to move to take up a job offer and to those who may be benefiting from *RMI* (France's welfare system).

Landlords cannot show your flat for more than two hours a day except on Sundays and holidays and they cannot show your flat in your absence unless you have agreed. Full rent must be paid up until the end of the period of notice, even if you decide to vacate the flat sooner.

You can be given notice by your landlord, but only within six months of your lease's end. You will receive a registered letter (*lettre recommandée avec accusé de réception*), drawn up by a bailiff and addressed to all occupants mentioned in the lease. You can leave at anytime thereafter, paying rent only until you move out. You can be given notice for any of the following reasons:

- because the property is being put up for sale. In this case you are given first refusal to buy it (*droit de préemption*)

- because the landlord, or one of his immediate family members, wants to make the flat his primary residence or use it as his place of work

Noise Problems

What to do when the neighbour's dog just will not stop barking? Or the frequent clicking of heels and loud voices coming from the apartment above yours keeps you from getting your ZZZ's? Any noise that is repetitive or of an intense or prolonged nature, and therefore considered to disturb the tranquillity of your way of life, is prohibited in France, especially those that occur between the hours of 22h00 - 07h00. These include (but are not limited to) noise from a TV, stereo or radio, an electrical household appliance, gardening or power tools, loud conversations and the barking/cries of domestic animals.

Most official sources will tell you the very first step to be undertaken is to try to work things out with the offending party in a calm and friendly manner. If you cannot resolve the noise problem in this way, it is advisable that you contact a third-party to mediate, such as your building's *Syndic* or *Copropriété*, your landlord (if you are renting), or even your building's concierge. If this fails, it is recommended that you file a complaint (*une main courante*) with your local *Commisariat de Police*. Make sure to keep a record of the offending noises and the dates and times of the occurrences to refer to. You will be asked to produce a piece of identity when filing your complaint.

Should the noise occur in the middle of the night and prevent you from sleep, such as noise from a party or a dispute, you should immediately call the *Commisariat de Police* and request that an officer be sent to your building to confront your neighbour. In some instances, if an officer is not available to come by, request that the police call your neighbours on the phone to inform them that a complaint has been logged.

If the problem is on-going and you must resort to police intervention, once you have amassed a certain number of complaints against your neighbour, the police will call him in for an in-person discussion to hear his side of the argument and warn him of potential fines should the noise continue. With an average fine costing €450, this is usually an effective means of getting results to your noise problems -- though keep in mind your personal relations with your neighbour will likely never be congenial again.

As the time of printing, the following website offers contact information for the *Commisiarat de Police* in Paris closest to you:

www.prefecture-police-paris.interieur.gouv.fr/infos_proxi/plan.htm

Administration

- if the landlord has "serious and reasonable cause", (i.e. late or non-payment of rent, trouble between you and other occupants)
- if the building is to be restructured
- if you sublease (*sous-louer*) your flat illegally

Further Information

If in need of professional advice you can contact the following:

Bureau de l'Information Juridique des Propriétaires et des Occupants (BIPO)

6, rue Agrippa-d'Aubigné, 75004 Paris
01.42.76.31.31
Office run by the Marie de Paris, giving free legal information for tenants and owners.

Centre d'Information et de Défense des Locataires

9, rue Severo, 75014 Paris
01.45.41.47.76
Information Centre for Tenants, focussing on defending tenants' rights.

Buying a Home

If you decide to purchase property in France, you will first want to determine the amount of money you can borrow. You can do this by either visiting one or more banks, or by using the websites 🖥 www.guideducredit.com or 🖥 www.meilleurtaux.com. Then, with your budget in hand, visit properties and review listings to get a feel for the market in the area you are looking at. Once you have decided on a particular property and have agreed a price with the seller, the actual process will involve three distinct stages: the pre-contract (*promesse de vente*), the deed of sale (*acte de vente*) and closing of the sale, and post-sale formalities. The first two stages of the process generally take at least three months to complete. At the point of agreeing to the price, you should revisit the banks to determine the best deal (it varies from bank to bank), or consult a *courtier*, (someone who brokers financial services transactions).

All of the formalities are prepared and signed in the presence of a French notary, who is the only person competent to draft and file property transfer documents. You can choose to have your own notary or share a notary with the seller; in either case the total fee remains the same, and is a percentage of the purchase price. (See Finding a Lawyer or a Notary, below.)

The *promesse de vente* is a holding agreement signed by both parties. As the buyer, you will probably be asked to pay a deposit at this stage (often 10%). You will also agree with the seller on a timescale for completing all the sale formalities. You then have a mandatory "cooling off" period of seven days if you wish to change your mind. Should you back out after this "cooling off" period, you may lose your deposit.

Between the signature of the *promesse de vente* and the final sale you will, if applicable, obtain your bank loan. At the same time, the notary will prepare the *acte de vente*. In order to do so, he must establish the origin of the house and ensure there are no outstanding mortgages or encumbrances on the property. He must also notify the local authorities of the intended sale (as it may decide to purchase the property for public purposes).

Once the *acte de vente* is prepared by the notary, you will have to meet in person with the seller and the notary to sign the document, after having been read the document aloud by the notary. The notary will then keep the original of the deed, which is the final sale contract.

After the sale contract is signed, the notary carries out all the financial and fiscal administration, and deals with registering the property. The notary has two months to register the *acte de vente* with the land registry. It can take from a few weeks to several months for the registry to issue the new deeds of ownership to the property. In the meantime, the notary will supply you with a document (*attestation*) to prove that you are the new owner.

Useful Information for Tenants

Financial Responsibility

Tenants are responsible for:

- minor repair costs to items provided by the landlord (cooker, refrigerator, etc.)
- minor repair costs when plumbing, electricity or heating fails
- maintenance costs necessary to keep things running smoothly (such as servicing the boiler and having the chimney swept)
- any freshening up of paintwork and replacement of wall/floor coverings before the end of a 10 year time period

Landlords are responsible for:

- repainting and replacement of carpets after 10 years
- replacing or repairing windows, shutters, furnaces, and taps and for redoing the façade after 10 years
- any damage caused by a manufacturing flaw, or if floor/wall/ceiling damage is caused by water infiltration
- any making good of decorating that was poorly done from the beginning (if you can prove this)

Other tips:

- Landlords cannot refuse normal house pets, but can draw the line at exotic animals
- Permission must be obtained when installing antennae and satellite dishes

Administration

FORMALITITES FOLLOWING A DEATH

Should you suffer a bereavement while in France, your consulate will be of great help, especially in the case of repatriation of the remains. Local undertakers (*pompes funèbres*) are also very helpful and deal quite often with repatriation. Bereavement is obviously a trying time, and you should not hesitate to ask for help even if you feel you do not yet have close friends in France, and particularly if your French is less than fluent. You will probably find that your neighbours and acquaintances will be willing to do whatever they can to help.

If you are a member of MESSAGE, fellow members can be of particular support. People may not hear of a situation immediately, so do phone and ask for help with childminding, interpreting, companionship, or whatever it is you need. If you do not yet know many members, call your area leaders first.

Registering a Death

If death occurs at home, you should immediately call the fire brigade (*sapeurs pompiers*) (dial 18) or your local doctor. It is recommended that you keep the room cool by closing curtains, windows and doors, and switching off any heating.

If death occurs in a hospital, it is likely that a department linked to the local *mairie* will look after the registration, and you will simply be asked to supply the deceased's papers, as well as their Social Security card and details of any health insurance (*mutuelle*). In the event that the hospital does not register the death, you will be given a form (*bon à régler*), which you should take to the *mairie*. The remains will be moved to the hospital mortuary and you can then arrange for transfer to a funeral home, or to your home, should you wish. This transfer must take place within 24 hours, (or 48 hours if the body is embalmed (*soins de conservation*) to preserve the remains.

A death must be declared within 24 hours at the *mairie* for the locality where the death occurred. Make sure you take the maximum amount of identification papers - not all of the following are obligatory but the more papers you have for the deceased person, the better:

- carte *d'identité* or *carte de séjour*
- passport
- *livret de famille* (required if the deceased is a minor)
- *fiche d'état civil*
- birth certificate (translated into French)
- wedding certificate (translated into French)
- death certificate (*certificat de décès*) which can be signed by any doctor

Also make sure you take your own identity papers. The *mairie* will give you an *acte de décès* and will send one to the consulate. It is advisable, however, to go to the consulate in person with the *acte de décès* to register the death.

When informing the deceased's employer, insurance, etc., you will need to send an *acte de décès* in each case, so ask for several copies from the undertakers or the *mairie*. You might also need a *fiche familiale d'état civil*, so ask for several at the time of registration.

Repatriation of a Body

The undertakers (*pompes funèbres*) can handle

this, and can contact undertakers in your home country if necessary. Each consulate has a department which deals with this situation and which can advise you (☞Living for consulate details).

Organ Donation

Depending on the circumstances of death, you may wish to donate organs for transplant. Further information is available from the *Fédération des associations pour le don d'organes*:

France ADOT
BP 35, 75462 Paris cedex 10
01.42.45.63.40
🖳 www.france-adot.org

Burial

Should you choose burial, this must also take place within six days of death, not including Sundays and holidays.

A full list of undertakers (*pompes funèbres*) is available from your local *mairie*, hospital or clinic. Many undertakers have websites (consult *Pages Jaunes* under *pompes funèbres* or visit the links at the *AFIF* website listed below).

Undertakers are obliged to give you a complete price list, supply a detailed written quotation and establish a written order. This order must differentiate between essential or obligatory services and optional extras (*prestations facultatives*).

Obligatory services include the coffin, its handles and seal, preparation and closing of the grave or tomb for burial, or the cremation itself and the urn. In some cases, optional services become obligatory – when remains are to cross international borders, for instance, coffins must be hermetically sealed. If you do not already possess a plot in a cemetery, you will need to buy one. The cost of plots is fixed, and must be charged to you by the undertakers without any additional costs or profit mark up. Any person is entitled to be buried in a Paris cemetery provided he or she lived in Paris, passed away in

Paris, or owns a plot in a Paris cemetery.

Optional services include embalming (*soins de conservation*), washing, grooming and make-up (*toilettage mortuaire*), accessories for the coffin, assistance with administrative papers, organisation of the funeral, extra personnel or vehicles, flowers, newspaper announcements and mortuary cards.

The *Association française d'information funéraire* has a website with useful information on all subjects related to bereavement. It includes a French-English-German dictionary of relevant terms, details of costs related to religious ceremonies, information on how to purchase a plot, details of fees charged by undertakers, articles on coping with bereavement, children and bereavement, and lists of recommended books.

AFIF
9, rue Chomel, 75007 Paris
01.45.44.90.03
Fax 01.45.44.99.64
🖳 www. afif.asso.fr

Cremation

Cremation in Paris takes place at the crematorium of *Père Lachaise* cemetery (01.43.15.81.81) and must take place at least 24 hours and at most 6 days (not including Sundays and holidays) after death. You will need to request an authorisation from the *mairie*, and enclose a medical certificate stating that cremation will not pose a medico-legal problem. The coffin must be closed in the presence of a police officer, and this involves a small fee. The urn containing ashes can be kept for up to two months at the crematorium without charge, allowing you time to decide about any final ceremony.

Religious Ceremonies

Contact your place of worship should you wish to organise a religious ceremony. Most burial places in France are Catholic, although your consulate should be able to inform you of the nearest facilities

Administration

for other religions (☞Organisations and Charities for details of English-speaking places of worship).

Financing Funeral Costs

You can make one withdrawal of up to €3,050 from the deceased's personal bank account to cover funeral costs (this does not apply to joint accounts). If the deceased was employed, Social Security should pay three times his or her last salary up to a certain limit. Private health insurance (*mutuelle*) may offer similar coverage. The deceased may also have had special insurance to cover funeral arrangements (*assurance obsèques* or *contrat de prévoyance*).

The *centre d'action sociale de la ville de Paris* (*CASVP*) has an office in each *arrondissement* and offers assistance to low-income families; your *mairie* can supply the relevant address.

Funeral costs are tax-deductible up to a limit, with receipts justifying the amount. Costs are generally deducted from inheritance tax (*impôts au titre de la succession*), but if there is no inheritance tax, the deceased's spouse or children may deduct costs from income tax.

After the Funeral

Within one week of the funeral, the following formalities should be attended to:

- inform Social Security and any private pension funds. The surviving spouse may be entitled to a pension (*pension de reversion*)
- formally notify the deceased's employer
- if the deceased was unemployed, inform the *Assedic*
- inform the deceased's insurance company and health insurance company (*mutuelle*)
- notify the bank
- notify the deceased's *notaire*
- if the deceased rented accommodation, inform the owner who will transfer the lease

to the surviving spouse
- if the deceased owned an apartment, inform the *Syndic de copropriété*

Within a month, the following should be notified:

- insurance companies such as car insurance, home insurance, etc.
- banks and lending institutions where the deceased held loans
- telephone (landline and mobile), electricity and water companies

Within six months, you may need to look after the following matters:

- transform any joint bank accounts to individual accounts
- change the *carte grise* for the car to the name of the surviving spouse (☞Living for information on *Cartes Grises*)
- send the *déclaration de succession* to the tax office and pay any tax due at the time of death
- a surviving spouse may need to obtain a personal Social Security number.

Inheritance

If a person's dies in France, the French courts decide which country's legal system should govern inheritance issues – the key element in this decision being the deceased's primary residence. If France was the deceased's primary residence, French law will apply to the estate – regardless of his nationality.

Under French law, inheritance follows the bloodline, i.e., children, parents and/or grandparents, rather than the spouse. A will (*testament*) can modify the traditional French succession and by doing so protect the surviving spouse. Life assurance (*assurance vie*) is one common way to ensure that the surviving spouse will be well provided for.

A *contrat de marriage*, signed before the wedding and kept by the *notaire* is another important way to express one's wishes in the case of death. There are three common kinds of prenuptial agreement in France: *communauté des biens*, *communauté réduite aux acquêts*, and *séparation des biens*, each with specific implications for succession.

Given the complexity of the issues involved in ques-tions relating to inheritance, wills and marriage con-tracts, it is important to take the time to settle these matters with your partner, and your *notaire*. Detailed information can also be found in *Vital Issues*, published by AAWE (see the Other Resources section at the end of this chapter). The *Chambre des Notaires de Paris* has also produced a booklet which may be of help. See 🖳www.paris.notaires.fr.

FINDING A LAWYER OR NOTARY

It is forbidden by law for the legal profession to advertise its services, so if you wish to consult a lawyer (*avocat*) or a notary (*notaire*) you will have to look for them. Most embassies provide general information about English-speaking *avocats* and *notaires*. For example, the American Embassy publishes such a list in its Guide for USA citizens residing in France. However, fluency in English is not verified.

Notaries

Notaries handle real estate transactions, wills and marriage contracts. Each region has a *Chambre des notaires*, a professional organisation of which every *notaire* is automatically a member. The Parisian *Chambre des notaires* has a useful website in both English and French (including a section on frequently asked questions), and staff can direct callers to English-speaking notaries.

Chambre interdépartementale des notaires de Paris
12, avenue Victoria, 75001 Paris
01.44.82.24.00
🖳 www.paris.notaires.fr
chambre@paris.notaires.fr

Lawyers

The legal profession in France is not split, as in the UK, between barristers and solicitors. Rather, *avo-cats* may represent you in court as well as advise you with regard to legal matters, draft contracts, negotiate on your behalf, etc. All French-qualified *avocats* are members of the bar where they prac-tice.

Free consultations on general legal matters relating to family law, labour law or tenants' rights are offered to Paris residents, daily at the *Palais de Justice* and one day per week at the *mairies* of each *arrondissement*. No appointment is necessary. If you do not live in Paris, contact the *Ordre des avocats du Barreau* for your *département* (see below) to find out where you might find such consul-tations in your area.

Palais de Justice
4, boulevard du Palais
Galerie de Harlay Escalier S
Mon – Fri 09h30 - 12h00
Free consultations, without an appointment, includ-ing during holiday periods.

SOS Avocats
0 825 39 33 00
Mon - Fri 19h00 - 23h30
Free consultations with Paris lawyers for residents of Paris, Hauts-de-Seine, Seine Saint-Denis and Val de Marne.

Administration

Here are the websites of the main *barreaux* in Ile-de-France, each of which offer a searchable directory of lawyers in the *département*, information regarding free consultations at local *mairies*, and information on obtaining legal aid (*aide juridictionnelle*).

Barreau de Paris
💻 www.avocatparis.org.

Barreau des Hauts-de-Seine
💻 www.barreau92.com

Barreau de Val de Marne
💻 www.ordre-creteil.avocat.fr

Barreau de la Seine-Saint-Denis
💻 www.avocats-bobigny.com
Barreau de Versailles
💻 www.avocats-versailles.com

If you do not have the financial means to pay a lawyer, legal aid can pay part or all of your legal fees. You can request legal aid either at your local *Tribunal d'instance* or by contacting the central office directly:

Bureau d'aide juridictionnelle
1, quai de Corse, 75194 Paris Cedex
01.44.32.76.61

OTHER RESOURCES

Vital issues: How to survive officialdom while living in France
(Association of American Wives of Europeans (AAWE))
💻 www.aaweparis.org (order forms can be downloaded)

Health Care Resources in Paris,
(WICE)

At Home in Paris,
(JSL)

Le Guide de L'Enfant and Guide Pratique de la Future Maman
Booklet available from the *Mairie de Paris*

Logement: Votre Conseiller Pratique
(PRAT (updated annually))

Les funerailles à l'église catholique
Booklet available from Diocèse de Paris
01.49.24.11.62

Les derniers devoirs – Le rituel juif du deuil
Booklet available from ACIP
01.49.70.88.00

Recueillir un héritage
Booklet available from the Chambre des Notaires de Paris
01.44.82.24.00

Le Guide des Obsèques
Booklet available from the Mairie de Paris

Formalités suite à un décès
Booklet available from the Mairie de Paris

Childcare

Compiled and edited by Miiko Anderson with contributions from Amy Terdjman

Whether you work outside the home or are a stay-at-home parent, you are bound to need outside childcare at some point. From occasional babysitters to full-time nannies, numerous childcare options exist for Parisian parents. We hope that some of your burning questions about childcare will be addressed here, and that you will find helpful information about where to find the care that best suits your child.

BABYSITTERS

Thanks to the Internet, you have a wealth of options for obtaining a babysitter, ranging from traditional agencies, electronic posting boards, university listings, to numerous governmental organisations.

Agencies

Finding a babysitter through an agency has many advantages, such as extensive pre-screened listings, English speaking babysitters, and last minute availability. However, bear in mind that you may have to pay dearly for these conveniences. Below is a list of agencies in and around Paris:

Babysitting Service
18, rue Tronchet, 75018 Paris
01.46.37.51.24

Allô Maman Poule
27, rue Raffet, 75016 Paris
01.45.20.96.96

Babychou
31, rue du Moulin de la Pointe, 75013 Paris
01.43.13.33.23
💻 www.babychou.com

Babysitting Services
4, rue Nationale, 92100 Boulogne Billancourt
01.46.21.33.16
💻 www.babysittingservices.com

Tidoudou
121, rue Marcadet, 75018 Paris
01.55.79.06.06
💻 www.tidoudou.com

Locating Student Babysitters

Hiring a student babysitter is a great option because the individual may be bilingual and flexible in terms of hours (although during school breaks, you may find yourself searching elsewhere).

International Student Organisations

Contact the following Anglophone schools directly to be placed in contact with a student babysitter:

Middlebury College
4, rue de Chevreuse, 75006 Paris
01.43.20.70.57

Sweet Briar College
101, boulevard Raspail, 75006 Paris
01.45.48.79.30

New York University
56, rue de Passy, 75016 Paris
01.53.92.50.80

In addition, 💻www.paris-anglo.com is a site that lists contact information for all Anglophone universities in Paris.

Local Student Organisations

If you decide to expand your babysitting search to local student organisations, where the students may or may not speak English, here are some options:

CIDJ (Centre d'Information et de Documentation Jeunesse)
101, quai Branly, 75015 Paris
01.44.49.12.00
💻 www.cidj.com
32 offices throughout the area.

C.R.O.U.S (Centres Regionaux des Œuvres Universitaires et Scolaires)
39, avenue George Bernanos, 75005 Paris
01.40.51.37.52
💻 www.crous-paris.fr

Childcare

Budget Babysitting Ideas

If you are really stuck for a babysitter at the last minute, and want to save on the cost of an agency, here are a few ideas:

- Try your child-free friends: they might enjoy the change of pace!
- Do any of your friends owe you a babysitting favour?
- Can you borrow a friend's regular babysitter for the night?
- Do your neighbours have responsible teenagers who would like to earn a few euros?

Alliance Française
24, rue Fleurus, 75006 Paris
01.42.84.90.00
💻 www.alliancefr.org

Institut Catholique
21 rue d'Assas, 75006 Paris
01.44.39.60.24
💻 www.icp.fr

YOOPALA
30, rue du Colonel Delorme, 93100 Montreuil-sous-bois
01.30.06.40.26
💻 www.yoopala.com

Useful Websites

If you would like to expand your babysitting search on the web, the following French babysitting websites may be of interest:
💻 www.magicmaman.com
💻 www.kidiweb.com
💻 www.abcpuericulture.asso.fr
💻 www.annonces-nounou.com

You can also find website listings on the Internet using a search engine, such as 💻www.google.fr and typing babysitting services or *garde d'enfant*.

Advertising for a Babysitter

Placing an advertisement is another option for locating a babysitter and, if you are a member of MESSAGE, the members-only classifieds on the MESSAGE website is a great place to post an advertisement.

Alternatively, you can post an ad on the following websites:
💻 www.fusac.fr
💻 www.parisfranceguide.com
💻 www.paris-anglo.com
💻 www.paris.craigslist.org

You might also consider placing an advertisement at your local bakery, church, *crèche*, or supermarket. Finally, you can advertise at the following locations:

American Church
65, quai d'Orsay, 75007 Paris
01.40.62.05.00
💻 www.acparis.org

American Cathedral
23, avenue George V, 75008 Paris
01.53.23.84.00
💻 www.americancathedral.org

Emergency Babysitting Services

There are several volunteer agencies that can address your emergency babysitting needs. These are French-speaking agencies and you may be asked to provide a donation.

Depann'Familles
23, rue de la Sourdière, 75001 Paris
01.42.96.58.32
For families registered with the *CAF* (*Caisse d'Allocations Familiales*).

SOS Urgences Mamans
56, rue de Passy, 75016 Paris
01.46.47.89.98

PART-TIME CHILDCARE

Halte-garderie

Halte-garderie is the perfect option if you are at home with your child, but want a few mornings or afternoons free. Considered to be more than a babysitting service, the professional staff use early learning activities to engage the children and prepare them for collective environments. Children from three months to 6 years of age are allowed to attend *halte-garderie*. The admission process and cost are similar to that of the *crèche* (see below); the only difference is the number of hours and days allowed. Children stay either several mornings or afternoons a week. The hours vary at each *halte-garderie* and during August, many close for the entire month.

There are two types of *halte-garderie*: state-run (*municipale*) and private (*associative*). The main difference is that for the *halte-garderie municipale*, you make your application through your local *mairie*, while you apply to the *halte-garderie associative* directly. The *halte-garderies associatives* may be more flexible in terms of the number of hours and days available, although the downside is that they are more expensive.

To obtain a list of *halte-garderies* in your area, consult your local *PMI* or search the *Mairie de Paris* website ▨www.paris.fr under the *petite enfance* section. Alternatively, consult *Tout-petit à Paris*, listed in the Other Resources section at the end of this chapter.

Several MESSAGE mothers have found success with the Petit à Petit and the AM STAM GRAM private *halte-garderies*.

Petit à Petit - Blomet
59, rue Blomet, 75015 Paris
M° Vaugirard
01.45.66.83.33
▨ www.petit-a-petit.fr

Petit à Petit - Vosges
6, rue Roger Verlomme, 75003 Paris
M° Chemin Vert
01.48.04.02.04
▨ www.petit-a-petit.fr

Petit à Petit - Neuilly
18, rue des Huissiers - Neuilly sur Seine
01.48.04.02.04
▨ www.petit-a-petit.fr

AM STRAM GRAM
Direction Générale
103 bis, rue Lauriston, 75016 Paris
01.53.65.78.26
▨ www.amstramgram.com
Check out their website for a list of locations.

◁ᴵⁱ TIP

Doudou is the generic French word for favourite cuddly toy, and most tots in France have one. Even if your child has not yet formed an attachment to a particular toy, take one along to nursery so he has something familiar from home.

COLLECTIVE CHILDCARE

If you are looking for full-time care, there are a number of collective childcare options available, from state-run *crèches* for young infants and toddlers, to private home childcare to preschools. A discussion of the main options follows, with the exception of preschools (*écoles maternelles*), which are covered in the Education chapter (☞Education).

Officially Recognised Childcare

Many of the options listed in this section are officially recognised, which means only trained professionals are employed and your child will be placed in a clean, safe, child-friendly environment. Working with officially recognised childcare can be time consuming and laden with bureaucracy, but you might benefit from tax breaks and other forms of financial assistance. To learn more about how to receive financial assistance with childcare, visit the *CAF* website (see the Other Resources section at the end of this chapter for details).

Crèches

There are three different types of full-time childcare: *crèche collective*, *crèche parentale*, and *crèche familiale*. Each *crèche* or nursery employs a *directrice*, who is a licensed nursery school nurse (*infirmière-puericultrice*). The *directrice* works directly with doctors, early childhood specialists, certified nursery school attendants, and psychologists to monitor the progress of each child.

To obtain a list of *crèches* in your area, search the *Mairie de Paris* website 🖳www.paris.fr under the *petite enfance* section. Alternatively, consult *Tout-petit à Paris*. If you are a member of MESSAGE, you can request information on childcare centres in Paris and in the suburbs from the Education Coordinator by emailing education@messageparis.org.

General Information

Opening Times

Most *crèches* are open from Monday to Friday all year round and closed on weekends and public holidays. During the summer, some *crèches* may close for a month. Drop-off and collection times are expected to be adhered to and the hours may vary from *crèche* to *crèche*. At a *crèche familiales*, children may not stay more than 10 hours a day.

Registration (l'inscription)

To maximise your chances of obtaining a place at one of the municipal facilities, you should register as early as possible during your pregnancy. To register your child for a place at municipal facility, enquire at the *service petite enfance* division of your local *mairie*. For other facilities, apply directly. Often, you are expected to provide a copy of your recent tax statement (*avis d'impots*), birth certificate (*copie integrale de l'acte de naissance*), child health booklet (*carnet de sante*) with current vaccinations,

---

What's in the Bag?

When you first take your child to nursery or halte-garderie, you might see other parents handing over a little rucksack to the staff. In case you are wondering, this magic little bag normally contains:

- snacks for your child
- favourite toy (*doudou*)
- a couple of nappies
- terrycloth mitt
- muslin square or diaper cloth
- a change of clothes in case of disaster (!)

especially the BCG and DT polio shots, and *livret de famille*.

Integration (l'adaptation)

The integration period is usually adapted to meet each child's needs and the *crèche* staff try to make the transition as smooth as possible. In the beginning, you may be asked to stay with your child at the facility. In the days that follow, your child may be left at the facility for increasing periods of time. If your child has a difficult integration period, the *directrice* may consider it more beneficial to return at a later date, when the child is ready.

Crèches Collectives Municipales

These are state-run *crèches* that operate according to rules outlined by the *Ville de Paris*. Places are only available to children (from two-and-a-half months to 3 years old) whose parents are both in either full time work or professional training, or who are looking for a job and registered with the *ANPE* (the French employment administration). Applications for places are made via your local *mairie* and fees are calculated according to your level of earnings and the number of children you have. The *mairie* will inform you if your child has been granted a place and, if so, which *crèche* has been allocated. If there is no place available, you can ask to be put on a waiting list.

Crèches Collectives Associatives

These are privately run *crèches*, and applications for places are made directly to the individual institution. The *directrice* of the *crèche* will give you details concerning application, registration requirements and fees. The regulations and opening times vary from institution to institution.

Crèches Familiales Municipales or Associatives

This is a system whereby a number of certified childcare assistants (*assistantes maternelles*) are employed directly by a local *crèche* to look after

Collective Care

In searching for collective care, it is helpful to visit any prospective facility and to keep in mind a list of questions along these lines:

- Do the children look happy?
- What is the staff-to-child ratio?
- What activities are the children doing?
- Is the centre clean?
- Do you have an overall positive feeling about the people?
- What do your instincts tell you?

small groups of children ranging from two-and-a-half months to 3 years of age in the privacy of their homes. The *crèche* provides a resource of early childhood specialists, doctors, psychologists and educators and once or twice a week, all the children meet at the *crèche* for group activities. In addition, the *directrice* of the *crèche* regularly visits the home of the *assistantes maternelles*. The parents, *assistante maternelle* and *directrice* agree on the hours and meals amongst themselves, so you may find more flexibility than in a *crèche collective*. Applications for places are made directly to the individual *crèche* and the fees are calculated according to your level of earnings and the number of children you have.

Crèches Parentales

These are parent-run *crèches* where the parents play an active role in the day-to-day operation, but qualified early childhood specialists are hired to help plan and organise the daily activities. Each parent is expected to work at the nursery at least half a day per week. As the rules are made by the parents, you may have more flexibility in terms of hours, menu choice, and curriculum input. Fees are set by the parent association, taking into account the length of time your child spends at the *crèche*, your level of earnings and the number of children you have.

Childcare

Childcare for Older Children (jardin d'enfant)

If your child is too old for *crèche*, an alternative could be a *jardin d'enfant*. *Jardins d'enfants* employ a certified *éducateur(trice) de jeunes enfants* and nursery school assistants to help young children prepare for *école maternelle*. There are three different types of *jardins d'enfants*: *municipaux, maternels*, and *l'OPAC* (*Office Public d'Aménagement et de Construction de Paris*).

At the municipal *jardins d'enfants*, a maximum of 60 children between the ages of 2 and 4 years old are welcomed. One advantage of selecting a municipal *jardin d'enfants* is that they are open from 07h30 - 19h00, even during school breaks.

The *OPAC jardins* operate under the umbrella of the *Ville de Paris* and welcomes young children between the ages of 2 1/2 to 6 years old during the school year.

Le jardin maternel accepts a maximum of 30 children between the ages of 18 months and 3 years

---

Adaptation: when the Going gets Tough

The first few weeks of leaving your child in a new environment are bound to be difficult. As you close the door on your screaming darling, here are a few things to keep in mind:

- The separation is probably tougher for you than your child
- The staff have dealt with this hundreds of times before and know what they're doing
- They will call if your child is getting too upset – no one wants her to scream for hours on end
- The chances are as soon as Mummy or Daddy is out of sight, she will play quite happily
- Every time gets easier – really!

---

who have not benefited from any other form of pre-school. Children who cannot go to preschool because their third birthday takes place after 1st January are also admitted to the *jardin maternel*.

Assistante Maternelle Libérale

An *assistante maternelle libérale* looks after a maximum of three children between the ages of two-and-a-half months to 3 years in the privacy of her home. Each *assistante maternelle libérale* is supported by the French Social Services *PMI* team, including social workers, doctors, and psychologists. All registered *assistantes maternelles liberales* have completed 60 hours of state-funded training, and the *PMI* has evaluated and approved their physical health and educational aptitudes. They have also certified that their homes are clean, safe and child-friendly environments.

Hiring an *assistante maternelle* means that you become an employer and you must declare your employee to the *URSSAF* and the *CAF*, establish a monthly pay slip (the *URSSAF* will automatically generate three of these for you each trimester), create a detailed work contract and determine the *assistante maternelle's* salary, which should reflect at least the minimum wage (*SMIC*). In addition, you must give the *assistante maternelle* a maintenance allowance to buy items such as baby wipes, nappies and formula.

For further information and assistance, contact the *URSSAF* and your local *CAF*. The *CAF* provides monthly reimbursements to families who hire an *assistante maternelle* and, unlike other forms of financial assistance, this is not subject to how much you earn.

To obtain a list of *assistantes maternelles* in your area, consult your local *PMI* (who can also offer advice about the employment process) or *mairie* (Paris residents can search the *Mairie de Paris* website ⌨www.paris.fr under the *petite enfance* section). Alternatively, consult *Tout-petit à Paris*.

Finally, the *Ville de Paris* and *CAF* recently created the *Paris Services Familles* division to answer questions relating to childcare and domestic childcare workers. Call 0 810 133 232.

◀)) TIP

Keep in mind that your local public preschool (*école maternelle*), not to mention many private bilingual preschools, may accept children as young as 2 years old. (☞Education).

INDIVIDUAL CHILDCARE

Nannies

Hiring a nanny to provide childcare at your home may be more expensive than a *crèche* or employing an *assistante maternelle*, but it is very practical, convenient, and full of benefits. You can choose hours to suit you and you may be eligible for tax refunds and childcare allowances. (Contact the *CAF* and the *Pajemploi* department of the *URSSAF* for details). Even if you do not qualify for allowances, it might be worth considering sharing a nanny with a neighbour or friend (*garde partagée*). As with the *assistante maternelle libérale*, you will be the employer and need make a declaration to the *URSSAF*. The nanny's salary cannot be less than the minimum wage.

To help you with the paperwork and any minor problems, you might want to consider using a service called *l'organisme mandataire*. For the convenience of this service, you may have to pay as much as €1,400 per year, but your money will be well spent because these organisations find you a nanny, provide a replacement if your worker is ill, and manage the payslips. You can find many *organismes mandataires* on the Internet.

Finding a Nanny

If you decide to employ a nanny, your next question will be how to find someone who is reliable and who gets on well with your children. The following section directs you to a number of helpful starting points for your search.

French Nannies

The quickest option for finding a French nanny is to use an agency. Although expensive, they should do all the vetting for you and may save you a long search.

ABC Puericulture
9, rue La Fontaine, 75016 Paris
01.40.50.13.64
🖳 www.abcpuericulture.asso.fr

Association Paris Prince
49, rue Marcadet, 75018 Paris
01.42.64.54.54

Asserdom
10, rue du Mont-Thabor, 75001 Paris
01.40.20.40.79

Childcare

Relais Famille
138, boulevard Murat, 75016 Paris
01.42.15.20.10

Générations Actives
129, rue de la Roquette, 75011 Pars
01.43.71.24.44

Prositting
8-10, rue de l'Eglise, 75015 Paris
01.44.37.91.11
💻 www.prositting.com

Alternatively, many nannies post advertisements on the following websites:
💻 www.garde-enfant.org
💻 www.nourrices.com
💻 www.allonounou.com

Finally, you may wish to post an advertisement on 💻www.famili.fr as French nannies regularly consult this website.

English Speaking Nannies
If you would prefer an English speaking nanny, then you can contact the following agencies:

Nannies' Working Hours

The rule of thumb for a nanny's working week is 50 hours. However, the reality can be far from this. According to French law, work over and above 45 hours must be paid at a higher rate. Here are some ideas for reducing overtime costs:

- *Halte-garderie* for one or two mornings a week
- Taking regular RTT days (☞Work)
- Sending the children on holidays with their respective grandparents / cousins
- Occasional care with a baby sitter or *assistant maternelle* (although this adds to child care budget).

CALID
06.86.55.06.96 (Christèle - French native speaker)
06.13.48.66.04 (Yannick - English native speaker)
paris.nanny@wanadoo.fr
This agency is run by two MESSAGE members and provides English and French mother tongue nannies, babysitters and au pairs.

Nannies Incorporated
8, rue du Dobropol, 75017 Paris
01.45.74.62.74
💻 www.nanniesinc.com

Soames Paris Nannies
64, Rue Anatole France, 92300 Levallois-Perret
01.47.30.44.04
💻 www.soamesparisnannies.com

Other good places to look include:

- Fusac magazine
- Anglophone churches around Paris (☞Organisations and Charities)
- Anglophone embassies (☞Living)
- the notice board in your local shops

Finally, if you are a member of MESSAGE, you will find it an excellent source of information for child-care referrals and contacts. Many of these individuals will have already worked for other MESSAGE members. For further information, consult 💻www.messageparis.org.

Au Pairs

The au pair system is a cultural exchange program designed to help unmarried individuals between the ages of 18 - 30 learn more about another country in exchange for taking care of children. An au pair (*Stagiaire Aide Familiale Etrangère, Au-Pair*) is not a domestic employee - she is considered a member of the family. Her role is to take care of the children by performing such tasks as giving them baths, taking them to school, preparing their meals, tidying their rooms, and playing games.

Childcare

Spotlight on the Garde Partagée Option

The *garde partagée* is an increasingly fashionable childcare solution in Paris and can be a rewarding and cost effective solution when managed thoughtfully. It combines some advantages of having a nanny in your own home with the advantages associated with collective care.

How it Works:

- A nanny in a *garde partagée* situation is employed separately by two families. Sample contracts and employer/employee responsibilities can be found on the FEPEM website (💻www.fepem.fr).
- Care of the children usually alternates between the two families' homes, usually on a weekly basis, but alternatives can be discussed with your partner family.
- The carer's main responsibilty is minding children, cooking their meals, regular outings and collecting them from *halte-garderie* or school. They may also be asked to keep play areas, children's rooms and kitchen clean and tidy. Occasional extras such as a bit of ironing, washing or running an errand may be agreed upon.

Tips on arranging a successful *garde partagée*:

- Make sure everything is clear to all parties from the outset – never assume anything!
- Consider choosing a neighbour (or friend) who lives very close to you. Think of the time you have available for drop-offs and pick-ups.
- Plan your holidays in advance, preferably at the same time as your partner family. This is particularly important if you do not have a family structure here to take the children while you work.
- Consider the age of the "other" children. You may prefer your baby to be with another baby of the same age, or to have the stimulation of older children for a toddler.

A *garde partagée* can be a fabulous childcare solution for very young children. Your baby has the luxury of staying in a calm, familiar and germ-reduced environment, where their individual needs and routines can be maintained. Additionally, the presence of other children can be fun, particularly for a first or only child. A full time nanny provides immeasurable peace of mind to a working mum, knowing your child will be cared for, even when sick.

However, the downside is that your childcare is reliant on all the continued participation of another family, the nanny and your responsibility as an employer. Furthermore, toddlers may need further activities and stimulation, so you may end up combining *garde partagée* with an *halte-garderie* or *crèche*.

Childcare

Employing an Au Pair

The family's role is to provide a private room, meals, pocket money, travel expenses and Social Security coverage. In return, the au pair works 30 hours per week, and provides two evenings of babysitting. She has one day off and follows 10 hours of language courses per week. During an au pair's stay, which may range from three to 12 months, she receives €225 - €270 per month (either the agency or the host family determines the exact amount), plus expenses.

Au pairs from EU-countries

An au pair who is from the EU needs only her passport or an identity card to enter the country. No other formalities are necessary and she no longer has to secure a work permit to live and work in France.

Au Pair Visa Requirements for Non EU Members

Hiring an au pair from a country outside the EU will require more of your time and effort because of the large amount of documents required:

- passport signed and valid for a period of three months after the last day of stay (plus photocopy)
- two long-stay visa application forms, completely and legibly filled out and signed
- two passport-size photographs, one for each form
- au pair contract from the host family in France approved by the local Labour Department in France (*DDTEFP - Direction Departementale du Travail, de l'Emploi et de la Formation Professionnelle*) (plus photocopy)
- proof of studies (plus photocopy)
- certificate of enrolment in a French language school (plus photocopy)
- visa fee

Before the au pair's arrival in France, a non-EU candidate must obtain from her host family the completed and signed Au Pair Placement Agreement forms (*accord pour le placement au pair*), provided by the Foreign Employment Service (*Service de la Main d'Œuvre Étrangère*). The au pair needs these documents to apply for a long-term visa (*visa de long séjour*), which she must have obtained before leaving her own country. She must then send to the host family photocopies of her passport and her secondary school record, translated into French, with proof of pre-registration for French classes (minimum of six months).

If unforeseen delays prevent all this administrative work from being completed before arrival, the French authorities allow an additional eight days after arrival to finalise the paperwork. When the au pair comes to France, she must go to the Foreign Nationals' Reception Centre (*centres de réception des étrangers*) at the local *Préfecture de Police* and request a residence permit (*carte de séjour*). The au pair must then take the residence permit, two copies of the contract, and proof of enrolment in a language course to the *Service de la Main d'Œuvre Étrangère*, who will grant her a temporary work permit.

Peace of Mind

When leaving your child with a childcare provider, you must feel at ease and not worry about whether or not you can trust the person. One of the best ways to ensure peace of mind is to hire someone who works with a friend or family member. If this is not an option and you have to hire a total stranger, you should call the individual's references, verify that you have the childcare provider's address and phone number, spend time with her beforehand, have her perform a practice run while you are there and trust your instincts.

Social Security

The family must declare the au pair as a *stagiaire aide familiale* to the *URSSAF* within the first eight days of her stay and afterwards to the Social Security. The host family must make a monthly contribution to *CPAM* (*Caisse Primaire d'Assurance Maladie*) which insures that the au pair receives Social Security benefits in the event of illness or accidents. These charges are not tax-deductible.

Administrative Addresses

Department du Travail de la Main d'Œuvre Étrangère
Central Paris
127, boulevard de la Villette, 75010 Paris
M° Jaurès
01.44.84.41.16

SSAE (Service Social d'aide aux Emigrants)
58 A, rue du Dessous-des-Berges, 75013 Paris
01.40.77.94.00
💻   www.service-public.fr

Préfecture de Police de Paris
💻   www.prefecture-police-paris.interieur.gouv.fr

Finding an Au Pair

Posting an Advertisement
One way to find an au pair is to place an advertisement (*une petite annonce*) on a local bulletin board. These can be found at the following locations:

American Church
65, quai d'Orsay, 75007 Paris
RER Pont d'Alma
01.40.62.05.00

American Cathedral
23, avenue George V, 75008 Paris
M° George V
01.53.23.84.00
💻   www.americancathedral.org

St. Joseph's Church
50, avenue Hoche, 75008 Paris
M° Charles de Gaulle-Etoile, Place des Ternes,
RER A Charles de Gaulle-Etoile
01.42.27.28.56

CIDJ (Centre d'Information et de Documentation Jeunesse)
101, quai Branly, 75015 Paris
M° Bir Hakeim, RER C Champ de Mars
32 offices throughout the area.
01.44.49.12.00
💻   www.cidj.com

Swedish Church
9, rue Mederic, 75017 Paris
M° Courcelles
01.44.29.70.00

If you are more comfortable with placing an electronic advertisement, you might want to consider using the following electronic posting boards:
💻   www.paris.angloinfo.com
💻   www.fusac.fr
💻   www.maman.fr
💻   www.parisvoice.com
💻   www.lady.co.uk
💻   www.messagesparis.org (members only)
💻   www.aaweparis.org

Au Pair Agencies
Some mothers prefer to find an au pair using an agency because of the level of security that this offers. Agencies can be a great help because they handle the paperwork, screen the candidates, and offer support when problems occur. Below is a list of various agencies:

L'Accueil International
2, rue Ducastel, 78100 St. Germain-en-Laye
01.39.73.15.25
💻   www.accueil-international.com

Au Pair Contact International
42, rue Monge, 75005 Paris
01.43.54.40.82 (mornings)
01.45.88.72.83 (afternoons)

Accueil Familial de Jeunes Etrangers (AFJE)
23, rue du Cherche-Midi, 75006 Paris
01.42.22.50.34

Europair Services
13, rue Vavin, 75006 Paris
01.43.29.80.01

Institut Catholique de Pari Service Social
21, rue d' Assas, 75006 Paris
01.45.48.31.70

Eglise Danoise de Paris Frederikskirken
17, rue Lord Byron, 75008 Paris
01.45.63.82.31 / 01.43.12.55.99

Accueil Franco-Nordique (AFN)
28, rue Vignon, 75009 Paris
01.47.42.45.04 / 01.42.66.53.02

Goélangues
26, rue Vignon, 75009 Paris
01.43.12.55.99
💻 www.goelangues.org

Entraide Allemande
2, rue Dorian, 75012 Paris
01.55.78.80.70
💻 www.entraide-allemande.org

Good Morning Europe
38, rue Traversière, 75012 Paris
01.44.87.01.22

Agence pour la Rencontre Culturelle avec des Hotes Etrangers (ARCHE)
53, rue de Gergovie, 75014 Paris
01.45.45.46.39

Association Nationale Franco-Quebecoise (ANFQ)
4, quai du Port, 94130 Nogent-sur-Marne
01.43.24.34.66
Carib-Pair Martinique
90, rue Perrinon, 97200 Fort-de-France
05.96.60.45.05

Helpful Au Pair Websites
If you would like to find an au pair on the Internet, the websites below should be of help:
💻 www.atout-fr-international.com
💻 www.butterfly-papillon.com
💻 www.goelangues.org
💻 www.perlangues.com

Tips for Working with an Au Pair

- assume nothing and discuss everything
- communicate
- make the au pair feel like a part of the family
- discuss the rules in advance
- write and post all rules
- do a dry run with your au pair during the first week
- explain how things work in this country
- give your au pair time to figure things out
- be understanding
- respect your au pair's time

CHILDCARE FOR SPECIAL NEEDS CHILDREN

All municipal *crèches*, *halte-garderies* and *jardins d'enfants* admit special needs children (*l'accueil des enfants handicapés*). As with any admission to a municipal childcare facility, the doctor on-site will examine the child and determine admission. If the doctor does not think the child will benefit from the childcare centre, he will direct the family to the centre that corresponds best to the family's needs.

The following private *haltes-garderies* are equipped to welcome children with motor and cerebral difficulties (*infirmes moteurs cérébraux*):

Les Trotte-Lapins
217, rue Saint Charles, 75015 Paris
M° Balard, Bir Hakeim
01.42.50.00.93

Le Chalet
11-21, rue du Chalet, 75010 Paris
M° Belleville
01.42.06.44.00

Ram'Dam
24, rue Frederic Schneider, 75018 Paris
M° Porte de Clignancourt
01.42.62.14.55

The following *haltes-garderies* and *jardins d'enfants* may be suitable for other special needs children:

Maison Dagobert
30, rue Erard, 75012 Paris
M° Reuilly Diderot
01.40.02.04.88

Petit Prince Lumiere
211, avenue Gambetta, 75020 Paris
M° Gambetta, Pointe des Lilas
01.43.61.64.00

Jardin d'enfants de l'école Gulliver
59-61, rue des Pirogues de Bercy, 75012 Paris
M° Cour St. Émilion
01.43.46.25.20

OTHER RESOURCES

Books

Le Paris des tout-petits: 6,000 adresses et conseils
(Mango)

SOS Jeune mère parisienne
(Parigramme, Collection Paris est à Nous)

Tout-petit à Paris: le guide de la naissance à la maternelle 2005/2006
Available from any Paris *mairie*

Organisations

Caisse d'Allocations Familiales (CAF)
- www.caf.fr
- www.adele.service-public.fr.
0 820 257 510 (at €0.11/minute)

Agence Nationale Pour l'Emploi (ANPE)
- www.urssaf.fr
- www.parisrp.urssaf.fr

OTHER VOCABULARY

I need a babysitter for today/this evening...........................*Je cherche un babysitter pour aujourd'hui/ce soir*

How much does it cost per hour? ....*Quel est le taux horaire?*

Do you have references?..*Avez-vous des références?*

She is asleep ....*Elle dort*

He has a nap at..*Il prend une sieste à…*

She has her bottle at...*Elle prend son biberon à*

He had lunch/supper at..*Elle prend le déjeuner/dîner à*

I will be back at… ....*Je reviens à…*

If there is an emergency, please call me on my mobile .....*En cas d'urgence, veuillez m'appeler sur mon portable*

What time can I drop him off/pick her up?..........................*A quelle heure puis-je lui déposer/venir la chercher?*

I am looking for a place at this nursery ....*Je voudrais inscrire mon enfant à votre crèche*

What is the enrolment procedure? ....*Comment fait-on pour l'inscription?*

Who will be looking after my child? ....*Qui s'occupera de mon enfant?*

What documents will I need to bring? ....*Quels documents faut-il que j'amène?*

He is allergic to..*Il est allergique à…*

She is ill today...*Elle est malade aujourd'hui*

Education

Compiled and edited by Sallie Chaballier, Lynna Tsou and Alexandra Wood

Your darling little one suddenly will be turning three, and it's time to sign him up for – gasp! – school. So soon? But he's so small! And aren't French schools horribly strict? Or, perhaps your in-laws are asking you where their adored granddaughter is going to *maternelle*, and are you sure if she goes there she'll be able to go to Henri IV for *lycée*? Or your dear husband frets that if you don't put Junior into the "right" bilingual school he'll have no chance of getting into Harvard...

The aim of this chapter is to give you a general overview of the education system in France and the schooling options available for your child. It also directs you to sources of more detailed information to help you make your choice.

CHOOSING A SCHOOL

Rule Number One: Don't Panic!

Take a deep breath and RELAX. First of all, school is not mandatory in France before the age of 6 (when it becomes compulsory until age 16). Nonetheless, most children in France start school at age 3, or even 2, and nearly all attend school by age 4. Why? Because they can. Residents of France are fortunate to be virtually guaranteed of a place in preschool for their children if they choose to send them.

The question for parents is then: which school? There are a number of educational options open to parents of bicultural or non-French children in and around Paris, and, while the choices can seem confusing, a bit a research can de-mystify the process and help you find the best fit for your child. Each type of school presents advantages and disadvantages. Since every family (and every child) is different, you will have to weigh several different considerations in choosing a school; language(s), location, price, teaching philosophy, your child's temperament, and your eventual plans for the future are but a few.

The three major categories of schools are French public (state-run), private *sous contrat* (within the French curriculum), and private *hors contrat* (outside the French curriculum).

French, English or Both?

A further wrinkle in the choice of a school is the question of language. Do you want your child to learn French? Do you feel a need to reinforce your child's English? Would you like your child to be truly bilingual? Depending on your family situation and your child's personality, these are vital considerations. Some non-French children adapt very quickly to French school and pick up the language with no problems, while others have difficulty understanding French and will not profit from the experience.

Families who are in France for a short time have to decide whether to expose their children to French - a potentially enriching experience, in a public, private or bilingual school - or whether to seek out instruction in their own national language. Parents can choose from monolingual French, bilingual French-English or French-other languages, and monolingual English or other languages. Almost all the bilingual schools at the nursery or primary level in the Paris area are private, with the exception of the Lycée International in Saint Germain en Laye and its partner schools. All monolingual non-French schools are *hors contrat*, as are Montessori schools, as they do not follow the French national curriculum.

Generally speaking, very young children (nursery school age) can adapt most rapidly to a French school, though a mature and motivated older child can also benefit from even one year in French primary school.

The choice of a French, bilingual, or monolingual school is an equation with many factors: linguistic, financial, logistical, philosophical and professional. For families living in France long-term, bilingual schools often provide the optimal solution for learning French while becoming literate in another language. However, many families do not live near a bilingual school, and small children may become tired-out by a long daily commute. Even modest tuition may present a financial burden for some families. Still, it is possible to find activities and playmates in English or another non-French language through MESSAGE and through more formal language instruction. As children grow older, they will need to learn to read and write in a second language if they are to be genuinely bilingual, but this CAN be accomplished (through an investment of time and/or money) for students enrolled in French public schools.

No Matter What School You Choose

The French national curriculum (see below) is academically rigorous, and the *Bacalauréat (Bac)* is an internationally respected academic credential. Students who hold a French *Bac* can be assumed to have a good level of general knowledge, and are sometimes awarded advanced placement or credits in foreign universities. Good students are respected by their peers – it is not considered "uncool" to do well in a French school. The downside of this emphasis on academic achievement is a good deal of stress and a lack of leisure time for extracurricular activities and other pursuits. The best public high schools can be highly selective and foster a "sink or swim" environment. However, a student who has been in the French system throughout his or her academic career is usually well-prepared to persevere and successfully pass the *Bac*. Students from French schools who attend university in, for example, the USA sometimes experience a "maturity gap" and find their foreign peers less well prepared for higher education.

However, if your child has learning difficulties or other special needs, or if you have an intellectually gifted child, the French system is not as accommodating as some other national curricula. Resources do exist in France for educating children with special needs, but parents often have to work hard to get the necessary information and support (see Special Needs Education below).

Tips on Deciding

When evaluating your decision, it may be helpful for you to review these questions:

- Has your child had any exposure to French?
- Would you feel comfortable speaking French with your child's teacher or school director?
- Can your child (and you) cope with a daily commute?
- Do you want your family to be part of your neighbourhood community?
- Is it imperative to you that your child learn English (or another language)?
- Does your child need a lot of structure or is he happier in an unstructured environment?
- Can you afford the expense of private school?
- Are you moving in a few years, or are you staying in France long-term?
- Where will your child attend primary school or secondary school if she attends a given preschool or primary school?

Make a list of your priorities for your child and for yourself: financial considerations, language(s) taught, your child's eventual educational path, transportation logistics, religious affiliation, etc. Unless you have ruled out your local public school as completely unacceptable, it is a good idea to register your child there as a fall-back solution so he will have a place at the *rentrée*. Ultimately, your goal is, of course your child's happiness and well-being. While there is no single, "magic formula" that will guarantee that your child will flourish in a given school, some preliminary research and making good use of the information resources available should help you to make the best choice for your child and family.

◀)) TIP

Parents' associations (*Associations de Parents d'Elèves*) exist in all schools, and can be an extremely useful resource. Get involved in your child's school as much as you can, both in order to understand what is going on in the school and to know the people involved (school administrators, teachers, and other parents). Some schools are more open to parental involvement than others, but all have some avenue for parents to participate in school life.

PUBLIC SCHOOLS

French public schools generally are excellent, with well-trained teachers. Education is taken seriously by parents and students alike. In contrast to some other countries, public schools by and large have a good reputation in France. They have the advantages of being free of charge and close to home. Sending your child to your local public school usually will mean that he or she will learn French, become socialised, make friends in your neighbourhood, and that you will meet French parents. Some families moving to France from abroad criticise French schools as being too strict, while others marvel at the high quality of free public schools. It is a matter of perspective and also a matter of each individual school and its director.

You can find out to which school you child would be assigned by consulting the *bureau des écoles* at your local *mairie.* If you would prefer that your child attend a different public school (for example, one closer to your workplace), you can request a *dérogation* (transfer). *Dérogations* must be approved by both the director of your assigned school and the director of the school you would like your child to attend. Be aware that a director of a school with low enrolment may be unwilling to give up a student, and that the director of an already crowded school may not accept a student from outside the school's catchment area.

Public schools do vary according to neighbourhood, and some have large classes with attendant discipline problems. If you know any other parents in your neighbourhood, talk to them about the local school. If you are a member of MESSAGE, there is an Education Directory which may provide feedback on certain specific public schools. Most importantly, make an appointment with the director of your local school to see it for yourself. Many foreign families have been pleasantly surprised by their local French schools and their children thrive there.

The French Curriculum - A Brief Overview

Preschool (*école maternelle*) provides children with a balance of creative activities (art and music), and physical activities. During the first two years (*petite section* and *moyenne section)* the emphasis is on playing, learning to cooperate with others and to become more autonomous. The last year of *maternelle* (*grande section*) is more structured, with activities to encourage literacy and numeracy, although learning through play still has a role.

Primary school (*école primaire* or *école élémentaire*) teaches children to read, write, and express themselves orally, acquaints them with the fundamentals of French grammar and of mathematics, introduces history and geography (treated as one subject in France) as well as science, and pro-

vides civic education. Schools also teach art, music, and physical education approximately once a week. Increasingly, French primary schools offer initiation in a foreign language, often English, beginning in *CE2*, and many schools offer some introduction to computers. Typically, students have one teacher for all subjects, except art, music, sports, and foreign language. The school day is a long one, and children do not have a great deal of after-school time for extracurricular activities, except for Wednesdays. Parents often arrange sports or artistic activities outside school to complement what is offered by the school curriculum.

Secondary school in France consists of *collège* and *lycée*. Whereas preschools and primary schools vary in size, most secondary schools are quite large. It is extremely difficult to receive a *dérogation* for *collège,* so most students in the public

Education

school system will attend *collège* according to their place of residence. Some schools have both a *collège* and a *lycée*, while some *collèges* feed into different *lycées*, depending on a student's choice of *Bac* orientation and his or her grades.

The change from *CM2* to *6ème* is a big one: students have different teachers for different subjects, and their schedules change from day to day and week to week. They are expected to plan their work in advance and are called upon to be responsible and autonomous at age 11. While most children make a smooth transition to *collège*, it can be stressful at first for students and parents alike.

Serious study of a foreign language begins in *6ème*, with the option of Latin in *5ème* and a second foreign language in *4ème* or *Seconde*. The study of physical science is added to natural science in *5ème*, as are interdisciplinary projects. In *3ème*, students have to start thinking seriously

about their course of study in *lycée* and which option of the *Baccalauréat* they will pursue. Towards the end of *3ème*, students take an exam to obtain the *Diplôme National du Brevet,* which measures the knowledge a student has acquired during *collège*.

The topics of *orientation* and passage into *lycée* could take up a lengthy article on their own, and parents concerned with the choice of a preschool or primary school need not worry about them anytime soon. Parents choosing a *collège,* however, may wish to give some thought as well to where their child will attend *lycée* at roughly age 15.

The type of diploma your child leaves school with determines the type of further training or education available afterwards. Not all high schools offer all options of the *Baccalauréat* (the general examination given at the end of secondary school in . France). French *lycée* programmes are either gen-

French School Years and USA/ UK equivalents:

French School	Age	Class Name	UK/USA equivalent
Maternelle	2-4	*Petite Section*	Early Learning
(Nursery school)	4-5	*Moyenne Section*	Reception Class
	5-6	*Grande Section*	Year 1/Kindergarten
Elémentaire	6-7	*Cours Préparatoire (CP) 11ème*	Year 2/1st grade
(Elementary School)	7-8	*Cours Elémentaire 1ère année (CE1), 10ème*	Year 3/2nd grade
	8-9	*Cours Elémentaire 2ème année (CE2), 9ème*	Year 4/3rd grade
	9-10	*Cours Moyen (CM1) 1ère année, 8ème*	Year 5/4th grade
	10-11	*Cours Moyen 2ème année (CM2) 7ème*	Year 6/5th grade
Collège	11-12	*6ème*	Year 7/6th grade
(Secondary School,	12-13	*5ème*	Year 8/7th grade
Middle School)	13-14	*4ème*	Year 9/8th grade
	14-15	*3ème*	Year 10/9th grade
Lycée	15-16	*Seconde*	Year 11/10th grade
(Secondary School,	16-17	*Première*	Year 12/11th grade
High School)	17-18	*Terminale*	Year 13/12th grade

eral, professional or technical. The general education programme - the most academic - has three tracks: science and maths (*Bac S*), economics and social sciences (*Bac ES*), or language and literature (*Bac L*). Students must choose one of the three during their year of *Seconde*, so their course of study will be mainly concentrated in those subjects for the last two years of *lycée*. Students with very strong English or other foreign language skills may wish to take the *Option International du Baccalauréat (OIB)*, which adds language, literature, history and geography at a bilingual level in the relevant language. At present, there are 12 national options for the *OIB* (including both American and British). However, only a few *lycées* in the Paris area offer the *OIB*, so families should bear this in mind in their educational planning.

Public School Enrolment Procedures

Enrolment for public schools takes place from September to March of the preceding year, although enrolment for an immediate entry into school occurs throughout the year. Precise dates for enrolment are posted at the *mairie*, schools and municipal *crèches*. Places may not be confirmed until June, as place allocations - at least at *maternelle* - are made according to the age of the child.

Ecole Maternelle

You should apply to the school's local *mairie* (to the *bureau des écoles*) armed with your passport or other recognised form of identity, your child's passport, a translation of his birth certificate or your family booklet (*livret de famille*) if you were married in France, proof of address (typically a *EDF/GDF* bill or a telephone bill), as well as the child's *carnet de santé* (☞Health and Medicine) or a certificate to show that they have had the obligatory vaccinations for their age, including the BCG.

The *mairie* will then supply you with a document (*le certificat d'inscription*) indicating the school your child may attend. This document is not a confirma-

tion of enrolment; you then need to make an appointment with the head of the designated school and take the form from the *mairie* with you, along with your *livret de famille* (or your child's birth certificate if you were not married in France) If there are enough places at your school, your admission may be immediate, but it might not be until June that you have confirmation and you may even have your enrolment transferred to a nearby school. You do not need to renew your enrolment every year, unless your child is changing schools.

Ecole Elémentaire

If your child attended *école maternelle*, he will be registered automatically at your local elementary school. If he did not attend *maternelle*, you will need to go through the procedure described above.

Collège and Lycée

Enrolments for *collège* and *lycée* are handled by your local Education Office (*Rectorat*). If your child was previously enrolled in elementary school, the head of that school will give you an admission form (*dossier d'inscription*) around March. You will be told which *collège* your child is eligible for, but that may change. You will be asked to nominate the formula for your child (half-board *cantine*, cafeteria (self-service) or having lunch outside of school) and to state his choice of first foreign language. You must return the form to the head of the elementary school by the beginning of April. The *collège* will then send you an offer of enrolment (*un avis d'affectation*). Upon receipt of this offer, you must either go in person to the *collège* within five days to confirm your acceptance or confirm by telephone or in writing to the head of the *collège*.

For the students in their last year of *collège*, the decision to go to *lycée* is taken in mid-May. If your child was not previously enrolled in a public school, contact your local *Rectorat* for an application form to enter into the public system. Your child will have to sit an examination as part of the enrolment procedure.

Other Information

Insurance & Health

All children need at least third party insurance (*l'assurance responsabilité civile*) in case of an accident at school causing damage to school property or injury to another student. They will also need medical insurance in case they injure themselves. Third party insurance is often covered by your household insurance policy. If your child eats at school, or attends after-school care, they will need personal comprehensive insurance (*l'assurance individuelle corporelle*). Some companies providing health insurance also provide school cover. The school needs to be given a certificate of insurance (*attestation*) from your insurer.

All students in the French public school system are eligible for government-funded medical examinations. Between the ages of 3 and 4, there is a test for vision, hearing and language development; between 5 and 6, a thorough examination (*bilan global*) is done, which is repeated between 13 and 14. Between 11 and 12, vision and hearing are checked again. (For details of other medical examinations ☞Health and Medicine)

Financial Contributions

While school is free, extra contributions are requested for the school cooperative (*l'Office Central de Coopération à l'Ecole - OCCE*). These contributions are for a range of things, including books, excursions or shows, mothers' and fathers'

A typical school day in *petite section*

The day begins with a roll call (*appel*) while the children play with the letters of their names. Then there is a snack (*collation*) which, at some schools, is supplied by the parents. There may be a roster outside the classroom for parents to fill in what they are going to provide for the class on their allotted day.

By 09h00, the children are ready to start their work. Because class sizes are so large with up to 30 children per qualified teacher, they are often divided into groups with the teacher focusing on one group at a time, while "helpers" (*dames de service)* help out with the other children. For example, one group may go to the library while another group does painting. They may join up for gymnasium or swimming, or tennis if the school offers it. On gym days girls should wear sports shoes (*baskets)* or other practical shoes and trousers rather than skirts or dresses.

There is a morning and afternoon recreational break (*la récréation* or *"la récré"*) of about 30 minutes at around 10h00 and 15h00. The *maîtresse* will get the children to put their coat on by themselves and send them out to play. Supervision may be very limited and they may fall over, get dirty - the normal kiddie things.

At about 10h30, it is time for written work (*travaux écrits*). Here the children work in groups again, possibly on a theme such as colours, stories, flowers, holidays, or the subject of their latest outing. They are taught to get used to holding a pen correctly and learn how to hold a pair of scissors. As your child's work may be posted on the walls of the classroom, you may not receive any of his work (except for Christmas projects, Easter eggs, mothers' and fathers' day presents) until the end of the school year.

At about 11h25, the teacher divides into those going to meet up with their parents for lunch, and those going to the *cantine*. For the children staying at school, they will go out to play at after lunch. At some point over the lunch period, children who still take a nap will do so at school. Then it is more class time until school is out between16h20 and16h30.

day presents (in *maternelle*) or any extra staff the school might provide, for example a pianist to accompany them while they learn their songs.

Similarly, school excursions (*sorties*) are generally extra. Parents are often encouraged to accompany the class on these trips and this can be a great insight into your child's school life. There may also be a cake sale, a book drive and a school *fête* to raise funds for the school.

School Life

The French school year runs from the beginning of September to the beginning of July. It consists of three terms with a holiday of about two weeks in the middle of each: *Toussaint* (late October to early November), winter and spring. There are also holidays breaking up the terms themselves - a short break for Easter, a longer one for Christmas. France has been divided up into three zones to stagger these holidays and most of Ile de France is in Zone C. The quickest way to find out the holiday dates for the current school year is on the Internet: search under *calendrier scolaire* on any French search engine.

The average school week in *maternelle* consists of Monday, Tuesday, Thursday and Friday, with the option of attending school on Saturday mornings if the school is open – although in practice, few parents send preschool aged children to school on Saturdays. In primary school and *collège,* students have a half day of classes either on Saturday mornings (in most public schools) or Wednesday mornings (most private schools). *Lycée* students usually will have classes both Wednesdays and Saturday mornings, according to their course load. Some school districts have instituted a four-day school week (*la semaine de quatre jours*), with shorter school holidays.

In *petite section,* it is possible for you to send your child to school just for the mornings. However, all children are usually expected to attend full days from *moyenne section* onwards. Some schools allow parents of children in *petite section* to accompany their child to the classroom until the *Toussaint* break. However, after *Toussaint,* all parents must be out of the school grounds by 08h30 and the door will usually be open for parents at around 11h30 and 16h30 to pick up their children and make informal contact with the teacher.

The little children are encouraged to take their security object (*doudou*) or dummy to school with them in a bag, and there may be a hanger with a special spot for it in the classroom. Like all other items that may be lost, it is wise to label the *doudou* with your child's name. The children need to be potty trained (*propre*) although accidents are largely tolerated. Similarly, they need to be able to take off and put on their shoes, so Velcro fastenings are ideal.

There are open nights at various points throughout the year to discuss your child's progress. Do not expect the teacher to linger at pick-up time to discuss this, even in the first year. The attitude is that if there is a problem they will tell you, and the best way to communicate with your child's teacher if you are worried is to make an appointment. Your child will be given a correspondence booklet (*cahier de correspondance*) in which all important announcements are communicated to parents over the course of the school year, and which you can use to communicate with your child's teacher.

Cantine & Garderie

If you work, your child may remain at school during the lunch break and eat at the school *cantine.* Even when one parent is not working outside the home, it may be possible to send your child to the *cantine* one day a week (or two or more, depending on the school if you are really lucky). If you are studying, it may be possible to send your child for more days provided you supply a certificate (*attestation*) to the head of the school when you apply. The *cantine* is charged on a sliding scale based on your adjusted household income, as calculated by the *mairie* after you have provided basic information and docu-

What to do during the School Holidays

Ever wondered what to do with the children do if you are not on leave during the school holidays? Here are some ideas:

Centres de Loisirs

Centres de Loisirs are municipal centres that organise activities for children aged 3 to 13 during the school holidays. They run in local schools or other public facilities, are open all day and you can enrol your child at the local *Centre de loisirs* for as many days as you like. A day costs at most €9.50 and you may get a reduction based on family income. Activities differ from centre to centre, but in good weather the children spend part of the day outdoors and they usually get to choose among several crafts/activities such as drawing, painting, group games and singing.

For more information, contact your local *mairie*, or, if you live in Paris, go to www.paris.fr and search under *centres de loisirs* or contact *Allô Scolaire* 01.42.76.23.45 or *Paris info mairies* 0 820 007 575.

Workshops

In addition to the various workshops (*ateliers*) and activities offered during the holidays and listed in ☞Activites, you may wish to contact the following organisations:

L'Esprit Culterelle
01.47.70.23.83
💻 www.lespritculturel.com
Organises cooking and art workshops and trips to museums and the theatre.

UCPA
0 825 820 830
💻 www.ucpa.com
UCPA organises supervised sporting activities in Paris and sports camps away from home for children aged 7 to 18.

Away from Home

Most *mairies*, including the *Mairie de Paris*, organise a wide variety of cultural or sports-oriented summer camps in July and August for children aged 4 to 16. The advantage of this set-up is that the holiday is heavily subsidised, even if you are paying the highest rate, and you can rest assured that the places you are sending your child to have been checked out. If you live in Paris, you can find more information by visiting www.paris.fr and searching under *Vacances-Arc-en-Ciel*. Or contact your local *mairie* for information.

For other summer camp options, consult the following websites:
💻 www.action-sejours.com
💻 www.aquarelle-sejours.fr
💻 www.compagnons.asso.fr
💻 www.temps-jeunes.com
💻 www.le-toupidek.com
💻 www.vmsf.org

For information on summer camps in other European countries and the USA, contact Tips on Trips and Camps (💻www.tipsontripsandcamps) at 0 871 721 491 or nancytipsontrips@gmail.com.

Education

ments relating to your household income and expenses (tax statements, pay stubs, number of dependents, etc).

Most schools also provide after-school care (*garderie*), and some have a recreation centre (*centre de loisirs*). The *garderie* is usually after school until about 18h30 and is charged according to a sliding scale. If your child attends the *garderie*, you will need to send along a snack (*goûter*) to eat at about 16h00. After school, the small children play, but from elementary school onwards, the *garderie* involves supervised homework time *(étude)*.

Further Information

The websites of the French education ministry, 💻www.education.gouv.fr and 💻http://eduscol.education.fr provide a wealth of information about administrative formalities and give an extremely detailed description of the French national curriculum. You can also find useful information on the regional education websites:

💻 www.ac-paris.fr (*Académie de Paris*)
💻 www.ac-creteil.fr (*Académie de Creteil*)
💻 www.ac-versailles.fr (*Académie de Versailles*)

TIP

Try to visit your *mairie* during the summer, when they are less busy, to have your household income calculated, to sign-up for *la cantine*, *la garderie* and/or *le centre de loisirs*, and to update your child's vaccination records.

PRIVATE SCHOOLS

Sous contract

Private schools that are *sous contrat* are partially subsidised by the French government and monitored by the French education ministry. Consequently, their tuition fees are modest compared to USA or UK standards, and their academic level is generally high. They teach the French national curriculum, but have leeway to add subjects or to teach some subjects in a language other than French.

Most religious schools (Catholic or other) are *sous contrat*, as are some of the better-known bilingual schools. In many cases, they have a less diverse student body than public schools. Some parents maintain, rightly or wrongly, that private schools provide greater discipline and academic rigor than public schools. Certain private schools actually may be more flexible and innovative in their teaching style than comparable public schools. Again, individual schools differ widely and parents must do their research to find out a particular school's profile and reputation.

Hors contrat

Hors contrat schools are not obliged to teach the French national curriculum, nor are they vetted by the French education ministry. Some may teach British, American, or other foreign programmes, others teach the International *Baccalaureate* curriculum, while still others offer Montessori or other education programmes. These schools are by far the most expensive, as they receive no state financing, and their student bodies are most likely to be largely expatriate. One advantage is that they usually have smaller classes than other schools. They may also have a greater component of arts and sports.

Education

If you plan on your child eventually attending a French public or *sous contrat* private school, he or she will have to be tested when transferring from an *hors contrat* school. On the other hand, if you will be returning to your home country and want your child to be educated in your national curriculum, you will most likely favour an *hors contrat* school.

Bear in mind, though, that when it comes to schools in France, "more expensive" does not necessarily mean "better". While many *hors contrat* schools have excellent teachers and facilities, others do not. This category probably has the greatest variation of standards, so it is wise to visit individual schools whenever possible.

Some private schools may open enrolments earlier than public schools, so be sure to check with the school. Enrolments for many bilingual schools are very competitive and places limited, so do not leave it too late.

To find out more about private schools, contact the following organisations:

C.I.D.E. (Centre d'Information et de Documentation sur l'Enseignement Privé)
84, boulevard Saint Michel, 75007 Paris
01.53.10.33.20
💻 www.enseignement-prive.org

C.N.E.P. (Centre National de Documentation sur l'Enseignement Privé)
Centre Fabert
20, rue Fabert, 75007 Paris
01.47.05.32.68
💻 www.fabert.com

Finally, for comprehensive information in English about private schools, consult the AAWE Guide to Education in France.

TIP

The AAWE Guide to Education in France is the most comprehensive source of information available in English about the French education system and schools in France. See the Other Resources section at the end of this chapter for details.

SPECIAL NEEDS EDUCATION

The AAWE Guide to Education in France has a full chapter devoted to resources for children with special needs, and the crucial organisations for Anglophone parents of children with learning difficulties are SPRINT and SPAN.

SPRINT (Sharing Professional Resources, Ideas and New Techniques)
01.34.86.93.41
http://sprint.france.free.fr
sprint.france@free.fr

SPAN (SPRINT Parents' Action Network)
06.14.67.04.50 (President: Carole Harrington-Fuhr)
01.47.23.85.46
(Secretary: Leslie Palanker-Dufresne)
SPAN@freesurf.fr

For children with physical or mental handicaps who cannot be mainstreamed:

Handiscol' (in French)
0 810 455 501
www.education.gouv.fr/handiscol
handiscol@cnefei.fr

For intellectually gifted children:

AFEP (Association Française pour les Enfants Précoces)
13 bis, rue Albert Joly, 78110 Le Vésinet
01.34.80.03.90
01.34.80.03.48
www.afep.asso.fr

ANPEIP (Association Nationale pour les Enfants Intellectuellement Précoces)
12, rue Xaintrailles, 75013 Paris
01.45.33.17.74
www.anpeip.org

HOME EDUCATION IN FRANCE

Although school of some sort is mandatory for children over 6 years old, parents wishing to educate their children at home may do so if they meet certain requirements.

Firstly, the home education must enable the child to acquire – by the end of the age of compulsory schooling - a good command of written and spoken French, as well as knowledge of French literature, history and geography, the basic principles of mathematics, science and technology and the ability to speak at least one foreign language (e.g., English). Art and sports must also be covered.

Secondly, the parents must choose to either enrol with a certified distance-teaching school or declare their intention to homeschool with their local *mairie* and *Inspecteur d'Académie*, at least two weeks before the start of school in September each year

(and eight days after moving to a new town).

Parents choosing to use a distance-teaching school need not file any declarations with the authorities (they are taken care of by the school). Rather, the child completes coursework sent by the school, and must return the work for grading by the school.

The CNED (*Centre national d'enseignement à distance*), found at www.cned.fr, is a state-sponsored option offering both full curriculum (for children not attending traditional school at all) and *à la carte* courses (helpful for families who might want to home-school certain courses only (e.g. English) while still enrolling their child in traditional school). Private institutions that have been certified to provide distance teaching also exist and can be found at www.cidj.com.

Education

Parents preferring to home educate without using such certified distance-teaching courses are required to make annual declarations to their *mairie* and *Inspecteur d'Académie*. Furthermore, both the *mairie* and the *Inspecteur d'Académie* may visit the home to confirm that the child is being taught in an appropriate environment and as required by law. In the event that the education being provided to the child is deemed to be insufficient, the parents will be given a probationary period to correct the problems cited, followed by another visit to confirm compliance. In the event of non-compliance, the parents may be required to enrol their child in school.

For further information about home education, contact the following organisations:

Les Enfants d'Abord
2, impasse Durot, 02130 Villers Agron Aiguzy
05.53.01.05.90
🖳 www.lesenfantsdabord.org

CISE (Choisir d'Instruire Son Enfant)
Le Village, 05130 Fouillouse
06.84.94.66.28
www.cise.asso.free.fr

Both the above organisations have an English version of their website.

CNED (Centre National d'Etudes à Distance)
boulevard Léonard de Vinci, Téléport 4, 86980 Futuroscope Cedex
05.49.49.94.94
🖳 www.cned.fr
The CNED is also very useful for families who leave France and want their child to keep up with the French curriculum.

BILINGUALISM

The first thing to note about bilingualism is that it is rather commonplace – about 20% of the population of France is bilingual, as is over half of the world's population. Bilingualism is the ability to function with native or native-like competence in two languages. For your children living here, dealing with two languages will simply be a normal part of life. For most of them, one language will dominate and this is not a cause for concern. Which language is the dominant one at any given time will largely depend on the quantity and quality of exposure to the two languages and the child's motivation to speak them.

All children have the potential to become bilingual. However, their eventual fluency in two languages will be influenced not only by environmental and motivational factors but also by individual aptitude. Siblings may therefore exhibit not only differences in their language preference but also in their linguistic proficiency, particularly in the less dominant language.

A young child just learning to speak may mix the sounds, words and grammar of his two languages because he has not yet differentiated between them. This can make for very interesting conversation! Parents can help their child to separate the languages by being consistent in their own language use. The "one parent, one language" approach in which each parent speaks his native language to the child is convenient and relatively easy to follow. When both parents are native English speakers, a context-based approach is advised. For example, English in the home but French in the community. The method selected must take into account the particular language patterns of the family and the child's community. The most important rule to remember is to be as consistent as possible, particularly with a very young child. The predictability of a particular language being spoken will help the young child to differentiate between the languages and to designate to whom he speaks which language. As the child develops, mixing will diminish until his languages are well differentiated. When mixing does occur the parent can simply repeat what he thought the child wanted to say. For example if the child says "I *veux* more" the English-speaking parent could respond with "Oh, do you want more?" or "Do you want more juice?" In the process of confirming what the child requested, the parent has modelled the correct form. Overt and constant correction is not only unnecessary but could be stressful for the child. Bear in mind that communication is the goal. Children learn languages simply by experience.

While most children do not have difficulty acquiring two languages, you should be concerned if your child's language development appears to be very slow and/or if he does not seem to understand as well as other children his age. Bilingualism does not cause language learning difficulties. But, there are bilingual children who – like children in the monolingual population – experience a specific difficulty in language function. If you have any doubts regarding your child's speech and language development, consult a speech therapist or orthophonist.

The important idea to remember is that bilingualism is as natural as monolinguism. It is a gift offered with living in a bicultural environment – for those who wish to take it.

Here are some suggestions for facilitating and maintaining bilingualism:

Provide opportunities for socialisation in both languages – for example a French *halte-garderie* and MESSAGE play groups. Later on, English story hours (for example at the American Library of Paris or Brentano's bookshop), Girl Scouts, sports and other organised activities in English, particularly for children otherwise immersed in French.

Read to your child in your native language (even when he starts school in a different language).

Show pride in your native language and the culture it represents. A child will quickly sense any reticence on the part of his parents in relation to their own use of language.

Encourage family visits – especially from monolinguals. A monolingual grandparent is a gift not to be underestimated!

Arrange some form of formal instruction for literacy skills if possible, as English reading is taught in French schools as part of the second-language programme.

Computer programmes and audio and video cassettes in English (or French) are popular with children of all ages. These are highly effective tools for improving comprehension.

Once reading and writing have been established, penpals or e-mail correspondence in the less dominant language can encourage further language progress in the older child.

Education

RESOURCES

AAWE Guide to Education in France
Association of American Wives of Europeans
(AAWE)
www.aaweparis.org (order forms can be downloaded)

L'Imagerie des tout-petits: La journée des petits,
(Editions Fleurus)

Elève à Paris de la maternelle au lycée
(Mairie de Paris)

Enfant Magazine: Il grandit 3-12 ans - Le guide de l'année scolaire.
Hors série No 3 Septembre Octobre 2005

Qu'apprend-on à l'école maternelle? (école primaire, collège, lycée)
(CNDP XO Editions)

The Bilingual Family: A Handbook for Parents
Edith Harding-Esch and Philip Riley
(Cambridge University Press)

The Bilingual Family Newsletter published in England by Multilingual Matters. For subscription information, or a free sample consult
www.multilingual-matters.com

Growing Up With Two Languages: A Practical Guide
Una Cunningham-Andersson and Staffan Andersson
(Routledge)

VOCABULARY

arithmetic	l'arithmétique
art class	l'art, le dessin
bell	le sonnerie
biology	la biologie
blackboard	le tableau
boarder	un(e) interne
boarding school	un internat
caretaker	le concierge
chemistry	la chimie
civics	l'éducation civique
classical languages	les langues mortes
classroom	une salle de classe
cloakroom	le vestiaire
college	une université
competitive exam	un concours
computing	l'informatique
corridor	le couloir
course	un cours

desk	*un bureau*
detention	*le retenue*
dining hall, cafeteria	*la cantine*
diploma	*un diplôme*
economics	*l'économie*
English	*l'anglais*
exam	*un examen*
French	*la français*
geography	*la géographie*
German	*l'allemand*
grade, mark	*une note*
grammar	*la grammaire*
Greek	*le grec*
gym	*le gymnase*
hall	*le hall*
headmaster (primary)	*le directeur*
headmaster	*le principal, le proviseur*
headmistress (primary)	*la directrice*
high school	*un lycée*
history	*l'histoire*
homework	*les devoirs*
junior high school	*un collège*
laboratory	*un laboratoire*
language laboratory	*un laboratoire de langue*
Latin	*le latin*
lesson	*un cours*
librarian	*le/la documentaliste*
library	*la bibliothèque*
literature	*la literature*
map	*une carte*
mathematics	*les mathématiques*
modern languages	*les langues vivantes*
music	*la musique*
note book	*un carnet, un cahier*
nursery school	*l'école maternelle*
oral	*un oral*
philosophy	*la philosophie*
physical education (pe)	*l'éducation physique et sportive (eps)*
physical science	*les sciences physiques*
physics	*la physique*
primary /elementary school	*l'école primaire*
primary school teacher	*un instituteur, une institutrice*
private school	*une école privée*
professor	*un professeur (always masculine)*
pupil (primary school)	*un(e) élève*
religious education	*l'instruction religieuse*

triangle . . . . *une équerre*
schedule . . . . *un emploi de temps*
school . . . . *une école*
school yard . . . . *la cour*
secretary . . . . *la sécretaire*
snack . . . . *le goûter*
Spanish . . . . *l'espagnol*
spelling . . . . *l'orthographe*
sports field . . . . *le terrain de sports*
staffroom . . . . *une salle des profs*
state school . . . . *une école publique*
student (secondary school) . . . . *un(e) étudiant(e)*
student desk . . . . *un pupitre*
study period . . . . *l'étude*
subjects . . . . *les matières*
teacher . . . . *un professeur (always masculine)*
technology . . . . *le travail manuel éducatif (TME)*
term/semester . . . . *un trimestre*
test . . . . *un examen*
to explain . . . . *expliquer*
to go to school . . . . *aller à l'école*
to know . . . . *savoir, connaître*
to learn . . . . *apprendre*
to repeat a year . . . . *redoubler*
to repeat . . . . *répéter*
to study . . . . *étudier*
to teach somebody something . . . . *enseigner quelque chose à quelqu'un*
to teach . . . . *enseigner*
toilets . . . . *les toilettes*
university . . . . *une université*
white board . . . . *une ardoise (Velleda is a popular brand)*
woodwork . . . . *le travail sur bois*
workshop . . . . *un atelier*
written paper . . . . *un écrit*

School Supplies

alphabetical notebook . . . . *un répertoire*
assignment notebook . . . . *le cahier de textes*
backpack . . . . *un sac à dos*
ball-point pen (biro) . . . . *un bic*
binder . . . . *un classeur*
book . . . . *un livre*
book covers (transparent) . . . . *protège-cahiers transparents*
calculator . . . . *une calculatrice*
cardboard folder . . . . *une chemise cartonnée*

chalk.	*la craie*
chalkboard	*un tableau*
compass.	*un compas*
copy-book	*un cahier*
crayons	*les crayons de couleur*
diary.	*un agenda*
dictionary	*un dictionnaire*
dividers (for files)	*intercalaires*
drawing paper	*le papier Canson*
eraser.	*une gomme*
exercice book	*un cahier (d'exercice)*
folder with elastic grommets	*une chemise / pochette à élastique avec rabats*
fountain pen	*un stylo à plume*
markers	*les feutres*
paintbrush	*un pinceau*
highlighter	*un surligneur*
paper	*le papier*
pen	*un stylo*
pencil.	*un crayon*
pencil case	*une trousse*
pencil sharpener	*une taille-crayon*
pencil	*un crayon*
piece of paper	*une feuille de papier*
pumps, slippers	*les chaussons*
roll of transparent paper.	*un rouleau de papier transparent*
rough book.	*un cahier de brouillon*
rubber	*une gomme*
ruler	*une règle, un double-décimètre*
schoolbag, satchel.	*le cartable*
scissors	*une paire de ciseaux*
sheet of paper	*une feuille de papier*
smock.	*un tablier*
text book	*un manuel*

Notes

Health & Medicine

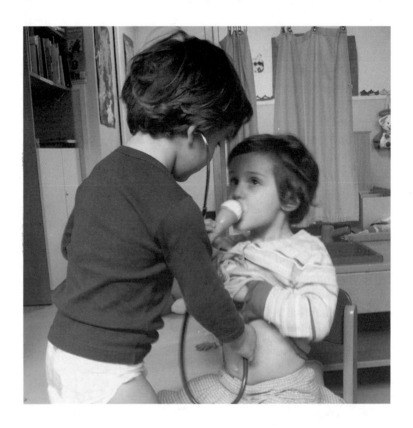

Compiled and edited by Claire Varnica

France is a country with excellent medical facilities. However, any health system that is new to you can be bewildering and intimidating. For example, how do you register with a doctor, and what do you do if your child needs to see a doctor in the middle of the night? This chapter aims to guide you through some of the intricacies of the French health-care system, covering the following topics:

Health & Medicine

CHILD ABUSE

The following are associations you can call if you have witnessed or know of a case of child abuse. Do not be embarrassed or afraid to report known or suspected violence or gross neglect, your call will remain anonymous. All that is needed is the name of the child and the town of residence.

English Speaking

SOS Help
01.46.21.46.46
An English-speaking crisis line open every day from 15h00 - 23h00.

French Speaking

Allô Enfance Maltraité
11, boulevard Brune, 75014 Paris
119
0 800 559 557
💻 www.allo119.gouv.fr
This is a state-run service for children, parents or other adults who are witnesses to abused or neglected children. The telephone line is open 24 hours a day, is free, and the number will not appear on an itemised telephone bill. In urgent cases, the service can investigate and intervene within 24 hours. They call upon a team of psychologists, jurists, etc, for relevant cases.

SOS Familles en Péril
9, cours des Petites Ecuries, 75010 Paris
01.42.46.66.77
Mon - Fri 08h30 - 18h30
Free help for all child/parent problems.

Croix Rouge Ecoute
0 800 858 858
Mon - Fri 10h00 - 22h00
Listening service where you can discuss a problem and be directed you to a relevant organisation if necessary.

Enfance et Partage
0 800 051 234
Mon - Fri 09h00 - 20h00
This association offers psychological advice. They can direct you to a relevant organisation or report a case to the local authorities. They also have lawyers available who can give free legal advice if necessary.

Health & Medicine

CHILDHOOD ILLNESSES

Due to rigorous vaccination campaigns, most children in France are now immunised against the most severe diseases and, therefore, these have become much less common. A calendar for vaccinations can be found at the back of your child's health booklet (*carnet de santé*). However, should you suspect that your child is suffering from an infectious disease you should contact your doctor or pædiatrician who can confirm the diagnosis.

Bronchiolitis

Bronchiolitis, a respiratory disorder that causes the child to struggle for breath, is a viral disease often caused by the VRS virus, but is also related to passive smoking, urban pollution and allergies.

Repeated episodes may bring on childhood asthma. Incidences of this disease are increasing and in the Paris area a specialist network has been set up to deal with winter epidemics of bronchiolitis. If you need to contact a doctor out-of-hours, a call centre is available on 0 820 800 800. The call centre is open from mid October to mid March from 12h00 - 20h00 on Fridays and on the day before bank holidays, and from 09h00 - 18h00 on weekends and bank holidays.

You can also take your child directly to the *Hôpital Robert Debré, Service de Rééducation Fonctionnelle* without an appointment Mon - Fri, 18h00 - 23h00.

The treatment depends on the severity of the disease: physiotherapy may be prescribed (see Physiotherapy, below), or perhaps drugs such as steroids if your child is having great difficulties in breathing.

For more details in French, you can consult www.reseau-bronchio.org.

Chicken Pox

A chicken pox vaccine has been available in France since September 2004 but is not prescribed systematically. You should therefore consult your doc-

tor if you wish your child to be vaccinated, and bear in mind that the vaccine is not reimbursed except in particular circumstances.

A child is not allowed to return to school or *crèche* in France until all spots have crusted over. The disinfectants available in France for dabbing on the spots include *Hexomédine, Septéal* and *Eosine*. Anti-itch potions include Calamine gel and Parkipan pomade. Baking soda (*bicarbonate de sodium*) can be bought from a pharmacy, and is useful when dissolved in tepid water for a soothing bath to decrease itching.

Useful Websites

www.cdc.gov
A USA website with detailed pages on infectious diseases and children.

www.petitweb.com/pediatrie
A French-language website with useful information and a question and answer section.

www.parentsoup.com
A comprehensive parenting site including an "ask the experts" section which allows users to e-mail a pædiatrician with questions.

www.kidshealth.org
A USA-based site with information on medical problems, nutrition and fitness, growth and development.

www.babycentre.co.uk
A UK based website with useful information.

CHILD HEALTH CLINIC

Centres de PMI (la Protection Maternelle et Infantile) were set up in France shortly after the Second World War, with the aim of reducing infant mortality. Their role is to provide health care for children from birth to 6 years, including carrying out necessary vaccinations. The *PMI* stocks the vaccines that a child needs to have in France. Other optional vaccines can be administered, but must first be purchased on prescription from a pharmacy. While minor coughs and colds may be treated, the *PMI* is not for sick children, who should be taken to their doctor or pædiatrician.

The *PMI* combines a team of specialists that includes doctors, pædiatricians, midwives and psychologists. Services are completely free of charge and available to all, irrespective of French Social Security cover. Most centres also have agreements with local hospitals to provide free antenatal and postnatal care for women, again irrespective of Social Security cover.

In France, it is recommended that babies up to six months have monthly check-ups (see the section on Doctors and the French Medical System). You can choose for these to be done at the *PMI*, where the baby is weighed and measured by a nurse, and then undergoes a full examination by a pædiatrician. It is possible to see the same pædiatrician at each visit.

Centres de PMI are usually located in the centre of town and you can find them in the (*les Pages Jaunes* (🖳 www.pagesjaunes.fr). They usually operate on an appointment system (*rendez-vous*), but also have set times when no appointment is necessary (*consultation*).

Centres de PMI can also offer information leaflets, nutritional advice, mother and baby meetings and activities for children. This can be a good way to meet other young mothers in your area (☞ Activities). Waiting rooms are usually well equipped with toys, and some centres have a notice board where you can place and consult advertisements for childcare or baby equipment. The *PMI* can give you a list of the GPs (*médecins généralistes*) and pædiatricians in your area, and also a list of midwives who dispense antenatal classes and postnatal physiotherapy. They will also put you in touch with childminders (*assistantes maternelles* ☞ Childcare).

You must take your child's *carnet de santé* with you each time you visit. No other identification is required.

Health & Medicine

CIRCUMCISION

Circumcision (*circoncision*) is the surgical removal of all or part of the foreskin of the penis. It is very common in the USA, quite common in the UK, but is rarely practised in France (except when it is done for religious reasons). If you wish to have your baby circumcised, you should discuss this with your doctor during pregnancy.

Assuming your baby is in good health, you can have him circumcised non-religiously in any French hospital, clinic or maternity facility before you leave, either by an experienced obstetrician, pædiatrician, or, in certain cases, by an urologist (*urologue*). Discuss pain relief with the practitioner you are considering, as well as with your child's pædiatrician: it may be that if, for example, the obstetrician or gynaecologist who performs the circumcision at the maternity does not want to use anaesthesia, then EMLA cream (*la crème EMLA* - a readily available

local anaesthetic that is easy to use and provides at least some pain relief) could be applied before the procedure.

For an older child that needs to be circumcised for reasons such as phimosis (foreskin too tight), the procedure is done under general anaesthesia by an urologist.

Jewish Religious Circumcision

If you are looking for a Rabbi who can perform a ritual Jewish circumcision, contact the following organisation:

Consistoire Israélite de Paris
17, rue St Georges, 75009 Paris
01.40.82.26.26

CONTRACEPTION & TERMINATION

Contraception

France offers the same methods of contraception as other developed countries, except the diaphragm, which is very rarely prescribed. You can seek contraceptive advice from a GP, a gynæcologist or a family planning centre. For information and the address of your closest family planning centre contact:

Mouvement Français pour le Planning Familial
Centre de Documentation,
4, square Ste Iréné, 75011 Paris
01.48.07.29.10
Mon - Fri 09h30 - 17h30
Your enquiries can be handled in English here. They also have an excellent documentation centre for women's issues, with a good selection available in English.

If you take the pill or use another form of hormonal contraception, the doctor will check your blood pressure before renewing the prescription. It is also likely that you will be prescribed a blood test to check your blood sugar, cholesterol and triglycerides.

For new mothers who intend to breastfeed, the midwife can prescribe an appropriate mini-pill before you leave the maternity after your child's birth.

The morning after pill is available without a prescription in a pharmacy, but will only be reimbursed if you have a doctor's prescription. It is free of charge if you go to a family planning clinic, and free for girls under 16 from pharmacies or school health nurses.

Sterilisation

For men, vasectomy can be carried out by an urologist. One hospital which handles this procedure is the *Hôpital Bicêtre*. Tubal ligation for women, can be carried out by a gynæcologist who also does surgery (*gynécologue-accoucheur*).

Useful Websites

🖳 www.obgyn.net
An English-language website for women (patients and medical professionals) - all you need to know about being a woman.
🖳 www.femiweb.com/core.htm
A French-language website for women - all you need to know about being a woman in France!

🖳 www.contraceptions.org
A French-language website for practical information on the different contraceptive methods.

Termination

A therapeutic abortion (*l'interruption thérapeutique de grossesse, ITG*) is legal in France at any point of the pregnancy if the life of the woman is in danger, or if the risks are high that the baby will be born with a severe or incurable ailment. However, after ten weeks of pregnancy (the legal delay for an abortion), the opinions of two doctors are necessary. One of these must be a public or private hospital doctor, the other must be a specialist.

For a voluntary abortion (*l'interruption volontaire de grossesse, IVG*), the following conditions apply under French law:

• The abortion must be performed before the end of the 10th week of pregnancy (12 weeks after the last normal period). The age of the fœtus will be confirmed by a blood test and/or ultrasound scan. It must be carried out by a doctor in an authorised public hospital or private clinic

• The patient must receive two counselling sessions to allow time for reflection. The first is to explain the medical procedure involved and the second is carried out by a social worker or marriage counsellor (the address will be given during the first counselling session), who will inform the patient of her rights and support services available, should the woman decide to continue with the pregnancy

In both cases the operation is reimbursed by Social Security. A foreigner must provide proof of residence in France of more than three months on the day of the abortion. If the pregnant woman is under 18 and unmarried, agreement from one parent or guardian is mandatory.

French law provides a conscience clause that allows the doctor to refuse to perform an abortion. In this case, the doctor would refer the woman to one of his colleagues.

Health & Medicine

DENTISTS

In France, you can consult any dentist you choose. Social Security will reimburse routine dental work at a rate of 70% standard costs. Orthodontic dental work is not well reimbursed unless you have private complementary health insurance.

For dental work to be reimbursed, you must first ask for authorisation from your *CPAM (Caisse primaire d'Assurance Maladie)*. The dentist will explain this procedure to you and fill in a form called *Demande d'entente préalable*, which you send to your *CPAM*. If you do not receive a reply within 15 days, then, you have their tacit agreement that the dental work can go ahead. You pay the dentist directly after your treatment and claim reimbursement from Social Security on a green form called a *feuille de soins bucco-dentaires* or via your *carte vitale* (☞ Administration). From the beginning of the sixth month of pregnancy, all routine dental work is reimbursed at 100%.

For Children

In Paris, the campaign *Paris Sourire* has been launched for children aged between six and nine, for whom Social Security will fully reimburse two visits to the dentist per year together with any resulting routine dental treatment. A special dental health book (*carnet de suivi bucco-dentaire*) is sent to each Parisian child. This scheme has not yet been extended to the rest of France. For further information (in French) call free on 0 800 881 670.

School children will have periodic check-ups at school, where they will be recommended any treatment that should be carried out by the family dentist. You can ask your pædiatrician or local *PMI* to recommend a dentist used to dealing with children. Alternatively, the following websites have a list of English-speaking pædiatric dentists in Paris:

- 💻 www.intransit-international.com
- 💻 www.parisfranceguide.com

Fluoride

Fluoride is not added to the water supply in France and a fluoride supplement is highly recommended for children from birth until 10 to 12 years of age. Take note of the recommended dosage as fluoride is added to toothpaste and too much fluoride can result in discoloured teeth. Fluoride is also added to some brands of table salt, so if your child is taking fluoride supplements it is best to buy table salt that has only iodine added to it.

Emergency Treatment

Apparently the most common dental emergencies for children are: broken or knocked-out teeth, fillings that have fallen out or orthodontic equipment that has broken. Should you or your children require emergency treatment, contact the emergency department of your local hospital and ask for *les urgences dentaires*. They will be able to tell you the nearest centre to go to in your area. If you live in Paris, you can also contact:

SOS Dentaire
87, boulevard de Port Royal, 75013 Paris
M° Glacière, Gobelins or RER B Port Royal
01.43.37.51.00
01.43.36.36.00
Call for an appointment between 21h00 - 23h40 on weekdays. On weekends, bank holidays, and school holiday periods, call between 09h30 - 12h30, 14h30 - 19h30 or 21h00 - 23h30.

Urgences Dentaires de Paris
01.47.07.44.44
Open every day including weekends 08h00 -

22h00. An operator will take your call and a dentist will call you back within 15 minutes.

American Hospital of Paris
63, boulevard Victor Hugo, 92202 Neuilly-sur-Seine Cedex
01.46.41.25.25
Provides complete dental services by appointment and 24-hour on-call emergency cover.

Conseil de l'ordre des chirurgiens-dentistes
01.42.61.12.00
A recorded message lists dentists on call for emergency dental treatment on Sundays and bank holidays.

DOCTORS AND THE FRENCH MEDICAL SYSTEM

If you require a doctor in an emergency, you should call:

SOS Médecins
01.43.37.77.77
01.47.07.77.77

SAMU (the ambulance service)
15

(For other numbers, see the Emergency Numbers section at the end of the book)

Medecin Traitant

The French medical system is undergoing major reforms in order to reduce spending costs. Since 1st July 2005 you must formally register with one doctor (*médicin traitant*) who can then refer you to a specialist if need be. You usually register with a GP, but it is also possible to choose a specialist (*médecin spécialiste*), especially if you have to see one regularly for an ongoing condition. You should receive a form from the Social Security to sign and have signed by the doctor with whom you choose to register. This form can also be downloaded from 🖳 www.ameli.fr.

French Social Security will reimburse 70% of standard medical costs (minus €1, which is a token participation in reimbursing the current French Social Security deficit). If you consult a GP other than your *médicin traitant*, or if you go directly to a specialist, this rate of reimbursement will be reduced. This move is an attempt to prevent patients from consulting specialists over minor conditions rather than visiting a GP. However the rule does not apply to:

• children under 16 years old
• pædiatricians, gynæcologists, ophthalmologists and dentists

If you attend a group practice (*cabinet de groupe*), you still have to nominate a particular doctor but, should that person be unavailable and you need to be treated by another member of the practice, the rate of reimbursement will be maintained. Members of the same family can have a different registered doctor. You can change your doctor by simply submitting a fresh declaration, which will cancel your existing one.

Payment and Reimbursement

In France, you pay the doctor directly at the end of the consultation and then claim your reimbursement from Social Security (☞ Administration). The cost of a consultation will vary, depending on how your doctor or specialist is categorised:

Health & Medicine

Conventionné

If your doctor is *conventionné*, it means that the treatment undertaken will not cost more than the limits set by Social Security (i.e. €20 for a GP and €27 for a specialist).

Conventionné Honoraires Libres

Doctors or specialists who are *conventionné honoraires libres* charge what they want. In this case, Social Security will only refund up to their limit, but your private complementary health insurance (*mutuelle*) may refund the difference.

Non-Conventionné

If your doctor is *non-conventionné* (20% of doctors in France), it means that Social Security will reimburse only a token part of their fee. Again, your private insurance may cover the rest.

It is advisable to find out in advance what affiliation your doctor or specialist has with Social Security. Further explanation of the various categories of charges can be found in "Health Care in Paris" (see the Other Resources section at the end of the chapter).

Medical Records

According to French law, a patient is entitled to access to all of his/her medical records. If you change doctors, your records will not be forwarded automatically, but it is common practice for your new doctor to request a copy of your records from your previous doctor. Be aware that, if you have used the services of an "on-call" doctor, he/she will not automatically inform your regular doctor unless they are in the same medical practice. Similarly, a specialist will not automatically inform your GP of any results unless your GP referred you in the first place. As part of the current Social Security reform, a computerised medical record system is planned for introduction in France in July 2007.

Children and Doctors

In France, a personal healthcare booklet (*carnet de santé*) is given to each child at birth. This details the child's medical history from birth to 21 years of age. Your doctor, pædiatrician or *PMI* will record details of all visits, including measurements of height, weight and head circumference, together with the results of any physical examinations required. Any medication prescribed and all vaccinations are also recorded (remember to show the *carnet de santé* to on-call doctors). The vaccinations section must be kept up-to-date as certain vaccinations are mandatory for entry to *crèches*, pre-schools or schools etc. If your child was not born in France, you can obtain a *carnet de santé* from your local *mairie* and the *PMI* will update it with the necessary information.

Compulsory Visits for Children

From birth to 6 years, children should be regularly followed up by a GP, pædiatrician or the *PMI* in order to detect any problems in development. The following medical examinations are obligatory in France and are fully reimbursed (or free of charge if you choose to go to the *PMI*):

- 8th day of life, 1st month, 2nd month, 3rd month, 4th month, 5th month, 6th month, 9th month and 12th month visits
- 16th month, 20th month and 24th month visits
- A visit every 6 months from 2 to 6 years

For the visits on the 8th day, 9th month and 24th month, the doctor should fill out and sign a corresponding health certificate that is found in the child's *carnet de santé*.

Home Visits

In France, doctors are willing to make home visits, but they will not always come to you after hours or in emergencies. A home visit will cost more than a visit to the doctor's office and, if you wish your doctor to visit you at home, you should telephone early in the morning to request it.

All doctors must participate in the local duty rota. This is called *service de garde*. If you need a doctor outside normal surgery hours, you should contact your doctor's *service de garde* and you will be given the telephone number of the doctor on duty. Otherwise call *SOS Médecins* (see the Emergency Numbers section at the end of the book).

English-Speaking Hospitals/Medical Centres

American Hospital of Paris
63, boulevard Victor Hugo, 92202 Neuilly-sur-Seine
01.46.41.25.25
01.46.41.27.27 (English speaking operators)
💻 www.american-hospital.org
Most specialists and staff should be able to converse in English.

Hôpital Franco-Britannique
Hertford British Hospital
3, rue Barbès, 92300 Levallois-Perret
01.46.39.22.22
💻 www.british-hospital.org
There are two British GPs and the nursing staff should be able to converse in English. Any visiting British citizen needing medical care in France will have free treatment provided he/she has a European Health Insurance Card (EHIC). This card entitles you to reduced-cost (sometimes free) medical treatment that becomes necessary while you are in a European Economic Area (EEA) country or Switzerland. The quickest and easiest way to get a card is to apply online: 💻 www.ameli.fr (search under *la carte européenne d'assurance maladie*). Alternatively, you can pop into your local *CPAM* and ask for the card. You should receive it in 10 days or so, and it lasts for a year.

The English Medical Centre
8 bis, rue Quinault, 78100 St Germain-en-Laye
01.30.61.25.61
English-speaking GP provides a full general service and health check ups for men, women and children.

Free Medical Check-Up

The *bilan de santé* is a general physical examination which is offered free of charge if you are insured by the general organisation (*régime général*) of the French Social Security system.

Adults

Adults are entitled to one check-up every five years. This involves blood and urine analyses, an electrocardiogram, x-ray of the lungs and a detailed clinical examination. More specific examinations may be requested. To make an appointment, you should call the head office of the Social Security in your area (see list below) and request the relevant form (*demande d'inscription au bilan de santé*). This form should be returned to the *CPAM*, who will then send you an appointment along with a detailed questionnaire to fill out and take with you on the day of your appointment.

CPAM de Paris
21, rue Georges Auric, 75948 Paris Cedex 19
0 820 904 175
www.paris.ameli.fr
Mon - Fri 08h30 - 17h00
Telephone enquiries: Mon - Fri 08h30 - 17h30

CPAM des Hauts de Seine
113, rue des Trois Fontanot, 92026 Nanterre Cedex
01.41.45.20.00
💻 www.cpam92.fr
Mon - Fri 08h30 - 17h15

CPAM de l'Essonne
boulevard François Mitterrand, 91039 Evry Cedex
0 820 904 125
💻 www.evry.ameli.fr
Mon - Fri 08h30 - 17h15
Telephone enquiries: Mon - Fri 08h00 - 18h00

CPAM de Seine-Saint-Denis
195, avenue Paul Vaillant-Couturier, 93014 Bobigny Cedex
0 820 904 193

🖳 www.bobigny.ameli.fr
Mon - Fri 08h30 - 17h00
Telephone enquiries: Mon - Fri 08h30 - 17h00

CPAM du Val de Marne
1/9, avenue du Général de Gaulle, 94031 Creteil
Cedex
0 820 904 156
🖳 www.cpam94.fr
Mon - Fri 08h30 - 16h00
Telephone enquiries: Mon - Fri 08h30 - 17h30

CPAM du Val d'Oise
2, rue des Chauffours - Immeuble Les Marjoberts,
95017 Cergy-Pontoise Cedex
0 820 904 128
🖳 www.cpam95.fr
Mon - Fri 08h30 - 17h30
Telephone enquiries: Mon - Fri 08h00 - 18h00

CPAM des Yvelines
92, avenue de Paris, 78014 Versailles Cedex
0 820 904 102
🖳 www.versailles.ameli.fr
Mon - Fri 08h30 - 17h00
Telephone enquiries: Mon - Fri 08h00 - 20h00

Family medical check-ups can also be done privately at the American Hospital of Paris, the Hertford British Hospital and the English Medical Centre in St Germain-en-Laye.

Children

Children are entitled to a *bilan de santé* at 12 - 18 months and at 3 1/2 - 4 1/2 years. These examinations are separate from the obligatory visits carried out by the child's pædiatrician, GP or *PMI*. For the child, this involves a laboratory examination (blood and urine), a review of full clinical history, measurements of height, weight and blood pressure, auditory examination, consultations with a pædiatric ophthalmologist, ENT specialist (ears, nose and throat), child psychologist and a pædiatrician. You should allow at least three and a half hours to complete all the different examinations and one of the parents must accompany the child.

A full report detailing the results of these examinations is sent to both the parents and to the child's pædiatrician (or other designated doctor) approximately one month after they are carried out. This report may be inserted in the child's *carnet de santé*.

An appointment form may be sent to you automatically by the *Centre des Bilans de Santé*. However, you should follow up by phone to make sure you are given an appointment within the strict age limits as the demand is so great you could miss out on the check-up. If you do not receive an appointment and would like to find out if your child is eligible, contact the *CPAM* offices listed above.

Further Information

For further information and detailed explanation of French health care services, including a directory of hospitals and English-speaking medical professionals and an explanation of French qualifications and credentials, see "Health Care in Paris" (details in the resources section at the end of the chapter).

If you are a member of MESSAGE, the Medical Practitioners Directory has information on doctors and medical specialists (many of whom speak English). For further information, consult
🖳 www.messageparis.org, or contact
medical@messageparis.org.

Embassies of English-speaking countries may also provide a list of English-speaking doctors in the Paris area, and you can also consult the following websites:

🖳 www.intransit-international.com
🖳 www.paris.angloinfo.com
🖳 www.parisfranceguide.com

HOMEOPATHY

Homeopathy (*homéopathie*) is a specific branch of natural medicine that, unlike conventional medicine, treats the person rather than just the symptoms or illness. Because homeopathic remedies come from plants, minerals, and other natural substances, they are reputed to be safe, gentle, and natural – thus ideal for babies, children and pregnant or breastfeeding women. Homeopathic remedies are found at most pharmacies in France and can often be bought without a prescription, although it is best to use a pharmacy indicating *homéopathie* outside, since these are more likely to have a full variety of remedies in stock. Some remedies require prescriptions or are reimbursable by Social Security, in which case it is necessary to see a doctor.

The practice of homeopathy is restricted to doctors in France who identify themselves as homeopaths (*homéopathes*). Many blend conventional medicine with homeopathy or another alternative medicine. To find a qualified homeopath, check the *Pages Jaunes* (⌨*www.pagesjaunes.fr*) under *Médecins: médecine générale orientation homéopathie*. Alternatively, your local pharmacist may be able to recommend a homeopath in your neighbourhood.

The following medical centres are specialised in homeopathic medicine:

Centre Médical de l'Hôpital Saint Jacques
37, rue des Volontaires, 75015 Paris
M° Falguière, Duroc, Cambronne
01.53.58.40.80
This centre also offers acupuncture.

Dispensaire Homéopathique Hahnemann
99, rue Augusté Blanqui, 75013 Paris
M° Glacière
01.45.80.15.03
Children up to 16 years old can consult a homeopathic pædiatrician by appointment on Tuesday and Thursday mornings.

The following centres can offer recommendations:

Centre d'Etudes Homéopathiques de France
228, boulevard Raspail, 75014 Paris
M° Raspail
01.43.20.78.96
A training college which can provide details of your nearest homeopathic doctor.

Groupement des Pédiatres Homéopathes
2, square Henry-Paté, 75016 Paris
M° Mirabeau
01.42.88.11.31
A group which will provide a list of homeopathic pædiatricians.

A Few Homeopathic Basics You can Get from Your Local Pharmacy are:

Arnica
Available as granules and as Arnican cream. Given for bumps, bruises and injuries where the skin is not broken.

Meurtripan
Similar to Arnica but can be used on injuries where the skin is broken.

Calendula Cream
For skin irritations, including small cuts, diaper rash and sunburn.

You might also like to consult the *Guide Familial de l'Homéopathie* see the Other Resources section at the end of the chapter.

Institut National Homéopathie et Maternité
77, boulevard de Grenelle, 75015 Paris
M° Duplex
01.47.34.32.30

HOSPITALS FOR CHILDREN

Should your child need to go to hospital for a routine procedure, you will be given a referral by your doctor. You are not restricted to using your local hospital. For an emergency visit to the hospital, make sure you take your child's *carnet de santé and carte vitale* (☞ Administrative).

In recent years, pædiatric units in Paris have made efforts to make a child's stay in hospital as pleasant as possible. Many now propose entertainment or activities, and some have toy libraries (*ludothèques*). School lessons are also organised for long-term patients.

If your child does have to go into the hospital, consider buying *Enfant à l'Hôpital? Suivez le Guide* (see the Other Resources section at the end of the chapter), which explains (in French) what is likely to happen.
Sometimes it is possible for parents to stay at the hospital. Conditions vary from unit to unit, so ask the staff about facilities (*les structures d'accueil*), but, keep your expectations low. Treatment at home is sometimes possible under the *HAD* scheme (*Hospitalisation à domicile*). Ask the hospital you are considering whether these options are possible in your case.

For more detailed information on hospitalisation in general, see "Health Care in Paris", and *Le Paris des Tout-Petits*. The *Mairie de Paris* provides a free booklet in the *Prevention Santé* series called *L'Hospitalisation*, available from the town hall of any *arrondissement*. *Association Sparadrap* also publishes brochures for children about illness, operations and hospitalisation (see the Other Resources section at the end of the chapter). Their website has a full list of the brochures (*livrets*) available, or they can be contacted at: 🖳 www.sparadrap.asso.fr.

Main Pædiatric Hospitals

There are four specialised state pædiatric hospitals in Paris:

Hôpital Necker-Enfants Malades
149, rue de Sèvres, 75015 Paris
M° Duroc
01.44.49.40.00
Specialist cardiology, neurology, surgery units.

Hôpital Robert Debré
48, boulevard Sérurier, 75019 Paris

M° Pré-St Gervais, Porte des Lilas
01.40.03.20.00
Specialist hand and burns units. The hospital also has an associated residence for accompanying families, providing full psychological/information services from medical personnel:
Maison des Parents
78, rue de Romainville, 75019 Paris
01.48.03.33.60

Hôpital St. Vincent de Paul
82, avenue Denfert-Rochereau, 75014 Paris
M° Denfert-Rochereau, RER B Denfert-Rochereau

or Port Royal
01.40.48.81.11
Specialist neurology, pædio-psychiatry, surgery units.

Hôpital Trousseau
26, avenue du Dr. Arnold Netter, 75012 Paris
M° Bel-Air, Picpus
01.44.73.74.75
Specialist burns unit.

Other state hospitals with specialised pædiatric units in the Paris area are:

Hôpital Antoine Béclère
157, rue de la Porte-de-Trivaux, 92141 Clamart Cedex
01.45.37.44.44

Hôpital Bicêtre
78, rue du Général Leclerc, 94275 Le Kremlin-

Bicêtre Cedex
M° Le Kremlin-Bicêtre
01.45.21.21.21
Specialist emergency, liver, neurology, surgery units.

Hôpital Jean Verdier
avenue 14 Juillet, 93140 Bondy
01.48.02.66.66
01.48.02.60.36 (for emergencies for children.)

Hôpital Louis Mourier
178, rue Renouillers, 92700 Colombes
01.47.60.61.62

Hôpital Ambroise Paré
9, avenue Charles de Gaulle, 92100 Boulogne Billancourt
01.49.09.50.00

INFERTILITY

In France, a couple is generally considered to be having fertility problems if they have not conceived after two years (with twice-weekly intercourse). However, different doctors have varied standards, and one may be willing to begin treatment after only six to eight months of trying to conceive, especially in the case of women who are over 35 and trying for the first time.

Treatment

To find out about fertility treatment, you can make a direct approach to a gynæcologist (there is no need for a referral from your *médecin traitant*). Bear in mind that all French gynæcologists have a diploma in sterility, awarded after a year's theoretical course, so the best way to find someone may be through word-of-mouth or a recommendation from your GP. If you are a member of MESSAGE, you can consult the MESSAGE Medical Practitioners Directory.

In the first instance, a number of routine tests will be carried out to determine possible causes for a lack of conception: temperature charting *(une *

courbe de température), ultrasound *(échographie)*, testing of hormonal levels *(prélèvements hormonaux)*, sperm count *(le spermogramme)*. Ovulation prediction kits *(tests d'ovulation)* are available from pharmacies, but they are expensive and not reimbursed by Social Security.

If the cause for the infertility is not found in the initial tests, then further examinations will be performed, such as a hysterographie or a coelioscopie (a surgical intervention), which permit a closer look at the uterus and the fallopian tubes.

Depending on the results of the tests, your doctor may suggest that your next step is to try artificial

Health & Medicine

insemination (*l'insémination artificielle*). If there is serious difficulty in conceiving, then your doctor may also suggest that you try IVF treatment *(In-Vitro Fertilisation)* (*FIV - la fécondation in vitro*).

Social Security

French Social Security reimburses fertility treatment at a rate of 100%, provided the service you use is *conventionné* (see the section on Doctors and the French Medical System for further details). This includes tests, exams, operations, medication and up to four IVF treatment attempts per pregnancy. This means that if you become pregnant, you would still be eligible for reimbursed fertility treatment in the future. Similarly, in the event of a miscarriage, you would still be eligible for four further IVF treatments.

Support and Information

If you would like further information in English on infertility and possible treatments, a good place to start is ⌨ www.fertilethoughts.com.

If you are looking for support, Circle of Friends is an English-speaking women's support group in Paris offering information, counselling and fellowship to those concerned with infertility, pregnancy loss and adoption. Call 01.47.20.00.03.

LABORATORIES

In France, it is rare for a doctor to take samples at the surgery, so laboratories play a vital role in medical investigations. Your doctor will give you a prescription (*ordonnance*) detailing any tests to be done. It is then up to you to choose a laboratory facility – or ask your doctor for a recommendation – and to make your own appointment. Laboratories are listed in the *Pages Jaunes,* (⌨ *www.pagesjaunes.fr*) under *Laboratoires d'Analyses,* or there may be facilities attached to your local hospital or clinic. Specialised pædiatric laboratories also exist – again, you can ask your doctor for a recommendation.

For certain blood tests you should not eat or drink anything (*être à jeun*) on the morning of the test - check this with the laboratory beforehand. The laboratory can supply you with the appropriate container for urine or stool samples.

You will be asked for your *carte vitale* to prepare the necessary documentation for the tests. You will be required to pay for the tests either upfront or when collecting the results. If the tests have been performed with a prescription they will be partially or fully reimbursed ☞ Administration.

If owing to ill health you are unable to visit the laboratory, a nurse working for the laboratory can visit you at home. You must have a written prescription to be able to receive this service.

Results

You can ask to have results sent to you at home with a copy sent to your doctor (this is standard practice), or you can collect them from the laboratory yourself. Even if you have asked to have the results sent to you, you can still call the laboratory to get the results over the phone (they will send the paperwork anyway). You can also call your doctor about the results if it concerns an illness for which prompt treatment may be required (a urinary tract infection, for example).

Laboratories and Pregnancy

When you are pregnant, you will be using the services of the laboratory regularly, as the French probably investigate more frequently than in the UK or the USA. (☞ Pregnancy, Birth and Newborn).

Your doctor may perform a cervical smear test or vaginal swab to check for infection and you may be asked to deliver it to the laboratory. If the facility is closed, make sure you refrigerate the sample and deliver it first thing the next morning. Sometimes the sample can be sent by post to a specialised laboratory. Cervical smear tests can also be carried out at a laboratory.

LEAD POISONING

Lead is one of the most toxic metals known and lead poisoning (*le saturnisme*) is of particular concern in an older city like Paris, where lead paints and lead-lined pipes were in common use until recently. Paris has the added disadvantage of serious air pollution, including toxins from the continued use of leaded petrol, which causes lead contamination in soil (and sandboxes in playgrounds) near busy roads. One reason lead is particularly dangerous is that its effect is cumulative: unless the digestive system excretes it immediately, it circulates in the blood and is absorbed directly from the blood into other tissues. Also, the body treats calcium and lead as though they were the same, so when lead leaves the blood it is stored in the bones, where it accumulates over an entire lifetime. At times of biological stress, including pregnancy and menopause, it can re-enter the blood and cause symptoms.

Symptoms

Children's symptoms can appear over a period of days (in adults it is usually weeks) and usually include severe gastrointestinal colic. Their gums sometimes turn blue and they may have muscle weakness. Other symptoms include diarrhœa, anxiety, loss of appetite, fatigue, tremors, seizures, vertigo, insomnia, learning disabilities, confusion and arthritis. If untreated, lead poisoning can eventually lead to paralysis of extremities, blindness, loss of memory, mental retardation, impotency, infertility, liver failure and, in chronic cases, coma and death.

Risks for Children

Children (and pregnant women) are especially vulnerable to lead poisoning because they absorb more calcium, and therefore more lead. They are also more susceptible because their activities bring them into closer contact with the lead in the environment. In addition, pregnant women who have high lead levels can pass the lead to the unborn child. These children suffer from growth retardation and disorders of the nervous system.

Tests

If you suspect lead poisoning in your child, or simply want to make sure your child is not at risk, you should obtain a prescription for a blood test from your pædiatrician. The test is called *dosage de plombémie*. Here is a list of the main laboratories in Paris that test for lead:

Hôpital Fernand Widal

Laboratoire de Biochimie-Toxicologie: R. Boundon
200, rue du Faubourg St Denis, 75010 Paris
M° La Chapelle, Gare du Nord, bus: 42, 43, 46, 47, 48, 49, 65
01.40.05.42.19 (reception)
01.40.05.42.25 (biochemistry)
01.40.05.42.23 (toxicology)
01.40.05.42.28 (metals)

Laboratoire Vaugirard, Laboratoire d'Analyses Medicales

11, rue Cambronne, 75015 Paris
M° Cambronne
01.47.83.28.75

Le Laboratoire d'hygiène de la Ville de Paris
(LHVP)
11, rue George-Eastman, 75013 Paris
M° Place d'Italie
01.44.97.87.87

Body Temperature Conversion Chart

Fahrenheit	Celsius
95	35.0
96	35.5
97	36.1
98	36.6
99	37.2
100	37.7
101	38.3
102	38.8
103	39.4
104	40.0
105	40.5
106	41.1
107	41.6
108	42.2
109	42.7
110	43.3

Steps to achieve a lead free environment:

• Be wary of lead soldered cans – particularly in imported foods from countries which may not have regulations against lead

• Make sure children wash their hands before eating and after outdoor play

• Keep painted surfaces in good repair so those older layers are not exposed, chipping or peeling

• Wet clean your floors often and consider having them refinished and sealed if dusty cracks are visible

• Have your water tested if you suspect your building has lead pipes

• Let water run for at least three minutes in the morning before you use it. Never boil water longer than necessary as this concentrates contaminants. Do not use hot water from the tap for drinking or cooking

• If your children play in a garden or park near a busy street, or you garden often, have your soil checked for lead contamination

• Avoid sandboxes right next to heavily travelled streets

• Try to avoid keeping your child at auto exhaust pipe level (i.e., in the pushchair) on the most heavily travelled streets. Use side streets when possible, or better still, carry your child in a backpack

MEDICINES FOR CHILDREN IN FRANCE

Medicines used, and the ways of administering them vary from country to country. The biggest difference in France seems to be the amount of medicines you are prescribed! Suppositories are more widely used here and their usefulness is unparalleled when treating a child who is vomiting or refusing to take any other form of medicine. Glass ampoules are frequently used for packaging liquid medication in France. To use these, break off the tip on one side, then hold the unopened tip over a glass or cup. When you break the second tip off, the medicine should flow out easily.

If your child has been on a regular treatment prescribed outside France, take the manufacturer's details contained in the box and show this to your pharmacist. The same medication may well exist in France under a different brand name. If in doubt, ask your doctor or pharmacist.

Medicines Available Over the Counter at the Pharmacy

This information is a general guideline and does not replace proper medical advice. Please check with your doctor or pharmacist before giving any medication to your child.

Paracetamol

The mainstay of pædiatric medication, given for fever, pain etc. Available as *Doliprane* or *Efferalgan* as sachets to mix with water, suppositories or in a syrup form. All forms are available in different strengths according to age and weight.

Aspirin

Given for fever, pain and inflammation. It is sometimes recommended for children in France, though may not be used in other countries because of the very rare complication of Reye's syndrome. Available as *Catalgine* or *Aspégic* in sachets to mix with water.

Ibruprofen

Given for fever, pain and inflammation. Available in liquid form as *Nureflex* or *Advil*. Should not be given

if chicken pox is suspected.

Coughs and Colds

- *Sérum Physiologique* - saline solution for blocked noses or bathing sticky eyes.
- *Stérimar* - saline solution in an atomiser spray.
- *Prorhinel* - a modified *sérum physiologique* in the form of nose drops for stuffy noses.
- *Soframycine* – local antibiotic nose spray, but should only be used for a few days as it can sensitise the lining of the nose.
- *Actifed* - dries up runny noses which helps stop the cough following a cold. Contains antihistamine which can make a child sleepy. Not suitable for very young children as it can make them excitable.
- *Sudafed* - similar to Actifed but without the antihistamine. Not suitable for children under 12 as it can make them excitable.
- *Rhinathiol* - cough mixture. It makes sticky secretions thinner and therefore stops the tickle which makes the child cough.
- *Camphopneumine* or *Trophires* - similar to Vick's/Pediacare. It is an all-natural medication whose main ingredient is eucalyptus, in suppository form for very young children. This medication clears nasal passages and chest so the child is able to breathe more easily.

Nappy (Diaper) and other Skin Rashes

- Eryplast and Oxyplastine - protective creams for mild nappy rash. Both very similar to Sudacrem in the UK and Desitin in the USA.
- Mitosyl - a cream for a more severe rash, though it smells awful (fish liver oil and zinc oxide)
- Eosine - red liquid to paint on the skin in order to dry out and disinfect lesions. Stains everything (but does wash out)
- Daktarin or Homéoplastine - anti-fungal creams which are often necessary if the rash has been present for a few days. Homéoplastine should not be used on children under 30 months of age

Eczema and Dry Skin

- Huile d'Amande Douce - almond oil for the dry skin of young babies
- Savon de Marseille - pure soap for washing babies and their clothes
- Oléatum - a range of products for babies and children with dry skin and eczema. Available as:
  - Crème - protective cream especially for young babies' cheeks
  - Emollient - to put in the bath, but be careful as it makes the bath and baby very slippery
  - Savon - a very mild soap which also moisturises

Vomiting and Diarrhœa

Fluid replacement sachets containing glucose and electrolytes are available at the pharmacist to mix with water. They help prevent dehydration. Several makes are available, e.g., *Alhydrate, Adiaril*
- Diaralac - a capsule that can be used by adults and children for diarrhœa relief. For children, you dissolve the recommended dosage in liquid

Cuts and Bruises

- Hansaplast solution antiseptique cutanée - disinfectant spray for cleaning cuts
- Stéristrip - small strips of sticky tape to hold together the edges of a cut, enabling it to heal more quickly and be less likely to leave a scar. Often used in hospitals in place of stitches for small cuts
- Cetavlon - same as Savlon antiseptic cream for cuts
- Hexomédine - spray for disinfecting cuts

Allergies and Itching

Primalan - antihistamine which can be given to children.

Head Lice

Products used to eradicate head lice fall into two categories:
- *Les Organochlores* - products with a base of DDT (pesticide): *Benzochloryl, Lentinol,* or *Lindane, Aphitina, Elentol* and *Elenol.*
- *Les Pyréthrines* - some of which are natural: *Marie-Rose, Spray-Pax,* and some of which are compositions: *Hegor, Parapoux, Defipux, Itam, Parasidose, Pyréflor, Itax.*

Worms

Fluvermal is a de-worming syrup effective against threadworms and roundworms. One dose usually kills all the worms and eggs, but a repeat dose must be taken two weeks later. The whole family should be treated at the same time. Ask your doctor or pharmacist for more information.

OPTICIANS AND OPHTHALMOLOGISTS

Your GP or pædiatrician will regularly check your baby's eyes during routine visits up until the age of 6. The child's *carnet de santé* includes a specific but succinct eye question for the 4 month, 9 month and 24 month visits. An eye test is also done during the final year of pre-school (*grande section de maternelle*).

If you have any grounds for concern you should talk to your child's doctor, who can refer you to an eye specialist (*ophtalmologue*). Although there are many ophthalmologists in Paris and its suburbs, only very few are able to detect visual disorders before the age of three - the crucial age when disorders can turn into more severe handicaps. It is important therefore to ask your doctor for a recommendation, or to contact one of the specialist units in Paris:

Hôpital Necker Enfants-Malades - Service d'ophtalmologie
149-161, rue de Sèvres, 75015 Paris
M° Sèvres Lecourbe, Duroc, Falguière
01.44.49.45.02

Fondation Ophtalmologique Adolphe-de-Rothschild
25, rue Manin, 75019 Paris
M° Bolivar, Buttes Chaumont
01.48.03.65.68 or 01.48.03.65.30

Hôpital Lariboisière - Service d'ophtalmologie
2, rue Ambroise Paré, 75010 Paris
M° Gare du Nord, Barbès Rochechouart
01.49.95.65.65

In case of an eye emergency, you can contact:

Hôpital Hôtel Dieu
Service d'ophtalmologie
1, place du Parvis de Notre Dame, 75004 Paris
M° Cité, St Michel
01.42.34.83.56
01.40.92.93.94 or 01.48.07.22.00 (out of hours)

Privately Practising Ophthalmologists

If you are a member of MESSAGE, the Medical Practitioners Directory has information on ophthalmologists. See the Support Services page of the latest MESSAGE Magazine.

Opticians

If glasses are required, you will need to go to an optician who specialises in making and fitting eye wear for children. The ophthalmologist will give you a prescription for the proper lenses. The amount reimbursed by French Social Security is determined by the prescription, and reimbursement from your complementary health insurance varies considerably depending on your policy. For Social Security reimbursement, the number of pairs per year is unlimited for children under 6 (and adults over 18), but is limited to one pair per year for children from 6 to 18 years of age.

The following opticians specialise in children's frames and their shops have a child-friendly lay-out:

Lissac Opticien
114, rue de Rivoli, 75001 Paris
M° Chatelet
01.44.88.44.44 (ask for other store locations near you)

Destray
96, avenue Victor Hugo, 75116 Paris
M° Victor Hugo
01.45.53.90.40
and
53, rue de Passy, 75016 Paris
M° Passy
01.46.47.77.66

Poncelet Optique
25, rue Poncelet, 75017 Paris
M° Ternes
01.43.80.59.50

PHARMACIES

Pharmacies or chemists (*pharmacies*) in France are independent businesses governed by the *Ordre de Pharmaciens*. The symbol for a pharmacy in France is a green cross, usually neon and flashing when open, making it easy to locate. Sometimes you will see another sign called a *caducée* (a staff with two entwined serpents), denoting the order of pharmacists.

Pharmacists train for seven years and are qualified to give medical advice. For minor illnesses, visit your local pharmacy rather than rushing off to your doctor. A pharmacist can administer first aid and either call the emergency services or direct you to the nearest emergency hospital or specialist if necessary.
France is quite restrictive in the distribution of medication: many drugs that may be non-prescription in other countries are strictly prescription drugs here. Commonly used medication such as paracetamol, bought in supermarkets in the UK or the USA, are only available from a pharmacy in France.

Services Offered by the Pharmacy

Medicines

You can buy all medicines prescribed by your doctor and, if you have forgotten your prescription, the pharmacist may accept telephone confirmation from your doctor. If the medicine you want is temporarily out of stock, the pharmacist may order for delivery later the same day or next day for you to collect. Pharmacies can still mix ointments or potions, but this is done less and less. All prescription medicines are sold at a recommended retail price, as set by Social Security. The pharmacist is authorised to substitute a medicine prescribed by your doctor with the same medicine in a cheaper, generic form, the

aim being to reduce French Social Security spending.

Non-prescription medicines are not usually displayed, so you may have to describe your symptoms (See Medicines for Children in France, above, for help with this).

Vaccinations

You must buy the necessary vaccinations from the pharmacy with a prescription from your doctor or pædiatrician.

Baby Milks and Nappies

Pharmacies sell baby milk formulæ and nappies, should you need an emergency supply on Sunday or in the middle of the night. Pharmacies also sell baby milks specially formulated for babies suffering from diarrhœa or vomiting.

Baby, Health and Beauty Products

Pharmacies usually sell a range of baby, healthcare, feminine hygiene and beauty products, but these can be very expensive. The same products are also available at parapharmacies, which do not dispense any medicines but usually carry a good range of recognised baby, cosmetic and beauty brands at discounted prices. Pharmacies also sell hot water bottles and bicarbonate of soda, which can be difficult to find elsewhere.

Reimbursement of Medicines

To claim either a percentage or the full cost of medicines from the *CPAM,* you must purchase them on prescription. If you have a *carte vitale*, you pay only the part which is not reimbursable. Otherwise you pay the total cost and the pharmacist will prepare a form (*volet de facturation*) for you to send to your local *CPAM* for reimbursement (☞Administration).

On the medicine packet or box, there are detachable labels (*vignettes*) that you must peel off and attach to the space provided on the form. You will not be reimbursed if the *vignette* is missing. You must send the form to the *CPAM* together with the carbon copy of your prescription. Medicines are reimbursed at different rates: 65% for a white *vignette* and 35% for a blue one. If you have complementary insurance, this may cover the remainder of the amount.

Tiers Payant

It is worth registering at your local pharmacy in order to take advantage of the third-party payment (*tiers-payant*). This means the pharmacy claims

payment on your behalf directly from the Social Security and from your provider of complementary health insurance, so you pay nothing when you collect your prescription. You simply need to take your *carte vitale* and details of your complementary health insurance policy to your local pharmacy. You can of course do this at any pharmacy at any time, but it is time consuming and inconvenient to have to carry the relevant documents around with you.

Repeat Prescriptions

You should keep the original of the doctor's prescription carefully in order to buy more medicine, as the pharmacist is normally only allowed to dispense a month's supply. It is sometimes possible to buy further supplies without a prescription, but then you will not be reimbursed by Social Security. Any medicine whose packet has a red or green frame (at the bottom of one side) can only be purchased on prescription. The pharmacist will be able to advise you on this.

Equipment Hire

Pharmacies can organise the rental of cribs, scales, and breast pumps (☞ Pregnancy, Birth and Newborn). Some pharmacies have scales on the premises for you to weigh the baby.

Other Services

Pharmacies can supply lists of nurses, laboratory personnel, doctors and pædiatricians etc., in your area and they sell medicines for pets on prescription from the vet. Pharmacists are also qualified to identify any wild mushrooms you may have gathered!

Returning Unused or Unfinished Medicines

Most pharmacies will accept any unused drugs, either for safe disposal or for handing over to aid organisations such as *Pharmaciens sans frontières* for use in developing countries or war-torn areas.

Opening and Emergency Hours

Most pharmacies are open 6 days a week from around 08h30 - 20h00, usually not closing at lunch time. Most are closed on Sundays. If you need medical supplies out-of-hours, your local pharmacy will have a sign posted in the window detailing out-of-hours pharmacies in your area. To find the nearest pharmacy on emergency duty (*pharmacie de garde*), you can also contact your local Police Station (*Commissariat de Police*) or consult 🖳 www.doctissimo.fr.

24 hour Pharmacies in Paris

Pharmacie des Champs-Elysées (Pharmacie Dérhy)
84, avenue des Champs-Elysées, 75008 Paris
M° George V
01.45.62.02.41

Pharmacie Européenne de la Place de Clichy
6, place de Clichy, 75009 Paris
M° Place de Clichy, bus 80, 68, 30, 74, 54, 95, 81
01.48.74.65.18

Grande Pharmacie Daumesnil
6, place Félix Eboué, 75012 Paris
M° Daumesnil
01.43.43.19.03

Late Night Pharmacies in Paris

Pharmacie des Halles
10, boulevard de Sébastopol, 75001 Paris
M° Chatelet
01.42.72.03.23
Mon - Fri until midnight, Sun until 22h00.

Pharmacie du Drugstore des Champs-Élysées
133, avenue des Champs-Élysées, 75008 Paris
M° George V
01.47.20.39.25
Every day until 02h00.

Pharmacie du Drugstore Matignon
2, rue Jean Mermoz
Rondpoint des Champs-Elysées, 75008 Paris
M° Franklin Roosevelt, bus 80, 28, 83, 73, 42, 49
01.43.59.86.55
Mon - Sat 08h00 - 02h00, Sun and holidays 10h00 - 02h00.

Pharmacie Internationale
5, place Pigalle, 75009 Paris
M° Pigalle
01.48.78.38.12
Every day 08h00 - 23h00 (including bank holidays).

Grande Pharmacie de la Nation
13, place de la Nation, 75011 Paris
M° Nation, RER A
01.43.73.24.03
Every day until midnight.

Pharmacie Forum Santé
86, boulevard Soult, 75012 Paris
M° Porte de Vincennes
01.43.43.13.68
Every day until 02h00.

Pharmacie Italie Tolbiac
61, avenue d'Italie, 75013 Paris
M° Tolbiac
01.44.24.19.72
Every day until midnight.

Pharmacie des Arts
106, boulevard Montparnasse, 75014 Paris
M° Vavin
01.43.35.44.88
Everyday except Sun, 09h00 - midnight.

Pharmacie Centrale
52, rue du Commerce, 75015 Paris
M° Commerce, Emile Zola
01.45.79.75.01
Every day until midnight.

Pharmacie Mozart
14, avenue Mozart, 76016 Paris
M° La Muette, RER Boulainvilliers
01.45.27.38.17
Mon - Fri until 21h00, Sat until 20h00.

Pharmacie Basire
143, rue de la Pompe and 118 bis, avenue Victor Hugo, 75016 Paris
M° Rue de la Pompe
01.47.27.88.49
Mon - Sat until 21h00, except bank holidays

Pharmacie Exelmans
77, boulevard Exelmans, 75016 Paris
M° Exelmans
01.46.51.23.92
Mon - Sat until 22h00, except bank holidays

Pharmacie des Sports
2, place du général Koening, 75017 Paris
M° Porte Maillot
01.45.74.31.10
Mon - Sat until midnight

Espace conseil
64, boulevard de Barbès, 75018 Paris
M° Château Rouge
01.46.06.02.61
Every day until 02h00.

Pharmacie Battail
6, rue de Belleville, 75019 Paris
M° Belleville
01.46.36.67.42
Mon - Fri until 21h30, Sat until 21h00.

English-Speaking Pharmacies In Paris

British & American Pharmacy
1, rue Auber, 75001 Paris
M° Opéra
01.47.42.49.40

Pharmacie Anglaise
62, avenue des Champs Elysées, 75008 Paris
M° Franklin Roosevelt
01.43.59.22.52
01.43.59.82.30

Pharmacie Anglo-Américaine
37, avenue Marceau, 75016 Paris
M° George V, Alma Marceau
01.47.20.57.37

Pharmacie Anglaise de Montmartre
98, boulevard de Rochechouart, 75018 Paris
M° Anvers
01.53.28.06.08
01.53.28.06.77

It can Pay to Go to the Doctor...

Did you know some medication you might normally buy over the counter (e.g. pain killers, some cold remedies and cough mixtures) can be partially reimbursed by Social Security if you have a prescription from your doctor? Bear this in mind if you find you are spending a lot of money on basic medication - it might be worth asking your doctor if he can prescribe them for you.

PHYSIOTHERAPY

The French word for a physiotherapist/physical therapist is *kinésithérapeute*, a difficult word to pronounce so most people just say *kiné*.

Antenatal

There are antenatal exercise classes available in and around Paris given by private instructors, but it is quite difficult to find them (☞ Pregnancy, Birth and Newborn). Birth Preparation Classes are helpful, but you will be attending these just before the birth of the baby and you might want to be thinking about starting antenatal exercises earlier in your pregnancy.

MESSAGE provides antenatal classes in English to its members. For more information ☞Pregnancy, Birth and Newborn.

Postnatal

Postnatal physiotherapy is 100% reimbursed by Social Security in France and is an exceptional benefit. You are entitled to 10 sessions for the re-education of the pelvic floor (or perineal) muscles and the stomach (or abdominal) muscles. However, if you need a further course, this may not be reimbursed. You should ask your doctor, gynæcologist, obstetrician or midwife for a prescription and they may be able to recommend a physiotherapist to you. You can also do the physiotherapy sessions with an independent midwife.

For full reimbursement, you must complete your course of physiotherapy before the first year after the birth. The exercises are less effective the longer you delay them.

The norm in France is to start the postnatal sessions six weeks after the birth of the baby. When you are choosing your physiotherapist, be sure that he or she is at a location convenient to you and that you can take your new baby with you if you wish. Usually a bouncy chair and some toys are provided.

Some therapists may visit you at home.

Treatment often involves manual and electrical stimulation of the pelvic floor. The physiotherapist will insert her fingers or an electrical probe into your vagina and tell you where and how to contract the muscles. A peronmeter, which gives a pressure reading when you contract your pelvic muscles, may be inserted to assess progress. The electrical probe can also send electrical impulses to your muscles which contract them for you. Sometimes a combination of these methods is used. Be reassured that this is all totally painless, and all part of a day's work to the physiotherapist. Peronmeters can be bought privately, as can vaginal cones, and sometimes your doctor will prescribe them if progress is slow.

Respiratory Therapy

When a baby or toddler has bronchiolitis and has very congested tubes, it is quite common for doctors to prescribe sessions of respiratory physiother-

Why do those Kiné Sessions?

- You get your general fitness back more quickly after having your baby
- It affords your pelvic floor muscles a much better chance to recover (especially useful if you want to have another baby)
- You have to tone your abdominal muscles
- It helps reduce the risk of incontinence as you get older
- It is free!

apy. In this case, you should ask your doctor to recommend a physiotherapist for your child, or contact the local *PMI* for a recommendation. For further information you can contact the *Service de Kinésitherapie Respiratoire* at *l'Hôpital Necker.*

If your child needs respiratory physiotherapy on a weekend or public holiday, you can call the following number:

Réseau Kiné Bronchiolite Ile de France
0 820 820 603
This service puts you in contact with physiotherapists working in their offices during weekends and bank holidays from 09h00 - 18h00. However, it is only in operation from mid October to mid March, when bronchiolitis epidemics generally occur.

SPECIAL NEEDS CHILDREN

Excellent care exists in France for children with physical, mental or learning disabilities, but it is often difficult to know where to start. If you are a member of MESSAGE, a good place is the MESSAGE Support directory, which should be able to provide details of useful organisations. For further information, contact support@messageparis.

For information in French, you can obtain a copy of *Paris Pratique - Personnes Handicapée*, a free booklet from your local *mairie* (see the Other Resources section at the end of the chapter). In it, you will find information on medical care, schooling, specialised schools and services, employment, social service entitlements, accessibility for people in wheelchairs, transportation, housing, culture, leisure, and sports activities, as well as the names and addresses of the major associations for people with disabilities.

For information about childcare facilities for children with special needs ☞ Childcare. For further information about the educational facilities available ☞ Education.

Therapy

If you feel your child needs speech, motor or psychological therapy, you can either choose a private specialist (you will need a doctor's referral and prescription for speech and motor therapy), or look for specialised centres providing therapy for special needs and learning disabled children. There are three types of centres: *CMPP (Centre Médico-Psychopédagogique), CMP (Centre Médico-Psychologique),* and *CAMSP (Centre d'Action Médico-Sociale Précoce).* Your local Social Security office, *CPAM* or *mairie* should be able to give you the name and address of the nearest child therapy centre.

Many local hospitals also provide out-patient therapy (*Hôpital de Jour*) for children, especially for chil-

Health & Medicine

dren needing psychological or psychiatric therapy.

Another alternative for children whose disabilities require more intensive therapy is a *SESSAD (Service d'Education Specialisée, Soins à Domicile)* where therapists work with the children in their natural settings (home, *crèche*, school). To obtain the name and address of the nearest *SESSAD*, usually run by a parents' association for mentally disabled children, contact the *Plate-forme d'Accueil et d'Information* (details below).

Disability Benefits

If you are eligible under French Social Security and if your child is certified to have a disability of more than 80% (your doctor will fill out the form and testify on your behalf to Social Security), you may be eligible for any or all of the following:

- Total coverage of therapy and related medical expenses
- Special Education Allowance from the CAF (Caisse d'Allocations Familiales)
- Free transport for your child to and from specialised schools and institutions (usually by taxi)
- A free car tax disc (vignette) - contact your Bureau d'Aide Sociale and ask for a Carte d'Invalidité
- An extra tax deduction - indicate on your annual tax return that your child has a disability of more than 80%

Further Information

For more information about facilities for special needs children, contact the *Plate-forme d'Accueil et d'Information*. Created by the *Marie de Paris*, this service aims to help people with disabilities by advising them on administrative requirements and giving referrals to associations for specific disabilities.

Plate-forme d'Accueil et d'Information
94-96, Quai de la Rapée, 75012 Paris
0 800 033 748
www.paris.fr
plateformhandicap.dases@paris.fr

VACCINATIONS

At two to three months of ages, most French pædiatricians will expect your baby to begin an immunisation programme. Make sure that all vaccinations are recorded and stamped by your doctor or clinic in your child's *carnet de santé*. The reason for this is that in France, you will be asked to provide proof of immunisation before your child is allowed to attend most childcare facilities, schools or sports programmes such as swimming classes. If you move to another country before your child's vaccination programme is complete,the *carnet de santé* will provide a useful record for your new doctor to work from, as vaccination programmes vary from country to country.

How and Where to Buy Vaccines

Unless you choose to go to a *PMI*, you must first buy your vaccines from the pharmacy on a doctor's prescription and then take it to your doctor who will administer your injection. Keep in mind that shortages of vaccines do occur occasionally; you may want to ask your local pharmacist if this is the case several days before your appointment, and order it if need be. If you are not going directly to your doctor from the pharmacy then be aware that most vaccinations need to be stored in the refrigerator until use, otherwise they become less effective. Vaccines are reimbursed by Social Security. (☞Administrative)

Calendar of Vaccinations (Guideline only)

Below is the standard list of vaccinations approved by the French government medical authorities, and a guideline as to the age at which it is advisable to have them done. In cases of epidemic, other vaccinations may be required.

- **1 month**: Tuberculosis (BCG) (in high risk areas)

- **2–3 months**: Diphtheria, Tetanus, Whooping Cough, Polio and Hæmophilus Influenza b (1st)

  Hepatitis B (depending on the medical practitioner) (1st)

- **3–4 months**: Diphtheria, Tetanus, Whooping Cough, Polio and Hæmophilus Influenza b (2nd)

  Hepatitis B (2nd)

- **4–5 months**: Diphtheria, Tetanus, Whooping Cough, Polio and Hæmophilus Influenza b (3rd)

- **9 months**: Measles (for children attending nursery)

- **9–12 months**: Hepatitis B (3rd)

- **12–15 months**: Measles, Mumps and Rubella (combined injection – "ROR")

- **16–18 months**: Diphtheria, Tetanus, Whooping Cough, Polio and Hæmophilus Influenza b (booster)

- **Before 6 years**: BCG (if not already done)

- **3–6 years**: Measles, Mumps and Rubella (booster)

- **6 years**: Diphtheria, Tetanus and Polio (booster)

  Whooping Cough or acellular Whooping Cough

- **11–13 years**: Diphtheria, Tetanus, Whooping Cough or acellular Whooping Cough and Polio (booster)

  Measles, Mumps and Rubella (if not already done)

  Hepatitis B

- **16–18 years**: Diphtheria, Tetanus and Polio (booster) acellular Whooping Cough

  Rubella (if not already done)

BCG Vaccine

In the UK, the BCG is given at age 13 except in some high risk areas. In France, a child is expected to have had the vaccination before entering a *crèche, halte garderie* or school, and it is administered at any time from birth to 6 years old, by which time it is compulsory.

As the BCG is not administered in the USA or Canada, you will need to discuss this with your doctor before your child has the vaccine. If you return to North America and your child is tested for TB in a routine school or summer camp test, the positive result may cause confusion. It is possible (but not easy) to obtain a waiver if your child will only be in France for a few years, but whether or not the waiver is accepted is entirely up to the individual *crèche, halte garderie* or school.

Chicken Pox

A chicken pox vaccine has been available in France since September 2004, but is not prescribed systematically. You should therefore consult your doctor if you wish your child to be vaccinated.

Whooping Cough Vaccine

A new whooping cough vaccine is now available called acellular pertussis (*coqueluche acellulaire*), which causes milder and fewer side effects. In France, it is often used for the 18 month booster and for the boosters at 6 and 11 - 13 years, but is not yet common practice to use it for the first series of whooping cough vaccines. This means that if you decide you want your child to have this vaccine from the start, it may not be reimbursed by Social Security. Acellular pertussis is not available except in combination with several other vaccines, so the decision to use it must be made before the start of a vaccine series.

Health & Medicine

VITAMIN AND MINERAL SUPPLEMENTS

During Pregnancy

Different countries have differing policies on giving pregnant women vitamin and mineral supplements. In France, you will probably be prescribed supplements of iron, calcium and fluoride by your doctor or gynæcologist.

Vitamin Supplements for Infants

Vitamin D

This is essential for the satisfactory metabolism and absorption of calcium and phosphorus used in the building of bones. It is usually prescribed (and reimbursed) to babies and children in France because it is not added to foods (such as milk and bread).

Vitamin D is given until the age of five years. If you are breastfeeding, vitamin supplements are not essential until six months of age. Vitamin D can be given in different forms: daily as drops, as a phial every 6–12 months, or by injection.

Fluoride

Fluoride strengthens the enamel and helps prevent tooth decay during the formation of the teeth (it has no effect on formed teeth). It must be prescribed and will also be reimbursed by the *CPAM*. Fluoride is available either as tablets or as drops. Tablets can be crushed and added to the food or drinks of younger babies. Older children can suck the tablets as the fluoride will stay in contact longer with the teeth.

OTHER RESOURCES

Books

Glossary of Medical, Health and Phramacy Terms (French-English, English-French)
Alan. S. Lindsey
(Hadley Pager Info)

Association Sparadrap Booklets
Available from 🖳 www.sparadrap.asso.fr

Enfant à l'hôpital ? Suivez le guide
Apache
(Ed. Gallimard Jeunesse)

Guide familial de l'homéopathie
Alain Horvilleur
(Hachette Pratique)

Health Care in Paris - A Resource Book in English
A 200-page reference book produced by Health Network International in collaboration with WICE
Available from 🖳 www.hni-paris.org

L'Hospitalisation
A booklet available from your local mairie

Paris Pratique - Personnes Handicappée conseils
(Marie de Paris)

Le Paris des tout-petits: 6000 adresses et conseils
(Mango)

OTHER VOCABULARY

Childhood Illnesses

bronchiolitis .... *bronchiolite*
chicken pox .... *la varicelle*
childhood asthma .... *asthme de nourrison*
ear infection .... *l'otite*
German measles .... *la rubéole*
head lice .... *les poux*
hives .... *les urticiares*
head lice/nits .... *pédiculose or poux*
laryngitis .... *la laryngite*
measles .... *la rougeole*
mumps .... *les oreillons*
pinworms .... *oxyurose*
rosiola .... *la roséole*
roundworms .... *ascaris*
scarlet fever .... *la scarlatine*
strep throat .... *la pharyngite*
threadworms .... *oxyurose*
whooping cough .... *la coqueluche*
worms .... *les vers*

Contraception

blood sugar .... *glycémie*
blood test .... *prise de sang*
capsules placed under a woman's skin .... *micro pastille*
cholesterol .... *cholésterol*
condom .... *préservatif*
contraception .... *contraception*
family planning centre .... *Centre de Planning Familial*
GP .... *médecin généraliste*
gynæcologist .... *gynécologue*
hormone implant .... *implant hormonal*
IUD .... *dispositif intra-utérin*
mini-pill .... *micro-pilule*
morning-after pill .... *pilule du lendemain*
patch (hormonal contraceptive) .... *patch contraceptive hormonal*
pill .... *pilule*
ovulation predictor kit .... *test d'ovulation*
spermicides .... *spermicides*
sponge .... *éponge or tampon*
triglycerides .... *triglycérides*

tubal ligation ....*ligature des trompes*
urologist ....*urologue*
vaginal ring ....*anneau vaginal*
vasectomy ....*vasectomie*

Dentists

bonding/composite..*composite*
brace ....*bague*
cleaning ....*détartrage*
crown/cap..*couronne*
dentist ....*dentiste*
filling ....*plombage*
orthodontic treatment...*ortodentie*
plate ....*palais*
tooth...*dent*

Laboratories

anaemia ....*l'anémie*
antibodies..*les anticorps*
blood group..*le groupe sanguin*
blood sample..*une prise de sang*
blood sugar level..*le taux de glycémie*
haemoglobin ....*l'hémoglobine*
hepatitis...*l'hépatite (Hbs)*
HIV (AIDS) ....*VIH (SIDA)*
laboratory...*un laboratoire d'analyses*
Rhesus factor..*le facteur Rhésus*
rubella ....*la rubéole*
smear test ....*un frottis*
specimen bottle..*un flacon*
swab..*un prélèvement*
syphilis ....*la syphilis, la tréponématose*
toxoplasmosis ....*la toxoplasmose*
urine sample ....*échantillon d'urine*
Is it necessary to be fasting?...*Faut-il être à jeun?*

Medicines for Children

adhesive tape...*sparadrap*
bandage...*une bande Velpeau, une bande de gaze élastique,*
un pansement
bruise ....*bleue*
burn...*brûlure*
cotton wool..*coton hydrophile*

cut, wound..*coupure, plaie*
de-worming syrup ....*vermifuge*
disinfectant...*une solution antiséptique*
first -aid kit ....*une trousse à pharmacie de premiers secours*
graze..*écorchure, égratinure*
needle ....*une aiguille*
plasters, Band-aids ....*des pansements adhésifs*
safety pin..*une épingle de sûreté*
scar ....*une cicatrice*
scissors ....*une paire de ciseaux*
sterile gauze...*une compresse stérile à gaze*
stitches...*les pinces*
thermometer...*un thermomètre*
tweezers...*une pince à épiler*
wound ....*plaie*

Opticians

amblyopia or "lazy eye", ...*amblyopie*
astigmatism..*astigmatism*
contact lenses ....*lentilles*
farsightedness..*hypermétropie*
frame ....*monture*
glasses ....*lunettes*
lenses (for glasses)..*verres*
nearsightedness ....*myopie*
ophthalmologist..*ophtalmologue*
optician...*opticien*
prescription ....*ordonnance*
strabismus, "crossed" or "turned" eye ....*strabisme*

Pharmacies

ailments treated by the product ....*indications*
baby milk formulæ ....*laits pour nourrissons/laits de suite*
baking soda..*bicarbonate de sodium*
breast pump ....*tire-lait*
by mouth ....*voie orale*
capsules...*gélules*
cold ....*rhume*
cough ....*toux*
diarrhœa ....*diarrhée*
do not exceed prescribed dosage ....*ne pas dépasser la dose prescrite*
dosage ....*posologie*
drops ....*gouttes*
earache ....*mal à l'oreille*

first aid ....*premiers secours/soins*
headache ....*mal de tête, migraine*
hot water bottle ....*bouillotte*
indigestion..*indigestion*
injections ....*piqûres*
inner ear infection ....*otite*
lozenges...*tablettes*
method of use ....*mode d'emploi*
motion sickness ....*mal des transports*
not for use by children under age... ....*ne convient pas aux enfants de moins de...*
packets of soluble powder ....*sachets*
pharmacist ....*pharmacien*
powder ....*poudre*
prescription ....*ordonnance*
private complementary health insurance ....*mutuelle*
salve...*pommade, onguent*
scales (electronic or with weights)......................................*balance (électronique or mécanique)*
side effects...*effets secondaires*
suppositories..*suppositoires*
syrup ....*sirop*
tablespoon ....*cuillère à soupe*
tablets ....*comprimés*
teaspoon ....*cuillère à café*
vial, small bottle ....*flacon, ampoule*
warnings, precautions ....*contre-indications, précautions*

Physiotherapy

pelvic floor muscles physiotherapy ....*rééducation du périnée*
stomach (or abdominal) muscles ....*rééducation abdominale*
physiotherapist/physical therapist ....*kinésithérapeute, kiné*
complementary health insurance ....*mutuelle*
prescription ....*ordonnance*
independent midwife ....*sage-femme libérale*
electrical probe ....*sonde*
respiratory physiotherapy ....*kiné respiratoire*
physiotherapy...*rééducation*

Vaccinations

Chicken Pox vaccination..*vaccination antivaricelle*
Diphtheria vaccination..*vaccination antidiphtérique*
Haemophilus Influenza vaccination ....*vaccination antihaemophilus*
Measles Vaccination ....*vaccination antirougeoleuse*
Mumps Vaccination..*vaccination antiourlienne*
Polio Vaccination..*vaccination antipoliomyélitique*

Rubella vaccination	*vaccination antirubéolique*
Tetanus vaccination	*vaccination antitétanique*
Tuberculosis vaccination	*vaccination antituberculeuse*
Whooping cough vaccination	*vaccination anticoquelucheuse*

Vitamin and Mineral Supplements

calcium	*calcium*
fluoride	*fluor*
folic acid	*acide folique*
iron	*fer*

Useful Phrases

My child is sick/vomitting/coughing	*mon enfant est malade/vomit/a une toux*
My child has an ear ache	*mon enfant a mal aux oreilles*
My child has diarrhea	*mon enfant a la diarrhée*
My child's throat is sore	*mon enfant a mal à la gorge*
My child has a fever	*mon enfant a de la fièvre*

Is it contagious?	*Est-ce que c'est contagieux ?*
Can I send my child to school/garderie?	*Je peux l'envoyer à la garderie/école?*

Taking medication	*Prendre de médicament*
How often?	*Combien de fois par jour?*
For how long?	*Pour combien de jours?*
Should it be taken with food or drink ?	*Avec de la nourriture/avec une boisson?*
Are there any side effects ?	*Y'a-t'il des effets secondaires?*
I am allergic to	*Je suis allergique au…*

Do I need a prescription for this ?	*Est-ce que j'ai besoin d'une ordonnance?*
Is it reimbursed by Social Security ?	*Est-ce que c'est remboursé?*

I'd like to make an appointment	*Je voudrais prendre rendez-vous*
Is the doctor conventionné ?	*Est-ce que le medecin est conventinoné?*
It's an emergency. Can I come sooner ?	*C'est un urgence. Je peux venir plus-tôt?*

Notes

Living

Compiled and edited by Samantha Steed

This chapter deals with some of the day-to-day aspects of life in Paris, from eating out with the kids, to setting up your home technology to navigating public transport. You will also find useful information such as embassy contact details and emergency services numbers.

ECO FAMILY

With the increasing awareness of the need to safeguard our environment, Paris and surrounding areas now have their share of "environmentally friendly" products for children and families. This term encompasses recycled and recyclable products, to vegetables grown without chemical fertilisers or pesticides.

The guiding principle behind the new ecological consciousness is choosing not to "over consume", but rather to re-use, exchange, repair and recycle wherever possible. When choosing a cleaning product or detergent, for example, look for those that are biodegradable *(biodégradable)*, low in or without phosphates *(sans phosphates)* and in a recyclable container (indicated by a circle of three folded arrows:♲). You may frequently come across another symbol, of interlocking arrows:🔃. This does not indicate that the packaging is in fact recyclable, but that the supplier has paid an environment tax associated with its disposal.

Clothing can be dyed with environmentally friendly water-based dyes or made with 100% organic cotton. Children's toys can be made from recycled materials, wood from managed forests and lead-free paint *(peinture sans plomb)*.

Environmental Labelling

Products which comply with French or European environmental norms bear the following labels:

• *NF Environnement*

• *Eco-Label Européen*

Further information is available at 🖥www.afnor.fr. The *Prix Ecoproduit* is an award given by the French government *(Ministère de l'Ecologie et du Développement Durable* – Ministry of Ecology and Sustainable Development) to articles which respect the environment throughout their life cycle.

Cloth Nappies (Couches Lavables)

The use of disposable products still creates a problem in respect of the huge amount of landfill created. Millions of disposable nappies are thrown away each day and about 90% of them end up in landfill, where they will take centuries to decompose. With this in mind, you might be persuaded to use reusable nappies - it may even save you money: the Women's Environmental Network suggests a saving of more than €700, even after taking into account laundry costs.

There are also some "eco-disposable" nappies available, such as Tushies or Tendercare, for those who want the convenience of a disposable nappy. Unfortunately, at the time of publication, there do not seem to be any nappy laundering services available in Paris or the suburbs.

For more information consult the following organisations:

WEN, the Women's Environmental Network
PO Box 30626, London E11 TZ, UK
00 44 207 481 9004
Fax 00 44 207 481 9144
🖥 www.wen.org.uk
Lots of useful information on real nappies.
🖥 www.theclothresource.co.uk
Information and reviews on nappies and nappy sellers.

Organic Produce

Organic produce *(bio)* can be found in all of the main supermarket chains and at many traditional street markets. There are also many specialist organic supermarkets and a number of organic markets held on a weekly basis in and around Paris. (☞Shopping). In addition, there are even specialist services which will deliver a basket of in-season fruit and vegetables, or a full range of organically produced goods to your door:

- 🖳 www.lespaniersduvaldeloire.fr
- 🖳 www.biofrais.com
- 🖳 www.acheterbio.com

Cleaning Products

Look out for these brands at the supermarkets: *Ecover, Génération Verte, Maison Verte, Monoprix verte, Rainet, Sonett*. Genuine organic and/or 100% biodegradable cleaning products can be found in all the organic supermarkets and through some mail order companies. (☞Shopping). Check out 🖳www.vigitox.org (in French) for information on what your cleaning products contain.

Crèches

Some *crèches parentales* serve organic food regularly or occasionally. As these type of *crèches* are run by the parents, you may have a say in the kind of food served. Call the specific *crèche* for more precise information (☞Childcare for detailed information on *crèches parentales*).

Annual Trade Fairs

Salon du Bien-être et des Médecines douces
Porte de Versailles, Paris Expo, 75015 Paris
M° Porte de Versailles
🖳 www.spas-expo.com
Big fair, usually held in January or February, with all products and services concerning health, welfare and beauty.

Salon Marjolaine
Parc Floral de Paris, Bois de Vincennes
M° Chateau de Vincennes
🖳 www.biogourmand.com/marjolaine
The largest European organic product fair, the first week in November.

Vivez Nature
La Villette, Cité des Sciences et de l'Industrie
M° Porte de la Villette
🖳 www.vivez-nature.com
In spring and autumn, a medium-sized fair with food, toys and clothes.

Vivre Autrement
Espace Auteuil, 75016 Paris
M° Porte d'Auteuil
In March, a "friendly" sized fair with organic food, clothes, etc.

Salon International de l'Agriculture
Porte de Versailles, Paris Expo Paris 75015
M° Porte de Versailles
🖳 www.salon-agriculture.com
Huge annual agricultural show, held every February with a whole hall devoted to ecology.

Household Waste and Recycling

Household Waste

In Paris, household waste is picked up every day except 1st May. The service is free, and special green dustbins are used. Pickup times vary by *arrondissement*. Dustbins must not be put out more than one hour before pickup and must be brought back in within a quarter of an hour. In Parisian apartment blocks, it is usually the caretaker (*gardien*) who will put out the communal bins, not the individual tenants. In the suburbs, rubbish is normally collected twice a week and in some areas recyclable materials are collected directly from your home on specific days.

Large Items

There are several options for disposing of cumbersome objects. The city of Paris has a free pick-up service by appointment. There are also 250 large bins *(caissons)* placed around the city from time to time. Call *Allô Propreté* on 0 801 175 000 for an appointment or for information on current locations of the nearest *caissons*. Large objects are also accepted at the recycling centres.

Paper, Cardboard, Tins and Plastic

A green dustbin with a yellow lid is used specifically for recycling paper, cardboard, tins, plastic and certain other household items. There is a picture on the lid to tell you exactly what you can and cannot put in it. Most buildings have at least one of these dustbins, but if you wish to request a dustbin or have any questions, call *Allô Propreté*. Pickup is at specified times, usually once or twice a week.

Glass

About 1,000 large green plastic containers (*conteneurs* or *colonnes à verre*) are scattered around Paris for collecting glass for recycling. Most are strategically placed close to a supermarket. Some apartment blocks have a green dustbin with a white lid for glass, which are usually emptied once a week.

Used Car Batteries and Engine Oil

You can obtain a list of garages which accept these items, called *La Liste des Relais-Verts-Auto,* by telephoning 01.40.99.55.00.

Small Batteries and Button Batteries

These can be recycled at many collection points in photo and electronic shops such as FNAC, Nature et Découvertes, and Photo Station, as well as at all Monoprix and Prisunic and Carrefour supermarkets.

Recycling Centres

In Paris, there are four major recycling centres (*déchetteries*) and two neighbourhood recycling drops (*espace propreté*). Specific containers are set up to receive recyclable objects such as metal, wood, cardboard, paper and glass. Dangerous materials such as motor oil, car batteries, household batteries, CFCs (refrigerator coolant), solvents and other toxic substances should also be brought to the centres rather than put in household waste bins. You may also bring tyres, large objects such as furniture and a small amount of debris resulting from

household renovation. They will not take chemical waste, hospital waste or some other poisonous wastes. For more information contact:

Direction de la Protection de l'Environment
Documentation Centre,
2 rue Beaubourg, 75004 Paris
Mon - Fri 09h00 - 12h00
01.42.76.49.54
0 801 175 000

Location Of Recycling Centres

Déchetterie de la Poterne des Peupliers
8, rue Jacques Destrée, 75013 Paris
(under the exit ramp of the *périphérique exterieur*)
M° Porte d'Italie
Open daily 09h30 - 19h00 except 25th December, 1st January and 1st May
01.46.63.38.59

Déchetterie du Quai d'Issy-les-Moulineaux
voie AD 15, 75015 Paris (under the overpass connecting the quai d'Issy to the *périphérique*)
M° Place Balard, RER Boulevard Victor
Open daily 09h30 - 19h00 except 25th December, 1st January and 1st May
01.45.57.27.35

Déchetterie de la Porte de la Chapelle
17-25, avenue de la Porte de la Chapelle,
75018 Paris
M° Porte de la Chapelle
Open daily 09h30 - 19h00 except 25th December,
1st January and 1st May
01.40.37.15.90

Déchetterie de la Porte des Lilas
rue des frères Flavien, 75020 Paris
M° Porte des Lilas
Open daily 07h30 - 12h00 and 12h30 - 19h30
except 1st May
01.43.61.57.36

Mini-déchetterie
1, rue Fabert and rue Paul et Jean Lerolle,
75007 Paris (under the *Esplanade des Invalides*,
near the police station and the quai d'Orsay)
M° Invalides
Open Mon morning and 07h30 - 19h30 Tues - Sat
except 1st May.
01.45.51.23.68 or 01.47.53.90.52

For more information on recycling centres, check
with your local *mairie*.

For further information about protecting the environment have a look at the Other Resources section at
the end of this chapter.

DRIVING IN FRANCE

Driving Licence (Permis de Conduire)

Exchanging your Licence
Holders of EU licences no longer need to exchange
their licence for a French one. All other foreign long-
term residents need to exchange their existing
licence and it is important to get the process under
way as quickly as possible as you may face serious
fines for driving without a French licence. Shortly
after receiving your *carte de séjour*, you should go
to the *Préfecture* or *Sous-Préfecture* (according to
local procedure) and acquire a licence. You will
need some identification, your original licence translated into French, a proof of residence less than
three months old, and three photos (wearing spectacles if you need them for driving). Since January
2000, there is no charge for a French driving
licence, it can be used in all EU countries and is
valid for life.

A straight (and speedy) exchange may be possible
if your country has a reciprocity agreement with
France and your *Préfecture* or *Sous-Préfecture* will
tell you whether this is possible. Typically, this
exchange is only allowed within the first year of resi-

dency in France, so you should apply for the license
exchange as soon as possible after obtaining your
carte de séjour.

Obtaining a French License
All other unlucky souls must follow the more lengthy
and expensive route of enrolling in a driving school
(auto-école) and passing both the written *(code de
la route)* and road *(conduite)* tests.

If you would like lessons in English, you can contact
the following organisation:

Fehrenbach Driving School
53, boulevard Henri Sellier, 92150 Suresnes
01.45.06.31.17
Fax 01.47.28.81.89
www.frenchlicense.com

Loss of Licence
Should you misplace your licence or have it stolen,
declare the loss to the police, carry the *déclaration*
provided by the police with you and ask for a duplicate licence from your local *Préfecture* or *Sous-
Préfecture*.

Vehicle Registration (Carte Grise)

The vehicle registration document must be carried with the vehicle at all times, as must your insurance documents and driving licence. It is issued by either your *Préfecture* or *Sous-Préfecture* and should be applied for within 15 days of acquiring the vehicle. If you buy a new car, the garage will organise the application for you. If you purchase a second-hand car *(d'occasion)*, you must organise the change of registration yourself. Your *Préfecture* or *Sous-Préfecture* will give you the correct form to be completed and advise you which documents are required.

If you have brought your car with you to France, you will need to register it here. If you arrived from another EU country, then contact your local tax office *(services fiscaux)*. Arriving from outside the EU, you must await passage of the vehicle through customs *(douane)* and the receipt of documents stating customs clearance. With either the tax office or customs documents, go to your *Préfecture* or *Sous-Préfecture* with your former vehicle registration documents and passport or *carte de séjour*. You will need to file an application *(remplir un dossier)*, which will be sent on for safety and standards equivalency tests. This process can be long, time-consuming and costly and involves very extensive paperwork, even by French standards!

Change of Address

If you move to a new home, you must change the address on your *carte grise* within one month of moving. To do this, go to your new *Préfecture* or *Sous-Préfecture* with identification, proof of your change of residence (printed rent receipt, water, telephone or electricity bill, home insurance or car insurance), and the latest road test.

Loss of Carte Grise

Should you misplace your *carte grise* or have it stolen, declare the loss to the police, carry the *déclaration* provided by the police with you, as well as your identification and latest road test *(contrôle*

technique), and ask for a duplicate *carte grise* from your local *Préfecture* or *Sous-Préfecture*.

Insurance and Tax

Do not forget that you are legally required to arrange for insurance. You must display proof of current insurance by affixing a stub (provided by your insurer) to your windshield. In addition, every vehicle must display an up-to-date tax disc *(vignette)*, which can be obtained either from a *tabac* or from your local tax office *(hôtel des impots)*. The *vignette* lasts for one year and must be purchased annually between 1st November and 1st December in the *département* where the vehicle is registered. You will need to produce your *carte grise*. The *vignette* has two parts: an adhesive *timbre* that must be displayed on the windscreen of your car, and a receipt that you must keep with your vehicle documents.

Vehicle Testing

All vehicles over four years old are required to pass a road test called *un contrôle technique*. This must be carried out by an approved test centre *(centre de contrôle technique)*. It is up to you to organise this and it must be carried out during the six months preceding the vehicle's fourth "birthday", and every two years thereafter. Lists of approved test centres can be found on ⌨www.pagesjaunes.fr under *contrôle technique,* or on ⌨www.utac-otc.com.

Road Safety

If you have recently moved to France from a country that drives on the other side of the road make sure your children, who may have learnt the "look right, look left, look right again" rule, re-learn their road skills.

Using the Pedestrian/Zebra Crossing in France

In France, a driver is legally obliged to stop if someone is on the pedestrian crossing *(passage piéton)*.

Living

While this is widely ignored, *passages* are still the safest places to cross. At crossings controlled by traffic lights *(feux de signalisation),* be aware that there is often a filter light for cars coming round the corner, who could ignore your priority as a pedestrian. Never count on cars coming to a stop for a red light as many drivers routinely "run" red lights.

In Your Car

Safety belts are compulsory in the front and back of the car. The driver is responsible for passengers who are 13 years of age and younger not respecting this law. Children under 10 must sit in the back with a safety belt on, and/or (depending on their age and weight) in a special child/baby seat which conforms to French safety laws. (For information on car seats ☞Shopping, Travel).

Certain French Traffic Rules

Here is a by no means exhaustive overview of French traffic rules most likely to differ from driving "back home":

Traffic moves on the right. When there is no yield sign or flashing orange light, you must give way to traffic coming from your right. Be careful on main roads, as this rule applies and is the cause of many accidents in France. On the motorway, you do NOT yield to traffic coming from your right, except on the *Boulevard Périphérique* (the ring road round Paris).

When you drive into a roundabout (or traffic circle) you do NOT have the right of way. Cars already in the roundabout have priority EXCEPT around the Arc de Triomphe. There you must give priority to the traffic coming on to the roundabout.

Americans and Ontario Canadians note: there is no right turn on a red light except when you have a green/orange arrow indicating that you may do so. Also note that a flashing yellow light means you can go (and those behind you will certainly let you know if you do not!).

On Two Wheels

A helmet is not compulsory on bicycles but is strongly recommended. A helmet is compulsory for mopeds and motorbikes, both for drivers and passengers.

Drinking and Driving

The legal blood alcohol limit is 0.5g/litre. A safe limit would be about one glass of wine for a person weighing 50kg, or two glasses for a person weighing 70 - 80kg, if driving immediately.

For further information on driving in France ☞Travel.

Parking in Paris

Parking in Paris is rarely easy and can often be quite a headache. To park your car, you have the choice between finding a spot to park on the street or in an underground parking garage. You may not double park, park in a no-stopping zone (*axe rouge*), or in spaces reserved for the disabled or for deliveries (*livraison*).

Assuming you manage to find a spot, you must pay for parking from Mondays to Saturdays from 9h00 to 19h00 (though parking is generally free on public holidays and during the month of August – if so, this will be indicated on the parking meter by a yellow sticker). To pay for parking, you have to purchase a

Paris Carte, available at tabacs for €10 to €30 – parking fees range from €3 per hour in the centre of Paris to €1 per hour on the outskirts. You then insert your Paris Carte in the parking meter, and the meter will produce a ticket that you must place in your windshield, clearly visible from the outside. Street parking is limited to two hours, so if you need to leave your car for more than two hours during the day, it is best to park in an underground car parking garage.

If you return to your parking spot to find your car missing, this probably means you have run afoul of the parking rules and your car has been towed (mise en fourrière). In this case, you will need to find out where it has been taken, which you can do by inquiring at the nearest police station (commis-sariat de police) or by checking online at www.prefecture-police-paris.interieur.gouv.fr (only for French-registered vehicles). In either case, you will need to provide the vehicle's registration number (numéro d'immatriculation).

Once you have located your car, you should quickly retrieve it, as fees are charged by the day. To do so, present your driver's license and the vehicle registration (carte grise) and, if the car belongs to someone else, a power of attorney (pouvoir) from them authorizing you to retrieve the car, along with a copy of their proof of identity. You will have to pay a towing fee of about €126, and €10 for each day the car is impounded. Plus the parking ticket!

FOOD AND WATER

France has a well-deserved reputation for having some of the best food in the world, both in restaurants and in its shops and markets. This section is a brief guide to the baby food you can expect in France and, for those days when you just do not feel like cooking, details of some child-friendly restaurants. Bon appétit!

Baby Food

You may find that the French diet differs quite a bit from that of your country, and might be surprised at the meals proposed for babies.

The most popular brands of baby food in France are Blédina and Nestlé. Both brands can be found in most supermarkets, and both produce a large variety of products, ranging from puréed food for babies, to more lumpy varieties for older babies (petits plats). They also produce fruit drinks, soup and cereal mixes, and a variety of biscuits and snacks and ready-to-heat soups. However, nearly all of the Blédina and Nestlé products contain additives such as salt, sugar and emulsifiers, which some parents may prefer not to give to their young babies.

Cereals tend to be wheat-based (i.e., contain gluten), and many are also very sweet and flavoured (generally chocolate, vanilla, or honey). Gluten-free cereals exist, but are difficult to find - Gallia makes one (slightly sweet but unflavoured) which you can find in pharmacies. In France, it is very difficult to find baby cereals that do not have to be mixed with formula or milk.

Jars of fruit often contain a mixture of two or more varieties. Apples, pears and bananas are available individually, but strawberries, blueberries, and even prunes are invariably mixed with other fruits.

Additive-Free Baby Foods

Organic baby food is available in health food stores and some supermarkets (☞Shopping). If you want to avoid foods with added sugar, look for jars labelled sans sucre ajouté. However, many brands claiming not to add sugar have added honey

Living

instead, which should not be given to children under 12 months so check the ingredients before buying. Materne, a French brand of fruit desserts, produces a limited line of puréed fruits with no added sugar. Be aware that some fruits are mixed with cereal and may contain gluten. If you want to avoid this, look for jars marked *sans gluten*.

If you want to to avoid using foods containing genetically modified ingredients (GM foods, or *OGM - organismes génétiquement modifiés*) consult the list compiled and frequently updated by Greenpeace France at 🖳www.greenpeace.fr.

Hipp, a German organic brand, can be found in an increasing number of stores such as Le Bon Marché, Auchan, G20 and Champion, and in some organic and health food stores. (☞Shopping). Hipp is sometimes in the specialised food section (*diététique* or *produits biologiques*) rather than on the baby food shelves. It contains vegetables and fruit which have not been treated with pesticides or fertilisers. Many of their savoury and sweet varieties have no additives. The savoury recipes that contain no salt are clearly marked *sans sel ajouté*. The brand also produces a range of sugar-free fruit juices fortified with vitamin C.

Babybio is a line of organic sweet and savoury baby foods available in many organic food stores. Products include formula and puréed fruits and vegetables with no refined sugar, salt or other additives.

Nestlébio is another organic brand which can be found in Carrefour, who also stock their own-brand organic range called Carrefour Bio.

Other Suggestions

It is possible to buy portions of frozen puréed vegetables (*purée de légumes en galets*) in most supermarkets. These come in the form of large pellets, making it easier to cook small amounts. A number of varieties are pure vegetables, but check the ingredients list, as some contain a variety of extras such as salt, *crème fraîche*, rice, etc. Picard

(☞Shopping) sells frozen pellets of pure fruit (*purée de fruits*), organic frozen vegetables and soups frozen in pellets, some of which are specifically labelled as having no added salt or fat. In the health food section (*produits diététiques*) of many supermarkets, there is usually a wide range of biscuits with added vitamins, extra fibre, and reduced or unrefined sugar. Some varieties of rice cakes have no added salt and sugar and can be used as an alternative to biscuits. Another idea is to use bread sticks (*grissini* or *gressins*). Specialised organic and health food stores also carry a large selection of these types of products.

Preparing Homemade Food

There are a number of electrical gadgets on the market in France for cooking and puréeing baby food. The most versatile of these is the Babycook by Beaba, which will steam and then purée fruits, vegetable, meats and fish all in one small bowl. This sells for around €99 in appliance stores. Tefal make a similar gadget which sells for around €60. Cheaper alternatives include a mini food chopper (*hachoir*) which will purée small amounts of food very efficiently, a hand mouli-grinder (*mouli*) or a food processor with a small bowl and blade.

For ideas of recipes especially designed for the younger palate, you might like to consult the

MESSAGE Cookbook available from 🖥www.messageparis.org or have a look at the Other Resources section at the end of this chapter for other inspiration.

Useful Telephone Numbers and Websites

Babybio
05.57.96.56.60
🖥 www.kidbio.com/vitagermine

Danone (Blédina, Gallia)
0 801 111 213
🖥 www.groupedanone.fr

HIPP France
04.72.91.81.00

Nestlé
0 801 633 242,
🖥 www.bebe.nestle.fr

Child-friendly Restaurants

Many restaurants in France happily welcome children and you will often see French families eating out together, especially for Sunday lunch. However, if you need to keep to early hours, or you feel more comfortable in a restaurant that caters specifically to children, here are a few ideas:

Restaurants which have more than one branch in Paris are marked with an *

Altitude 95
Located on the 1st floor of the Eiffel Tower
M° Bir-Hakeim
01.45.55.20.04
🖥 www.tour-eiffel.fr
This restaurant is a very good choice for kids. They offer a children's menu and high chairs. Kids will be mesmerized by the ascent to the restaurant and the view of Paris from their seats! No changing facilities.

Bistro Romain *
26, avenue des Champs Elysées, 75008 Paris
M° Franklin D. Roosevelt
01.53.75.17.84
🖥 www.bistroromain.fr
This chain restaurant prides itself on its family service and children's menu. Kids can enjoy burgers and fries, while mum and dad enjoy classic French dishes. Courtyard seating is available in some locations – particularly on the Champs Elysées.

Buffalo Grill *
1, boulevard Saint Germain, 75005 Paris
M° Sully-Morland
01.56.24.34.49
🖥 www.buffalo-grill.fr
Children's menu, high chairs, booster seats. Large non-smoking section. Balloons, crayons, cut-outs, fun decor, birthday parties. Some locations outside Paris have indoor play areas. No changing facilities.

Café de la Jatte
60, boulevard Vital Bouhot, Ile de la Jatte, Neuilly sur Seine, 92000
M° Levallois Becon
01.47.45.04.20.
🖥 www.cafelajatte.com
Sunday brunch with children's buffet and entertainment for the kids (face painting, crayons, children's show). No high chairs or changing facilities.

Café de la Paix
12, boulevard des Capucines, Paris 75009
M° Opera
01.40.07.36.36.

Wonderful views of the Opera await you at this famous café/restaurant. Children's menu, high chairs, and changing tables are available.

Chicago Meatpackers

8, rue Coquillière, 75001 Paris
M° Châtelet-Les Halles
01.40.28.02.33
Children's menu, high chairs, booster seats, plastic bibs. Changing table in women's toilets. Large non-smoking section. Balloons, crayons, fun decor (electric train suspended from ceiling) and entertainment Wednesdays and weekends.

Chicago Pizza Pie Factory

5, rue du Berri, 75008 Paris
M° Charles de Gaulle-Etoile, George V
01.45.62.50.23
Children's menu, booster seats. Changing table in women's toilets. Large non-smoking section. Balloons, crayons, friendly and helpful staff. Entertainment on Sundays and for birthdays.

Festival Disney

Disney Village (outside the entrance to Disneyland Paris), 77000 Marne-la-Vallée
RER A Disneyland Paris
Multiple, mostly American-themed, family restaurants. Facilities vary.

Flunch *

5-7, rue Pierre Lescot - Forum des Halles
75001 Paris
M° Châtelet-Les Halles
01 42 33 52 35
🖳 www.flunch.fr
Self-service cafeteria. Children's meal with toy, high chairs, booster seats, microwaves. Changing table in women's toilets. Large non-smoking section. Birthday parties possible.

La Halle Saint Pierre

2, rue Ronsard, 75018 Paris
M° Anvers
01.42.58.72.89
Situated in the *Musée en Herbe/Musée d'Art Naïf*

Max Fourny at the foot of *Sacré Cœur*. Children's tables and chairs. Relaxed café with space for kids to play. Closed in August.

Hippopotamus *

42, avenue des Champs-Elysées, 75008 Paris
M° Franklin D. Roosevelt
01.53.83.94.50
🖳 www.hippopotamus.fr
This is a very child-friendly chain of restaurants, located all over Paris. Children's menus and high chairs are available. You can ask for balloons,

Tips (étrennes)

Although tipping in restaurants in France is easy because service is included, what do you do about Christmas tips and gifts? Here is some guidance taken from discussions on the MESSAGE members' website:

- the postman, who visits just before Christmas with calendars for you to "buy": €5 - €10
- the dustmen: €5 - €10
- the firemen: €10 - €15
- the gardien: opinion ranges from ¤30 - ¤100, some with a bottle of Champagne thrown in.

And here is what the French do:

- the postman: €5 - €8
- the dustmen: €4 - €8 (although apparently they are forbidden by law to ask for tips!)
- he firemen: €5
- the cleaner: depends on what she does and how long she works for. For a full-time cleaner about €45, but a carefully chosen present is also acceptable.
- the gardien: 10% monthly rent. And do not wait for a visit – put it in an envelope in their mailbox.

crayons, colouring books, games and puzzles from the friendly staff. Large non-smoking section. Lifts to toilets but no changing facilities.

L'Ile

Ile-Saint-Germain, 170, quai Stalingrad
92130 Issy-les-Moulineaux
RER C Issy Val-de-Seine
01.41.09.99.99
Sunday brunch: children's menu, cushions (no high chairs). Large non-smoking section. No changing tables, but counter space available. Crayons, drawings to colour. Face painting and children's show (magic, puppets, etc.).

Restaurant Justine

Hôtel Le Méridien Montparnasse
19, rue du Commandant René Mouchotte
75014 Paris
M° Montparnasse-Bienvenue, Gaîté
01.44.36.44.00
Sunday "Baby Brunch": children's menu, high chairs, cushions (no booster seats). Face painting and children's show (magic, puppets, balloons, gifts, etc.). No changing tables, but no problem using one of the sofas. Non-smoking section. Birthday parties possible. Also organises special event brunches (e.g., Carnival).

Kentucky Fried Chicken *

213, boulevard Vincent Auriol, 75013 Paris
M° Place d'Italie
01.53.79.06.85.
Children's meal with toy, high chairs. Ask at counter to heat bottle or baby food. No changing facilities.

Léon de Bruxelles *

131, boulevard Saint Germain, 75006 Paris
M° Saint Germain-des-Près, Mabillon
01.43.26.45.95
🖳 www.leon-de-bruxelles.fr
Children's menu, booster seats, high chairs. Balloons, pictures to colour (no crayons though), sweets. No changing table, but counter space available. Some branches in the suburbs have children's play areas.

Lina's Sandwiches in Galeries Lafayette

40, boulevard Haussman, 75009 Paris
M° Chaussée d'Antin
01.45.26.41.72.
The children's level of the Galeries Lafayette has a section specially set up for kids. On Wednesdays and Saturdays, buy your lunch at Lina's and eat while the kids are engrossed in a food workshop (which must be reserved in advance). It is well set up with the children's area covered in puzzles and activities. Children's menu and high chairs are available.

Monte Carlo

9, avenue de Wagram, 75017 Paris
M° Charles de Gaulle-Etoile
01.43.80.02.20
Self-service cafeteria. Children's menu, high chairs, microwaves. No changing tables, but small counter space available.

Pavillon des Oiseaux au Jardin d'Acclimatation

Bois de Boulogne, 75016 Paris
M° Les Sablons
01.45.02.11.61.
This café restaurant in the middle of the *Jardin d'Acclimatation* (☞Activities) offers a family buffet on Saturdays and Sundays with animation for the children. Kids can enjoy face painting, clowns, and magic tricks as well as their own buffet with chicken nuggets, pizza, and French fries. Children's menu offered all other days of the week. High chairs and changing tables available.

Pizza Hut *

1, place Joachim du Bellay, 75001 Paris
M° Châtelet-Les Halles
01.42.33.71.43
🖳 www.pizzahut.fr
Children's menu with toy, high chairs, booster seats. Place mats to colour, crayons. No changing facilities.

Pizza del Arte *
2, boulevard Haussmann, Paris 75009
01.42.26.67.77
M° Richelieu-Drouot
Children's menu, high chairs. No changing facilities.

Pizza Pino *
43, rue Saint Denis, 75001 Paris
M° Châtelet-Les Halles
01.40.26.39.07
Children's menu, high chairs and booster seats. No changing facilities.

Quai Ouest
1200, quai Marcel Dassault, 92210 Saint Cloud
M° Pont de Saint Cloud
01.46.02.35.54
Sunday brunch: children's menu, booster seats, lots of cushions (no high chairs). Large non-smoking section. Lounge near toilets with changing pads and large comfortable chairs (great for breastfeeding). Crayons, drawings to colour. Face painting and children's show at 13h00 (magic, puppets, etc.).

Spicy Restaurant
8, avenue Franklin Roosevelt, 75008 Paris
M° Franklin Roosevelt
01.56.59.62.59
www.spicyrestaurant.com
Central Parisian restaurant. Offers a special family brunch on Sundays from 12h30 - 15h00, with cartoons playing on TV screens and a clown to entertain the kids.

Ty Breiz
52, boulevard de Vaugirard, 75015 Paris
M° Montparnasse-Bienvenue, Pasteur
01.43.20.83.72.
A low-priced *crêperie* at Montparnasse. Choose from a wide range of *crêpes* – salty or sweet. High chairs available.

T.G.I. Friday's
8, boulevard Montmartre, 75009 Paris
M° Grands Boulevards
01.47.70.27.20

Children's menu, high chairs. Changing table in disabled persons' toilets. Large non-smoking section. Balloons, children's kit, fun decor and birthday cake possible.

Universal Resto
Le Carrousel du Louvre
99, rue de Rivoli, 75001 Paris
M° Palais Royal-Musée du Louvre
01.40.20.04.04
www.universal-resto.com
Food court with variety of foods from around the world, including a health food bar. Some counters with children's menus, microwaves available to warm baby food or bottles. Large non-smoking section.

Other Ideas

The large department stores have multiple restaurants including self-service cafeterias. Facilities vary, but most have microwaves and high chairs.

Weights and Measures

Ever been at the *marché* and wondered how much a kilogram is? Here are some handy conversion formulae to ease the frustration!

To Convert:	Multiply by:
Inches to Centimetres	2.540
Feet to Metres	0.3048
Yards to Metres	0.9144
Miles to Kilometres	1.609
Imperial Gallons to Litres	4.546
Ounces to Grams	28.35
Pounds to Grams	453.6
Pounds to Kilograms	0.4536
Centimetres to Inches	0.3937
Metres to Feet	3.281
Metres to Yards	1.094
Kilometres to Miles	0.6214
Litres to Imperial Gallons	0.22
Grams to Ounces	0.03527
Grams to Pounds	0.002205
Kilograms to Pounds	2.205

Stores such as IKEA and certain shopping centres in the suburbs have baby-friendly restaurants and even children's play areas. Examples include Bercy II (Charenton), Paris Nord II (Aulnay-sous-Bois), Créteil Soleil (Créteil), Art de Vivre (Eragny), Les Portes de Taverny (Taverny) (☞Shopping).

Do not forget about outdoor restaurants in the parks during warm weather *(Parc Floral, Jardin de Luxembourg, Tuileries*, etc.) or restaurants at child-oriented locations *(Cité des Sciences et de l'Industrie, Jardin de l'Acclimatation,* etc.). (☞Activities).

Water

Bottled Water

Bottled water is very popular in France, and you will find a wide variety of brands available in all small and large supermarkets in and around Paris. Although many people prefer to use bottled water for formula preparation and for drinking water during pregnancy, it comes with no guaranteed assurance of safety. Controls are very strict, but accidents have happened, even with popular brands.

Mineral Water (eau minérale)

The mineral content of this kind of water has been adapted to fall within set values, and it is purified but not sterilised. Some brands are suitable for infants – look for the words *convient aux bébé*s.

Spring Water (eau de source)

This is water bottled from natural springs and the mineral content may vary. It is tested for contaminating bacteria but otherwise it is natural, and generally not suitable for infants.

Carbonated Water (eau gazeuze)

There is also a wide range of carbonated waters available, e.g. Perrier, Badoît. This is not suitable for infants due to the high sodium content.

Tap Water and Lead Contamination

Tap water is safe to drink but it is advisable to take certain precautions due to the possible lead content. Lead in water presents a serious danger to babies, small children and the unborn child in pregnant women. (☞Health and Medicine). Lead in water comes not only from the water companies but also from lead pipes or lead solder in the plumbing in individual buildings. It is now illegal to fit buildings with lead pipes and the water companies have replaced all old lead pipes with PVC ones. However, this measure has only been taken up to the metre point in houses and residential buildings - any piping beyond this point is the responsibility of the owner. Therefore the lead content of water may vary from building to building and even from apartment to apartment, despite the strict legal controls regarding lead content in the water leaving the processing plant.

You can find out more about the quality of your water from your local *Direction Départmentale des Affaires et Sociales (DDASS) - Service Hygiène du Milieu* at ⌨www.ile-de-france.sante.gouv.fr.

Water for Infants

There is some debate and confusion over the usage of various waters for infant formula preparation. Some authorities recommend that particular mineral waters be used during the first four months, while others state that these give no added benefit over tap water. Discuss this with your paediatrician or doctor.

If tap water is chosen, it should always be boiled and cooled. Do not repeatedly boil the same water, as this causes concentration of the minerals. If your tap water is being passed through a domestic water softener or jug water filter, it is important to check with the manufacturer's instructions before using for baby formula preparation, because there have been problems with deposits of silver being left in the water.

Living

MOVING WITH CHILDREN

Moving house is never easy, especially when you have babies or young children. Whether you are moving to or away from Paris, or simply changing apartments in Paris or the suburbs, most children find the experience unsettling. The following tips should help to keep stress to a minimum for all members of the family:

Organising the Move

Choosing a Removals Firm

To find one of the many companies in and around Paris specialising in international removals, consult 💻www.pagesjaunes.fr or look in Fusac magazine. You can also contact the *Chambre Syndicale des Enterprises de Déménagements et Garde-Meubles de France* to obtain a list of registered moving companies and an advice booklet on how to organise your move:

Chambre Syndicale des Enterprises de Déménagements et Garde-Meubles de France
73/83, avenue Jean Lolive, 93100 Montreuil
0 800 010 020
💻 www.csdemenagement.fr

Relocation Agencies

These are agencies that provide services in English to help you with the entire logistics of your move:

Cosmopolitan Services Unlimited
64 boulevard Malesherbes, 75008, Paris
01.44.92.10.10
💻 www.cosmopolitanservices.com

Relocation Resources International
1 rue Gâtes Ceps, 92000, Saint Cloud
01.46.02.45.59

You will find similar agencies advertised in the Fusac magazine.

Getting Rid of Excess Items

If you want to cut down on your possessions in the weeks and months before the move, consider contacting organisations which will accept (and come to collect) donated items (☞Organisation and Charities for details).

The Fusac magazine has a large classifieds section for expats selling good quality furniture and appliances.

If you are a member of MESSAGE, you can advertise items for sale on the MESSAGE website, or you can organise a stand at either the spring or autumn Bring and Buy sale.

Whom to Notify When You Move:

- Owners' Association *(syndic)* or *gardien* of the building, if applicable
- Post office *(bureau de Poste)*. Ask about the mail forwarding service
- Water, gas *(GDF)* and electric *(EDF)* companies. Call two weeks before moving date to make an appointment
- Telephone company
- School
- Other administrative bodies, e.g. Social Security, Tax Office *(Hotel des Impôt)*
- Bank
- Insurance company, etc.

Documents that Need to be Reissued with Your New Address:

• National Identity Card or Resident Card (if applicable)
• Passport (French passport – change at your new *mairie*)
• Voter's card
• Car papers (*carte grise*)

Involving the Children

Decide on a strategy for involving your children in the move – this will depend on their age and the distance you are moving. If you are moving out of the area or to another country, your children will have to cope with the news that they will be leaving their friends behind and will have to adapt to a whole new environment. As a general rule, it might be best not to tell younger children until the preparations are well under way (provided they do not sense that something is going on), as they might find months of waiting for the change to occur difficult to cope with. On the other hand, older children might be able to deal with the news more positively if involved in the process right from the start. Books aimed at your children's age group might help them to understand and accept the process of moving house. To give you some ideas, a selection of such books is included in the Other Resources section at the end of this chapter.

Younger children will be very unsettled by the sight of all their toys and belongings being packed away, so it might be best to pack their things up very gradually, whilst they are asleep or out of the house. If you start this process several weeks before the move, it has the added benefit of many of their toys appearing new when you unpack them again, as they will have forgotten all about them in the meantime! If a toddler has a friend who is moving out, or makes a new friend who is just arriving, try to expose your child to a little bit of the friend's experience. Stop to watch and talk about movers you see working on the street.

Older children will appreciate being involved in the process of packing – even if it takes longer, try to leave them in charge of their own boxes if they are old enough, or let them decide what to pack in each box and which items to keep on one side until the last minute. Some children might also enjoy drawing on the boxes, especially if you ask them to help with the labelling. They might also enjoy helping to prepare change of address cards to give to their friends.

If you are moving within the same area, try to take your children to visit your new home as often as possible before the move. Even babies and young toddlers will find the transition easier if they have been familiarised with their new surroundings. If you are moving to a different country, gradually try and interest your children in their new environment by showing them pictures of interesting places and customs and telling them about different things they will enjoy doing in their new country.

At the same time, help them to say goodbye to their current surroundings by asking them which favourite places they would like to visit before you leave. Taking photos of your current home, their school or nursery and their friends for a scrapbook or for decorating their new room will also help them to realise that their feelings are important and that you understand how much they are leaving behind.

Planning for the last few days is crucial. Whether you are moving locally or switching countries, the day of the move is very upsetting for younger children so it is always preferable to arrange for someone to look after them away from the home. If practical, it is often easier for one parent to leave for the new home with the children before the removals firm arrives.

If your children are very young, it is also advisable to child-proof your new home before you move in (or ask someone else to do so for you if moving overseas) as toddlers are likely to be even more inquisitive than usual in a new house. It is especially important to get a stair gate fitted if you are moving

Living

to a house from an apartment, since younger children will probably be unfamiliar with the new skills required when going up and down the stairs and you may not be able to watch them as closely as you would like whilst the removals van is being unloaded.

However you plan the "big day", make sure that you pack a small survival kit for feeding and keeping the children occupied over the first couple of days, as it is always difficult to locate vital equipment amongst a mountain of removals boxes.

Finally, be prepared for a few days (or weeks!) of unsettled behaviour from your children. Babies and toddlers may react to the change in environment with disturbed eating and sleeping patterns. However difficult it may be to do so during the first few chaotic days, try to keep to their usual meal/bath/bedtime routines, as this will ease the transition and ensure that they settle down as quickly as possible.

📢 TIP

Some international removals firms also offer children's activity packs (including board games and colouring books about moving) specifically designed to interest children in the move and keep them occupied whilst your possessions are being packed up.

PUBLIC TRANSPORTATION

RATP

The *RATP (Régie Autonome des Transports Parisiens)* runs the public transport system in Paris and the suburbs, namely the *métro*, *RER*, tramway and bus services.

Maison de la RATP

54, quai de la Rapée, 75599 Paris Cedex 12
0 892 687 714 (timetable and service enquiries)
🖥 www.ratp.fr

Although neither the *métro* nor *RER* facilities are particularly user-friendly for mothers with young children, largely due to the amount of steps, you can always ask a fellow passenger or a staff member for help. Though help may not be offered (respecting your privacy), most people will lend a hand if asked.

As for barriers and passageways, they are theoretically standardised, so if your pushchair fits through one, you ought to be able to manage them all. There are "reserved" seats on the public transport systems, indicated by a heart, four per carriage in trains and four on buses. These are given in order of priority to: military and civilians with disabilities, blind people and finally to pregnant women or women with young children, but you may have to ask for a seat if you fit into one of these categories.

Métro

The *métro* runs from 05h30 to about 00h30. There are no changing facilities in any of the *métro* stations and most have a least one flight of steps with no escalator option. In theory, if pushchairs and prams are collapsible, they must be collapsed, but

Seasoned MESSAGE Public Transport Users' Tips:

Métro, RER, or Tramway

• Avoid the pushchair altogether and put a baby or toddler into a front or back carrier.

• Take the baby out of the pushchair and put him into a baby sling while you collapse the pushchair and continue your journey through the public transport system.

• Most lightweight, folding pushchairs (e.g., MacLaren brand) are narrow enough to fit through the barriers at *RER* or métro stations. If you are on your own, go through the turnstile backwards with the baby/child still in the pushchair. Tilt the pushchair backwards so the baby is almost lying flat to fit under the turnstile.

• For larger, or double (side-by-side) pushchairs ask at the ticket office for the exits reserved for disabled persons to be opened.

• Ask a fellow passenger for help going up/down stairs. You may even obtain a spontaneous offer of assistance (especially if you have twins).

• Look out for *métro* stations with escalators (they often have them going up if not down). It is often worth travelling an extra stop if you know that the next station has an 'up' escalator.

Bus

• When getting on the bus using the front door next to the driver, take the steps on the left as these do not bend so sharply at the top and there is more room to manoeuvre a non-collapsed pushchair.

• Seat your child first, and then go and validate your ticket (*composter votre billet*).

• For getting off the bus, learn how to say "please press the button and hold the doors open for me" ("*veuillez appuyer sur le bouton et tenir les portes ouvertes, s'il vous plaît*").

• Bus route map books are available at newstands and bookstores.

---

in practise you can ask the staff to open the special door reserved for disabled persons, provided you put your ticket through the turnstile first. If your pushchair is narrow enough to go through the turnstiles you can usually leave your child in it. At rush hour, you may find the trains too crowded and will need to fold the pushchair to board.

RER

The *RER* runs from 05h30 to 01h00. In the *RER* stations, things are easier as most Parisian stations are equipped with lifts, and escalators are more common. Most *RER* turnstiles are simpler to negotiate as well, but remember that you need your ticket to exit as well as to enter the system!

Buses

In theory, you must collapse your pushchair before boarding buses, but in practice the driver will rarely ask you to fold the pushchair, and will sometimes open the back doors so you can get on more easily (you may have to ask). On the longer, "bendy" buses on some routes, there are several doors, including one for wheelchair/pushchair access – for getting on, as well as getting off the bus. There is a reserved space on all buses for pushchairs and anyone standing in it should make room for you, although you may have to ask them to. Although buses run less frequently and take longer to get to their destinations, you have the advantage of no stairs to deal with and you are able to see where you are going.

Lost Property

For any item lost on public transport, taxis or in the street visit the:

Bureau des Objets Trouvés
36 Rue de Morillons, 75015 Paris
0 821 002 525
Mon - Wed 08h30 - 17h00, Tue - Thu 08h30 - 20h00, and Fri 08h30 - 17h30
If you cannot visit the offices they will accept written enquiries.

Reduced Ticket Prices

On the *SNCF* (trains), *RATP* (*métro* and tramway)

and *RER* systems, children under the age of 4 years travel free, and children from 4 - 10 years of age travel for half price (*tarif reduit*). You can buy a packet of 10 tickets (*un carnet*) for the *métro, RER,* bus and tramway at *métro* and *RER* stations and at your local *tabac*. Buying them this way saves a significant percentage of the purchase price of single tickets.

If you frequently use the public transport systems ask at the ticket offices for information on reduced travel rates *(tarif réduit)*.

For further information on SNCF travel, ticket prices and discounts, including reduced rates for *familles nombreuses* (families with three or more children).
☞Travel.

Jumping the Queue

Have you ever been standing at the back of a very long queue, fuming as someone sails right to the front? Well, in France there are certain situations where jumping the queue is practically a right! To make sure you do not miss out on a time-saving opportunity remember this:

If you are pregnant, you can ignore the queue in the Post Office, the supermarket (if you are brave enough!) and the train station. Even in other places, you are often waved to the front by genial Parisians - never refuse!

Anyone travelling with a child under four can jump the taxi queue at stations and airports. If you have ever stood in one of those queues with a travel-weary toddler you will know what a lifeline this is!

SAFETY IN THE HOME

If you have just moved to France with young children or your baby has turned toddler and is beginning to explore, be aware of the dangers that your "foreign" environment may present.

Electricity

The domestic electricity supply in France is 220v AC/50Hz compared with 110v AC/60Hz in the USA and 240v AC/50Hz in the UK. To use electrical appliances from the USA in France, it is possible to buy a transformer *(transformateur)* to reduce the voltage of the French mains power to that required by your appliance. Adapters *(adaptateurs)* are available to enable the plugs on your UK appliances or USA lamps (just change the bulb to a 220v bulb) to work from the French mains supply. However, since the voltage in France is lower than that required by a UK appliance, it will run more slowly. Adapters and transformers can be bought from any hardware store, including *BHV* and furniture stores *Castorama* and *Ikea* (☞Shopping).

Unplug transformers when not in use so as to avoid overloading sockets. Note that total wattage drawn should be no more than 2,000 watts at each normal household socket (10 amperes).

If you find that the electrical installation has not been recently updated in your home or flat, you may wish to have it checked out by a specialist. Expenses can be deducted from your income taxes if any work is done to put things in conformity with today's standards.

Promotelec
01.41.47.10.80,
🖥 www.promotelec.com
This is an association that comes to the home and writes up safety assessments.

Finally, you may want to invest in French plug safety covers to prevent curious little fingers poking into sockets (these are available from most major supermarkets and hardware stores).

Gas

The gas distributed by *GDF (Gaz de France)* does have a smell. Should you suspect a gas leak either in the home or a public place, call the Fire Service (dial 18) and open the windows immediately. For any other problems regarding your gas supply, call the telephone number indicated on your gas bill for emergency repair services *(dépannage)*. Remember to regularly change the rubber gas pipes connecting your appliance to the mains - they usually have a use-by date stamped on them.

Fire

If you live in a flat, check the fire procedure with your *gardien* (if you have one) and learn what the escape routes are. If you are in a house, have a plan and make sure that everyone understands what to do. Also make sure you have your heating system checked annually, as well as all chimneys swept out. This is not only as a safety measure – it also is necessary in order to obtain insurance cover in case of a fire. Smoke, gas and carbon monoxide detectors, fire blankets and small fire extinguishers suitable for the kitchen can be bought at IKEA, BHV, or any other major hardware store (☞Shopping).

Windows and Balconies

Do not put furniture in front of windows for little ones to climb. If you have radiators under them which children will climb, put locks on the windows. If you wish to install a child-safe barrier on your balcony or window railing, you must get permission from the landlord or tenants' association. Though the request is rarely refused, you may be required to use certain materials or colours and this expense is usually not covered by landlords.

Living

Bathrooms

Many Paris apartment buildings have extremely hot tap water. It is unlikely your landlord will lower the temperature, so you must be extremely vigilant about bath temperatures. If you control your own water temperature, 50° - 55° C or 120° - 130° F is the recommended maximum for safety. Always run the cold tap before turning on the hot, to help avoid accidents.

Kitchen

European ovens are less insulated than American ones, resulting in many burned little hands each year from the *outside* of the oven door.

Poisons

In case of an emergency, never give your child anything to drink, including the syrups to induce vomiting, until you have checked with the Poison Control Centre *(SOS Anti-Poison)* on 01.40.05.48.48. They have English speakers who can handle your call. If the situation is serious, call the SAMU for ambulance assistance. Remember, cleaning products are not the only poisonous things found in a household and you may not notice or be able to understand warning notices on products in French. Keep an eye out for words such as *nocif* (harmful) or *toxique* (poisonous).

Out for a Walk? Keep your Eyes to the Ground...

There are around 220,000 dogs in Paris. That is about one for every ten people. And they all have to be taken out each day, to "do their business". Dog-owners are, in theory, obliged to clean up after their pets - including from the gutter or in parks and gardens. However, despite government advertising campaigns over recent years, the reality is that many do not.

The result is that wherever you choose to take a walk with your child, you need to watch out for where your pushchair wheels, toddler feet, children's bikes or skateboards go. Hone your slalom skills; the chances are you are going to need them - unfortunately.

Some individuals and local (French) mothers' groups have carried out commando operations in order to clear up their local park, or quartier, circling the offending mess with spray paint, and piling up the evidence in heaps, writing to the town hall, putting up notices. This is a hot topic for parents, disabled people in wheelchairs, cyclists... and not only in and around Paris, but all over France.

A team of Cleaning Inspectors (*Les inspecteurs du CAPP - centre d'action pour la propreté de Paris*) is responsible for looking out for and fining miscreants (average fine : €183). However, there are less than 100 inspectors for the whole of Paris, and they intervene only in areas where there has been a poster awareness campaign. Fines went up three-fold between 2001 and 2003, and this is expected to rise further when traffic wardens also have the power to fine offenders.

In the meantime, watch where you walk – and feel free to contact your local *mairie* for more information on this issue in your area.

TECHNOLOGY

Telephone

Although France Télécom is the service provider for your telephone installation and line rental, you can choose from an ever-increasing number of discount telephone operators in Paris. Thanks to new technology like Voice Over IP, discount providers such as neuf.fr or free.fr offer low monthly calling plans that include unlimited free calls to many international destinations. To subscribe to any of these operators, you should contact them and they will liaise with France Télécom to become your service operator.

A very useful website is
www.budgetelecom.com. It allows you to fill in details of a specific call (destination, time of day, length of call) and then offers a comparison of what the various operators would charge.

Another option for international calls is to subscribe to a callback service. Callback companies offer substantial reductions on international phone calls (often 40% or 50% cheaper than the normal rate), by routing calls through the most competitive operator for each destination.
It is also worth considering making your telephone calls over the Internet, using software that allows you to make calls if you have a broadband connection.

Useful Numbers

France Telecom free English-language helpline
0 800 364 775 (Mon - Fri 09h00 - 17h30)

France Telecom local agency
10 14 (free from a fixed line)

Telephone repair service 10 13

France Télécom International directory enquiries 32 12

The single, historical number for national directory enquiries (*12 – le douze*) was gradually phased out from the end of 2005 as this service was privatized. There is now a choice of numbers (and companies) to call. They are all six-figure numbers, beginning with *118*. A total of 27 companies were assigned numbers; the following are the most well-known at the time of printing:

National Directory Enquiries

Scoot France 118 000
Le Numéro
(subsidiary of the UK's The Number) 118 218
France Télécom 118 712
Bouygues Télécom 118 812

The governing telecoms body in France requires that these numbers provide the equivalent service to the *pages blanches*, or white pages, i.e. fixed and mobile private numbers; Internet telephone numbers; freephone numbers; commercial numbers beginning with 08.

The 118 XYZ numbers are free to offer additional services, such as professional numbers, international numbers, the reverse directory (*l'annuaire inverse*, where you give a telephone number and they tell you to whom it belongs), putting you through to the number required, or sending information to you by e-mail or text/SMS.

Living

However, the pricing for these services is set freely by the operators, and you may find it difficult to compare any one with the other competitive offerings available. The only exception to this rule is the historic incumbent, France Télécom, which will continue to offer the full gamut of services.

You can also find telephone numbers on the internet, with the France Télécom services 💻www.pagesjaunes.com (for professional numbers) and 💻www.pagesblanches.com (for private individuals).

Numbers Beginning with 08

Many companies use special numbers to offer services such as technical support, customer services, competitions and prize draws, or simply information. In France, these calls are often more expensive than regular calls. The tariff should be given with the number, but here is a brief guide:

Numbers beginning	Cost (from a fixed line as of August 2005)
0 800	Free call (numéro vert)
0 810	same price as a local call, minimum 1 minute (numéro azur)
0 820 20 / 0 820 22	€0.09 per minute including VAT (numéro indigo)
0 820	€0.118 per minute including VAT (numéro indigo)
0 825	€0.15 per minute including VAT (numéro indigo)

Principal Telephone Operators

France Télécom
10 14 (free from a fixed line)
💻 www.francetelecom.com

Cegetel
0805 805 805 (free from a fixed line)
💻 www.cegetel.fr

Tele2
💻 www.tele2.fr

Neuf telecom
💻 www.neuf.fr

Television

Channels

With cable, satellite and digital television developing all the time, you have a mind-boggling array of channels available to you in France. Fortunately, there are also numerous comprehensive TV guides to tell you what is on, such as *Télérama*, *Tele Z*, *TéléLoisirs* and *Telestar*, all available from your local newsstand or supermarket. There are also specialized guides for subscribers to cable and users of satellite TV such as *Télé Cable Satellite Hebdo*.

Standard Channels

The five standard terrestrial channels are TF1, France 2, France 3, 5e/Arte and M6. Children's programmes feature on all of the five channels and sub-titled films in English appear regularly on the 5è/Arte channel.

Canal +

Canal + is available by subscription and you need a decoding device to be able to watch it (although a few programmes are broadcast unscrambled). On Canal + you will find many newly released films (in English and other languages) and some special sports coverage. To subscribe to Canal +, contact a local television store or consult 💻www.canalplus.fr.

Cable Television

These days, most of Paris and the suburbs area are connected to the cable network. Channels are selected by the particular network operator and presented to the subscriber in the form of bundled options (*bouquet*) and subscriptions range from less than €20 to over €60 per month. You will definitely find programmes in English for you and the children on the BBC and Sky channels.

Satellite Television

For access to this service, you will need at least one satellite dish and southern exposure to your house or apartment to mount the dish on the roof, balcony or side wall. Permission from the landlord (*propriétaire*) or your residents' association (*assemblée des co-propriétaires*) is necessary before mounting the dish on the building or in the garden, and there may also be local area restrictions which apply.

Canal Satellite
0 891 391 111
💻 www.canalsat.fr

TPS
32 99
💻 www.tps.fr

These are the two main (digital) satellite providers in France. TPS offers Euronews, Bloomberg, BBC World, BBC Prime and NBC Super Channel C while Canal Satellite offers EuroNews, CNN International,, Bloomberg, BBC World and CNBC. Sky TV is the satellite system from the UK. You can purchase Sky TV from most satellite shops in and around Paris and through many online sites.

If you have a satellite dish pointing at the correct satellite, English language channels are also available without subscription. This includes all BBC channels, Bloomberg TV, CNBC (business chan-

nels), Channel 5 (UK general entertainment), CNN International, ITV 3 (back-catalogue entertainment), Sky News (news channels), Eurosport, Quantum, QVC, Screenshop, TNT (classic movies) and Travel. The following guide gives you information concerning cable and satellite operators and television broadcasting companies classed by country:

Internet Guide to Radio and Media
01.49.55.01.30
💻 www.comfm.fr

Digital Terrestrial TV

Introduced in early 2005, the TNT digital terrestrial service covers most of the major towns and cities in France, with a package of 14 French-language channels including the main ones plus some specialist channels. There is no monthly charge, but you do need a decoder, which is available from most audio/visual shops. A replacement aerial may

---

Too Much TV?

The question of whether children should watch television, for how long and from what age is open to debate. An introduction to nursery and primary education published by Bayard Presse offers six guidelines regarding viewing with young children:

• Never install a television set in your child's bedroom

• Consult programme guides to select programmes

• As often as possible, watch the programme with your children

• When the programme is finished, discuss it with your children

• Always let them watch a programme right to the end

• Prevent them from "zapping" by withholding the remote control!

also be necessary. For more information, consult 💻www.tnt-gratuite.fr.

Video and DVD

If you wish to make use of the widest selection of English language video cassettes available in France, your video player *(magnétoscope)* needs to be able to read PAL (European), NTSC (USA and Japan) and SECAM (French) systems. Your television must also be multi-system and your DVD player should be multi-region. Both Darty and FNAC offer expert advice in this field and addresses and contacts are also to be found in the many video/hi-tech magazines available.

Video and DVD Libraries

Some videos (in PAL and NTSC) and audio cassettes are available for loan from the American Library (☞Activities). If your children attend the American School of Paris, you can borrow video-tapes (NTSC) from the large collection managed by the Parent Faculty Association. Many local libraries around the Paris area now stock several videos and DVDs in foreign languages.

Video and DVD Clubs

There are lots of video and DVD clubs dotted in and around Paris so there is bound to be one not far from you. Many video clubs have a *VO (version originale* - soundtrack in original language) section and even the *Cinébank* dispenser machines offer a small range of titles in English.

An English language video club with free membership:

Prime Time Video
24 rue Mayet, 75006 Paris
01.40.56.33.44
12, rue Léone Reynaud 75116 Paris
01.47.20.50.01.
💻 www.prime-time.org/paris

Buying Videos and DVDs

WHSmith has a wide selection of English language videos and DVDs (☞Shopping) and many DVDs you buy in France have a menu allowing you to select the English soundtrack. You may also find a wide array of English language videos and DVDs at www.amazon.fr and 💻www.play.com (a UK site that ships free to France).

Internet

Competition is forcing prices down for all types of Internet access. Most service providers now offer unlimited dial-up access, including telephone charges, for a fixed monthly fee.

Broadband

Broadband connections share your telephone or cable TV line, so you can still receive and make telephone calls while online. Broadband comes in two flavours: cable and ADSL.

You will find prices for broadband access vary from operator to operator, with France Télécom being one of the more expensive providers. You will also find that it is generally cheaper if you bundle your telephone service and Internet access together.

A wide range of Internet service providers *(four-nisseurs d'accès)* is available and each one provides different access packages. Quality and price comparison is difficult since each service differs in speed, local charges, technical support, hours and timing of access and availability of English support and/or documentation. When calling providers, if you do not respond to the automated choices and stay on the line, eventually an operator will answer who will usually be able to transfer you to someone who speaks English. Below are the telephone numbers of several providers. Club-Internet, Wanadoo, and AOL had English speaking staff available at the time of printing.

Club-Internet

32 04

 www.club-Internet.fr

Free

 www.freetelecom.fr

Neuf

 www.neuf.com

Wanadoo

36 08

 www.wanadoo.fr

Public Access

La Poste

The Post Office has a service called *Cyberposte* in 800 post offices across France. You use a special Internet card and pay as you go (€7 for the first hour and then €4 per hour to recharge your card).

Around 30 of the bigger post offices in Paris offer this service.

The Town Hall (Mairie)

Offering a similar service to the Post Office, the *mairie* is a good place to check if you live in the suburbs and do not have a local *cybercafé*. Not all *mairies* have points of Internet access, so call before you visit.

Cybercafés

There are many *cybercafés* across Paris, majority of which advertise in Anglophone publications such as the Fusac magazine. Prices and services vary, and some have staff who speak English. Usually drinks and meals are available, with music and exhibitions if you are lucky. Call before you go, as they do not always stay in business very long.

Living

EMERGENCIES

Emergency Services

For quick reference to Emergency Numbers go to the inside back cover of this book.

This section provides a guide on how to use the French emergency services, which number to call and what kind of help you can expect. You can call all the emergency numbers free of charge from any public, private or mobile phone. When calling emergency services, make sure you give clear instructions as to where you are. Fill in these details (in French and perhaps phonetically) and stick them somewhere prominent so that your children are able to call the emergency services if necessary.

Fire Brigade (*Sapeurs Pompiers*) . . .dial 18
Ambulance (*SAMU*) . . . . .dial 15
Police (*Police*) . . . . .dial 17

Your Name:
Building Number:
Door Code:
Floor:
Address:
Telephone Number:

Fire Service (18)

The *sapeurs pompiers* are primarily fire fighters but can also be called out to most emergency situations such as accidents, asphyxia (drowning, hanging, gas poisoning), gas leaks and saving animals (cats stuck up a tree, etc.).

It is a public service and their aid is free of charge. They are very well trained in cardio-pulmonary resuscitation and basic life support and are equipped with semi-automated defibrillators (machines which provide an electric shock to restart an arrested heart). If needed, an on-call doctor can join the team of *pompiers* and start ACLS (advanced cardiac life support) or provide medical support for the *sapeurs pompiers* ambulance. The *sapeurs sompiers* and the *SAMU* work closely together to provide the most appropriate assistance.

Ambulance Service (SAMU) (15)

It is generally easier to find someone who speaks English at this number. Located in each *département* is a *SAMU Centre (Service d'Aide Médicale Urgente)* which receives emergency medical calls and arranges the dispatch of an appropriate emergency medical team and vehicle. It is a public service and is free of charge for private individuals. The *SAMU Centre* can trace all calls made to them. All emergency calls pass through a switchboard staffed by permanent auxiliary medical personnel who may, depending on the nature of the call, pass the call to a doctor who asks brief and precise questions to evaluate the seriousness of the case and arranges the appropriate medical service. This will be one of the following:

• Medical advice over the telephone
• A general practitioner, a doctor from *SOS Médecins* or a specialist (pædiatrician, heart specialist, psychiatrist, etc.) will be sent
• A first aid assistant or ambulance from either the French Red Cross, Civil Defence volunteers or a private ambulance will be sent
• A mobile emergency resuscitation unit (*SMUR - Service Mobile d'Urgence et de Réanimation*) will be sent

Police Service (17)

The police force in France is made up of three different organisations:

La Police Municipale

This is the police force provided by the town council. Their officers do not have the power of arrest, are not armed and deal mainly with traffic and parking offences, helping schoolchildren across the road, etc.

La Police Nationale

This is the force which deals with serious crime and operates in Paris and surrounding areas, crossing city and *départementale* boundaries. The officers are armed and deal with any kind of situation, e.g. road accidents, burglaries, street crime, domestic problems, lost children. The *Police Nationale* also includes the anti-riot police and services such as surveillance of official ceremonies. In small towns and villages outside the Paris region, these services are provided by the *Gendarmerie*.

The following website offers contact information for your local police station (*Commissariat de Police*) in Paris closest to you 💻 www.prefecture-police-paris.interieur.gouv.fr/infos_proxi/plan.htm

La Gendarmerie

This is a paramilitary police force, officially part of the army, which operates mainly in small towns. They also patrol the roads and motorways.

Wednesday Alarm

Every first Wednesday of the month at noon, an air raid siren wails mournfully across Paris. The French are testing their sirens again – they have been doing that at the same time every month since the Second World War. If you hear it at that time, there is no need to pay any attention apart from to notice it is still working. We are all supposed to know that if it goes off at any other time then it is not a drill - there is serious danger of some sort. We are meant to go back to our home as soon as possible, switch on the radio or television and await further advice from the authorities.

Living

Useful Telephone Numbers

Here is collection of some handy telephone numbers. You might find it useful to fill in your personal and local contact numbers in the spaces below and put this list somewhere prominent in your home. For a quick reference to emergency numbers, turn to the back of the book.

My office:
My partner's office:
Our family doctor/GP (*Généraliste*):
Our doctor's stand-by (*Service de garde* - from your doctor):
Our pædiatrician:
Our pædiatrician's stand-by (*Service de garde*):
Our dentist:
Our dentist's stand-by (*Service de garde*):
Our nearest hospital with emergency facilities:

Practical Help

Our babysitter/babysitting agency:
Our school(s):
Our garderie/crèche:

Emergency Child Minding Services
SOS Urgences Mamans (01.46.47.89.98)

Pregnancy Problems
SOS Grossesse (01.45.84.55.91)

Lost And Found
Lost Carte Bleue (0 892 705 705)
Objets trouvés (0 821 002 525)

Administration
Our local Caisse Primaire d'Assurance Maladie:
Our Social Security Number:
Our local Caisse d'Allocations Familiales:
Our CAF number:

Specialist Services

Burns
Hôpital Cochin (Paris 14th - adults) ☎ 01.58.41.26.49
Hôpital Percy (Clamart 92) ☎ 01.41.46.60.00
Hôpital d'Enfants Armand Trousseau (children) ☎ 01.44.73.74.75

Children's Hospital
Hôpital Necker Enfants Malades (Paris 15th) ☎ 01.44.49.40.00

Children's Medical Emergency
Urgences pédiatriques (after 20h00) ☎ 01.43.94.35.01

Counselling Services
SOS Help ☎ 01.46.21.46.46

Dentistry
SOS Dentaire 24h/24 ☎ 01.43.37.51.00

Doctors 24h/24
SOS Médecins (Paris 75) ☎ 01.47.07.77.77
SOS Médecins (Yvelines 78) ☎ 01.39.58.58.58
SOS 92 (Hauts de Seine 92) ☎ 01.46.03.77.44

Drug Addiction
Drogues, alcool, tabac info service ☎ 0 800 231 313

Eyes
Urgence Oeil Hôpital des Quinze Vingt ☎ 01.40.02.16.80

Heart
SOS Cardiologie ☎ 01.47.07.50.50

Mental Illness
Urgences Psychiatrie 24h/24h 7/7 ☎ 01.47.07.24.24

Poison
Centre anti-poison, Hôpital Fernand-Widal (Paris 10th) ☎ 01.40.05.48.48

Veterinary
Our vet:
Our vet's stand-by *(Service de garde)*:
24h/7 Home visits *(Vétérinaire à domicile)* ☎ 01.47.55.47.00
Emergency Service *(Urgences vétérinaires)* ☎ 0 892 689 933

Living

EMBASSIES

American Embassy
2, avenue Gabriel, 75008 Paris
M° Concorde
01.43.12.22.22
💻 www.amb-usa.fr

American Consulate
2, rue St Florentin, 75008 Paris
M° Concorde
0 810 204 626
💻 www.amb-usa.fr

Australian Embassy & Consulate
4, rue Jean Rey, 75015 Paris
M° Bir-Hakeim
01.40.59.33.00 (embassy)
01.40.59.33.06 (consulate)
💻 www.austgov.fr

British Embassy
35, rue du Faubourg St Honoré, 75008 Paris
M° Concorde
01.44.51.31.00
💻 www.amb-grandebretagne.fr

British Consulate
18 bis, rue d'Anjou, 75008 Paris
M° Madeleine
01.44.51.31.02
💻 www.amb-grandebretagne.fr

Canadian Embassy & Consulate
35, avenue Montaigne, 75008 Paris
M° Franklin D. Roosevelt or Alma-Marceau
01.44.43.29.00
💻 www.amb-canada.fr

German Embassy
13-15, avenue Franklin D. Roosevelt, 75008 Paris
M° Franklin D. Roosevelt
01.53.83.45.00
💻 www.amb-allemagne.fr

German Consulate
13-15, rue Marbeau, 75116 Paris
M° Porte Dauphine
01.53.83.46.40

Irish Embassy & Consulate
4, rue Rude, 75116 Paris
M° Charles de Gaulle-Etoile, Argentine
01.44.17.67.00
💻 www.embassyofirelandparis.com

New Zealand Embassy & Consulate
7 ter, rue Léonard de Vinci, 75116 Paris
M° Victor Hugo
01.45.01.43.43

South African Embassy & Consulate
59, Quai d'Orsay, 75007 Paris
M° Invalides
01.53.59.23.23 (embassy)
01.47.53.99.70 (consulate)

OTHER RESOURCES

Books

Paris est à nous, Vivre Bio à Paris
Catherine Mercadier (Parigramme)

A Life Stripped Bare: Tiptoeing through the Ethical Minefield
Leo Hickman (Eden Books, Transworld)

A Good life: The Guide to Ethical Living
Leo Hickman (Eden Books, Transworld)

The Little Book of Living Green
Mark Hegarty (Nightingale Press)

Reduce, Reuse, Recycle!: An Easy Household Guide
Nicky Scott (Green Books)

New Complete Baby and Toddler Meal Planner/Superfoods for Babies and Children
Annabel Karmel (Ebury Press)

First Foods and Family Meal Planner
Sara Lewis (Lorenz Books)

Moving House Ltd (Usborne First Experiences Book)
Anne Civardi and Stephen Cartwright (Usborne Publishing)

Moving Molly (Red Fox Picture Book)
Shirley Hughes (Red Fox)

We're Moving House
Heather Maisner and Kristina Stephenson (First Time Stories - Kingfisher Books)

Expat Survival Guide
Free from English-language bookshops and stores iin Paris. Pdf version available online from
www.expatica.com

Almost French: A New Life in Paris
Sarah Turnbull (Nicholas Brealey Publishing)

French or Foe: Getting the Most out of Visiting, Living and Working in France
Polly Platt (Culture Crossings)

60 Million Frenchmen Can't Be Wrong
Jean-Benoit Nadeau & Julie Barlow (Robson Books)

Magazines

Fusac
(France USA contacts)
bi-monthly, free
www.fusac.fr

OTHER VOCABULARY

Telephone line	Ligne téléphonique
Internet Connection	Connexion à internet
Service Provider	Fournisseur
Subscription	Un abonnement
What is the monthly charge?	Quel est le tarif mensuel?
Television channel	Chaîne de télévision
Cable TV	La télévision cable
Satellite TV	La télévision satellite
Satellite Dish	Le parabole
Digital TV	La télévision numerique
Technical support	Le service technique
My connection doesn't work	La connexion ne marche pas
Does anyone speak English?	Y a t-il quelqu'un qui parle anglais ?
A packet of 10 tickets please	Un carnet, s'il vous plaît
Please can you help me with the pushchair?	Pourriez-vous me donner un coup de main avec la poussette, s'il vous plaît ?
Please can you open the gate?	Veuillez ouvrir la grille s'il vous plaît
Please can I get on through the back doors?	Puis-je entre par les portes arrière?
This space is for pushchairs	Ici, c'est la place aux poussettes
I would like to sit down	Je voudrais m'asseoir, s'il vous plaît
I have lost...	J'ai perdu...
I have moved...	J'ai démenagé...
I need to exchange my driving licence	Je voudrais échanger mon permis de conduire
I would like to enquire about driving lessons	Je voudrais me renseigner a propos des cours de conduite
There has been an accident	Il y a eu un accident
It is an emergency	C'est une urgence
Someone is badly hurt	Quelqu'un est gravement blessé
Someone is very ill	Quelqu'un est très malade
II would like to make a complaint	Je veux porter plainte

Organisations & Charities

Compiled and edited by Cathy Delattre

Places of worship and charitable organisations can provide a great opportunity to meet people. This chapter provides the background to and the names, addresses and opening times of a wide variety of organisations, both in Paris and the surrounding area. It might also inspire you if you have time on your hands and would like to get involved with voluntary work.

VOLUNTEER ORGANISATIONS

If you have some hours to spare, there are many organisations in Paris that would be happy to have your help. All the organisations in this chapter need volunteers, but the following are organisations that specifically place volunteers.

Siège Social du Centre de Volontariat de Paris
130, rue des Poissoniers, 75018 Paris
M° Marcadet-Poissoniers
Mon - Fri 14h00 - 17h00
01.42.64.97.34
This is the central office of a clearinghouse for volunteers that can direct you, in person or by phone, to the affiliate in your neighbourhood. Either at the main office or the affiliate, you will be interviewed to determine your interests and availability before a volunteer assignment match is made.

Junior Service League of Paris (JSLP)
01.47.20.00.03
Welcomes and trains women wishing to contribute as volunteers in the areas of health and child welfare, cancer and infertility support groups, excursions and toy collections for underprivileged children, training courses for child minders and lunches for the unemployed.

Volunteering in Hospitals and with the Disabled

American Hospital Volunteers
01.46.41.25.48
volontaires@ahparis.org

British Hospital Volunteers
Apply in writing to:
La Direction
Hertford British Hospital
3, rue Barbès
92300 Levallois Perret

Fondation Claude Pompidou
01.40.13.75.00
www.fondationclaudepompidou.asso.fr
Places volunteers for work with disabled children and in hospitals.

Orgs & Charities

CHARITIES

Giving to Charity

Another way to help those in need - and help yourself - is to clear out your unneeded clothes, shoes, books, toys, furniture and bric-a-brac and donate them where they will earn income for charitable organisations, or go directly to those in need.

Charities which will Collect Used Items Directly from your Home

ASSODEM (Association de Solidarité et de Soutien aux Rhis Démeris)

21, rue Mademoiselle, 75015 Paris
01.44.19.61.84
Helps those in exile from Africa. Will pick up anything, anywhere in Paris. Call for collection.

La Croix Rouge (The Red Cross)

Mon, Tue, Thu, Fri 14h00 - 16h00
01.47.05.57.40
💻 www.croix-rouge.fr
Accepts clothing only. Flyers are posted in entrances of residential buildings giving collection dates, or phone to arrange a collection in Paris.

L'Armée du Salut (Salvation Army)

12, rue Cantagrel, 75013 Paris
01.53.61.82.00
💻 www.armeedusalut.fr
Specialises in lodging for the homeless and social reintegration.

Les Orphelins Apprentis d'Auteuil

40, rue La Fontaine, 75016 Paris
M° Eglise d'Auteuil, bus 52, 70
Mon - Fri 09h30 - 12h30, 13h30 - 17h00
01.44.14.75.75
💻 www.fondation-auteil.fr
Founded in 1866 by the *Abbé Roussel*, this organisation takes in young people without families or resources and gives them a home and

vocational/technical education. Today, there are 30 "houses", which take in 4,000 young people. They collect clothes, books, and any objects that can be resold. There is only one collection point for Paris (the address above) or call to arrange a collection. There is a small park and children's play area. Beautiful table linens at bargain prices are sold in the adjacent shop as well as clothes, bric-a-brac and books. There is also a separate bookshop that has a good selection of greeting cards.

Emmaüs

First founded by the Abbé Pierre during the particularly severe winter of 1954, there are now many communities in Paris and the suburbs. Emmaüs sales outlets can be good sources of very inexpensive household items, furniture and clothes. Some specialise in a certain range of items and will only collect or accept donations in this range. Each will also only collect from a particular geographic area. Call the central number (below) for the phone number in your *arrondissement* to arrange a pick-up, and receive updated information on new communities; they seem to change often.

Union Centrale des Communautés Emmaüs
32, rue des Bourdonnais, 75001 Paris
M° Chatelet
01.42.36.06.99
💻 www.emmaus-france.org
This community will collect anything: furniture, crockery, clothing, books, household electrical appliances, bathroom appliances, bicycles, etc. by appointment only. Items are repaired and resold or distributed to the needy.

Emmaüs, "Le Vestiaire"
4, rue Georges Pitard, 75015 Paris
M° Plaisance
Mon - Fri 08h30 - 17h30
01.44.19.83.12
Accepts clothing donations at this location.

Communauté de Bougival
7, Ile de la Loge, le Port Marly, 78380 Bougival
RER A St. Germain-en-Laye, then bus 158 to La Machine
01.39.69.12.41
Collection from Paris 8th and 16th *arrondissements* and the western suburbs. Collects and sells anything and everything in usable condition.

Communauté de Longjumeau
15 bis, rue de Chilly, 91160 Longjumeau
SNCF Chilly-Mazarin
01.60.49.13.60
Collects from Essonne and southern suburbs. Collects anything in usable or repairable condition. Sells everything except electrical appliances.

Communauté de Neuilly-sur-Marne
15, boulevard Louis-Armand
RER A Neuilly-Plaisance, then bus 127, get off at Louis-Armand
Wed - Sat 09h30 - 12h30, 14h30 - 17h30
01.43.00.05.52
Collection from Paris 1st, 2nd, 5th, 7th, 9th, 12th, 17th, and 19th *arrondissements*, and far northeast suburbs.

Communauté de Charenton
2 bis, avenue de la Liberté, Quai des Carrières, 94220 Charenton Le Pont
M° Liberté, bus 24, 180
01.48.93.25.33
Call for collection area. Specialises in bric-a-brac, dishware, small appliances, books, records and antiques.

Communauté du Plessis-Trévise
41, avenue Lefèvre, 94420 Le Plessis-Trévise
01.45.76.10.79
Collection from Paris 6th *arrondissement* and far eastern suburbs. Collects and sells everything.

Communauté de Bernes-sur-Oise
9, chemin Pavé, Bernes-sur-Oise
95340 Persan-sur-Oise
SNCF Persan-Beaumont

01.30.28.67.20
Collection from Paris 18th *arrondissement* and northern suburbs. Collects and sells everything.

Communauté de Neuilly Plaisance
38, avenue Paul-Doumer, 93360 Neuilly-Plaisance
RER A Neuilly-Plaisance, then bus 114, get to square Jean-Mermoz
01.43.00.14.10
Fax 01.43.00.09.47
Collects from Paris 3rd, 4th, 10th, 11th, 13th, 14th, 15th, and 20th *arrondissements* and from the eastern and south-eastern suburbs, except Neuilly-sur-Marne. Collects and sells everything.

Communauté de Dennemont
Route de Sandrancourt, 78520 Limay
Autoroute Paris-Rouen, sortie Mantes-la-Jolie Est (sortie S11)
01.30.92.05.31
Collection from North-West Yvelines, South-West Val-d'Oise, far western suburbs and Eure. Collects and sells everything.

Communauté d'Ivry-sur-Seine
23, rue Denis Papin, 94200 Ivry-sur-Seine
RER C Ivry-sur-Seine, bus 180, 125 or 325
Next to Carrefour
Mon - Fri 13h30 - 17h30, Sat 09h30 - 17h30
01.49.60.83.83
Specialises in furniture, rugs, office equipment and office furniture. Call for collection area.

Communauté d'Ivry-sur-Seine
73, boulevard de Brandebourg, 94200 Ivry-sur-Seine
RER C Ivry-sur-Seine, located next to station – exit to the Ivry-Port side, bus 325, 323, 123, 180, 132, 182
Mon - Sat 13h00 - 17h00
01.46.71.95.31
Specialises in clothing, accessories and toys. Call for collection area.

Orgs & Charities

Communauté de Maisons-Alfort
145, rue Marc Sangier, 94700 Maisons-Alfort
M° Maisons-Alfort les Juilliottes
01.42.07.22.00
Collects and sells everything.

Communauté de Sucy-en-Brie
91, rue du Genéral Leclerc, 94370 Sucy-en-Brie
RER A Sucy-Bonneuil
01.49.82.47.06
Collects and sells anything and everything in usable condition.

Charities which Do Not Collect from your Home

GAS (Groupe d'Acceuil et Solidarité)
17, Place Maurice Thorey, 94800 Villejuif
 M° Villejuif l'Aragon
01.42.11.07.95
💻 www.gas.asso.fr
Helps those seeking political exile in France. French language courses are offered along with meals for families lodged in hotels without kitchens. Accepts kitchen and electronic goods as well as furniture, rugs, books and toys (clothing not accepted).

Le Secours Catholique
106, rue du Bac, 75007 Paris
M° Rue du Bac
Mon - Fri 09h00 - 18h00
01.45.49.73.00
💻 www.secours-catholique.asso.fr
This is the biggest charity in France in terms of scope and financial turnover and was founded in 1946 by Monseigneur Rodhain. It has 106 delegations in the various *départements* and many more teams working all over France. You can deposit clothes and household linen as well as small bric-a-brac, books, small furnishings and small appliances at the address above. To get the address of the team closest to you or any further information, ask your local Catholic church or call the Paris headquarters on the central number (above). Larger furniture can sometimes be collected with prior arrangement.

Le Secours Populaire
9-11, rue Froissart, 75003 Paris
M° Goncourt
Daily 09h00 - 17h30
01.44.78.21.00
💻 www.secourspopulaire.asso.fr
A charity founded fifty years ago, particularly oriented towards disadvantaged children. They receive clothes and toys in perfect condition at the above address.

Les Petits Frères des Pauvres
33 & 64, avenue Parmentier, 75011 Paris
M° Goncourt, Parmentier
01.49.23.13.00
A charity founded sixty years ago with offices throughout Paris. It helps the elderly living alone by providing volunteers who visit their homes to prepare meals, converse, and take them on outings around the neighbourhood.

Other Charities

Local St. Vincent de Paul societies accept clothes, toys and household goods for distribution.

Pharmacies are required to take back unused/unfinished medicines or pharmaceutical items (in their original packaging) for redistribution through the local *Ordre de Malte* or *Pharmaciens sans frontiers*
01.55.43.36.36

Local hospitals, PMI, schools and childcare facilities may accept donations of toys in good condition.

Your *mairie* or local church may have suggestions for other charities.

Lastly, some of the English-speaking churches organise annual fundraising bazaars with a variety of stalls. Contact the one of your choice (For details see Places of Worship, below).

Orgs & Charities

WOMEN'S AND SOCIAL ASSOCIATIONS

Listed alphabetically below are some English-speaking women's and social organisations in Paris. Most charge membership fees and all offer a range of social and cultural opportunities.

American Catholic Women's Organisation (ACWO)

St. Joseph's Church
50, avenue Hoche, 75008 Paris
M° Charles De Gaulle-Etoile
01.42.27.28.56
💻 www.stjoeparis.org
iThe American Catholic Women's Organisation is a non-profit organisation offering activities, services, and resources for the English-speaking community in Paris. ACWO activities include cultural visits within Paris, French and cooking lessons, bridge clubs, pilgrimages, and a Lenten retreat. ACWO welcomes all nationalities and faiths into its association.

American Women's Group In Paris (AWG)

32, rue du General Bertrand, 75007 Paris
M° Duroc
Mon 13h30 - 16h30, Tue - Thu 10h00 - 12h30 and 13h30 - 16h30
01.42.73.36.74
💻 www.awgparis.org
Founded in 1949 to assist American women living overseas, today AWG Paris offers educational, cultural and social programs to its membership. Open to English speakers of all nationalities.

Association of American Wives of Europeans (AAWE)

34, avenue de New York, 75116 Paris
M° Iéna
01.40.70.11.80
💻 www.aaweparis.org
Regular membership is open to women who are USA citizens by and who are, or have been, married to, or living maritally with, a citizen of a European country.

Association of Irish Women in France

24, rue de Grenelle, 75007 Paris
M° Rue du Bac
01.45.48.83.21
💻 www.irishwomenfrance.org

Australian Women's Group

c/o The Australian Embassy
4, rue Jean Rey, 75724 Paris Cedex 15
01.40.59.33.00
01.40.59.35.61 Community Liaison Officer
CLO@dfat.gov.au

British & Commonwealth Women's Association (BCWA)

8, rue de Belloy, 75116 Paris
M° Boissière, Victor Hugo
Mon - Fri 10h30 - 15h00
01.47.20.50.91
💻 www.bcwa.org
The BCWA's clubrooms host a library and lunches as well as a range of activities and classes. Membership is open to those who are, or are married to, British or Commonwealth nationals.

British Council

9-11, rue Constantine, 75007 Paris
M° Invalides
01.49.55.73.00
💻 www.britishcouncil.org/France.htm

The Caledonian Society of France

18, rue Grange Batelière, 75009 Paris
M° Le Peletier, Grands Boulevards
01.47.70.67.71

Orgs & Charities

Canadian Women's Group in Paris

Cultural Services of the Canadian Embassy
35, rue Constantine, 75007 Paris
M° Invalides
01.44.43.21.03

MESSAGE Mother Support Group

01.58.60.00.53
💻 www.messageparis.org
A network of and for English-speaking parents and pregnant women living in and around Paris. Meetings and activities for parents and children, help and information on all aspects of pregnancy and parenting. Also offers support to its members. See support groups below.

The Paris Welsh Society

31, rue d'Alouettes, 94470 Boissy Saint Leger
RER A Boissy St. Léger
01.45.69.21.56 (John Evans, President)
pariswelshsociety@free.com
Several social meetings a year including meals, entertainers and guest speakers from Wales, pub nights, and St. David's day celebrations. Non-Welsh members most welcome. Contact the president, John Evans, at johnevans@wanadoo.fr for more information.

Women's International Club (WIC)

3 bis, ville Emile Bergerat, 92522 Neuilly sur Seine
M° Les Sablons
01.34.46.01.14
http://pariswic.free.fr
The Women's International Club provides an opportunity when moving from one country to another to find friends with an international background. This English language club unites 40 different nationalities, including French.

Women's Institute for Continuing Education (WICE)

20, boulevard Montparnasse, 75015 Paris
M° Duroc, Falguière
Mon - Fri 10h00 - 16h30
01.45.66.75.50
💻 www.wice-paris.org

Provides cultural and educational programmes and services to the international community in Paris.

Women of The American Church in Paris (WOAC)

The American Church
65, quai d'Orsay, 75007 Paris
M° Invalides, RER C Pont de l'Alma
01.40.62.05.00
💻 www.woac.net
The WOAC sponsors four outreach programs: "Bloom Where You're Planted"/"Bloom While You Work" orientation programs each March and October; Bloom Neighbourhood coffees; Sunday welcome table at the American Church and an Information Centre at the American Church.

Other useful sources of information: your Embassy, your local *mairie* and local Town Guide, *les Pages Jaunes*.

PLACES OF WORSHIP

The following places of worship have been included as they provide English-speaking services. Most of them also provide childcare facilities and/or activities. Many of these religious institutions are very active and offer support services, Bible studies, musical groups and various other religious and social outlets. The information included here gives only an idea of what is offered. For more information and to confirm service times, enquire at your chosen place of worship.

Paris

Adath Shalom Synagogue
(Jewish conservative congregation)
8, rue Georges Bernard Shaw, 75015 Paris
M° Dupleix
01.45.67.97.96
💻 www.adathshalom.org
Services in English, Hebrew and French.

Adath Shalom – Est
119, rue des Pyrenees, 75020 Paris
M° Maraichers, Gambetta

The American Church in Paris
(All Protestant denominations)
65, quai d'Orsay, 75007 Paris
M° Invalides, RER C Pont de l'Alma
01.40.62.05.00
💻 www.acparis.org
Services: Sun 09h00 and 11h00. Sunday school for nursery to primary school-aged children, as well as a nursery service for up to 2 year olds.

The American Cathedral
(Episcopal/Anglican, Cathedral Church of the Holy Trinity)
23, avenue George V, 75008 Paris
M° Alma Marceau
01.53.23.84.00
💻 www.americancathedral.org
Services: Sun 09h00 and 11h00. Sunday school and nursery 10h45. Also weekday services.

Church of Christ
(non-denominational)

4, rue Déodat-de-Séverac, 75017 Paris
M° Malesherbes
01.42.27.50.86
Sun 17h00 Bible class in English. Sun 18h00 worship in English. Home Bible studies available.

Church of Jesus Christ of Latter Day Saints
(Mormon)
64-66, rue de Romainville, 75019 Paris
M° Porte des Lilas
01.42.45.28.57
Service in French and English, Sun 09h00 - 12h00

First Church of Christ Scientist
36, boulevard St. Jacques, 75014 Paris
M° St. Jacques
01.47.07.26.60
Services in English: Wed 18h00, Sun 11h20, both with a nursery for under 5 year olds. Sunday school 10h00. Reading room: Mon - Sat 12h30 - 18h30, Sun and public holidays 15h00 - 18h00.

Kehilat Gesher
(French-Anglophone Jewish congregation of Paris and Saint-Germain-en-Laye)
7, rue Léon Cogniet, 75017 Paris
M° Courcelles
10, rue de Pologne, 78100 Saint-Germain-en-Laye
01.39.21.97.19
💻 www.kehilatgesher.org
Services alternate between Friday night and Saturday morning between the two venues. Services are in French, English and Hebrew.

Liberal Synagogue
(Synagogue Union Libérale Israélite de France)

Orgs & Charities

24, rue Copernic, 75116 Paris
M° Victor Hugo
01.47.04.37.27
💻 www.ulif.com
English service Fri 18h00.

Liberal Jewish Movement of France (Mouvement Juif Libéral de France)
MJLF-Beaugrenelle
11, rue Gaston de Caillavet, 75015 Paris
M° Charles Michel, Bir-Hakeim, RER C Kennedy
Maison de la Radio
01.44.37.48.48

MJLF-Surmelin
24, rue Surmelin, 75020 Paris
M° Pelleport
01.40.30.18.60
💻 www.mjlf.col.fr
Two of the three Rabbis are fluent in English.
Regular religious services are Kabbalat Shabbat, Fri 18h15 and Shaharit Sat 10h30 at both addresses.

St. George's Anglican Church
7, rue August-Vacquerie, 75116 Paris
M° Kleber
01.47.20.22.51
💻 www.stgeorgesparis.com
Services: Sun 08h30, 10h30 with Sunday school and *crèche*. Sun 12h00 first Sunday of the month young families' communion.

St. Joseph's Church
(Roman Catholic)
50, avenue Hoche, 75008 Paris
M° Charles De Gaulle-Etoile
01.42.27.28.56
💻 www.stjoeparis.org
Services: Sat 18h30. Sun 9h30, 11h00 (family mass), 12h30 and 18h30.

St. Michael's Church
(Anglican)
5, rue d'Aguesseau, 75008 Paris
M° Concorde, Mirosmesnil
01.47.42.70.88

💻 www.saintmichaelsparis.org
Services Sun 09h30, 11h15 with *crèche* for up to 3 year olds and 19h00 Sunday clubs for children 4 - 14 years old.

St. Patrick's Chapel
(Roman Catholic)
5, rue des Irlandais, 75005 Paris
M° Place Monge, Cardinal Lemoine, RER B Luxembourg
01.58.52.10.89
Services: Sun 11h30

The Scots Kirk
(Church of Scotland/Presbyterian)
17, rue Bayard, 75008 Paris
M° Franklin D. Roosevelt
01.48.78.47.94
💻 www.scotskirkparis.com
Services: Sun 10h30 family service and Sunday school for 3 to 11 year olds. Possibility of a *crèche* for under 3 year olds. Youth groups.

Second Church of Christ Scientist
58, boulevard Flandrin, 75008 Paris
M° Porte Dauphine, RER Foch
01.45.22.29.60
Reading Room
38, rue de Turin, 75008 Paris
Mon - Fri 10h30 - 18h30; Sat 14h00 - 18h00
💻 www.cs2paris.org
Services: Sun 11h15 (English); Wed 19h00 (bilingual). There is a nursery for the very young and Sunday school in English and French.

Third Church of Christ Scientist
33 bis, boulevard Bourdon, 75004 Paris
M° Bastille
01.42.78.61.93
Services: Sun 11h15 (English); Wed 19h00 (bilingual).

Trinity International Church of Paris
(Protestant Evangelical Christian congregation)
58, rue Madame, 75006 Paris
M° Notre Dame des Champs, St. Placide

01.56.23.08.05
www.trinity-paris.org
Services: Sun 17h00; Nursery care for under two's as well as Children's Church.

Unitarian Universalist Fellowship of Paris
Foyer de l'Ame
7 bis, rue du Pasteur Wagner, 75011 Paris
M° Breguet-Sabin
01.30.82.75.33
www.uufp.info
Services: 12h15 one Sunday per month. Religious education classes for children during services.

Suburbs

Chapel of the Lycée Saint Aspais
18, boulevard Andre Maginot, 77300 Fontainebleau
01.64.24.62.30
www.fontainebleauchurch.org
Services in English: Sun 10h30 with *crèche* and Junior church (Sunday school) and a monthly all age service.

Emmanuel International Church
(Baptist)
56, rue des Bons Raisins, 92500 Rueil-Malmaison
01.47.51.29.63
www.ebcparis.org
Services: Sun 09h00 and 11h00; Sunday school at 10h00. Nursery as well as children and youth ministries.

Holy Trinity Church
(Anglican)
15, avenue Carnot, 78600 Maisons Laffitte
01.39.62.34.97
www.htcml.com
Services: The schedule changes through the year, but on most Sundays at 10h30 is a family service with Sunday school groups for 3 year olds to school leaving age, as well as a *crèche* for up to three's. Tues 10h00 mother and toddlers group.

Kehilat Gesher
(French-Anglophone Jewish congregation of Paris and Saint-Germain-en-Laye)
See above, under Paris, for details.

St. Mark's Church
(Anglican)
31, rue du Pont Colbert, 78000 Versailles
01.39.02.79.45
01.41.15.01.99 (Maggie Simmons - children)
www.netministries.org/see/churches/CH03904
Services: Sun 10h30 with *crèche* for under three's. Sunday school for 3 years and over.

St. Paul's Church Gif-sur-Yvette
(see St. Mark's Church, above, for contact details)
Centre Culturelle St. Paul, place du Marche Neuf, Chevry 2
Services: Sun 17h30 (not in July or August)

St. Peter's Church
(Anglican)
7A, avenue du Bouteiller, 60500 Chantilly
03.44.58.53.22
Services: Sun 10h30 with *crèche* and Sunday school. Youth groups.

SUPPORT GROUPS

Living far from home in a non-English speaking environment can be an isolating experience. Be assured that not only are you not alone, but there is probably an English-speaking support group that can help you in your time of need.

Alcoholics Anonymous
01.46.34.59.65 for meetings at the American Church
01.53.23.84.00 for meetings at the American Cathedral
Meetings also held at Eglise St. Paul (Chapelle), Centre St. Léger, St. George's Church, and the American Hospital in Paris.

American Aid Society
US Embassy, Consular Section
2, rue Saint-Florentin, 75001 Paris
M° Concorde
01.43.12.48.07
annisah@state.gov
Helps Americans in difficulty in France. Grants for elderly, disabled or sick Americans residing in France.

Association of American Residents Overseas (AARO)
34, avenue de New York, 75116 Paris
M° Iéna
01.42.04.09.38
www.aaro.org
Worldwide organisation defending the rights of American citizens residing outside of America, especially on issues to do with citizenship, voting, social security, Medicare and tax.

CESC (Council for the English Speaking Community)
http://cesc.online.fr
An informal organisation for the exchange of news and information between more than 80 English-speaking service groups and associations in the Paris region.

Counselling Centre at the American Cathedral
23, avenue Georges V, 75008 Paris
M° Georges V
01.47.23.61.13
Individual, family and couple counselling; also themed support groups led by the centre's psychologists and social workers.

English Cancer Support Group
Mona Bismarck Foundation
34, avenue de New York, 75116 Paris
M° Alma Marceau
01.45.51.26.93
Open to English-speaking cancer patients and led by a trained and qualified volunteer facilitator. Sponsored jointly by the Association of American Wives of Europeans and the Junior Service League.

Health Network International
06.23.27.34.24
01.42.79.90.97
www.hni-paris.org
A network of English-speaking health professionals practicing in France. Organises an annual health fair, provides speakers and seminars for the community. Organises several American Red Cross Infant, Child and Adult CPR and First Aid courses each year.

International Counselling Service
The American Church
65, quai d'Orsay, 75007 Paris
M° Invalides
01.45.50.26.49
Individual, family, couple and group therapy for adults, adolescents and children.

La Leche League Paris (Breast Feeding Supporters, English Group)
01.39.68.10.81 Lea Cohen
01.55.76.69.86 Margaret Crick
01.39.58.45.84 for emergencies in French only
(select 5 in recorded menu for English)
💻 www.lalecheleague.org
leadersp@wanadoo.fr (Lea Cohen)
mcrick@noos.fr (Margaret Crick)

MESSAGE Mother Support Group
01.58.60.00.53
💻 www.messageparis.org
info@messageparis.org
Offers birthing and parenting classes, breastfeeding support and directories of medical and education resources. Excellent parent-to-parent support via website and meetings.

Narcotics Anonymous

American Church in Paris
M° Invalides
01.40.62.05.00
Meetings in English and French, Sat 19h00

58, rue Madame, 75006 Paris
M° St. Placide
Meetings in English, Wed19h30

St. George's Anglican church
M° Etoile/Kleber
01.47.20.22.51
Meetings in English, Mon 19h30
💻 www.na.org
Also support groups in French in Boulogne, Saint Cloud and Versailles. Email helpline@nafrance.org for more imformation.

Overeaters Anonymous
Meetings at the American Church
65, quai d'Orsay, 75007 Paris
01.43.47.21.90 (Diane)
06.14.32.11.33 (Tina)
💻 www.oa.org/index.htm
Tue 19h00 - 20h00

Sat 11h00 - 12h00
English-speaking group for those struggling with compulsive overeating, undereating or dieting, binge-starve cycles, bulimia and anorexia.

SOS Help
BP43, 92101 Boulogne CEDEX
01.46.21.46.46 daily 15h00 - 23h00
💻 www.soshelpline.org
A help crisis line in English if you are worried, in a crisis, or just need someone to talk to in confidence. Call for assistance or if you wish to volunteer.

SPRINT - Special Professional Resources, Ideas and New Technologies
Jacquelyn Todd-Morel
02.33.21.48.16
http://sprint.france.free.fr
Professional organisation of English speaking educators and therapists who work with children with special needs. Email sprint.france@free.fr for more information.

SPAN - Sprint Parents' Action Network
01.39.59.10.64
02.33.21.48.16
A group of English-speaking parents of children with special needs. SPAN members provide a support and information exchange about therapy, medical attention and educational needs through an information help-line and regular meetings. Publishes "Finding help in France for your child with special needs." (contact SPAN@freesurf.fr)

Orgs & Charities

OTHER VOCABULARY

Are you interested in taking my... ?	*Seriez-vous intéressé par mes/mon/ma... ?*
When can you pick them up?	*A quel moment pourriez-vous venir les chercher?*
When can I drop them off? And where?	*A quel moment pourrais-je les livrer? Et où?*
When are you open?	*Quels sont vos horaires d'ouverture?*

Pregnancy, Birth & Newborn

Compiled and edited by Sara Abraham

Planning to have a baby or just found out you are pregnant and wondering what to do next? No need to panic! This chapter provides key information about being pregnant, giving birth and looking after a new baby in Paris. It also points you towards other valuable sources of information on maternity units, alternative births and many other topics. However, you will still need to arm yourself with general pregnancy and baby-care manuals, a list of which can be found in the Other Resources section.

PREGNANCY

Initial Information

If you need information on infertility, contraception or termination of pregnancy ☞Health and Medicine.

Pregnancy Testing

If you want to find out whether or not you are pregnant, you can get a pregnancy test kit from your local pharmacy - ask for *un teste de grosesse*.

Seeing a Medical Practitioner

Once you find out you are pregnant, probably one of the first things you will want to do is arrange to see a doctor. If this is the first time you have encountered the French health system, the prospect of arranging this may feel a little overwhelming. You may want some general information about the system (☞Health and Medicine) and will want to know how you pay and claim for medical expenses (☞Administration).

In France, you can choose to be under the care of your family doctor up to the sixth month of your pregnancy and then transfer to the care of an obstetrician or gynæcologist at your chosen maternity facility. Alternatively, you can go directly to an obstetrician or gynæcologist without a referral from your family doctor. However, even if you choose to go with a gynæcologist from the outset, your first port of call may still be your family doctor if you would like guidance in choosing both your specialist and your maternity facility.

If you are not yet registered with a doctor in France, and need some information about medical practitioners, consider contacting an Anglophone place of worship (☞Organisations and Charities) or consulate, which can probably provide you with a list of English-speaking medical practitioners (☞Living for consulate details). MESSAGE also has information available to members about medical practitioners (many of whom speak English) and hospitals or clinics.

Administrative Considerations

If you are covered by French Social Security and wish to claim benefits (☞Administration), your pregnancy must be officially confirmed by either your general practitioner or your gynæcologist before the end of the 14th week of pregnancy (dated from the first day of last period) and a declaration sent to French Social Security. Seven antenatal visits at monthly intervals are then compulsory in order to obtain benefits. These visits can be with your family doctor or with the gynæcologist or obstetrician (*obstétricien or gynécologue-accoucheur*) at your chosen maternity facility. If you choose to employ an independent midwife (*sage-femme libérale*), she is authorised to carry out the monthly visits and to sign any benefit forms requested by the *Caisse d'Allocations Familiales* (*CAF*) (☞Administration).

Due Date

In France, the date of the pregnancy is calculated from the first day of the last period, and 280 days, or 40 weeks, are added. In practice you are usually given an estimated due date (*date, prévue de l'accouchement*) of 41 weeks, which represents the lat-

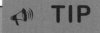 **TIP**

Start thinking about booking your place at a hospital or clinic as soon as possible, as many maternity facilities (particularly the French ones) get booked up a long way in advance.

est date the baby is expected to be born. Labour is usually induced after this date, although if all is well you may be allowed to wait a few more days with daily monitoring.

Miscarriage

Miscarriage (*fausse couche,* or *avortement spontané*) occurs very frequently and it is thought that as many as three fertilisations out of five end in miscarriage, often even before the woman realises she is pregnant.

If you are bleeding during early pregnancy, contact your doctor or gynæcologist, who may recommend you have an ultrasound scan or a blood test to ascertain the state of the pregnancy. If it is in the middle of the night or at the weekend and you feel you need urgent attention, call the *SAMU* (15) or *SOS Medicins* (0 820 332 424).

If you have suffered a miscarriage and would like to talk to someone about your experience, you can contact the following organisation:

Circle of Friends
01.47.20.00.03
A support group offering information, counselling, and fellowship about infertility, pregnancy loss, and adoption.

If you are a member of MESSAGE, you can contact the Support Co-ordinator for support and advice. You can find the relevant contact details in your latest MESSAGE Magazine.

Medical Care During Pregnancy

If you are new to the French health system, this section gives you an idea of what you can expect in terms of usual medical care in France during your pregnancy.

Monthly Visits

At your first visit, expect to be weighed and your

blood pressure to be checked to get a base reading. In France, blood pressure is measured in centimetres of mercury (millimetres in the UK and USA). An internal examination (*toucher vaginal*) will also be done to confirm the pregnancy and check the shape of your pelvis and the condition of the cervix. A swab (*prélèvement*) is often done at the same time to check for infection, and a cervical smear (*frottis du col*) may also be offered if you are due to have one. Your breasts may also be examined. You will be given a prescription (*ordonnance*) to have both blood and urine tests done at a laboratory (☞Health and Medicine). Urine is tested for sugar levels (to check for diabetes) and the presence of bacteria or proteins. Blood is usually tested for the following:

• blood group and Rhesus factor
• antibodies to Rubella (German measles)
• antibodies to toxoplasmosis
• evidence of syphilis
• HIV (all pregnant women are tested anonymously for HIV for statistics, but results are provided by request only)
• hæmoglobin level as a base to check for anæmia

At each subsequent visit, you will be weighed (French doctors generally seem to be more fussy about excessive weight gain than those in the UK or USA) and you will have your blood pressure taken and urine tested. You will be given a prescription for monthly blood tests if your initial tests showed you to be rhesus negative or rubella negative, or that you do not have toxoplasmosis antibodies (see below). At one of your visits, your blood will be tested again for hæmoglobin, and also for Hepatitis B.

It is usual for an internal examination to be done at every visit, together with external palpations of your abdomen to check the size, position, and presentation of the baby, and also the condition of the cervix. If you feel uncomfortable about internal examinations, some doctors may be sympathetic and agree not to perform them. You may be expected to undress completely for these examinations, and you may be alone with the doctor.

You may be offered vitamins and mineral supplements - iron, calcium and fluoride (*fluor*) (☞Health and Medicine) and you may also be offered folic acid. If you are having contractions, you may be prescribed antispasmodic drugs (*anti-spasmodiques*).

Ultrasound Scans (Echographie)

In France, it is routine to have three ultrasound scans during a normal pregnancy: the first between 8 and 12 weeks, the second between 20 and 24 weeks and the final scan between 34 and 35 weeks. In private clinics and hospitals, the scans are usually done as part of your monthly visits. In public hospitals, or if you are under the care of your family doctor, you will probably be given a prescription for you to have your scans in a private ultrasound clinic. Ask your doctor to recommend a clinic.

Ultrasound scans for pregnancy are reimbursed by Social Security at normal rates until the 6th month. After the 6th month, or if the scan has been done to investigate a possible problem, they are reimbursed at a rate of 100%.

At a private ultrasound clinic, you will be given a copy of the results for your doctor and/or for the hospital/clinic. On many systems, it is now possible for the operator to print off a photograph or even make a recording of the image for you, so you may want to take along a blank video cassette or DVD. The best images for a video recording are seen during the second scan, as the foetus is active but not yet too large.

Foetal Doppler (Echo-Doppler)

This is a common procedure in France, and it is done during routine ultrasound scans. It uses sophisticated equipment to check the pattern of the blood flow through the umbilical cord. This is partic-

ularly useful if the mother has high blood pressure, or if the baby seems not to be growing well.

Internal Ultrasound Scans

In addition to the three standard scans, you may have a number of internal scans (*sonde échographique intravaginale*) in the early stages of your pregnancy. These scans are done with a small probe about the size and shape of a toothbrush which is inserted into the vagina. This is totally painless and you do not need to drink any fluid beforehand. The definition and image of the pregnancy is better as the probe can get closer to the uterus than the external ultrasound scan at this stage.

Pelvic X-rays

If, in the last month your baby is presenting by the breech (bottom or feet first) (*position siège*) or appears to be larger than average for your body size, you may be offered a pelvic x-ray (*pelvimetrie*) to determine whether the baby has a good chance of fitting comfortably through your pelvis. Some doctors in France offer to turn a breech baby manually from the outside (*version*).

When taking the *métro* or a bus during your pregnancy, do not hesitate to request one of the seats marked with a heart (which are reserved for passengers who are pregnant, disabled, elderly or accompanied by small children). Simply ask *"pourriez-vous me céder votre siège, s'il-vous plait ?"*

Visit to Anesthetist

You will probably be asked to make an appointment with an anesthetist (*anesthésiste*) during the last month of your pregnancy, in case you need an epidural or general anaesthetic during labour (see below). He or she will ask you to do a blood test to double check your blood type and your blood clotting ability. Your back will be examined to check that a needle can be inserted easily between two vertebrae.

Antenatal Tests

In addition to the routine checks, your doctor may recommend antenatal screening or diagnostic tests in the following circumstances:

- a known genetic risk for an inherited disease or disorder
- the birth of a previous child with a disability
- your age (38 years and over)
- an at-risk pregnancy (Rh incompatibility, life-threatening infection etc.)

A screening test will only give an indication of a possible abnormality that may require further investigation. A diagnostic test will confirm the presence of an abnormality.

Maternal Serum Screening

A number of blood tests are useful in predicting the likelihood of a woman bearing a child with a chromosomal abnormality or a neural tube defect such as spina bifida. Certain biochemical markers in a pregnant woman's blood, in combination with her age, give a risk factor for that woman. These are:

- alpha-fetoprotein (AFP)
- human chorionic gonadotrophin (hCG)
- unconjugated œstriol (uE)

These together make up what has been developed in some countries as the Triple Test. Most hospitals/clinics in France do a blood test at 15 weeks to assess the risk of Down Syndrome (*Trisomie 21*). If the result indicates that the risk is greater than 1 in 250, then an amniocentesis is advised. In these circumstances, the amniocentesis is not reimbursed by Social Security. However, some hospitals charge a slightly higher fee for the blood test, which includes an insurance premium so that if an amniocentesis is required, you do not have to pay for it. While AFP and hCG can be measured in any laboratory, it is a good idea to be tested at a centre where a high number of tests are carried out, and where experienced personnel will easily recognise what is normal and what is not.

Amniocentesis (Amniocentèse) and Chorionic Villus Sampling (CVS) (Chorioncentèse)

Amniocentesis is usually performed between the 16th and 18th weeks of pregnancy, but it can be done as early as the 12th week in large obstetric hospitals such as Hôpital Robert Debré and Port Royal (both in Paris).

CVS is done between the 9th and 12th weeks of pregnancy, and results are available in three to four days. However, it is a much more difficult procedure, with a higher risk of miscarriage (about 2%), bleeding and infection. In France, doctors usually prescribe one week's medical leave after the procedure to reduce the risk of miscarriage.

These tests are not performed routinely in France and will not be prescribed or paid for by Social Security if you are under 38 years of age unless you have a known risk for chromosomal abnormalities. The medical establishment justifies this on the statistical basis that 97% of pregnancies result in healthy babies. Nonetheless, if you believe you have reason to be concerned, you should speak frankly to your gynaecologist about it. The American Hospital of Paris is one of the very few laboratories willing to do the tests in such cases.

Other Health Issues during Pregnancy

Listeriosis (la listeriose)

Listeriosis is relatively common in France, with around 300 cases per year. Though harmless to the general population, listeriosis is extremely danger-ous for pregnant women, newborn babies, the elderly and those with weakened immune systems. A pregnant woman may have no symptoms, or she may have some fever, aching muscles, headaches, nausea and general flu-like symptoms, which can appear anywhere from one to ninety days after eat-ing infected food. If undertaken early, antibiotic treatment is successful, both for pregnant women and newborn babies. Do consult a doctor immedi-ately if you have fever during pregnancy.

Listeria is a bacteria which can continue to grow in refrigerated food, survives freezing, but is killed by sufficient heat. It is found in raw meat, raw vegeta-bles, unpasteurised milk as well as processed food such as soft cheese, paté, smoked meats and fish. High-risk foods are those which have a long shelf-life and can be eaten without thorough reheating. Cross-contamination can also occur where these foods are stored, cut or handled near other foods. Full details of precautions to take to avoid listeria infection can be found in most pregnancy guides.

Toxoplasmosis

Toxoplasmosis (toxoplasmose) is an infection car-ried by a parasite that, although not dangerous to a healthy adult or child, can cause serious damage to the unborn fœtus if it is contracted by the mother during pregnancy. In France, toxoplasmosis is rou-tinely tested for during pregnancy because conti-nental Europe has one of the highest rates of toxoplasmosis infection in the world. If your initial blood test is positive, this will usually indicate you have at some stage in the past contracted the dis-ease and made your own antibodies to it. In some cases, a repeat blood test may be taken 10 days later to establish whether the antibodies are as a result of a new or an old infection. If you have had the infection in the past, you cannot contract toxo-plasmosis again and, unless you suffer from an immune deficiency, you need not concern yourself with toxoplasmosis any more.

If the initial blood test is negative this indicates that you have not had toxoplasmosis in the past and must be extremely careful not to contract the dis-ease during pregnancy. You will be required to have repeat blood tests at monthly intervals to check that you have not contracted the disease. If you do con-tract toxoplasmosis, you will be given an antibiotic called Rovamycine to take for the duration of your pregnancy. Depending on when in pregnancy toxo-plasmosis is contracted, you may be offered an amniocentesis and a cordocentesis to test whether the baby has been infected in the womb.

The toxoplasmosis parasite is most commonly found in raw or undercooked meat and cat faeces, so avoid eating raw or undercooked meat (in restaurants, request that your meat be cooked *bien cuit* and handling cat litter. Full details of precau-tions to take to avoid contracting toxoplasmosis can be found in most pregnancy guides. Alternatively, for further (free) information in English contact:

Tommy's The Baby Charity
www.tommys.org

Antenatal Classes (La préparation à l'accouchement)

"Traditional" Preparation Classes

Many (but not all) hospitals and clinics offer prepa-ration classes to mothers booked to give birth at their facility. In addition, most independent midwives (*sage-femmes libérales*) give preparation classes to their clients as well as assisting them in labour, whether this is in the hospital/clinic or at home.

Up to eight classes held by midwives or other pro-fessionals on hospital premises are reimbursed by Social Security. These usually take place weekly in the last two or three months of pregnancy, often during the day. However, some hospitals and clinics hold special Saturday sessions or evening classes – this appears to be a growing trend so it is worth asking at your facility.

Classes vary greatly in content, but generally include some or all of the following: explanation of types of birth, perhaps with a film; exercises and relaxation; information about the maternity unit, including a visit; feeding and care of the new baby. The emphasis may vary depending on the speciality of the midwife who runs the sessions. Attending these classes can be helpful for asking questions or picking up useful vocabulary and information about hospital policy.

MESSAGE Preparation for Parenthood Classes

As one of its services to members, MESSAGE offers Preparation for Parenthood classes in English. The qualified instructors normally cover the end of pregnancy, breathing and relaxation, labour and types of delivery, the role of fathers, pain relief, medical interventions, feeding and caring for a new baby and postnatal issues. For further information, consult info@messageparis.org.

Other Birth Preparation Options

Haptonomy (haptonomie)
This method uses touch as a basis for getting to know the baby in utero, making it easier to accept the pain of labour and bond easily with the newborn infant. A list of practitioners is available from:

CIRDH (Centre de recherché et de développement de l'haptonomie)
04.68.39.42.23
⌨ www.haptonomy.org

Psychoprophylaxis/Lamaze method (préparation classique/accouchement sans douleur)
This method de-dramatises birth by giving accurate information as well as training the body to respond to the stimuli of labour through conscious relaxation and breathing techniques. It forms the basis of

many hospital classes, although in France it is generally assumed that you will have an epidural and will not solely rely on these techniques.

Sophrology (sophrologie)
This is a form of active relaxation and visualisation which, when applied to pregnancy and birth, enables the woman to understand her body, relax deeply and control her pain. It is recommended to begin sessions from the fourth month of pregnancy. Some midwives are also sophrologues. For more information, visit ⌨ www.sophrologie-francaise.com.

Antenatal Singing Classes/Groups (chant prénatal)

Si Ça Me Chante
5, rue La Vega 75012 Paris
M° Michel Bizot
01.43.40.99.54
⌨ www.sicamechante.com
Music school offering singing sessions for pregnant women and their partners, as well as for new parents and their babies. Details, including dates, times and fees, available on the website (in French).

Association Française de Chant Prénatal
0 871 745 654
⌨ www.chant-prenatal.com
Sessions are in French, but the selection of songs is international. May be able to recommend English-speaking antenatal singing group leaders.

Prenatal Exercise

Pregnancy Gymnastics (La gymnastique prénatale)
Exercise classes for pregnancy may be offered at the hospital and privately in your area by qualified instructors, though classes are rather difficult to find. A good starting point is the Fusac magazine or, if you are a member of MESSAGE, the latest Magazine or the website.

Water Exercise (La gymnastique aquatique)
Some municipal swimming pools offer classes for pregnant women. For a list of these pools consult 💻www.fael.asso.fr. Classes are also available at theHertford British Hospital (*Hôpital Franco-Britannique*) and many private organisations such as:

Le Carré Faber
1, rue Bausset,75015 Paris
01.40.45.71.36
💻 www.carrefaber.com

Yoga
You may be lucky and find your chosen hospital offers prenatal yoga classes. Otherwise there are yoga centres in Paris which run prenatal classes:

Ashtanga Paris
64, avenue d'Italie, 75013 Paris
M° Place d'Italie, Tolbiac
01.45.80.19.96
💻 www.ashtangayogaparis.fr

Centre de Yoga du Marais
72, rue du Vertbois, 75003 Paris
M° Arts et Métiers
01.42.74.24.92
💻 www.yogamarais.com

Hatha Yoga
41, rue du Faubourg Montmartre, 75009 Paris
M° Le Peletier
01.48.24.77.82

GIVING BIRTH IN FRANCE

Deciding how and where to give birth is probably the most important decision you will make during your pregnancy. This section tells you how matenity facilities are classified in France and where to find out more about individual facilities, specialists and alternative birth options. It also provides information about what to expect in the hospital, pain relief options and post-partum health.

Maternity Facilities

Most obstetricians and midwives tend to practise at a certain facility. You can either choose a doctor and go where he or she delivers, or choose a facility and ask for a list of doctors who deliver there. In France, maternity units are split into three different categories according to their facilities:

Level 1

This is the most common type of maternity facility, where most normal births (i.e. those with no foreseeable complications) are carried out. There is no pædiatric department.

Level 2

This type of facility can cater for "slightly" more risky pregnancies (maternal hypertension, growth retardation, multiple births). All level two facilities have a neonatal department where your baby can be taken care of if there are any complications after the birth.

PBN - Birth

Pregnancy To-Do List

As soon as the pregnancy is confirmed
Investigate and visit hospital or clinic maternity facilities, interview doctors and book yourself into a hospital/clinic. If you have registered with a doctor at a particular facility, this may be done automatically, but you should ask for confirmation of this.

Depending on your location, you may need or want to consider reserving a place in a crèche as soon as possible by contacting your local mairie (☞Childcare).

At 3 Months
Remember to have the pregnancy certified before the 14th week by a doctor, gynæcologist or obstetrician and declared to Social Security.

At 5 Months
Think about starting to buy (or borrow) baby equipment. Remember that when you take your baby home from the hospital, s/he will have to be strapped into an appropriate car seat.

Sign up for an antenatal class at your hospital/clinic or through MESSAGE.

At 8 Months
Arrange advance childcare for older children and consider what you will do if your labour begins in the middle of the night.

Pack your bag for the hospital stay, following the list supplied by your hospital or clinic or your pregnancy manual. (If you are a member of MESSAGE, do not forget to pack the telephone number of your MESSAGE Breastfeeding Supporter or any other information on MESSAGE services that may be of use to you).

Make sure you have all necessary telephone numbers close at hand: doctor, hospital/clinic, SAMU.

If you will be driven to hospital in your own car, do a trial run to find the best route and time how long it takes.

In order to make your return home easier, it may be helpful to have some extra meals frozen and ready. If you have never tried items from the large French frozen food stores Picard Surgelés or Gel 2000, this is a good time to get acquainted.

This is also a good time to locate a pædiatrician or generalist to see the baby at the recommended two week visit (☞Health and Medicine).

PBN - Birth

There are three subgroups:

- 2-a: can care for a sick baby before transfer to another hospital
- 2-b: equipped with incubators and material required for phototherapy
- 2-c: equipped with intensive care department where artificial respiration can be given for 24-48 hours

Level 3

These are often university hospitals where most "high-risk" pregnancies will be followed up (risk of premature birth before 32 weeks gestation, fœtal malformation needing immediate care). These hospitals have an intensive care neonatal department where very premature babies and babies with serious complications can be looked after.

The pregnant woman (or the mother and new baby) can be transferred to a hospital of a different level, if necessary, due to a complication during the pregnancy or a premature birth. It may be that just the baby is transferred to another hospital, but, where possible, separation is avoided.

All maternity hospitals have a medical team, but the constitution of this team varies according to the annual number of births at the facility:

- Under 1,500 births per year, only midwives are required to be permanently on site. The obstetricians, anesthetists and pædiatricians are only on call, but have to be reachable 24 hours a day
- Over 1,500 births per year, all the medical team is obliged to be on site 24 hours a day
- Over 2,000 births per year, there should be one anesthetist assigned to just that facility
- Since July 2001, any maternity facility delivering less than 300 babies per year has been closed down for safety reasons – e.g., lack of sufficient practical experience

In making your decision, you should find out whether the maternity unit you are interested in is part of a public hospital, a *clinique conventionné* or a totally private clinic. This classification dictates how much of the cost of your stay will be reimbursed by Social Security and your health insurance, and what will have to come out of your own pocket (☞Administration).

In a public hospital (*hôpital publique*), most costs and charges incurred for antenatal appointments and delivery are paid (directly to the hospital) by Social Security. Some extra costs, e.g., private room, television and telephone, will be payable by you. It is sometimes possible to "go private" within a public hospital if you would like your chosen obstetrician to deliver your baby. Charges for this should be negotiated directly with your obstetrician and the hospital, and must be paid by you to the hospital and obstetrician directly when you leave the hospital.

In a *clinique conventionné*, the rates are set by Social Security and, before the 6th month, you pay 35 % of the charges. All costs incurred for antenatal appointments after the 6th month and for delivery are paid directly to the clinic by Social Security, although you are responsible for any extra costs, e.g. telephone, television or private room. Be aware that your chosen obstetrician may be classed as

The *Nouvel Observateur* magazine supplement (20 June 2003), in partnership with the website www.maman.fr, compiled a list of the best maternity hospitals in the Île-de-France region. The six best Parisian *maternités* according to the enquiry were:

1. *Hôpital des Diaconesses* (12th arr.)
2. *Clinique Villa Isis* (13th arr.)
3. *Institut mutualiste Montsouris* (14th arr.)
4. *Hôpital Saint-Vincent-de-Paul* (14th arr.)
5. *Hôpital Necker - Enfants malades* (15th arr.)
6. *Maternité Sainte-Félicité* (15th arr.)

PBN - Birth

conventionné honoraires libres, meaning that the difference between what he charges and what Social Security pays is your responsibility (☞Health and Medicine). Make sure you know what you will need to pay for at the end of your stay.

In a private clinic or hospital (*clinique agréée non conventionnée*) the main charges for your stay, the renting of the birth room or the operating theatre for a cæsarean and the vast proportion of charges for the obstetrical team, including the anesthetist, will not be covered by Social Security. Social Security will pay a percentage of costs directly to the facility and the remainder will be your responsibility, although this may be covered by your private medical insurance (*mutuelle*).

Questions To Ask When Choosing Your Maternity Facility

Payment and Costs

- Is the facility fully or partially reimbursed by Social Security?
- How much will a routine delivery and stay cost?
- What are the charges for extras, private room, telephone calls and television?
- Do they expect any payments in advance?
- What type of medical insurance does the facility accept? (If you have private insurance in another country, be sure to discuss the coverage in detail with your insurer and find out exactly what documentation they will require from the hospital, doctor, and other medical professionals before they will pay. Then discuss your insurance requirements with the hospital to make sure that the necessary documents will be supplied.)

Services and Facilities Available

- What category is the facility?
- Do they have English-speaking doctors, midwives, nursery nurses (*puéricultrices*) or pædiatricians?
- Is there a premature baby or neonatal unit on site; if not, where would the baby be cared for and can you be transferred too (if necessary)?
- Do they have equipment to help you pump breast milk for a premature baby?
- Do they have any special security measures to guard against baby snatching?
- How long can you expect to stay in the hospital after the birth?
- Do they offer instruction on how to care for the baby (changing nappies, bathing and umbilical cord care)?
- Does the hospital provide nappies, sanitary towels, breast pads etc?
- Is physiotherapy offered after the birth?
- Can partners stay overnight in your room, and have meals provided?
- Do they offer any antenatal classes (in evenings?) and do these include a tour of the facilities?
- What are the visiting hours for: partners, siblings (can siblings under 14 years visit at all?), family members or friends?
- Are the washing and toilet facilities private or must you share?
- Are there bedside telephones or televisions?
- Are you allowed to have flowers in your room?

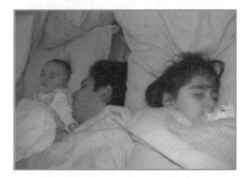

As the idea of a "birth plan" does not strictly exist in France you may wish to probe the facility in depth about its policies and medical procedures:

Hospital/Clinic Policies

- Are women permitted to give birth in the labour room (*salle de travail*) or must all births take place in the delivery room (*salle d'accouchement*)? Or, do labour and delivery take place in the same room?
- Is giving birth without medication encouraged?
- Are women allowed to be out of bed during labour?

Administrative Items You Should Take with You:

- Maternity booklet from the *CPAM* (*Carnet de maternité*)
- Identity documents (*Pièce d'identité officielle, livret de famille*)
- Blood group card (*Carte de groupe sanguin et facteur Rhésus*)
- Family allowance registration number (*Numéro d'allocations familiales*)
- Social Security card (*Carte Vitale*)
- Your partner's Social Security number (*Numéro de Sécurité Sociale du conjoint*)
- Laboratory results (*Résultats d'analyses*)
- X-Rays (*Radiographies*)
- Ultrasound scans (*Echographies*)
- Your private medical insurance details (*la prise en charge de votre mutuelle*)
- Some money and cheque book (sometimes laboratory technicians call round for payment)

- Can you choose your own position for birth?
- Do midwives deliver the baby?
- Are partners permitted to be with the woman throughout labour and delivery? If he is away, can a friend be present?
- In the case of a cæsarean, planned or emergency, can the partner be present during the procedure? If not, can he give the baby its first bath?
- What routines and tests are there for the baby directly after the birth?
- Is your own private pædiatrician permitted to examine the baby?
- Can the baby stay with you directly after the birth?
- Can the baby stay in your room day and night?
- If you are tired, can the baby stay in the nursery?
- If breastfeeding, are there staff trained to help you get started breastfeeding? How soon after the birth can you start, can you feed the baby on demand, can you insist the baby is fed only breast milk day and night?

Medical Routines

- What methods of pain relief are available during labour?
- Do they routinely give women an intravenous solution?
- Do they use electronic fœtal monitoring? If so, is it used for the entire labour or only periodically?
- How frequently are episiotomies done?
- What is the percentage of cæsarean births in the hospital/clinic?
- Are cæsareans performed with general or local anæsthetic?

The Final Decision

To help with your decision, you might find it helpful to consult the following resources:

www.topdesmaternites.com

A site containing information from the French Ministry of Health about all maternity units in France. Also has comments from mothers who have given birth in the facilites.

Bien Naître à Paris

Explains the different classifications of maternity units and gives details of the facilities in Paris and the surrounding area (see the Other Resources section at the end of this chapter).

MESSAGE Medical and Prenatal directories

If you are a member of MESSAGE, you can consult the MESSAGE Medical and Prenatal directories. These directories contain information on doctors and medical specialists (many of whom speak English). For further information, ☞ Organisations and Charities.

Alternative Birth Options

As many French hospital and clinics have a reputation for a high level of intervention during childbirth, it is not surprising that more and more women are becoming interested in alternative options, where they have more say in their childbirth experience. If you are interested in alternative childbirth, it is a good idea to investigate all the possibilities and discuss your wishes with several practitioners before deciding on how you will proceed.

Women in France who opt for a more "natural" approach to childbirth have four main options:

- support from a doula in a traditional medical setting
- choosing a clinic whose practitioners opt for less intervention
- placing themselves under the care of a midwife throughout the pregnancy and birth with the birth taking place in a clinic/hospital
- home birth

Remember, you can always discuss alternative childbirth options (not wanting an epidural or an episiotomy, kangaroo care vs. incubator, etc.) with your gynæcologist/obstetrician, or the medical team of a traditional clinic/hospital. In some cases, it may be possible to negotiate a less medicalised birth within a "standard" medical setting.

Doula

A doula (or childbirth assistant) offers emotional and practical support to a woman (or couple) before, during and after childbirth. The goal of the doula is to foster a sense of safety and calm in the expectant mother, allowing her to have the most satisfying and empowered time she can during pregnancy, birth and the early days of motherhood. Studies have shown that women supported by a doula during labour are less likely to request an epidural or analgesia for pain relief, and are also less likely to have a cæsarean or forceps delivery.

A doula may have professional qualifications, but is NOT a medical practitioner, so her presence during the actual birth is not a substitute for a midwife and/or obstetrician. Further information on doulas can be found through the following organisations:

www.doulas.info

This site has information on the doula profession, as well as contact details for doulas in Paris, four of whom are English-speaking.

www.dona.org

This doula organisation has over 5,000 members, and its website offers detailed information and resources, a discussion forum and an online doula-locator service.

Clinics or Medical Practitioners with a Less Interventionalist Approach

Some clinics in the Paris area have significantly lower cæsarian and epidural rates and encourage greater freedom of choice for women during child-birth (freedom of movement during labour, choice of birthing position, etc.). The two clinics best known for this approach are the *Maternité des Bluets* 💻www.bluets.org and the *Maternité des Lilas* 💻www.maternite-des-lilas.com.

To find out about doctors who subscribe to a more natural approach to childbirth, a good place to start is *La Leche League* and, if you are a member of MESSAGE, enquiring on the website forums.

Accompaniment by a Midwife Throughout Pregnancy and Birth

It is possible to arrange to be monitored by a mid-wife(*sage-femme*) throughout your pregnancy. She will provide birth preparation classes, support and monitor you throughout the labour and birth, and also offers post-natal care (which can be in your home). As with doctors, a good way to find out about *sage-femmes* with a policy of less interven-tion is via *La Leche League* and, if you are a mem-ber of MESSAGE, enquiring on the website forums. You can also contact the following organisation:

Organisation Nationale des Syndicats de Sages-Femme (O.N.S.S.F)
7, rue Rougemont, 75009 Paris
01.48.24.50.20
Fax 01.47.70.17.89

Home Birth

The percentage of women in France who give birth at home is low and it can be difficult to find a doctor or midwife who will accept the responsibility of a home delivery, although it is possible provided the pregnancy is considered low-risk.

Your chosen midwife and/or doctor will follow you throughout your pregnancy and you will have the normal ultrasounds and, for a first baby, perhaps an x-ray to check the width of your pelvis. For the birth, the doctor will usually not be present, but the mid-wife will have all the necessary equipment and the medical emergency services must be notified to be on stand-by. The midwife will perform the first medi-cal examinations for the baby and stitch an epi-siotomy or any tears you may have. A home birth is reimbursed at a rate of 100% by Social Security. There are a dozen or so midwives who provide pre-natal care throughout a pregnancy and deliver in the home (as well as at clinics/hospitals in the Paris area). A list of these midwives and their contact details is available on 💻www.perinatalite.info (click on *répertoire*). MESSAGE members can also con-tact the person coordinating the MESSAGE Prenatal directory for a list of midwives or doctors willing to perform home births.

Further Information

For more information on alternative childbirth, con-tact the following organisations:

Libres Naissances
99, avenue Raspail, 94250 Gentilly
01.45.47.96.71
The main aim of this association is to provide par-ents with sufficient information so they can make more informed choices with regard to the birth of their child. They are currently in the process of compiling a list of midwives and doctors who deliver in the home.

Féderation Nationale des Parents Naissance et Libertés
Naissance et Libertés
7, rue de Cherbourg, 31300 Toulouse
06.87.80.43.95
💻 www.fraternet.org/naissance
This organisation groups associations from all over France who share the philosophy of associations such as *Libres Naissances*.

La Leche League (See the section on breast-feeding, below)

The *La Leche League* library, available to members, includes books on the subject of home birth.

💻 www.accueilnaissance.fr

Paris-based organisation for parents and future parents interested in natural birthing and alternative health and childcare. (In French.)

http://maternage.free.fr

Paris-based association whose website provides detailed information on home birthing and other natural parenting topics. (In French.)

What to Expect in Hospital

On the whole, France favours an interventionist approach to childbirth. You can expect to be monitored frequently during labour and should not automatically assume that you will able to move around. It is generally assumed that you will want pain relief - epidural rates are among the highest in the world, and women who opt for natural childbirth are the exception rather than the norm. Be aware that the concept of a birth plan does not really exist in France, so your doctor will probably be quite bemused to be presented anything detailing how you would like your labour to progress! This section contains details of the pain relief options available in France, a summary of standard French birth and cæsarian procedures and what to expect after the birth.

Pain Relief

Listed below are the various methods of pain relief available in France, but your chosen hospital/clinic may not offer all of them:

Epidural Anæsthesia (la péridurale)

This is the most common method of pain relief during labour (accounting for 97% of all births in France) and is now 100% reimbursed by Social Security. Many facilities recommend and (strongly) encourage its use.

Pudendal Block (l'anesthésie par infiltration des nerfs honteux internes)

This is a local anæsthetic for the lower vagina, vulva and perineum which can be used for a forceps delivery.

Spinal Block (rachianesthésie)

This is similar to epidural but goes direct to the spinal fluid. Unlike an epidural, this is a single injection, and wears off after two or three hours.

For the more natural methods of pain relief described below, be prepared to do your own research and be ready to insist on using your chosen method!

Gas and Air (l'analgésie par inhalation gazeuse - Entonox)

Gas and Air does exist in France, but it is not used as a form of obstetric analgesia. It is never requested by French women and the staff are unlikely to know how to use it, even if they can find the equipment stashed away at the back of a storeroom. If you would like to use Gas and Air, the British and American hospitals and other hospitals and clinics inclining towards 'natural birth' would probably make it available on request, but you will definitely have to make it very clear in advance that you want to use it.

TENS (Trans-cutaneous Electrical Nerve Stimulation--TENS)

A TENS machine consists of a small box, about the size of an audio-cassette case with a clip on the back so you can attach it to whatever you are wearing in labour. Leading out of the box are four wires connected to sticky pads, which you place on your back. The machine gives out little pulses of electrical energy. These pulses prevent the pain signals from your womb and cervix from reaching your brain and also stimulate your body to release its own, natural "feel good" substances, called endorphins. TENS works best if you start using it at the very beginning of your labour because it takes about an hour for your body to respond to the electrical impulses by releasing endorphins. The TENS

Getting to Hospital

Unless your hospital or clinic is within walking distance (and even in that case), you will want to consider how you plan to get there when the time comes. If you do not have a car, or someone to drive you, and are not able to take public transportion, you will need to call an ambulance (the on-call ambulance (SAMU), or a private ambulance company) or take a taxi.

It has been reported that a taxi may refuse to take you if they know you are in labour, and the SAMU will only take you to the closest maternity facility. That said, here are some experiences MESSAGE members have had:

"Our plan was to call a private ambulance - we called before I was due and they told us they will take me wherever I want to go, any time of the day or night. Anyway, when my contractions were close, my husband made the call only to be told that things have changed and the private ambulances will not take you at night time, that we should call the SAMU. I too had heard that the SAMU will take you to the nearest hospital, not your clinique, however, the options were dwindling for me as the contractions were pretty close. Anyway, after all that, the SAMU did take me to my clinique and they were great. We didn't even have to pay anything, just gave them my carte vitale. They were lovely men and the only complaint I had was when they were driving over all the cobblestones mid-contractions." -- Alice S., Australian mother of one.

"If you call SAMU, they will try to take you the nearest hospital. We did this, and they tried to take me to Hotel Dieu, but my husband raced alongside the ambulance in his motorcyle and forced them to take us to Antoine Beclere, which is way out in Clamart! They were freaking out, but they did it, driving 120 km/h the whole way like maniacs. Then sent a huge bill." -- Janine D., American mother of one.

"I couldn't drive our car yet because I was still in the process of getting my French DL. When my water broke 3 weeks before the due date, I threw together a bag and called a taxi. The driver asked me in the cab whether I would be delivering soon and I said YES and smiled. I was a little afraid he might freak out if I told him just how soon it was! I didn't have any problem with the taxi driver, but that's probably because he didn't know that the address I gave him was a Maternité until we got there. He did have a pretty funny expression as he pulled my bag out of the trunk in front of the Maternité." -- Denelle T., American mother of one.

machine is available for hire to MESSAGE members. For more information contact info@messageparis.org.

Electric Anæsthetic (anesthésie éléctrique)
Similar to TENS machines, three electrodes are placed on a particular part of the body. May be offered in some facilities.

Acupuncture (l'acupuncture)
This is practised by some midwives, especially the independent ones and those doing home deliveries.

Vaginal Labour and Birth

When you decide it is time to go to hospital, you will be admitted straight away, so be very sure that you are at the stage of your labour where you want to be under medical supervision. When you arrive, you will be taken to a labour room (*salle de travail*) and you will be asked for a sample of urine, which will be tested for protein and sugar. You will be asked to undress and put on either a gown provided by the hospital/clinic or your own T-shirt. An electronic fœtal monitor (*le monitoring*) will be attached to your abdomen. The monitor may be left in place until delivery, or you may be able to be monitored intermittently.

You will be regularly examined internally to verify the degree of dilation (*dilatation*) until your cervix is fully dilated.

You may also be attached to an intravenous drip (*perfusion*) in your hand, which contains either a saline or glucose solution to prevent dehydration. The setting up of the drip is routine in France as a precautionary measure should medication need to be given quickly. Your labour can be accelerated with oxytocin (*oxytociques*) via the drip if necessary.

Most hospitals/clinics do not allow any food or water intake during labour.

When you are fully dilated, you will be prepared for the delivery of your baby (*l'expulsion*), possibly in a

The Pros and Cons of the TENS Machine

Pros:
- Portable, non-invasive and entirely under your control
- Easy to use
- Does not stop you being mobile
- Use it for as long as you want and then take it off — no lasting side-effects
- Not thought to have any effect on babies
- Can be used for a home birth

Cons:
- May only help in the first half of labour
- May have to be removed for electronic monitoring of your baby's heart, although the risk of TENS interfering with a fetal heart monitor has been described as only "slight". Taking the machine off interrupts the release of endorphins

separate delivery room (*salle d'accouchement*). In France, is it usual to lie on a delivery table with your legs in stirrups (*étriers*), but if you prefer to adopt a more upright position ask the staff - some hospitals allow more "natural" birth positions.

As soon as the baby is born, he will probably be placed on you briefly unless you have had a cæsarean. The staff will perform the first tests and may either clean the baby up in front of you or take the baby away to another room. The baby may have any mucus suctioned (*l'aspiration*) from its nostrils, mouth and throat.

PBN - Birth

The staff will assess the baby's general condition three times using the Apgar Score. The baby will be weighed and its length and head circumference will be measured. The results of the tests and measurements are recorded in the baby's *carnet de santé* (☞Health and Medicine). The baby's temperature will be taken to check that he can maintain his own body heat. If not, then he may be placed in a heated cot (*couveuse*) for a while. The hips are checked for dislocation (*luxation de hanche*) and then the first bath will be given (if you want your partner to be present for this, make it clear to the staff). The baby's reflexes will then be tested, the mouth checked, antibiotic eyedrops given and the umbilical cord bandaged. Whilst all this is taking place, your placenta will be delivered (*la délivrance*) and any episiotomy or tears sewn up (*recoudre*). The baby will be dressed and given back to you. If you, your partner want to be left alone with your baby at this point, make it clear to the staff. You may be required to stay in the delivery room for up to two hours before being moved to your room.

As soon as the baby is born, be ready with your selected name, as in France you must register the birth within three days at the *mairie* of the town in which the baby was born (☞Administration).

Cæsarean Section

In France, 14% of births are by cæsarean section (*césarienne*). The decision to perform a cæsarean is sometimes made during the pregnancy, when there is doubt as to the relative sizes of the maternal pelvis and the fœtal head or possibly in cases of placenta prævia, pre-eclampsia or a difficult breech presentation.

In preparation for a planned cæsarean (*césarienne prévue*), you will be given nothing to eat for several hours before the operation. For both planned and emergency cæsareans (*en urgence*) you may be shaved and your abdomen painted with antiseptic. An intravenous drip (*perfusion*) and urinary catheter (*sonde urinaire*) are inserted at the beginning of the operation and are not removed until the following day.

The operation itself is carried out by an obstetrician in an operating theatre (*salle d'opération/bloc opératoire*) either under general (*anesthésie générale*) or epidural. Your partner is usually unable to be present during the procedure as any supplementary presence in the theatre increases the risk of infection. However, check with your doctor as policies vary, and some hospitals or clinics may allow him to be present if you have an epidural rather than general anæsthetic.

After the operation, the baby will probably be shown to you briefly if you have not had a general anæsthetic and then moved quickly to a warmer area than the operating block to be given routine examinations by the staff. At this point, your partner may be able to give the baby its bath, although some hospitals and clinics wait until the next day before bathing the baby to avoid abrupt changes in body temperature. You will be reunited with your baby and partner after some time spent in the recovery area.

A cæsarean is a major abdominal operation, so make sure you get plenty of assistance from the nursing staff, both for your own comfort and with caring for the baby. For example, you may need help to position the baby for breastfeeding. If you are feeling too much pain or discomfort, ask for pain relief (*analgésie*).

Subsequent Pregnancies
If you have had a cæsarean, subsequent births can often be by normal delivery. This is known as Vaginal Birth After Cæsarean (VBAC). If avoiding a subsequent cæsarean is important to you, be aware that some doctors in France are more supportive than others. If you are a member of MESSAGE, the MESSAGE Prenatal directory is a good source of advice about doctors supportive of VBAC.

Other good sources of information are:
- www.lalecheleague.org
- www.childbirth.org

Post-Natal Care

For the first night, most hospitals/clinics will keep the baby in the nursery (*nurserie*) so the mother can have a good sleep and then, if you wish, each night, for the rest of your stay. If you are breast-feeding make it clear that the baby should be brought to you when hungry and that you do not want her to be given any milk from a bottle (it may be a good idea to attach a note to the cot to avoid any confusion). Be aware that, unless you specifically request otherwise, the baby may be given a drink of glucose water from a bottle by the nursery nurses (*les puéricultrices*) the first night.

The staff on the ward will bath and change your baby, and will be happy to show you how to change nappies and how to clean and take care of the umbilical cord. You can ask if your partner could also attend a bathing and umbilical cord care session. Some hospitals make the parents responsible for all bathing and changing after a training session.

At three days, a sample of blood will be taken from the heel in order to screen for certain inherited disorders. The baby will have a full examination after at the end of your stay, either by the hospital's pædiatrician or your chosen specialist who you can ask to attend the hospital. A special form will be completed which you need to send to the *CAF* to receive benefits (☞Administration). If you leave the hospital before this examination takes place, you must take the baby to your pædiatrician.

(If you would like information regarding circumcision ☞Health and Medicine).

Once the pædiatrician is happy that the baby is doing well, (and your doctor feels you are, too), you will both be discharged. Expect this to be three or four days after a normal delivery, and five or six days after a cæsarean.

Going Home After the Birth

It is completely normal to feel uneasy about leaving the relative calm and safety of the hospital/clinic for home. The beginning of parenthood can be a very demanding time both physically and emotionally, especially if you are away from family and close friends. On top of this, it is not usual in France to have follow up visits once you are at home with the baby. To help ease your worries, be sure to ask both your doctor and the pædiatrician about any special requirements or restrictions for you and the baby. Also make sure you have the relevant telephone numbers and contact names, as you will probably have further questions to ask once you return home.

If you are a member of MESSAGE, try to get out to a meeting as early as you feel able - talking to other parents and discussing any worries, fears or ideas can be very reassuring. MESSAGE also provides a wealth of support for new mothers, including breastfeeding advice and a "Helping Hands" services, where members help out by cooking a meal or assisting with shopping to ease you through the first few days.

Post-Partum Check-up

Six weeks after the birth, you will be expected to arrange an appointment with your doctor or midwife, who will give you an internal examination to check that your uterus has returned to its correct size and shape, and will also check that your episiotomy or cæsarean incision has healed properly.

You may also be given a prescription to see a *kinésithérapeute* (☞Health and Medicine) to help strengthen your abdomen and perineal muscles (using Kegel exercises, internal probes and/or manual strength tests). These sessions, which are virtually unheard of in the UK and the USA, may help with problems such as urinary incontinence and painful intercourse, and are fully reimbursed by Social Security. Perineal reeducation (*re-education perineale*) sessions may also be offered by independent midwives (*sage femme liberale*).

Post-Natal Depression

What you should know:
- As many as 10% of all new mothers develop post-natal depression.
- Depression is not a sign of weakness – it is an illness and can be treated.

What you should do:
- Seek medical help immediately! Take someone with you to the doctor's if possible.
- Contact SOS Helpline, an English-speaking help service available on 01.46.21.46.46 from 3pm - 11pm every day.
- Get help with your baby. Do not struggle on alone because you feel you "should" be able to manage. You are ill. If you had a broken leg, you would not be able to cope alone, would you? Try and see depression like that.
- Talk to other women who have had post-natal depression, who know what it is like and who can reassure you that you will get better. If you are a member of MESSAGE, you can contact other members who have experienced post-natal depression by contacting the MESSAGE Support Coordinator, whose details are listed on the "Key Contacts" page in the latest MESSAGE magazine.
- Find out as much as you can about post-natal depression.
- Try and get out and see other people who are sympathetic. Stay away from people who make you feel worse.
- Be kind to yourself; try being at least as kind to yourself as you are to other people.
- Get as much rest as you can; tiredness seems to make depression worse.
- Eat properly; low blood sugar can make things worse.

The French Social Security will often also cover visits to specialists to take care of varicose veins and the little spider veins that can come out on the face as a result of either pregnancy or labour.

Post-Natal Depression

Usually, we think of the birth of a baby as a joyful event. But what can you do if you find yourself weepy, irritable or down and having difficulty coping with the demands of a young baby?

Post-natal depression comes in several forms:

Baby Blues (*le bébé "blues"* or *la déprime après l'accouch motement*) happens to most mothers. Around the third or fourth day after the birth the mother finds herself ready to burst into tears about anything and everything. Confusion and lack of concentration are other symptoms. This may last for several days and generally disappears around the eighth to tenth day.

Post-Natal Depression (*la déprime post natale*) occurs when the "baby blues" persist beyond that time into the weeks and months following the birth. Characteristics of post-natal depression are feelings of despair, anxiety or even panic, irritability, obsessive or inappropriate thoughts, difficulty sleeping, lack of appetite, lethargy and difficulty in coping.

Post-Partum Psychosis (*Psychose Puerpérale*) is fortunately very rare. In this case the mother loses touch with reality and may have delusions and hallucinations. Admission to a psychiatric hospital is usually necessary.

It is now generally agreed that the baby blues are related to the enormous hormonal changes which occur in the days following the birth, as the mother's body makes the change from pregnancy to a non-pregnant state. No special treatment is needed beyond support and understanding from family and medical staff.

The treatment for post-natal depression may be hormones, anti-depressants, tranquilisers or psychotherapy, or a combination of these.

What Others Can Do to Help

Ensure that a medical practioner has been involved. Accept that the new mother is unwell and cannot be jollied out of it (though counselling, particularly cognitive therapy can help). Women who are suffering from post-natal depression will often refuse offers of support, but may dislike being left alone. You can help just by staying in touch with them for low-key activities such as a walk in the park, or by cooking them a meal. Their partners are also likely to be suffering as a consequence of the depression, so may appreciate an ear or a shoulder. The APNI (see below) is a good source of advice for those wanting to support a friend suffering from post-natal depression.

Help is also available from the following services:

APNI (Association for Postnatal Illness)
25 Jerdan Place
London SW6 1BE
United Kingdom
00 44 207 386 0868
Mon - Fri 10h00 - 17h00
If you write to them, enclose a self-addressed envelope and international reply coupon available at the post office.

International Counseling Service
65, quai d'Orsay, 75007 Paris
01.45.50.26.49
Mon - Fri 09h30 - 19h00
Sat 09h00 - 13h00

SOS Help
An English-language telephone support line with trained listeners.
01.47.23.80.80
Every day 15h00 - 23h00

Croix Rouge Ecoute
01.05.21.48.88
Mon - Fri 10h00 - 22h00
This is a support line for families, to give psychological support, and you can have follow-up over several calls, while remaining anonymous.

NEWBORN

Once you have got through the pregnancy and birth, you might be quite daunted to find yourself at home with a brand new baby. This section gives you an idea of what to do about medical examinations, where to find the equipment you need and where to go if you need support.

Medical Examinations

To be eligible for full benefits from Social Security, in addition to the 8 day check up, the baby must have two further medical examinations at 9 months and 24 months. In addition, his *carnet de santé* includes a timetable of optional visits over the next two years for vaccinations and, for the first six months, to check the baby's weight and measure his length and head circumference (☞Health and Medicine). All this information will be recorded in the *carnet de santé*, as are details of any other medical examinations.

Weighing the Baby

As the weight of the baby will not be monitored from when you leave hospital until his next check-up, you may wish to rent scales from a pharmacy or rental company (☞Shopping). Alternatively, some pharmacies will weigh your baby for you on their own scales and there are *PMI* centres all over France, which offer weighing and measuring of your baby free of charge and as often as you wish (☞Health and Medicine).

Breastfeeding

While most hospitals and clinics in France now claim to be in favour of breastfeeding, the information and support offered to breastfeeding mothers varies a great deal. If breastfeeding is important to you, choose a pædiatrician or doctor who is well informed about breastfeeding and ask him or her what percentage of his or her clientele is breastfed, for how long they are breastfed, and what sources the doctor uses for seeking solutions to difficulties, (for example up-to-date references on compatibility

of medications and breastfeeding, access to information resources at available websites, current professional breastfeeding publications).

When choosing a doctor, you may find talking to other mothers helpful or, if you are a MESSAGE member, consult the list of health professionals on the Medical Practitoners Directory. You can also consult a list of medical practitioners (*associes médicaux*) at *La Leche League*.

If you would like to talk to a lactation consultant (a health care professional who specializes in the clinical management of breastfeeding), you can find a board certified lactation consultant in Paris by visiting 🖳www.ilca.org.

Breastfeeding Support

Mother-to-mother support groups exist to help with breastfeeding, providing information and support both during pregnancy and after the birth. It is very helpful and reassuring for the mother or mother-to-be to talk to other women who are going through, or have already experienced, the same things. Such support has been found to be vital to the ease and success of breastfeeding. MESSAGE members have support from trained Breastfeeding Supporters, who can answer any breastfeeding related questions, such as breastfeeding after a cæsarean or successfully feeding a premature baby, as well as the more mundane questions of how often to feed and for how long. All Breastfeeding Supporters speak English and several of them speak French. Check the Support Services pages of a recent MESSAGE magazine for contact details.

La Leche League, an international breastfeeding information and support group, also has English-speaking leaders available in Paris. To contact the English-speaking *La Leche League* group, visit 🖥️www.lllfrance.org or call their emergency number 01.39.58.45.84.

For further information on breastfeeding, you might like to refer to a specialist book, some of which are listed in the Other Resources section at the end of this chapter. *La Leche League* has a small English-language library available to its members, with books on breastfeeding, homebirth and parenting. The MESSAGE library also has a number of relevant publications available to its members.

Breastfeeding and Illness

If you contract a minor illness – flu, tummy upset, cold, tonsillitis, etc. – while breastfeeding, you should continue feeding. In fact, breastfeeding your baby will help protect her from what ever bug you have and, if she does get ill, it should be with a milder version of what you have. If you need medication, tell the pharmacist you are breast-feeding. If they are unsure what to give you, they will refer you to your doctor.

Many French medical practitioners receive little breastfeeding training and are therefore, with the best will in the world, ill-equipped to help with problems such as blocked ducts or mastitis, and may suggest you stop breastfeeding unnecessarily. If you should find yourself in your doctor's surgery with a breast disorder requiring antibiotics, do not hesitate to request one compatible with breastfeeding. Such drugs do exist but sometimes you have to insist to get them. As well as conventional medicine, there are homeopathic remedies that can help with breastfeeding problems; consult your pharmacist or a homeopath for specific advice. Should the doctor suggest weaning as the solution to any given problem, discuss your feelings about the importance of breastfeeding, get a second opinion, or consult your MESSAGE Breastfeeding Supporter, as weaning may not be necessary.

Donating Breastmilk

If you would like to donate your breastmilk, which can be used to nourish premature babies still in hospital, contact:

Solidarilait
Lactarium de Paris, Institut de Puériculture
26, boulevard Brune, 75014 Paris
M° Porte de Vanves
Mon - Fri 08h30 - 16h30
01.40.44.39.14
01.40.44.39.16
They will explain what you need to do, provide the necessary equipment and collect the breastmilk from your home. There are also lactariums in Versailles, Evreux and other parts of France.

Equipment

The equipment and products available for breastfeeding mothers are the same in France as in other

Social Attitudes to Breastfeeding in France

Socially, French attitudes to breastfeeding are mixed. Many French women feel that breastfeeding is a wonderful thing in theory, but that it is not for them. The breastfeeding mother is regarded, if not as an interesting oddity, then as someone who is performing above and beyond the call of duty.

However, despite the fact that so many people think breastfeeding is a rather quaint pastime, few people in France actually object to it in their presence, and the breastfeeding mother in Paris will not usually find herself being requested to leave cafés or restaurants. The support groups mentioned above are especially helpful on living and socialising with your breastfed baby. With a little practice, babies can be fed anywhere – buses, parks, shops, even churches– and while people may give you a knowing smile they probably will not object.

countries. Almost all items are readily available from pharmacies, supermarkets and specialist baby shops (☞Shopping). For help with vocabulary when you are shopping, have a look at the vocabulary section at the end of this chapter.

Electric breast pumps (*tire-lait electrique*) are usually available to use while in the hospital and can be hired from pharmacies fairly cheaply thereafter (☞Shopping). If you have a prescription (*ordonnance*) from your doctor in the baby's name, Social Security will reimburse the hire charge. Medela's "Lactina" and Avent are two excellent electric pumps, and you can ask your pharmacy to order one of these for you. Alternatively, Medela also produce a "Mini-electric" smaller pump which can be plugged in or used with batteries. The Medela "Pump-in-Style" double electric pump is available for purchase as well, but only from Natal Service (☞Shopping). Note that Social Security will not reimburse the cost of purchasing a pump.

Manual pumps are available in France under the brand names Solustéril and Avent, to name but two. There is also a battery pump made by Solustéril which combines the best points of both electric and hand pump systems and is available from pharmacies.

Bottlefeeding

If you decide to bottle feed, most supermarkets, pharmacies (which tend to be more expensive), parapharmacies and baby equipment shops such as Prénatal, Natalys and Toys'R'Us, sell all the necessary equipment. Many baby shops stock the popular UK *Avent* range of equipment (☞Shopping).

Various manufacturers in France produce a wide range of teats (*tétine*) made of either silicone (*silicone*) or rubber (*caoutchouc*). The majority are interchangeable with different makes of bottle. There are teats for the newborn baby to three months old (*nouveau-né*) and a larger teat for the older baby (*deuxième âge*), as well as teats that simulate the nipple (*physiologique*). A baby who is

usually breastfed may accept an occasional bottle more readily if you use a *tétine physiologique*. Teats can have different flow rates (*à débit variable*), governed by the shape, size or number of holes in the teats, which allow increased flow to meet the demands of a growing baby. These can be described as *minimum/faible*, *moyen* and *maximum*. The teats with larger holes can also be used for milks with solids added (*bouillie*). Some teats are designed with integral valves to prevent the baby swallowing too much air while feeding.

Sterilising (stérilisation)

In France, the options for sterilising are:

Chemical or cold water (*stérilisation à froid*): Tablets or liquids are dissolved in water in a plastic container large enough to submerge completely all items being sterilised. This method takes around 15 minutes and the equipment can remain in the solution for up to 24 hours.

Steam (*stérilisation à la vapeur*): Units (*stérilisateur électrique*) are available from supermarkets and baby shops. It is also possible to hire these (☞Shopping).

Microwave (*stérilisation micro-ondes*): A specially adapted unit for microwave sterilisation. This is the quickest method.

Boiling Water (*stérilisation à chaud*): Clean bottles, teats, caps, discs and breast pumps are completely submerged in a saucepan of boiling water and simmered for 25 minutes, then stored in a sterilised container.

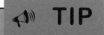

◀» TIP

If you find that you need an electric breast pump but cannot get out to get it, Natal Service (01.58.09.89.00) delivers, generally by the next day.

PBN - Newborn

Baby Milk (Manufactured)

Baby milks, or infant formulæ (*lait maternisé*), are manufactured in individual countries and are controlled by strict government nutritional guidelines. The same brand names of formula milk exist in different countries, but each country may use slightly different recipes.The formulæ are developed in response to the medical opinion and the market trends of each country. To check which milks guarantee not to use genetically modified ingredients (*OGM - organismes génétiquement modifiés*), consult the list compiled and frequently updated by Greenpeace France on 💻www.greenpeace.fr, or 01.53.43.85.70.

There are two main types of French baby milk - the *premier âge*, and the *deuxième âge*. Both are modified cow's milk casein-based feeds. The usual recommendation is to use the *premier âge* until the baby is five months old and then change to the *deuxième âge*, which has a slightly higher protein content to meet the needs of the older infant. In the *premier âge* range, there is a special section for babies with low birth weight (*nouveau né - faible poids de naissance*). Both types of milk are fully vitaminised and a wide variety of brands are readily available from supermarkets or pharmacies.

More Specialised Milks

Hypoallergenic (*hypoallergique*) milks available from pharmacies are marketed as ideal for complementary bottle feeding when breastfeeding. These are cow's milk modified whey-based feeds whose composition is closer to breast milk than ordinary formula. However, the existence of these milks does not mean that the *premier* and *deuxième âge* milks are unsuitable for complementary feeding. There is also a vast selection of specialised milks available that should be used under medical supervision and prescribed by your doctor e.g. soya milks, specialised milks for babies suffering from diarrhœa, and anti-regurgitation formulæ.

Other Milks

A follow-on milk (*lait de croissance*) is a modified cow's milk formula designed for the older infant and child by having higher protein content and being fortified with vitamins and iron. They are recommended from 10 months to 3 years.

There is an organic milk available for *premier* and *deuxième âge* called Babybio 1 and 2. It is carried in some supermarkets and health food shps (☞Shopping). The supermarket Carrefour also offers its own brand of organic formula.

Premature Babies

Expectant mothers who know in advance that they are at risk of a premature birth should try to register at a maternity facility with an attached neonatal nursery. Only some of the major hospitals in the Paris area have these specialised maternity units (*maternités*):

Paris:
Hôpital Cochin
Hôpital Robert-Débré
Hôpital St. Michel
Hôpital St. Vincent de Paul

Suburbs:
Hertford British Hospital (Levallois-Perret)
Hôpital de Poissy (Yvelines)
Hôpital de Montreuil (Seine St Denis)
Hôpital de Créteil (Val de Marne)
Hôpital Antoine- Béclere, Clamart (Hauts de Seine)
Hôpital de Argenteuil (Val d'Oise)
Hôpital de Pontoise (Val d'Oise)

Premature Labour

A mother who arrives at a hospital/clinic in premature labour will usually be given drugs to slow or halt the contractions (*retarder l'accouchement* or *arrêter les contractions*). A few extra days or even hours in the uterus can help the baby's lungs (*poumons/bronches*) mature, and sometimes medication is administered to help with this.

Care of the Premature Baby

Immediately after birth, a premature baby will receive intensive care (*soins intensifs*), perhaps including respiratory assistance (*ventilation, incubation*) and intravenous (*perfusion*) nutrients and medicine. He will be placed in an incubator (*incubateur/couveuse*) and, if there is no neonatal unit at the maternity facility, an ambulance will be called to transport the baby to the closest unit that has space. The baby will be given temporary life-support until he gets to the neonatal re-animation (*service de réanimation néonatale*) or the intensive care ward.

Questions to Ask

It is advisable to arrange an appointment (if necessary) with the head neonatologist to discuss any questions or worries e.g.:

- What is the prognosis?
- Will there be any complications?
- What is the treatment?
- When can you begin to breastfeed?
- Can the baby be given your expressed breast milk in his feeding tube or from a bottle?
- Ask for a tentative release date.

Visiting Your Baby

Visiting hours are usually generous for premature babies, but normally restricted to the parents. Staff members at neonatology units generally encourage parents' involvement and presence. You may be asked to bathe your baby (*faire sa toilette*), sometimes limited to just a cotton pad to wipe his face or change his nappy. If your baby is doing very well, you will be allowed to hold him for short periods, but the staff will be there to remind you that the

best place for him is in the incubator, which helps to maintain the baby's body temperature. You should be allowed to stroke your 'preemie' through the incubator portholes and you can certainly talk and sing to him. Stuffed animals, music boxes and mobiles you bring to make the baby's crib or incubator more cheerful will be first sterilised by the hospital and then placed near him, helping to take your attention away from all the tubes and wires.

Breastfeeding a Premature Baby

It is possible to breastfeed a premature baby, and should be encouraged as the baby's mother's milk contains the precise elements the baby needs to continue growing outside the mother's uterus. The most important thing is not to be discouraged by nurses and doctors who may not be very supportive. If you are a member of MESSAGE, contact a Breastfeeding Supporter who can give you step-by-step advice on expressing and storing your breast milk and how to successfully feed your baby both in the hospital and once the baby has come home.

The milk should be stored in sterilised bottles, labelled with the baby's name, together with the name and address of the neonatology unit so, if it is necessary for you to be separated from your baby,

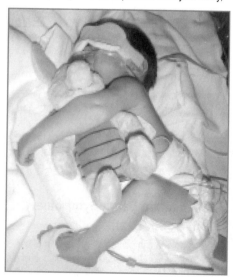

the milk will be taken to him. Some neonatology units provide special areas for mothers to express milk with electric breast pumps and sterilised bottles. A milk-bank (*Lactarium de Paris*) exists in Paris to provide breastmilk to fragile newborns.

Clothing for Premature Babies

Printemps department store stocks a line of baby clothes for premature and low birth weight babies for infants 1.5 kilos and up (☞Shopping).

Adorelle
13 rue Duchesnay, 92600 Asnières
01.47.93.22.47
Offers a selection of clothing and diapers for premature babies. All items are available by mail order and delivered within 48 hours. Call for a free catalogue.

Support

The days while the premature baby is hospitalised are long and, though you will want to spend time stroking and talking to your baby, try also to exchange feelings and information with other mothers you meet at the neonatal nursery, who will often, in turn, have stories to reassure you. Talking to the staff is also important; they have a lot of knowledge to share, as well as advice. Most facilities also offer the help of a trained therapist who is there to listen and answer the needs of anxious parents.

If you are a member of MESSAGE, there is a support service for mothers of premature infants. You can be put in touch with a MESSAGE mother who has been through the same thing. Contact the MESSAGE Support Co-ordinator (see latest MESSAGE magazine for details).

Sudden Infant Death Syndrome (SIDS) or Cot Death

Although no one can guarantee prevention of cot death (*mort subite du nourrisson*), knowledge of the factors which may reduce the risk has grown greatly in recent years. The most up-to-date research suggests ways in which you may be able to reduce the risk.

• Place your baby on his/her back to sleep
• Do not smoke during pregnancy and avoid exposing the baby to a smokey atmosphere
• Do not let your baby get too hot (or too cold). Around 19°C (65°F) is the ideal temperature for the baby's room. Babies can also become overheated because of too much clothing or bedding
• Put your baby to sleep with his/her feet at the end of the bed, not halfway down the bed. This prevents the child from wriggling down under the covers
• If you think your baby is unwell, always contact your doctor

As a general rule, health professionals in France follow the above guidelines. Campaigns to increase public awareness have been conducted in France.

Further information can be obtained from the following organisations:

Federation Naître et Vivre
www.naitre-et-vivre.org
This is a national federation which groups about 30 local associations including:

Naître et Vivre
5, rue La Pérouse, 75116 Paris
01.47.23.98.22
01.47.23.05.08 (24 hour hotline maintained by member parents)
Monthly discussion meetings and support groups.

The Foundation for the Study of Infant Deaths
00 44 207 222 8001 (General)
00 44 207 233 2090 (Helpline)
www.sids.org.uk

TWINS/MULTIPLE BIRTHS

Expecting twin/multiples can come as a great surprise. You may feel a bewildering mix of emotions, and have a great many concerns and questions as carrying multiple babies has its own set of issues and risks. This section addresses the particularities a mother of multiples will need to consider.

Support

Do not try to be superwoman and think that every-one expects you to cope all by yourself. If you can afford it, invest in some home help either with the cleaning, with childcare, or even to take the pressure off at night – the benefits of a full night's sleep on health and morale are well worth the expense of paying someone to do a night shift for you. Raising two (or more) babies at the same time is exhausting and you will need all the help you can get.

Information

The best way to gather information and practical advice is to make contact with a local group of mothers or parents of twins/multiples, as they will have knowledge and experience which can be very comforting and helpful to expectant parents. If you are a MESSAGE member, you can join the Twins and More support group (see latest MESSAGE magazine for details).

There are several other support groups that you can join, including:

Jumeaux et Plus – L'Association de Paris
2, rue Henri Ranvier, 75011 Paris
01.43.70.03.31
💻 www.jumeaux-paris.com
This is an excellent association providing practical advice, especially about which maternity to choose for giving birth to your multiples. The association is organised into different arrondissements in Paris and the suburbs, and you are able to contact your "area leader" to find out about meetings in your area or just for a general chat. Although most members are French, there are also English, Spanish

and German-speaking subgroups. The association will lend material such as car seats, double prams/strollers, double baby carriers, travel cots, etc. Every quarter, a gazette is published giving valuable information from health care professionals about specific multiples issues and also practical information about babysitters, administration, etc.

TAMBA (Twins and Multiple Births Association)
2 The Willows, Gardner Road
Guildford, Surrey, GU1 4PG
United Kingdom
0870 770 3305
💻 www.tamba.org.uk
This is a British organization, but its website contains a good deal of helpful information, as well as an extensive list of other organisations that offer support to parents of multiples.

MOST (Mothers of Supertwins)
💻 www.mostonline.org
International non-profit organisation that is a network of families with triplets, quadruplets or more.

Choice of Maternity Hospital

It is important to give careful thought to the hospital at which you will give birth, because half of all twins births and 90% of triplets births are premature. You will be advised to choose a hospital with a neonatal unit (level 2) or even an emergency neonatal unit (level 3), just in case the babies need intensive care. If there are no neonatal facilities at the hospital where you give birth, the baby or babies would have to be transferred to another hospital's neonatal unit and you would not be able to see them until you are fit to travel. This can be a traumatic experience for both mother and babies.

The following hospitals in Paris are equipped with neonatal units and hold special information sessions for pregnant women expecting twins or more:

- Notre-Dame-de-Bonsecours
- Port-Royal Baudelocque
- Saint-Vincent-de-Paul
- Robert Debré

These sessions give you a much better idea of what to expect from your birth and pregnancy than the regular singleton birth information sessions.

Medical Follow-up

In France, you will be closely followed during your multiple pregnancy, especially from the sixth month onwards, when the risk of a premature birth becomes a reality. You will see your obstetrician every month at the hospital and will probably undergo an ultrasound every month to check on the babies' growth rate. It is common practice in France to give steroid injections at around 35 - 36 weeks, in order to speed up the babies' lung maturation in case of premature birth. Some maternity hospitals have a network of midwives who will visit you at home on a regular basis and they are able to monitor the babies' heart beats.

After your babies are born, the pædiatrician may recommend having a hip ultrasound taken, since twins have an increased risk of developmental dysplasia of the hip (malformations), which if caught early enough can often be corrected. Such a screening is common practice for twins in France.

Breastfeeding

The experience of many women who have given birth to multiples in France is that medical practitioners and hospital/clinic staff have tried to dissuade them from attempting to breastfeed, often going so far as to say it is impossible. If you plan to breastfeed, be aware that you are likely to encounter this type of attitude, and prepare to be

firm. You may want to purchase a *DAL* (*dispositif d'aide à l'allaitement,* information available from *La Leche League*), which will help to prevent nipple confusion if your babies are fed by hospital or clinic staff. Many mothers also say that the breastfeeding "snake" pillow is indispensable for breastfeeding twins.

If you need to pump breastmilk, it is essential to have a hospital-grade double pump for twins. Good quality breastpumps, such as those made by Medela, can be hired from many pharmacies and, if done with prescription, it is not expensive. (See the discussion on Breastfeeding Equipment above.) Medela has the list of pharmacies participating on their website at 💻www.medela.fr. Another option popular with mothers of multiples is Natal Service in the 15th *arrondissement* as they deliver.

Best Ways to Get Around Paris with Multiples

Use *RER* A – the station at CDG Etoile has handicap elevator access at Carnot and all the way down to the quai, and AUBER is quite easy to get around, with street access and elevators.

Do not be afraid to use the handicap access on the elevators and buses – you are allowed. (Give priority to any disabled persons who may need to use them, of course!)

Try to avoid the *métro* if you can take the *RER* or bus instead. That goes double for using the *métro* at morning or afternoon rush hour!

For extra mobility, try carrying one baby in a babycarrier and push the other one in a single pushchair, this will open up new horizons.

Best of all, try to go out accompanied...

And keep in mind, people will help usually without being asked but do ASK and do not be afraid to ASK and smile and say *MERCI*!

If you are a member of MESSAGE, you can seek the help of a Breastfeeding Supporter during your pregnancy, to learn more about the specificities of breastfeeding multiples. You can also contact support groups such as *La Leche League* and/or consult the book Mothering Multiples, which is listed in the Other Resources section at the end of this chapter.

Mobility

The Paris public transportation system is infamously pram- or pushchair-unfriendly, and this becomes doubly troublesome when you have more than one baby to move around with. Choose a double pushchair that is as small and lightweight as possible, and bear in mind that side by side pushchairs are not practical if you live in central Paris, where the pavements are too narrow to let you pass, or the supermarket checkouts are not designed for wheelchair access. You may also want to plan trips quite carefully to ensure you are not faced with a hike up several flights of stairs in a *métro* or *RER* station.

The website of the Paris public transportation department (⌨www.ratp.fr) provides a detailed list of all stations equipped with lifts - but they cannot tell you when one is out of order. There is also an information line you can call to enquire about escalators, as these are not mentioned on the website 0 892 687 714.

Financial Aid

In addition to other forms of financial assistance you may qualify for (☞Administration), if you are expecting twins or more and have been a Paris resident for at least three years, you will be entitled to receive the *Allocation pour naissance ou adoption multiple*. You must request this benefit at your local *Centre d'action sociale* within six months of the births. If your request is approved, you will receive a one-time lump sum of €63. Full details of this benefit and how to request it can be found on the website of the *Mairie de Paris* ⌨www.paris.fr.

Working mothers are also granted a longer maternity leave if you give birth to twins or triplets. (☞Work)

Carte Paris Famille (Paris Family Card)

The *Carte Paris Famille* is available to families with at least three children, or with one handicapped child, who have been living in Paris for at least three of the last five years. (If you have been transferred within France by your company, then one year's residency in Paris is sufficient.) You must also have a valid French identity card, or a residence permit valid for 10 years.

The card, which is valid for one year and must be renewed each year, gives you reductions on entrance fees to municipal swimming pools, municipal parks and gardens, after-school activities and some museum exhibitions. The card-holder is allocated a credit of €305 annually, which can reimburse after-school activities, school dinner fees etc. Depending on your income, you may be entitled to a reduction in your electricity bills or financial aid for housing expenses.

Families with a handicapped child are also entitled to a monthly support payment of €153.

You can obtain the card either by post or in person from the *Centre d'Action Sociale de la Ville de Paris* situated in your *arrondissement*.

For more information on benefits ☞Administration.

PBN - Multiple Births

The *Caisse d'Allocations Familiales* (☞Administration) may also offer the services of a home help to steer you through the first weeks of the babies' arrival. You should contact them before you give birth so that they can schedule one of their *travailleuse familale* to come round to help you. The hourly rate depends on your income and how many children you have. If you have 3 children under the age of 3 at home you are entitled to 150 hours of home help entirely free of charge and irrespective of your income (you deserve it after all!). For information call Allo Social on 01.40.27.98.00.

Childcare

If you choose to return to work, the childcare options are the same as for any working mother. Unfortunately, there are no specific previsions for twins in the Paris childcare programme; you do not have priority for public *crèches* and getting two places at the same time is quite a feat. It can also be difficult to find an *assistante maternelle* with two free spaces. It is therefore worth calculating the cost of employing a nanny or au pair to come to your home (☞Childcare).

Equipment

Depending on where you live in Paris it may be worth considering moving, as some flats are up several flights of stairs with no lift. This is a problem later on in the pregnancy if you are house-bound (sometimes because of the effort of the stairs!), and certainly when you have your babies and have to leave one in the pram or inside the flat while you take the other one up or down the stairs. Ideally, measure the pram you buy to fit in the lift (not possible for old Parisian buildings) and also to fit through your doors!! You would be surprised at how variable the width of Parisian doorways can be. For the best choice of double prams consult the catalogue provided by the *Jumeaux et Plus* association (details above).

Among the many questions you probably want to ask veteran parents of multiples, enquire about

what equipment they found indispensable for twins. Some ideas include a bouncy seat (in which to put one twin while you feed or soothe the other) and, if you are planning to breastfeed, a breastfeeding pillow that can accommodate two babies. In the kitchen, the following come in handy: a dishwasher, tumble dryer, microwave, freezer and food processor. If you own a car, French law requires that you have two car seats (☞Shopping).

The double baby equipment that you will probably need to buy will stretch your budget considerably, and you may want to consider borrowing some equipment. *Jumeaux et Plus* (details above) helps parents of multiples by providing a catalogue of discounted baby supplies (eg formula milk, nappies, baby food jars, prams) that you can have delivered (very important when you lack mobility in the first months), and also lends some equipment. As a member of the association, you are entitled to discounts in some of the leading baby equipment stores such as Aubert (☞Shopping). Twice a year, the association holds a jumble sale at which you can buy cheap second-hand clothes donated by members of the association. MESSAGE also holds twice yearly Bring & Buys where you can pick up bargains in clothes, toys and equipment. Finally, the latest edition of *Paris pas Cher* (listed in the Other Resources section) can always be counted on for up-to-date information on the cheapest places in town for baby supplies and equipment.

As a member of the *Association Jumeaux et Plus*, you also have discounts with certain holiday organisations: Pierre et Vacances, Centre Parcs, UCPA, VVF, etc. (☞Travel)

Twins at School

It is standard practice in Parisian schools to split up twins, providing there are at least two classes of the same level. If you strongly object to this policy, you can try negotiating with the head of the particular school and you may be allowed to keep your children together.

OTHER RESOURCES

Books

What to Expect When You're Expecting
Arlene Eisenberg, Heidi E. Murkoff, Sandee E. Hathaway (Workman Publishing)

Conception, Pregnancy and Birth
Miriam Stoppard (Dorling Kindersley)

What to Expect the First Year
Arlene Eisenberg, Heidi E. Murkoff, Sandee E. Hathaway (Workman Publishing)

Complete Baby and Child Care
Miriam Stoppard (Dorling Kindersley)

NCT: Breastfeeding for Beginners
Caroline Deacon (Harper Collins)

What to Expect When You're Breastfeeding and What If You Can't
Clare Byam-Cook (Vermilion)

The Nursing Mother's Companion
Kathleen Huggins (Harvard Common Press)

Twins!: Pregnancy, Birth and the First Year of Life
Connie Agnew, Alan Klein (HarperCollins)

Mothering Multiples: Breastfeeding & Caring for Twins or More
Karen Gromada (La Leche League International)

Paris Pas Cher
Anne and Alain Riou (Seuil)

Bien Naître à Paris et dans sa region
(Parigramme)

OTHER VOCABULARY

Antenatal/prenatal check . . . . *L'examen/la consultation prénatale*
.... weeks pregnant . . . . *L'aménorrhée de .... semaines*
Abdominal palpation . . . . *L'examen abdominal*
Amniocentesis . . . . *Une amniocentèse*
Amniotic fluid . . . . *Le liquide amniotique*
Blood pressure. . . . . *La tension artériélle*
Cervical smear. . . . . *Le frottis du col*
Chorionic Villus Sample/CVS. . . . . *La chorioncentèse*
Date of conception. . . . . *La date de grossesse (DG)*
Delivery date . . . . *La date de l'accouchement prévue (DAP)*
Embryo. . . . . *L'embryon*
Engaged head . . . . *La tête engagée*
Fertilisation. . . . . *La fécondation*
Foetal movements . . . . *Les mouvements actifs (MA)*
Foetus . . . . *Le foetus*
Head (breech/transverse) presentation . . . . *La présentation céphalique (par le siège/transverse)*
Head down. . . . . *La tête en bas*
Heartbeat. . . . . *L'activité cardiaque*

PBN

Last period . . . . *Les dernières règles (DR)*
Long/closed cervix . . . . *Le col long/fermé*
Medical/obstetric history . . . . *Les intécédents médicaux/obstétricaux*
Pelvimetry . . . . *La radiopelvimétrie*
Pregnancy test . . . . *Le test de grossesse*
Pregnant . . . . *Enceinte*
Short cervix . . . . *Le col raccourci*
To be weighed . . . . *Se peser*
To take blood pressure . . . . *Prendre la tension*
Triplets . . . . *Les triplets*
Twin pregnancy . . . . *La grossesse gémellaire*
Twins . . . . *Les jumeaux(m)/jumelles(f)*
Ultrasound scan/sonogram . . . . *Une échographie*
Urine sample . . . . *Un échantillon d'urine*
Vaginal examination . . . . *Le toucher vaginal*
Vaginal swab . . . . *Le prélèvement vaginal*
Weight gain . . . . *La prise de poids*
X-ray . . . . *La radio(graphie)*

Blood Tests . . . . *L'analyse/le bilan sanguin*

Alfafetoprotein (AFP) . . . . *Alfafétoprotéine*
Anaemia . . . . *L'anémie*
Antibodies . . . . *Les anticorps*
Blood group . . . . *Le groupe sanguin*
Blood sample . . . . *La prise de sang*
Blood sugar level . . . . *La glycémie*
Haemoglobin . . . . *L'hémoglobine*
Hepatitis . . . . *L'hépatite (Hbs)*
HIV (AIDS) . . . . *HIV (SIDA)*
Rhesus factor . . . . *Le facteur Rhésus*
Rubella (German Measles) . . . . *La rubéole*
Screening . . . . *Le dépistage*
Syphilis . . . . *La syphilis*
Toxoplasmosis . . . . *La toxoplasmose*

Discomforts . . . . *Les inconvénients*

Cramps . . . . *Les tiraillements*
Fainting . . . . *Les évanouissements*
Haemorrhoids/piles . . . . *Les hémorroides*
Incontinence . . . . *L'incontinence (urinaire)*
Indigestion/heartburn . . . . *Les brûlures gastriques*
Insomnia . . . . *Les troubles du sommeil*
Itchy skin . . . . *Les démangeaisons*
Morning sickness . . . . *Les nausées/vomissements*
Oedema/swelling . . . . *L'odème/les gonflements*
Pain (abdominal/back) . . . . *La douleur (abdominale/lombaire)*

Pain on urinating . . . . *Les brûlures en urinant*
Painful ligaments . . . . *Les douleurs ligumentaires*
Stinging . . . . *Les picotements*
Stretch marks. . . . . *Les vergetures*
To swell up. . . . . *Engler/gonfler*
Vaginal discharge. . . . . *Les pertes vaginales*
Varicose veins . . . . *Les varices*

Complications . . . . *Les complications*
Bleeding (heavy) . . . . *Les saignements (abondants)*
Diabetes. . . . . *Le diabète*
Diabetic . . . . *Diabétique*
Ectopic pregnancy . . . . *La grossesse extra-utérine (GEU)*
Fungal infection . . . . *Les mycoses*
Glucose (in urine) . . . . *La glucosurie*
High blood pressure. . . . . *L'hypertension*
Low lying placenta/placenta praevia . . . . *La placenta bas inséré/placenta praevia*
Miscarriage . . . . *La fausse couche*
Pre-eclampsia/toxaemia of pregnancy . . . . *La pré-éclampsie/la toxémie gravidique*
Protein/albumin (in urine). . . . . *La protéinurie*
Termination of pregnancy/abortion . . . . *L'interruption voluntaire de grossesse (IVG)/L'avortement*
Threatened premature birth. . . . . *Le ménace d'accouchement prématuré*
Urinary infection. . . . . *Une infection urinaire*
Water retention . . . . *La retention d'eau*

Treatment/Medication. . . . . *Les medicaments*
Anti-spasmodic . . . . *Un anti-spasmodique*
Injection . . . . *La piqûre/l'injection*
Pessary . . . . *L'ovule*
Prescription . . . . *Une ordonnance*
Reimbursable by Social Security. . . . . *Prise en charge par la Securité Social*
Suppository . . . . *Le suppositoire*
Tablets . . . . *Les comprimés*
Thermometer . . . . *Le thermomètre*

Birth preparation. . . . . *La préparation à l'accouchement*
Breathing (deep) . . . . *La respiration (complète)*
Midwife (independent) . . . . *La sage-femme (libérale)*
Pregnancy exercises . . . . *La gymnastique prénatale*
Psychoprophylaxis/Lamaze method . . . . *L'accouchement sans douleur/La préparation classique*
To relax . . . . *Se détendre/se décontracter/se relaxer*
To stretch. . . . . *S'étendre*
Water exercise. . . . . *La gymnastique aquatique*
Yoga. . . . . *Le yoga*

PBN

Labour .... *Le travail*

Breaking of the waters...........................	*La rupture du sac amniotique*
Breathe in/out!................................	*Inspirez/expirez!*
Breathing	*La respiration*
Contractions.................................	*Les contractions*
Crowning	*L'apparition de la tête*
Delivery (second stage).........................	*L'expulsion*
Delivery of placenta (third stage).................	*La délivrance (du placenta)*
Dilation (first stage)	*La dilatation*
Early labour	*Le pré-travail*
Effaced cervix	*Le col effacé*
False labour................................	*Le faux travail*
Full dilation.................................	*La dilatation complète*
Home birth	*L'accouchement à domicile*
Multiple birth................................	*La naissance multiple*
Pain (tolerable)..............................	*La douleur (supportable)*
Painless	*Sans douleur*
Pant!......................................	*Soufflez!*
Premature labour............................	*L'accouchement prématuré*
Push!	*Poussez!*
Relax!.....................................	*Décontractez-vous!*
Soft cervix	*Le col souple*
The 'show'	*La perte du bouchon muqueux*
To cut the cord..............................	*Couper le cordon*
To give birth	*Accoucher*
To rub/massage	*Frotter/masser*

In hospital/clinic .... *A la maternité*

Birthing chair	*La chaise obstétricale*
Birthing pool................................	*La baignoire*
Catheter (for bladder)	*Le tuyau/catheter (la sonde urinaire)*
Delivery table...............................	*La table d'accouchement*
Electronic monitoring (continuous)	*Le monitoring (continu)*
Enema	*Le lavement*
Epidural	*La péridurale*
Fetal scalp monitor	*La sonde d'enregistrement/le scalp*
Gas & air (inhaled pain-killer)	*Le gas/l'analgésie par inhalation*
Glucose (in drip)	*Le sérum glucosé*
Induction (for convenience)	*Le déclenchement (de confort)*
Intravenous drip (routine)......................	*La perfusion (systématique)*
Labour/birth room............................	*La salle de travail*
Natural birth room	*La salle nature*
Oxytocin...................................	*Les oxytociques*
Pain relief..................................	*L'analgésie*
To break the waters	*Percer la poche d'eau*
To induce labour	*Provoquer/déclencher l'accouchement*

To lie down. . . . . *S'allonger/se coucher*
To shave. . . . . *Raser*
You are .... cms dilated . . . . *Vous êtes à ... cms de dilatation*
You will deliver soon . . . . *Vous allez bientôt accoucher*

Medical Interventions . . . . *Les interventions médicales*
A (small) tear . . . . *La déchirure (simple)*
Abnormal presentation. . . . . *La mauvaise présentation*
Caesarian section . . . . *La césarienne*
Episiotomy . . . . *Une épisiotomie*
Foetal distress . . . . *La souffrance foetale*
Forceps . . . . *Les forceps/les cuillères/les fers*
General anaesthetic. . . . . *L'anésthesie génerale*
Haemorrage. . . . . *Un hémorragie*
Lithotomy position . . . . *La position gynécologique*
Spinal anaesthetic . . . . *La rachis-anésthesie (péridurale??)*
Stirrups. . . . . *Les étriers*
Stitches . . . . *Les points de suture/les fils*
To stitch . . . . *Recoudre*
Vacuum extractor/ventouse . . . . *La ventouse*
Wound/scar . . . . *La cicatrice*

After the birth . . . . *Les suites de couches*
Afterpains. . . . . *Les contractions*
Baby blues . . . . *La dépression des accouchées/les blues*
Clots. . . . . *Les caillots*
Discharge. . . . . *Un écoulement*
Healing (of stitches). . . . . *La cicatrisation*
Lochia . . . . *Les lochies/saignements*
Nursery . . . . *La nurserie*
Painkiller . . . . *Un analgésique*
Physiotherapist . . . . *La kinésithérapeute*
Physiotherapy sessions . . . . *Les séances de kinésithérapie*
Salt bath. . . . . *Le bain d'eau salée*
Sanitary pad. . . . . *La serviette hygiénique*
Shrinking of uterus. . . . . *L'involution de l'utérus*
Sleeping pill . . . . *Le somnifère*
To firm up the stomach . . . . *Durcir le ventre*
To get up . . . . *Se lever*
To take temperature. . . . . *Prendre la température*
To tone up the pelvic floor . . . . *Raffermir le périnée*
Visiting times . . . . *Les heures de visite*

PBN

Useful phrases .... *Phrases*

Can I choose my position for birth?................. *Est-ce que je pourrais choisir la position d'accouchement?*

Can I deliver in a squatting (standing) position? .... *Est-ce que vous faites l'accouchement accroupi (debout)?*

Can I get up?................................. *Pourrais-je me lever?*

Can I move around? .... *Pourrais-je me déplacer?*

Can my husband/partner
be with me for a Caesarian under epidural? .... *Est-ce que mon mari/partenaire pourrait asister à une césarienne sous péridurale?*

Contractions are getting stronger .... *Les contractions deviennent de plus en plus fortes*

I have the urge to bear down....................... *J'ai envie de pousser*

I want to be more upright......................... *Je voudrais être assise/plus droite/rélevee*

I would like some pain relief .... *Je voudrais un analgésie*

I would like to be on my side..................... *Je voudrais me mettre sur le côté*

My contractions are coming every .. minutes .... *J'ai des contractions toutes les ... minutes*

My waters have broken .... *J'ai perdu les eaux*

What are the benefits?........................... *Quel en serait le bénéfice?*

What are the risks? .... *Quels en sont les risques?*

What do you have other than an epidural? .... *Qu'est-ce que vous proposez à part la péridurale?*

When can I go home? .... *Quand pourrais-je rentrer chez moi?*

Will I be monitored? (continuously) .... *Est-ce que j'aurai le monitoring (continu)?*

Will I be shaved?.............................. *Est-ce que vous rasez systématiquement?*

Will it make me sleepy?.......................... *Est-ce que cela va m'endormir?*

THE BABY . . . . *LE BEBE*

Newborn procedures . . . . *Le nouveau-né*
Apgar score . . . . *Le test d'Apgar*
Bandage . . . . *Le pansement*
Blood test (heel prick) . . . . *Le prélèvement de sang*
Circumcision . . . . *La circoncision*
Cord care . . . . *Les soins de l'ombilic*
Eye drops . . . . *Le collyre*
Guthrie test (PKU) . . . . *Le dépistage de l'hyperphenylaninémie*
Suctioning airways . . . . *L'aspiration*
Thyroid test . . . . *Le dépistage de l'hypothyroidie*
Vitamin K . . . . *La vitamine K*

Baby care . . . . *Les soins du bébé*
Breathing . . . . *La respiration*
Creases . . . . *Les plis*
Constipated . . . . *Constipé*
Cradle cap . . . . *Les croutes de lait*
Damp/wet . . . . *Mouillé*
Diarrhoea . . . . *La diarrhée*
Growth . . . . *La croissance*
Infant (0-3 months) . . . . *Le nourisson*
Meconium . . . . *Le méconium*
Nappy/diaper rash . . . . *Les fesses rouges/l'érythème fessier*
Spots . . . . *Les boutons*
Stools/bowel movements . . . . *Les selles*
To bathe . . . . *Donner un bain/faire la toilette*
To change nappy/diaper . . . . *Changer la couche*
To choke . . . . *S'étouffer*
To clean . . . . *Nettoyer*
To cry . . . . *Pleurer*
To hiccough . . . . *Hoqueter*
To rock . . . . *Bercer*
To rub/massage . . . . *Frotter/masser*
To scream . . . . *Crier*
To sneeze . . . . *Eternuer*
To Vomit . . . . *Vomir*
To weigh . . . . *Peser*
Weight gain . . . . *La prise de poids*

Breast (bottle) feeding . . . . *L'allaitment maternel (au biberon)*
A feed . . . . *Une tétée*
Baby milk/formula . . . . *Le lait infantile/la formule*
Bottle . . . . *Le bibéron*
Bottle warmer . . . . *Le chauffe-bibéron*

Colostrum. . . . . *Le colostrum*
Complementary feed . . . . *Le biberon supplémentaire/le complément*
Cracks (in nipples) . . . . *Les crevasses*
Demand feeding. . . . . *L'allaitment à la démande*
Dummy/pacifier . . . . *La sucette (la tetine)*
Electric breast pump . . . . *Un tire-lait (électrique)*
Engorgement . . . . *L'engorgement*
Inverted nipples . . . . *Les mamelons (ombiliques)*
Milk coming in . . . . *La montée du lait*
Natural shaped teat . . . . *La tétine physiologique*
Nipple shields. . . . . *Les bouts de sein*
Nursing bra . . . . *Le soutien-gorge d'allaitement*
Room temperature. . . . . *La température ambiante*
Teat/bottle nipple . . . . *La tétine*
Thrush (oral/nipple) . . . . *La candidose, le muguet*
To bottle-feed. . . . . *Donner le biberon*
To breastfeed. . . . . *Allaiter*
To position the baby. . . . . *Mettre le bébé au sein*
To sterilise . . . . *Stériliser*
To suckle . . . . *Téter*
To wean . . . . *Sévrer*
To wind/burp. . . . . *Faire le rot*
Weaning. . . . . *Le sévrage*

Useful Phrases . . . . *Phrases*

Can I give my baby a bath?. . . . . *Puis-je lui faire son bain?*
Can the baby go to the nursery?. . . . . *Le bébé peut-il aller à la nurserie*
Can the baby stay with me at night?. . . . . *Est-ce que le bébé peut rester avec moi pendant la nuit?*
Can you help me position the baby?. . . . . *Pourriez-vous m'aider a mettre le bébé au sein?*
He hasn't put on weight. *Il n'a pas pris de poids*
I Do not want my baby to have a bottle. . . . . *Je ne veux pas qu'on donne des compléments à mon bébé*
I'd like to put the baby straight to the breast . . . . *Je voudrais mettre le bébé au sein tout de suite*
I'd like to see the doctor/pediatrician . . . . *Je voudrais voir le médicin/le pédiatre*
I'm going to bottle feed . . . . *Je vais lui donner le biberon*
I'm going to breast feed. . . . . *Je vais allaiter mon bébé*
My breasts are engorged. *J'ai les seins engorgés*
My nipples are sore . . . . *J'ai mal aux mamelons*
Please bring the baby to me for night feeds . . . . *Pouvez-vous m'amener le bébé la nuit pour l'allaiter?*
The baby is (not) feeding well . . . . *Le bébé (ne) tete (pas) bien*
The baby is hungry . . . . *Le bébé a faim*
The baby is not well positioned . . . . *Le bébé est mal mis au sein*
The baby's weight is fine . . . . *Le bébé a un bon poids*
To sleep on side/on back/on front . . . . *Dormir sur le côté/sur le dos/à plat ventre*

Shopping

Compiled and edited by Rowena de Clermont-Tonnerre, with contributions from Meg Cutts

Paris offers a multitude of possibilities for shoppers, from grand department stores and specialist boutiques to small family-run shops and outdoor markets. There are numerous guidebooks available to help you make the most of your Parisian shopping experience, whether you are looking for *haute couture*, antiques or the best French foods.

However, if you are shopping while pregnant, or have recently moved to Paris with young children, you will probably want to save time and head straight to the shops where you can stock up on essential items for your family. In the first part of this chapter, you will find loads of information pertinent to shopping for a family in and around Paris, as well as by mail order and Internet.

Then, in the second half of the chapter, the Shopping Directory provides useful addresses for baby equipment, children's clothes, shoes, haircuts and so on, including details for each of the stores cited in the first half of the chapter.

BABY EQUIPMENT

Baby equipment, such as high chairs, baby baths, car seats, cots and pushchairs, can be found in a number of different types of shops in France. There are several stores that specialise in "baby paraphernalia" (*puériculture*), some of which also sell clothes, as well as department stores, mail order and Internet shops. Natalys is one of the best known chains selling baby equipment, clothes and maternity wear. The hypermarkets (such as Auchan, Carrefour, Leclerc) also stock a selection of baby products: pushchairs, cots, car seats, etc. The prices may be lower but you would not get the attentive and knowledgeable service of the specialist shops. Supermarkets also sell bottles, nappies, changing mats and other basic equipment. You may also want to visit Toys "R" Us who, although toy specialists, stock a good range of baby equipment.

Equipping yourself for a baby can be expensive: take advantage of any discount card (*carte de fidélité*) schemes the shops may offer. Many of the stores stock the same brands, so shop around for the best prices. A number of shops have a birth list (*liste de naissance*) service (similar to a "wedding registry") for clothes and baby equipment. Delivery may be free if you spend over a certain amount.

One item of equipment not widely seen elsewhere is the Buggy or Kiddy Board, a small rolling platform which attaches to the back of baby's pushchair for his older sibling to stand on for short journeys. This is available through the Graine d'Eveil catalogue.

Consumer Information

Before making any purchase, make sure that the item bears the NF (*Norme Française*) or EN (European) mark (or BS if buying British products). This is a certificate of safety and quality. The products are rigorously tested over and above the necessary legal safety limits by the LNE (*Laboratoire National d'Essais*) for AFNOR (*l'Association Française de Normalisation*, ⌨www.afnor.fr). The phrase *conforme aux exigences de sécurité* must appear on all items of baby equipment that have been officially approved. Before buying any expensive item (pushchairs, car seats, etc.) consider checking a consumer magazine for comments on the product. *Que Choisir* is equivalent to "Which" magazine in the UK and "Consumer Reports" in the USA. It is also worth looking at baby care magazines as they often run "tried and tested" features to help you select items of equipment.

Repairs

Also check the shop's policy on repairs (*réparation*)

and guarantees (*garantie*). A brand new pushchair will generally be covered under guarantee for one or two years. If, however, after this time, repairs are needed, try your local cobbler (*cordonnier*) for simple stitching work. If this does not suffice, then the manufacturer may suggest you post the pushchair to them for repairing (e.g. Maclaren's repair centre in France is in Meaux).

Nursery Furniture

Most of the shops selling baby equipment also sell nursery furniture such as cots and changing tables. The large department stores and several smaller shops in and around Paris sell "designer" ranges of furniture and nursery decoration. Many of the mail order catalogues, including La Redoute and Vertbaudet, also feature various co-ordinating ranges of furniture for children's bedrooms and play areas.

If you are looking for budget furniture, IKEA furniture stores (there are numerous stores in the Paris

Shopping

region) have a range of inexpensive cots, children's beds and bunks with mattresses, bedding and child-sized furniture. They also stock children's cutlery and crockery, baby baths and potties as well as a large selection of toys. Or try one of the larger out-of-town furniture warehouse stores such as Conforama or Fly (consult the *Pages Jaunes* for the store nearest to you).

Disposable Nappies

It is possible to save money when buying nappies by buying in bulk. The nappies are often unbranded, but are produced by major nappy manufacturers in France. Try Bébé Cash or Baby Couches. For information on reusable nappies (☞Living).

Safety Equipment

Chains such as Aubert, Natalys and Toys "R" Us, large department stores and the supermarkets Auchan and Carrefour sell safety equipment items such as electric socket protectors, locks, security gates, etc. IKEA sells a good range of drawer and cupboard locks, electric socket protectors, non-slip materials, security gates, etc. Hardware/home improvement stores like BHV, Leroy Merlin and Castorama carry security items pertaining to electricity, gas and fire such as smoke/gas detectors.

◀)) **TIP**

When shopping for a pushchair for a baby who will live in Paris, it is wise to take public transportation needs into account and give it a thorough "road test" in the shop. Make sure that you choose a pushchair narrow enough to fit through *métro* turnstiles or into small lifts and light enough to carry up and down stairs, and if it is collapsible, make sure you can fold it with ease.

Speciality stores in Paris that sell safety equipment include L'Avenue des Bébés and La Do Ré. Safety equipment can also be ordered from many of the popular mail order companies, such as La Redoute, 3 Suisses, Vertbaudet and Graine d'Eveil. Check their latest catalogues for further information.

Car Seats

It is illegal and dangerous to carry a child without proper restraint in the car. For further information in French, go to the website for *La Prévention Routière* (🖳www.preventionroutiere.asso.fr) to download a brochure called *L'enfant en voiture*. For information in English on choosing and fitting a child car sear as well as the legal requirements for different countries, visit the website 🖳www.childcarseats.org.uk. The site is endorsed by The Royal Society for the Prevention of Accidents, a British registered charity involved in the promotion of safety.

Taxis are obliged by law to accept car seats. Some airlines will accept the first stage car seat as a suitable form of restraint – be sure to request either an extra seat or bulkhead seating in order to have space to put the seat. If renting a car, some rental companies will also hire out seats suitable for your child.

Understanding the label
Approved (*homologué*) car seats that conform to European norms are marked with the letter E (in a circle) followed by a number between one and twenty-one (indicating in which EU country the car seat was approved).

Types of car seats
Car seats are sold according to the size and weight of the child; the ages indicated are merely guidelines. Be wary of second-hand car seats, since you should never reuse a seat that has been in a crash, or one that is cracked, has missing parts, or does not have a label.

First stage car seat (*Groupe 0*, under 10kg; *Groupe 0+*, under 13kg): Rearward facing car seats can be used either in the rear of the car or in the front pas-

What do you bring back from home?

Are you planning a trip home soon? You might be interested to know what MESSAGE members like to bring back to France from trips home – either because they cannot easily find the items here, or the items are much cheaper back home.

No matter where you are from, you will probably want to bring back some books (new and second-hand) and magazines for children and adults, English-language toys and board games, DVDs and CDs.

The **British** like to fill up their car boots with tins of Heinz and Campbell's soups, cheddar cheese, Branston's pickle, parsnips, deodorant, mint sauce, salad cream, Cadbury's chocolate, Marmite, cream crackers, mango chutney, underwear (mostly from M&S), Pim's, Ready Brek, Infacol, golden syrup and all types of biscuits from digestives and ginger nuts to chocolate hobnobs. And do not forget some Sudocrem to guard against nappy rash.

Americans claim to pack extra suitcases with as many of the following items as possible: candy, deodorant, underwear, flavoured coffee, electronic goods, chili powder for Texas-style chili, baking soda, cranberry juice, A&D ointment for nappy rash, stain remover, raisins in small snack boxes, buttermilk pancake mix, plain Cheerios, grits, craft items (stickers, glue, sequins, etc.), children's vitamins, ranch dressing powder mix, Pam cooking spray and cans of frosting.

Canadians bring back maple syrup (of course!) as well as sugar-free peanut butter, chocolate chips for baking, baking soda and powder, Reese's peanut butter cups, Jell-O, Trident chewing gum, Johnson & Johnson and Gerber baby products, Neocitron and popcorn seasoning.

Among the items that make the long journey in MESSAGE suitcases from **Australia** are vegemite, aluminium free deodorant, fluoride free toothpaste and kids' multivitamin chewable tablets.

MESSAGE families from **Singapore** bring back tiger balm plasters, laksa paste, sambal, dried mango, Chinese and Japanese teas, ginseng powder, Kicap black sauce, Keropok dry fish crackers, Goodaire air purifiers and solutions, Chinese herbs for soups, Chinese peanut brittle candy and cotton T-shirts.

Meanwhile the **South African** members stock up on butternut squash, cooking spray, Pronutro porridge, Braai salt, Bennetts cream, Woolworths underwear, Biltong, formula for 1+ in powder form, Rooibos tea, peppadews and Vidol (for teething).

Some of the items mentioned above can now be found in Paris – although they are generally more expensive here than at home. Check out the Shopping Directory for the addresses of shops selling international food or, if you are a member of MESSAGE, look at the discussion forums on the MESSAGE website for member recommendations.

senger seat, unless a front passenger air bag is fitted. Even if you do not own a car, a first stage seat is a good idea as apart from safely restraining your baby in a car (perhaps a taxi or friend's car), rearward facing car seats have become quite versatile. They can be used in the home as a rocking seat and as a way of carrying your baby around. Some also have the advantage of serving as the top part of a pushchair.

Second stage car seat (*Groupe* 1): The second stage car seat is generally for children aged between nine months and four years (9kg to 18kg). All car seats for older children are front-facing.

Third stage car seat (*Groupe* 2) (*rehausseur*): The third stage is a booster seat for a child aged four to eight years (15kg to 25kg). A booster seat does not have a harness but provides the extra height, which ensures that the child is positioned correctly in relation to the three-point seat belt of the car.

Equipment Hire

If you are looking for a scale to weigh your newborn baby for the first few months, or you have children visiting for a few days and need an extra high chair or an extra baby bed, the easiest and most economical solution may be to rent the items you need.

Baby Shows in Paris

The baby show *Le salon des Futurs Parents et du Petit Enfance* is held twice a year in Paris – in March at Paris Expo at Porte de Versailles and in October at the Parc Floral near Porte de Vincennes. This is a good opportunity to check out new products from leading baby equipment manufacturers, to try items such as car seats and to take advantage of special promotions. There is an entrance fee but you can buy tickets at a reduced rate if you book in advance online. Young children can go in for free. There are good baby-changing facilities, a baby-friendly restaurant and a play area. For more information, go to ⌨www.salonbaby.com

 TIP

Although you might prefer to purchase your own electric breast pump (and can do so at Natal Service), keep in mind that renting might make more sense economically, as rentals are reimbursed by Social Security (if you have a prescription from your baby's pædiatrician).

Every pharmacy can organise the rental of scales (*balance/pèse bébé*) - electronic or with weights (*électronique ou mécanique*) - and breast pumps (*tire-lait*). Be sure to let the pharmacist know if you want a specific model of breast pump. They will probably have to order the items in so you might have to wait 24 hours before you can pick them up.

Natal Service also rents a broad range of baby equipment and will deliver six days a week.

Your doctor, clinic or hospital will inform you about what can be reimbursed by Social Security and may recommend rental companies. In order to be reimbursed, you will need a prescription (*ordonnance*) (☞Administration, ☞Health and Medicine).

When hiring equipment you should verify the following:

- Does the shop deliver? (*est-ce que vous livrez?*) How long does it take? (*quels sont les délais de livraison?*)
- At what price? (*prix de livraison?*)
- Do you need to pay a deposit? (*une caution*). In most cases, you pay a deposit equivalent to the value of the item you rent. Some shops will ask for a cheque and will not cash it unless needed, while other shops will cash your cheque and return the money at the end of the rental period (*chèque*

encaissé et restitué).

- How can I pay: cash (espèces), cheque or credit card (carte bancaire)? Some stores do not accept credit cards, and some request bank account details (RIB or Relevé d'Identité Bancaire) in order to debit your bank account directly.

For details of companies that rent out equipment in Paris and the suburbs, consult the Shopping Directory.

Second-hand

The free English-language magazine FUSAC sometimes lists furniture and equipment (including nursery items and baby equipment) for sale by individuals. French-style jumble sales (garage sales), called vide-greniers or brocantes are especially popular in the spring and autumn. You can contact your local mairie to see when your area may be holding one or buy the magazine Aladin at any newsstand for information on dates and locations. Also look out for notices announcing sales in your local library, church or PMI (child health clinic). For rock-bottom prices, shop at the thrift shops run by charities such as Emmaüs (☞Organisations and Charities). If you are a member of MESSAGE, also check the MESSAGE magazine and website for Bring and Buy sales and items for sale by members.

CLOTHES

Children's Clothes

To newly-arrived expatriates, the price of children's clothes in Paris can seem exorbitant. However, alongside the many designer boutiques, there are also many ranges of cheap and cheerful clothes, as well as moderately priced good quality outfits. One advantage of Paris and the suburbs is the proliferation of factory/stock shops (boutiques d'usine, les stocks).

Collections for autumn/winter and spring/summer appear surprisingly early in the shops. Stocks can sell quickly (and are not necessarily renewed), especially just before the school term starts in September (la rentrée). Ask to be put on a shop's mailing list so you know in advance when the new season's clothes arrive, or when the sales start. Many shops hold regular promotions, but the main sales are held twice-yearly, at the end of June and at the beginning of January.

Check the shop's policy on returning or exchanging items if you are unsure about sizes (peut-on se faire rembourser ou échanger les articles?). Take an item of clothing with you that you know is a good fit and measure it up against a prospective purchase. Sizes can vary enormously between shops and manufacturers.

You are more likely to find expensive boutiques in residential areas like the 6th, 7th, 8th, 16th and 17th arrondissements, and less expensive shops in the 10th, 14th, 19th, and 20th arrondissements. The various suburban town centres around Paris such as Neuilly-sur-Seine, Levallois, Vincennes, Boulogne Billancourt, Versailles and St Germain-en-Laye also offer a good selection of clothes shops for children and there are many purpose built indoor shopping centres (centres commerciaux) outside Paris, many of which are listed in the Shopping Directory.

Supermarkets/Hypermarkets

It is worth investigating chains that have their own brands, such as Monoprix, Auchan, Leclerc and Carrefour for children's clothes. Prices are low, quality is good and outfits range from purely practical dungarees and T-shirts to stylish raincoats and pretty smocked dresses. These are also good places to stock up on underwear (Absorba, Petit Bateau and store brands).

Department Stores

The *grands magasins* of Paris (Galeries Lafayette, Printemps, BHV, Le Bon Marché) all have baby and children's departments. They all offer a choice of baby equipment and accessories (both French and imported) and sell clothes for babies and children. These tend to be in the medium to expensive price range, but offer a good choice for special outfits or presents.

Bargain Hunting

Stock Shops

Stock shops (*les stocks*) are a good source for factory seconds or the previous season's collections. There are a few in Paris, whereas the out-of-town factory centres (*usine centers*) listed in the Shopping Directory have several in one location. There are also various shops (especially in Paris) that sell seconds or leftover collections from various different designers (*magasins de dégriffe*). For addresses see *Le Paris des Touts Petits* or *Le Guide des Magasins d'Usine,* a useful guide to factory shops throughout France.

Troyes

Troyes, 150km east of Paris, is the capital of the French clothing industry: 30% of children's wear and 40% of babywear produced in France is manufactured there. There are over 150 textile firms around the city, and there is a large selection of factory shops open to the public. Among the labels produced there are Absorba, Aigle, Blanc Bleu, Burberry, Catimini, Mod 8, Nike, Sergent Major and Timberland, as well as a large selection of adult labels (Alain Manoukian, Armani, Cerruti, Kenzo). Prices drop even further during the bi-annual sales. You need a car to visit them as there are several sites. Alternatively, there is a coach service running from Place de la Bastille to the factory shopping centres in Troyes every Saturday (contact Eva Voyages by telephone (03.25.82.82.00) or look at www.eva-voyages.com for further information).

Second-hand

Second-hand shops provide a popular way of selling outgrown children's and adult clothing as well as offering designer outfits at more reasonable prices. A consignment shop (*dépôt-vente*) only accepts clothes in good condition, and usually from recent collections. Those specialising in children's clothes also sell used toys and baby equipment. Look for one near you, or consult the guides listed in the Other Resources section. It is also possible to borrow toys from a toy library (*ludothèque*) (☞Activities).

A chain of cheap second-hand clothing shops called Guérrisol operates in some *arrondissements*. Many items cost less than €10. If you are willing to dig through bins there are real bargains to be found.

Street Markets

Outdoor markets offer clothes at good prices if you look around. They often have seconds of Petit Bateau and other well known names and are also useful for gloves, hats, etc. in winter at reduced prices.

Private Sales (ventes privées)

Certain big-name brands will sell off old stock at reduced prices through discreet locations, or via their websites. Although access to such sales will often be only by invitation or limited to employees, you might be able to get on the distribution list or learn about a sale through word of mouth. See, for example, www.venteprivee.com, www.espacecatherinemax.com, www.espace-ngr.com. And if you are a MES-SAGE members, try posting a request on the MES-SAGE forums for information regarding upcoming sales, or if you need a sponsor (*parrain*) for a particular sale.

MATERNITY WEAR

You will probably find that your maternity wardrobe consists of a mixture of those items in your present wardrobe that will adjust to your growing abdomen, plus some specific maternity wear to get through the later months. For inexpensive items in large sizes try Etam, Kiabi, Promod, Camaieu and Pimkie - all chain stores found in most major shopping districts in and around Paris. For affordable maternity basics try shops such as H&M and C&A.

For a working wardrobe or a special event, you will probably want to go to a specialist maternity wear shop that offers a selection of good quality and elegant suits, trousers and dresses. Natalys is a good place to start (but the shops called La Maison de Natalys do not carry maternity clothes). Many of the maternity wear shops listed in the Shopping Directory have more than one outlet in and around Paris and/or concessions in the main department stores.

Second-hand Maternity Wear

There are also second-hand/consignment shops (*dépôt-ventes*) that specialise in maternity clothes. This is a good solution to finding quality garments at affordable prices and clothes in very good condition can be consigned for sale when you no longer need them. If you are a member of MESSAGE, check the classifieds on the MESSAGE website and magazine for members selling second hand maternity wear.

Maternity Underwear

For maternity tights, briefs, bras, swimsuits and support belts, try Euroform, Natalys, Formes and the department stores. Any of these shops should provide a fitting service. Your local lingerie shop may also have items in stock or can order items for you.

Maternity wear, including maternity underwear, is also available from a range of French and international mail order companies. Make sure that you know your size and check the returns policy before ordering from a catalogue or through a website.

◀)) TIP

You should be measured regularly during pregnancy by trained staff as your breasts may increase in size by as much as two bra sizes. Look for a bra that provides good support, preferably with wide shoulder straps and adjusting back to allow for later chest expansion. Front opening nursing bras will make breastfeeding easier. These are available in various designs with zip openings, clips or hooks. Bras in 100% cotton will be the most comfortable and will withstand frequent washes.

Shopping

Bra sizes conversion chart

USA	France	UK	Australia	International
32AA	85A	32A	10AA	70A
32A	85B	32B	10A	70B
32B	85C	32C	10B	70C
32C	85D	32D	10C	70D
32D	85DD	32DD	10D	70E
34AA	90A	34A	12AA	75A
34A	90B	34B	12A	75B
34B	90C	34C	12B	75C
34C	90D	34D	12C	75D
34D	90DD	34DD	12D	75DD
34DD	90E	34E	12DD	75E
36AA	95A	36A	14AA	80A
36A	95B	36B	14A	80B
36B	95C	36C	14B	80C
36C	95D	36D	14C	80D
36D	95DD	36DD	14D	80DD
36DD	95E	36E	14DD	80E
38AA	100A	38A	16AA	85A
38A	100B	38B	16A	85B
38B	100C	38C	16B	85C
38C	100D	38D	16C	85D
38D	100DD	38DD	16D	85DD
38DD	100E	38E	16E	85E
40A	105B	40B	18A	90B
40B	105C	40C	18B	90C
40C	105D	40D	18C	90D
40D	105DD	40DD	18D	90DD
40DD	105E	40E	18DD	90E

Women's clothes size chart

USA	France	UK
6	36	8
8	38	10
10	40	12
12	42	14
14	44	16
16	46	18
18	48	20

CHILDREN'S SHOES

There is a difference in opinion between France, the UK and the USA regarding first footwear. In France, you may be encouraged to put your child into shoes even before he is walking. By contrast, in the UK and the USA, the advice is to wait until your child has been walking for at least six weeks before putting him into shoes. Bare feet are said to be best for the developing foot and shoes are thought to be necessary only to protect feet rather than support them. Ill-fitting shoes can permanently deform feet. Try to find an independent shoe shop that carries a range of brands, giving you a better choice of designs and styles to suit your child's foot. If you are looking for shoes for particularly narrow or wide feet, try Start-Rite, which come in a range of different widths and fittings (available in the larger department stores).

Popular French brand names include: Aster, Babybotte, Kickers, Little Mary, Mod'8 and Pom d'Api. Specialist children's shoe shops include NA! and Till. The chain Petits Petons, which has several outlets in Paris and the suburbs, has a very good range of styles (many of which are seconds or surplus stock from the better-known brands) and makes shopping easier in that all the shoes in each size are the same price. It offers a particularly good selection in the smaller sizes in comparison with other stores.

You can find cheaper prices at certain shops specialising in shoes e.g. La Halle aux Chaussures, which are generally warehouse-sized and found in out-of-town shopping centres (although there are also locations in Paris). Alternatively, many of the mail-order catalogues selling children's clothes also stock shoes at competitive prices, but check the policy on returns before ordering. Consult *Le Paris des Tous-Petits* for further information on individual shops and for details of factory/seconds shops.

French (EU), UK and USA/Canada shoe sizes:

Children :

France	UK	USA / Canada
19	3	3.5
20	4	4.5
21	4.5	5
22	5.5	6
23	6.5	6.5
24	7	7.5
25	7.5	8
26	8.5	9
27	9.5	10
28	10.5	11
29	11.5	12
30	12	12.5
31	12.5	13
32	13.5/0.5	1
33	1	1.5
34	2	2.5
35	2.5	3

French (EU), UK and USA/Canada shoe sizes:

Women:

France	UK	USA / Canada
35	2.5	5
35.5	3	5.5
36	3.5	6
37	4	6.5
37.5	4.5	7
38	5	7.5
38.5	5.5	8
39	6	8.5
40	6.5	9
41	7	9.5
42	7.5	10

French (EU), UK and USA/Canada shoe sizes:

Men:

France	UK	USA / Canada
37.5	4.5	5
38	5	5.5
38.5	5.5	6
39	6	6.5
40	6.5	7
40.5	7	7.5
41	7.5	8
42	8	8.5
42.5	8.5	9
43	9	9.5
44	9.5	10
44.5	10	10.5
45	10.5	11
45.5	-	11.5
46	-	12
47.5	-	13

When buying shoes:

- Have the length and width of both feet measured by a trained fitter
- Choose shoes with square not pointed toes
- There should be at least 1cm of growing room at the end of the shoe
- Shoes should fit snugly around the heel, should have an adjustable fastening across the instep and soles should be flexible
- Leather uppers and linings are best as they allow the foot to breathe and take the shape of the foot
- The fit of the shoe should be checked every two to three months as feet grow in fits and starts

HAIRDRESSERS FOR CHILDREN

Some hairdressers will cut your child's hair free of charge hoping that you, the parent, will get a haircut at the same time. If you choose not to have a haircut yourself, leave a generous tip. The best way to find out about salons that offer this service is through word of mouth.

Specialised hairdressing salons for children have mushroomed all over Paris and slowly spread into the suburbs. See the Shopping Directory or consult Le Paris des Tout-Petits. These salons are usually designed to appeal to children, with colourful seats and mirrors shaped like aeroplanes or animals. Some show videos to keep their young clients entertained and some may offer play areas where siblings can play while waiting. If you are uncertain about communicating, take a picture of the haircut you want for your child or look in the salon brochure.

Some specialised and regular hairdressers will also come to your home. You have to pay an additional standard fee for transport (check in advance), but this might be a good idea if you have several children in need of a haircut. You could invite a friend and her children to make it worthwhile.

MAIL ORDER AND INTERNET

French Mail Order

Ordering from a catalogue (*VPC* or *vente par correspondance*) is extremely popular in France. The range of services available is vast – a selection of addresses specific to family life is listed in the Shopping Directory.

As well as the conventional method of filling in an order form, many companies offer phone and internet services. You can choose between home delivery (*La Poste* or special carrier), 24h/48h delivery, or collection from a central point in your neighbourhood or village (*relais-colis.*) Some companies have a direct delivery gift service (useful for new baby presents).

Smaller catalogues are usually free, but a charge is often made for the larger ones (offset by the first purchase). Once you are on a company's mailing list, you can often benefit from a variety of offers, services and free gifts.

Some of the suppliers below have boutiques in Paris and the suburbs where you can see and try items before purchasing. Look in your telephone directory or check the supplier's website for addresses close to you. You can often find bargains at sale times (June and January).

Conditions for exchanging or returning goods may vary depending on the company, but generally the procedure is very simple. However, when goods are returned, the initial delivery charge is rarely reimbursed.

Internet Shopping

The range of products available over the Internet continues to grow. In addition to the many Internet-only retailers, most well-known chains and department stores now have their own websites providing details of special offers, store locations and often including an on-line catalogue. As with any other form of retailing, prices for the same articles vary enormously from one site to another, and it is always worth shopping around. Of the sites listed in the Shopping Directory, those based outside France all offer international shipping services.

Extra Delivery Charges on items ordered from the USA

Be forewarned that duties are often levied by the French customs service on goods imported from the USA (but not the UK). These extra costs may negate the savings made by ordering from overseas. The imposition of duties is less likely if your package is sent directly to a corporate address. Companies such as Amazon.com and Lands' End have both USA and European sites and you will save unnecessary charges by ordering from the European site.

Books by Internet

Internet bookshops offer a vast selection of books catering for all ages and tastes, and are useful for tracking down rare or out-of-print editions. Prices are often a great deal lower than in traditional bookshops, and substantial savings can be made when placing large orders to offset the shipping costs. Books can usually be returned, but the shipping cost is not refunded. To save on delivery, first check the French online booksellers, such as Amazon.fr or fnac.fr, which offer a significant number of English books and may have what you are looking for. Otherwise, note that sites which operate out of the UK often stock the same books as their parent USA sites and delivery is usually quicker and cheaper, especially as there is no import duty.

TOYS AND CRAFTS

You can find most of the popular brands of toys in France: Duplo, Chicco, Fisher-Price, Lego, Little Tikes, Mattel, Playmobil, Tomy etc. French makes include Berchet, Clairbois, Nathan and Smoby.

Both Toys "R" Us and La Grande Récré stock a large selection of reasonably priced toys, as do most of the supermarket chains (either name or store brands), particularly in the run-up to Christmas. The main department stores in Paris have a good selection of toys, but are slightly more expensive. All these stores have wonderful Christmas window displays and there are sometimes special platforms so that small children can get a closer view. This is a traditional Christmas visit for French children, as is seeing the Christmas lights on Boulevard Haussmann, so they can get busy on Saturday afternoons in the lead-up to Christmas.

Craft supply stores include the Loisirs et Création chain and Rougier & Plé in the 11th arrondissement, as well as the Panduro Hobby website at 💻www.panduro.fr. In addition, Le Bon Marché has a particularly impressive selection of craft material, as do Truffaut and BHV.

Specialist local toy shops can be expensive but may stock unusual, wooden and/or educational toys, games and puzzles. For unusual presents, look for handcrafted wooden toys made in traditional styles from the Alps and Alsace. See *Le Paris des Tout-Petits* for a list of "old-fashioned" toy shops. Popular toy shops in Paris include Le Ciel est à tout le monde, Il était une fois, Pain d'Epice, Le Bonhomme du bois, Multicubes and Les Cousines d'Alice.

The guide *Paris Pas Cher* lists reasonably priced toy shops. *Le Paris des Tout-Petits* lists where to find particular types of toys: electronic, sporting, scientific, dolls and houses, drawing and art materials, outdoor toys etc., as well as toys by mail order and where to get toys repaired.

Toy Storage

Once your child is crawling (and maybe even before that!) you will probably find that your living space quickly becomes cluttered up with plastic building blocks, soft toys, books and puzzles. IKEA, Habitat and Pier Import all offer a range of colourful storage solutions, ranging from plastic stacking bins to durable wooden toy chests. Alternatively, try The Great Little Trading Company or Blooming Marvellous for ingenious storage ideas.

Toys - Safety Standards and Marks

When choosing a toy, look for the CE symbol denoting the toy complies with certain European Union (EU) safety standards. Toys cannot be manu-factured, imported, sold or given away within the EU without this mark. Any toys which are unsuitable for children under 36 months must be marked accordingly (*ne convient pas aux enfants de moins de 36 mois*) unless there is no possible ambiguity due to the toy's characteristics and functions.

Safety information on French toys and baby equipment is available from the French manufacturers' association:

Fédération Française des Industries Jouet Puériculture
💻 www.fjp.fr
4, rue de Castellane, 75008 Paris
01.53.43.09.10

BOOKSHOPS

If you do not visit your home country very often nor want to come back with your suitcases laden with heavy books, try the many bookshops in and around Paris that carry a range of books in English for children and adults.

Well-established shops on the Right Bank include the British WH Smith and the American bookshops Brentano's and Galignani, all of which also sell newspapers and magazines from the USA and UK, as well as the Red Wheelbarrow Bookstore. On the Left Bank, there is the Abbey Bookshop, and in the western suburbs there is Tridias in Le Vésinet, a typical British family bookshop. The San Francisco Book Co, Shakespeare & Co and Tea and Tattered Pages all offer a wide selection of second-hand books in English. Many bookshops also run events for children and adults (☞Activities).

In addition to these shops which specialise in English-language titles, there are some good French bookshops which have a large selection of books in English such as Attica, Nouveau Quartier Latin and Librairie Albion. The larger shops such as FNAC and Virgin also stock English-language books, although the selection tends to be restricted to current bestsellers and classics.

Many shops offer a discount to students and teachers on presentation of appropriate ID, and offer a general discount card.

FOOD

Supermarkets and Small Shops

Paris has many supermarkets of varying quality and size. Ed, Franprix, G20, Atac, Casino and Monoprix (in roughly ascending order price-wise) are *supermarchés*, while Carrefour, Leclerc and Auchan (located on the edge of Paris and in the suburbs) are *hypermarchés*, i.e. large surface (*grandes surfaces*) supermarkets specializing in cheaper goods and usually including more extensive non-food sections.

All these shops will deliver to your home, which makes life much easier if you do not have a car (or even if you do as parking is never easy in Paris) – or a lift. How deliveries are handled varies from shop to shop, even within the same chain: look for a cashier desk marked *Livraisons* or ask at the front of the shop what the policy is. Most shops will deliver for free above a certain amount spent (anywhere from €80 to €180); otherwise there is a €5 to €10

delivery charge (*frais de livraison*). Monoprix delivers for free regardless of how much you spend if you are pregnant, so be sure to point it out if you are (*Je suis enceinte et je voudrais une livraison gratuite, s'il vous plaît.*). In addition, most shops have an online shopping service that will deliver to your home within a time slot chosen by you when you place your order. If you are at home with a small baby or simply short of time, this is a very useful service.

If you live in a neighbourhood with a good butcher's (*boucherie*), cheese shop (*fromagerie*), grocer's (*épicerie*) and fishmonger (*poissonerie*), you may find it makes more sense to shop at one of the cheaper supermarkets for your dry goods and frequent the individual merchants for the rest of your food. This is a wonderful way to get to know to your neighbourhood and if you become a regular you will find the service in these small shops is incomparable. These merchants know that the only way they can compete with the larger, more convenient (and often cheaper) supermarkets is to provide better quality products and good service. Butchers will cut your meat as you like it, cheesemongers will offer to cut up your raclette cheese into wedges for you and will advise you on which cheeses to include in your fondue, and grocers will point out the fresh new fruits that have just come into season. Fishmongers will also prepare seafood platters (*plateau de fruits de mer*) in season if you order them in advance; they will not only open the oysters and other shellfish but put them on a presentation platter for you with ice. These shops also have one advantage over the major supermarkets in that they are often open on Sundays and holidays until 13h30. You should be aware that butchers with the *chevaline* sign sell horse meat. Some have a helpful little sculpture of a horse to make it obvious, but not all. You may want to purchase a little grocery trolley (*chariot*) to tote your goods home if you shop this way – Rolser is a popular, sturdy brand. All the major department stores carry them, as do most Monoprix stores.

A good range of frozen food, including frozen pureed vegetables, as well as good quality pre-prepared meals, is available from the chain Picard (they sell insulated bags to take your frozen goods home in). You can also order online from 💻www.picard.fr.

Takeaway

Paris does not have the same variety of take-away options as some countries. However, the traditional *traiteurs* are a very good source for a delicious hot meal at short notice. Typically, they have roast meats, potato salad, mashed potatoes, sausages, vegetables – basically all manner of classic French dishes that are easy to carry home and reheat. Aside from the French ones, there are a number of pizza outlets and many Chinese take-away places, though the latter vary enormously in quality. Lastly, a small number of Indian restaurants will make up meals to take away.

Organic Food

The Shopping Directory contains a list of supermarkets that specialise in organic products, which are generally marked *bio*. Les Nouveaux Robinson is a chain of organic supermarkets stocking all manner of organic products. The Naturalia and La Vie Claire chains of health food stores and Monoprix supermarkets also sell organic produce and eco-friendly household products. Several chain-stores such as Auchan, Carrefour and Casino have organic products often stocked in the *rayon diététique*. Brands include Cereal, Bjorg, etc.

Exotic Foods

Open air and covered markets are a good place to look initially for exotic spices and produce. Below are some further sources for ethnic products in Paris.

Indian

Passage Brady in the 10th *arrondissement* has a high concentration of Indian and Pakistani restaurants, as well as a small supermarket carrying everything you will need for an Indian feast. Indian spices, cans of mango, coconut milk, henna, PG-Tips, okra, etc., everything an Indian or anglo-Indian could want. M° Château d'Eau, Strasbourg St. Denis.

Chinese/Thai/Japanese

Paris' traditional Chinatown is in the 13th *arrondissement* near the edge of the city. Wander up the avenue d'Ivry where you will find a number of small

◁))) TIP

Although the merchants generally choose the vegetables or fruit for you, feel free to indicate how ripe or unripe you want the produce to be.

Shopping

shops and the mecca of oriental cooks at no 48: Tang Frères. M° Porte d'Ivry, Porte de Choisy.

North African/Chinese/Thai

The Belleville area of Paris in the 20th *arrondissement* has been the "new Chinatown" since the early 1990s. An exciting mix of North Africa and the orient, the neighbourhood is becoming increasingly hip. It remains a great place to pick up produce and spices and a wonderful source for good authentic oriental restaurants. M° Belleville.

American and British

Since shops specializing in American and British food often have an extremely high mark-up, it is worthwhile keeping an eye out in your local supermarket for your cherished products. Many American and British breakfast cereals and breads are available in the usual supermarkets and a variety of other products - from maple syrup to Heinz beans - show up from time to time as well. Supermarkets are also starting to promote seasonal items in keeping with non-French holidays, for example stocking cranberries around Thanksgiving or pumpkins at Halloween.

Another Source of Information

The *Guide du Routard* guide book series includes a small volume entitled *Paris Exotique* which has an up-to-date list of ethnic restaurants in Paris but also includes information on shops (food and otherwise)

Open Air and Covered Markets

No matter where you live in Paris, you will probably find an open air market or covered market within walking distance of your home. Although they may seem intimidating to the uninitiated, they really are worth visiting. It helps to be able to at least speak a few words of French but often you will find you can get by surprisingly well with hand gestures. In any case, if you become a regular, you will find your French improving as most of the stall keepers will find you a novelty and want to chat.

Grocers' stalls generally have cards above each of the produce bins with the price of the product by piece (*la pièce*) or by weight (per kilogram), the name of the fruit or vegetable (good for your vocabulary) and the origin. One of the delights of early spring is watching for your favourite vegetables as they come first from Morocco, then Spain, then the south of France, until finally you see they are coming from the Paris region and you know you are getting truly fresh local produce. When making your selection, it is not at all uncommon to ask for your vegetables by number, i.e. a dozen carrots if you do not know how many grams that would be. You will also find that one Imperial weight is still familiar to the stall-holders: the pound (*une livre*). If you ask for a pound of vegetables, you will receive just under half a kilogram.

In addition to the fresh quality of the produce, the real advantage of most markets lies in the exotic products available: spicy hot peppers, lemon grass, spices sold by weight etc. Most markets also have at least one or two organic stalls (marked *bio*). In addition, the markets at Batignolles, Brancusi and Raspail are completely organic. Open air markets are generally open two days a week: one weekend day and one day during the week. The hours are from 07h00 to 14h30 during the week and until 15h00 on the weekend. If you have the luxury of being able to shop during the week, you will find it is a lot less busy. To find a market in your neighborhood, go to http://www.paris.fr/fr/marches/ and click on your *arrondissement*.

Shopping

SHOPPING DIRECTORY

The Shopping Directory is intended only as a general guide to the many different types of store that might be useful for Anglophone parents living in Paris and surrounding areas. Nothing can beat visiting the shops in your neighbourhood, talking to friends and, if you are a member of MESSAGE, checking out the discussion forums on the members' only website for recommendations.

Locations and Opening Hours

Stores or shops followed by an asterisk (*) have more than one location, either in Paris or in the suburbs. Due to space restrictions, the contact details given below are only those for a centrally located branch of each shop. Phone the number given for the address of the location nearest you, as well as for further information on opening hours, access and parking. Where possible, website addresses have also been indicated as a useful source of information on locations, services and promotions.

Be warned that many shops are closed on Sundays, Mondays and public holidays. Opening hours may also change during the holiday months of July and August.

For all addresses and details, look in your *Pages Jaunes* (💻www.pagesjaunes.fr). For the addresses of shopping centres and supermarkets look under *Centres commerciaux et grands magasins* and *Supermarchés et hypermarchés*. Annual publications such as *Paris Pas Cher* and *Le Paris des Touts Petits*, as well as monthly parenting magazines, also contain detailed sections on clothes, shoes and baby equipment.

Baby Friendly Locations

Based on evidence to date, Paris does not yet seem to be as baby friendly to shoppers as many other European cities. However, with careful planning, it is usually possible to venture away from home whilst ensuring that your baby's needs can be met.

In general, the larger department stores (Galeries Lafayette, Printemps, etc.) and shopping centres/malls are baby friendly, offering a baby changing area and possibly further facilities. Most of the smaller boutiques and baby equipment shops do not.

When hunting out new places, beware of falling into the trap of thinking that establishments cateriing to

parents will offer baby facilities – or that baby supply stores must have somewhere to breastfeed – it is just not the case! Also, do not assume that the information you get by telephone or at the information desk will always be correct, as staff who do not work in the baby-care department are often completely unaware of the existence of changing facilities.

Baby Equipment (Puériculture)

Aubert*
11 Boulevard Poissonniere, 75002 Paris
M° Grands Boulevards
Wed - Fri 11h00 - 20h00, Sat and Sun 10h00 - 20h00
01.40.39.90.71
0 811 023 024 (general information and catalogue)
💻 www.aubert.fr
In addition to the Paris location, there are over 25 in Ile-de-France. Produces several catalogues a year and sells items through the website.

Autour de Bébé*
Centre commercial des Grandes Terres
78160 Marly le Roi
Mon 14h00 - 19h00, Tues - Sat 10h00 - 19h00
01.39.16.65.05
💻 www.autourdebebe.com

Avenue des Anges
💻 www.avenuedesanges.com
Gifts and gift baskets (including "mix and match" baskets) featuring quality baby items, many of which can be personalised.

L'Avenue des Bébés*
89, rue de Sèvres, 75006 Paris
M° Sèvres Babylone
Mon - Sat 10h00 - 19h00
01.40.26.09.05
💻 www.avenuedesbebes.com
Baby equipment and maternity wear. Good quality at reasonable prices.

Baby Couches

14, avenue du 6 juin 1944, 95190 Goussainville
Mon - Fri 10h00 - 13h00 and 14h00 - 19h00
01.39.88.81.16
🖳 www.babycouches.fr
Specialises in disposable nappies, which can be
ordered on the website. Also sells toys and baby
equipment.

Bébé Cash*

27, rue Picpus, 75012 Paris
M° Nation
Mon - Fri 09h30 - 12h30 and 14h00 - 18h30, Sat
10h00 - 17h00
01.43.43.32.14
Free delivery for orders over a certain amount.
Sells disposable nappies in bulk as well as clothes
and other reasonably priced baby equipment.

Bébé 9*

4, rue Saint-Ferdinand, 75017 Paris
M° Etoile, Ternes, Porte Maillot
Tues - Sat 10h00 - 19h00
01.45.74.48.41
🖳 www.bebe9.com
One shop in Paris and several in Ile-de-France.
Their range includes baby equipment, maternity
wear and baby clothes as well as prams and
strollers for twins.

La Do Ré*

356, rue de Vaugirard, 75015 Paris
M° Convention
Tues - Sat 10h00 - 19h00
01.42.50.26.47
🖳 www.ladore.com
A second store is situated on rue Lambert, also in
the 15th arrondissement.

Le Monde de Bébé *

71, rue du Commerce, 75015 Paris
M° Commerce
01.42.50.34.33
🖳 www.lemondedebebe.com

Natal Services

143 Avenue Felix Faure, 75015 Paris
M° Balard
Mon – Fri 09h00 - 18h30, Sat 09h00 - 13h00 and
14h00 - 17h00
01.58.09.89.00
🖳 www.natalservices.fr
Hires out breast pumps and baby scales, as well as
first stage car seats and other equiment. They will
deliver the same day to anywhere within Ile-de-
France if you place your order before 15h00. There
is a flat rate delivery charge. They also sell baby
equipment in the shop (and are the only place in
Paris carrying the Medela Pump in Style electric
breast pump).

Natalys* (M/E)

47, rue de Sèvres, 75006 Paris
M° Sèvres-Babylone
Mon - Sat 10h00 - 21h00
01.45.48.77.12
🖳 www.natalys.fr
Large number of shops in and around Paris.
Extensive range of prams, strollers, coordinated furniture and feeding equipment, as well as good-quality children's and maternity clothing. They produce
two catalogues a year. They will deliver and have a
mail order and gift service. It is also possible to
order through their website. The shops called La
Maison de Natalys specialise in nursery furniture
and decoration.

New Baby

106, rue de Meaux, 75019 Paris
M° Laumière
Mon 15h00 - 19h30, Tues - Fri 10h00 - 19h30, Sat
10h00 - 13h00 and 15h00 - 19h30
01.42.08.24.35

Oclio

0 892 353 532
🖳 www.oclio.com
Website dedicated to children's products, from car
seats and pushchairs to security items, sports
goods and toys.

Sauvel Natal*
24, rue Desnouettes, 75015 Paris
M° Convention, Porte de Versailles
Tues - Fri 10h00 - 19h00, Sat 9h30 - 18h30
01.42.50.47.47
💻 www.sauvel.com
A second store is located in La-Plaine-St-Denis.

Natural Mat
00 44 207 985 0474
💻 www.naturalmat.com
Natural fibre, made-to-measure cot mattresses, cotton bedding, fleeces and nursery furniture. Based in the UK. Overseas shipping charged at cost.

Clothing

Baby and Children's Clothes

Where possible, stores selling children's clothing are denoted as E (expensive), M (moderate), I (inexpensive). Please note that this is intended as a guide only and does not take regular sales or promotions into account.

Bonpoint* (E)
320, rue St-Honoré, 75001 Paris
M° Tuileries or Pyramides
Mon - Sat 10h00 - 19h00
01.49.27.94.82
💻 www.bonpoint.com
Seven shops in Paris. Elegant, durable clothes (0 - 18 years) for everyday wear and special occasions with matching accessories. Particularly good for little girls' party dresses. Prices can seem prohibitive but the seasonal sales are always a good value.

Catimini* (M/E)
114, avenue des Champs Elysées, 75008 Paris
M° George V
Mon - Sat 10h00 - 20h00
01.53.76.21.51
💻 www.catimini.com
Several shops in Paris and the suburbs. Colourful clothes for babies and children (0 - 14). Sizes tend to be small.

La Compagnie des Petits* (M)
10, rue Saint-Placide, 75006 Paris
M° Saint Placide
Mon - Sat 10h00 - 19h00
01.42.22.48.93
💻 www.lacompagniedespetits.com
Brightly-coloured and original baby and children's wear (0 - 10 years). Particularly good January and summer sales. Sizes run small.

Du Pareil au Même* (I)
1, rue St Denis, 75001 Paris
M° Châtelet
Mon - Sat 10h00 - 19h30
01.42.36.07.57
💻 www.dupareilaumeme.fr
There are three ranges available under the Du Pareil au Même label: DPAM *Bébé*, DPAM *Enfant* and DPAM *Chaussures*. *Bébé* stocks babywear (0 - 2 years) and a small range of equipment and furniture. *Enfant* sells brightly coloured and inexpensive clothes (0 - 14 years). New collections several times a year. Sizes are small but clothes can be returned for a refund within a month of purchase. *Chaussures* stocks shoes (including slippers, Wellingtons/gumboots and gym shoes) in sizes 16 - 38. The store listed above sells all three ranges.

Gap* (I/M)
36, avenue des Champs Elysées, 75008 Paris
M° George V
Mon - Sat 10h00 - 20h00
01.56.88.48.00
💻 www.gap.com
Babygap and Gapkids offer good-quality and stylish baby and children's wear from the famous USA chain. (Many of the Gap stores for adults have childrens wear sections.)

Jacadi* (E)
9, avenue de l'Opéra, 75001 Paris
M° Pyramides
Mon - Sat 10h00 - 19h00
01.49.27.06.29
💻 www.jacadi.fr

Chic baby and children's clothing, some equipment and bed linen.

Kiabi* (I)
rue de la Fontaine St Christophe, 94000 Créteil
Mon - Sun 10h00 - 20h00
01.56.72.16.90
www.kiabi.fr
Nine stores in the suburbs. Mainly discount clothes but also sells a small range of budget baby equipment.

Miki House* (E)
366, rue St Honoré, 75001 Paris
M° Concorde
Mon - Fri 10h00 - 19h00
01.40.20.90.98
Three shops in Paris. Very popular range of original, chic clothing in unusual colours.

Okaidi* (M)
115, rue Monge, 75005 Paris
M° Maubert-Mutualité
01.42.17.45.94
www.okaidi.com
Nine shops in Paris. Colourful, original clothing for kids.

Petit Bateau* (M)
Centre commercial des Halles
1, rue Pierre Lescot, 75001 Paris
M° les Halles
Mon - Sat 10h00 - 19h30
01.44.76.09.17
www.petit-bateau.com
Numerous shops throughout France. Baby and children's clothing in simple, classic designs. Emphasis on cotton. Particularly well-known for underwear and nightwear.

Petit Faune* (M/E)
13, rue de Mézières, 75006 Paris
M° St. Sulpice
Tues - Sat 10h00 - 19h00
01.42.22.63.69

www.petitfaune.com
Two shops in Paris. Popular, stylish clothing for children aged 0 - 12 years.

Sergent Major* (M)
5, place de la République, 75003 Paris
M° République
Mon - Sat 10h00 - 19h00
01.53.01.86.86
www.sergent-major.com
Good quality baby and children's clothing in both traditional and unusual designs.

Tartine et Chocolat* (E)
24, rue de la Paix, 75002 Paris
M° Opéra
Mon - Sat 10h00 - 19h00
01.47.42.10.68
www.tartine-et-chocolat.fr
Six shops, mainly in Paris. Chic baby and children's clothes, small range of baby equipment. Also offer a selection of coordinated wall coverings and fabrics for children's bedrooms.

Tout Compte Fait* (I)
170, rue du Temple, 75003 Paris
M° Temple
Mon - Sat 10h00 - 19h30
01.40.27.00.42
www.toutcomptefait.com
Brightly coloured basics.

Hanna Andersson
00 1 (880) 222 0544
www.hannaandersson.com
Brightly coloured, loose, practical clothes for babies, children and women from this company based in the USA. Many of the items are made from untreated cotton. Overseas deliveries are charged at cost.

Inch Blue
00 44 149 531 1123
www.inch-blue.com
A small company offering a range of brightly

coloured and original hand-made soft leather boots for babies and children from birth to approximately four years). Overseas deliveries are sent by airmail at an extra charge of £2.00.

Adult Clothes Stores with Children's Departments

C&A*(I)
49, boulevard Haussman, 75009 Paris
M° Chaussée-D'Antin
Mon - Fri 09h30 - 20h00, Thurs open until 21h00, Sat 09h30 - 19h30
01.53.30.89.33
💻 www.c-et-a.fr

Cyrillus* (M/E)
16, rue de Sèvres, 75007 Paris
M° Sèvres-Babylone
Mon - Sat 10h00 - 19h00
01.42.22.16.26
0 803 813 813 (general information)
💻 www.cyrillus.fr
Shops throughout Paris and the suburbs. Classic traditional style clothing for all the family, including a range of maternity wear, also available by mail order or Internet. Many of the stores provide a Lego table to keep younger children amused.

H&M (I)
120, rue de Rivoli, 75001 Paris
M° Châtelet
Mon - Sat 10h00 - 19h30
01.55.34.96.86
💻 www.hm.com/fr
Inexpensive baby and children's wear. Also maternity wear.

Tati* (I)
30, avenue d'Italie, 75013 Paris
M° Place d'Italie
Mon - Sat 10h00 - 20h00
01.53.80.97.70
💻 www.tati.fr

Four shops in Paris. Famous cut-price clothing stores selling clothes for all the family including children's and baby wear at extremely low prices. (However, the price is reflected in the quality of the fabrics, so be warned!)

Boden
00 44 208 328 7000
💻 www.boden.co.uk
Good quality separates for children and adults. Deliveries within Europe are charged at £6.00.

Lands' End
00 44 800 376 7974
💻 www.landsend.co.uk
0 805 111 360
💻 www.fr.landsend.com
Good quality basic but stylish casual clothing for all ages (from six months) at affordable prices. Excellent for winter gear and back-to-school range. Will gift wrap and monogram articles for an extra fee. Additional free services include trouser shortening and sending swatches, spare buttons etc. Delivery charged at cost. There is also a French website.

L.L. Bean Inc.
00 1 (207) 552 3028
💻 www.llbean.com
Sporty and classic clothes for all ages and sizes (including petite). Will ship items express, airmail or surface mail at cost.

Department Stores

Le Bon Marché
22, rue de Sèvres, 75007 Paris
M° Sèvres-Babylone
Mon - Fri 09h30 - 19h00, Thurs 10h00 - 21h00, Sat 09h30 - 20h00
01.44.39.80.00
💻 www.lebonmarche.fr
Underground parking. One of the more exclusive department stores and certainly one of the least

crowded. Excellent selection of foreign goods in the food department (💻www.lagrandeepicerie.fr) including most of the Hipp baby food range. Very good craft supplies and toy section in the basement. Large baby and children's wear department (also in the basement) stocks many designer labels and also offers a small range of prams and other accessories. There are several small flights of stairs within this area so look out for the ramp providing easy access for prams. Particularly impressive window displays for children around Christmas. Baby changing facilities situated in the basement of the main store. The entrance to this area is very discreet so you may have to ask a member of staff for directions. Comfortable chair provided in the changing area for breastfeeding.

BHV (Bazaar de l'Hôtel de Ville)*
14, rue du Temple, 75004 Paris
M° Hôtel de Ville
Mon - Sat 09h30 - 19h30, Weds open until 21h00
01.42.74.90.00
💻   www.bhv.fr
Underground parking, direct access from *métro*. Good range of furniture, clothes, school supplies and art materials. Baby equipment and children's clothes located on 5ᵗʰ floor, toys on 2ⁿᵈ floor. Baby changing facilities situated on 2ⁿᵈ floor. Good hardware/home improvement department. Also has locations outside Paris.

Galeries Lafayette*
40, boulevard Haussmann, 75009 Paris
M° Chaussée d'Antin or Opéra, RER Auber
Mon - Sat 09h30 - 19h30, Thurs 09h30 - 21h00
01.42.82.34.56
💻   www.galerieslafayette.com
Underground parking, direct access from *métro* and *RER*. Welcome service (English-speaking) on ground floor. Newly opened baby and children's department on the 5ᵗʰ floor. Good selection of clothing for babies and children ranging from their inexpensive in-house range to well-known brands (including Petit Bateau, Catimini, Gap, Ralph Lauren). Also sells a large selection of toys, a small range of baby equipment and nursery furniture and

decoration. Baby changing and feeding facilities are also situated on the 5ᵗʰ floor. Lafayette Maison has now opened on the opposite side of the boulevard. Also at Montparnasse and outside of Paris

Au Printemps*
64, boulevard Haussmann, 75009 Paris
M° Havre Caumartin, RER A Auber
Mon - Sat 09h35 - 19h00, Thurs open until 22h00
01.42.82.57.87
💻   www.printemps.com
Underground parking with direct access to store. English-speaking welcome service on the ground floor of the Mode building. The biggest beauty department in the world opened here in 2003. Offers a wide selection of clothing for babies and children (well-known brands include Petit Bateau, Jacadi and Catimini) and a good range of toys, equipment and furniture. Baby changing and feeding facilities are on the 5ᵗʰ floor. Other stores located at Nation, Place d'Italie and Parly 2.

Mail Order

La Redoute
0 892 350 353
💻   www.redoute.fr
Bi-annual bumper catalogue, selling clothes for all ages, baby equipment, household goods, sporting equipment, etc. Call the above number for details of the shop nearest to you.

Les 3 Suisses
0 892 691 500
💻   www.3suisses.fr
Similar services to La Redoute. Call for a catalogue.

Vertbaudet*
0 892 700 201
💻   www.vertbaudet.com
A very popular mail order company for baby clothes, equipment, children's clothes, toys and maternity wear. The catalogue is available from

newsagents or by telephone. There are also store locations in and around Paris

Seconds Shops

Guérrisol(I)
19-33, avenue de Clichy, 75017 Paris
M° Place de Clichy, La Fourche
Mon - Sat 10h00 - 19h00
01.42.94.13.21

Le Mouton à 5 Pattes*
138, boulevard St Germain, 75006 Paris
M° Odéon
Tues - Sat 10h30 - 19h30
01.43.26.49.25
Designer vintage and last season's collections for adults.

La Clef des Marques*
20, place du Marché Saint Honoré, 75001 Paris
M° Pyramides or Tuileries
Mon 12h30 - 19h00, Tues - Fri 10h30 - 14h30 and 15h30 - 19h00, Sat 10h30 - 13h00 and 14h00 - 19h00
01.47.03.90.40
Particularly good for athletic wear and swimsuits.

Unishop*
42, rue de Rivoli, 75004 Paris
M° Hôtel de Ville
Mon 12h00 - 19h00, Tues - Sat 10h30 - 19h00
01.42.72.62.84

BHV Ivry Entrepôts
119, boulevard Paul Vaillant Couturier
94200 Ivry-sur-Seine
Mon - Sat 09h30 - 19h00
01.49.60.44.00
Large warehouse of shop-soiled and sale furniture, white goods, electrical appliances etc. at discount prices (about 30% off). Many bargains to be found and items often only need cleaning.

Sportswear and Sporting Goods

Au Vieux Campeur
48, rue des Ecoles, 75005 Paris
M° Maubert-Mutualité
Tues - Fri 11h00 - 19h30, Sat 10h00 - 19h30
01.53.10.48.48

Decathlon*
23, boulevard Madeleine, 75001 Paris
M° Madeleine
Mon - Fri 10h00 - 20h00, Sat 9h30 - 20h00
01.55.35.97.55

Go Sport*
Centre commercial des Halles
1, rue Pierre Lescot, 75001 Paris
M° Châtelet les Halles
Mon - Sat 10h00 - 19h30
01.40.13.73.50

Maternity/Nursing Wear

Euroform
50 bis, rue de Douai, 75009 Paris
M° Blanche
Tues - Sat 10h00 - 12h30, 15h00 - 19h00
01.40.16.44.04
🖳 http://allaiter.free.fr
Maternity underwear and breastfeeding accessories.

Formes*
10, place des Victoires, 75002 Paris
M° Bourse
Mon - Sat 10h30 - 19h00
01.40.15.63.81
🖳 www.formes.com
Items can be ordered from their catalogue and website as well.

MamaNANA
01.56.68.09.89
💻 www.mamanana.com
Breastfeeding accessories, including cushions and clothes. Run by a MESSAGE family.

Neuf Lune*
42, rue du Cherche Midi, 75006 Paris
M° Sèvres-Babylone
01.45.48.33.63
💻 www.neuflune.com

1 et 1 font 3*
3, rue Solferino, 75007 Paris
M° Solferino
Mon - Sat 10h30 - 19h00
01.40.62.92.15
💻 www.1et1font3.com
Catalogue available.

Veronique Delachaux
69, avenue Ternes, 75017 Paris
M° Ternes
01.45.72.04.20
Mon 14h00 - 19h00, Tues - Sat 10h00 - 19h00
Also available in larger department stores and in Jacadi.

Blooming Marvellous
00 44 181 391 4822
💻 www.bloomingmarvellous.co.uk
Award-winning UK catalogue and website featuring stylish but practical maternity and nursing wear (including special breastfeeding shirts with hidden zips!). Also original baby accessories, gifts and equipment, storage solutions and good quality basic clothing for babies and children up to three years. Delivery to France is charged at £15.

Jojomamanbébé
00 44 163 329 4414
💻 www.jojomanbebe.co.uk
UK catalogue and website featuring extensive range of maternity wear, practical nursery products, toys and clothing. Delivery within Europe is charged at shipping cost.

Mothercare UK Ltd
00 44 192 324 0365
💻 www.mothercare.co.uk
The traditional UK chain store for baby equipment, clothing and maternity wear. Mothercare will only deliver certain items to France, charged at shipping cost.

Second-hand Maternity Wear

Les Années Troc
4, rue du Dr Goujon, 75012 Paris
M° Daumesnil
Mon 14h00 - 19h00, Tues - Fri 10h00 - 19h00
01.43.42.43.04
Maternity wear as well as children's clothes and baby equipment.

Bambini Troc
26, avenue du Bel Air, 75012 Paris
M° Nation
Tues - Sat 10h00 - 13h00, 14h30 - 18h30
01.43.47.33.76

Children's Shoes

La Halle aux Chaussures*
12, rue Brantôme, 75003 Paris
M° Rambuteau
Mon - Fri 11h00 - 14h00 and 15h00 - 19h00,
Sat 11h00 - 19h00
01.42.74.35.32

Il court, le furet
6 bis, rue Fourcroy, 75017 Paris
M° Ternes-Péreire
Mon 14h00 - 19h00, Tues, Thurs and Fri 10h00 - 14h00 and 15h00 - 19h00, Weds and Sat 10h00 - 19h00
01.43.80.28.08
Discounted children's shoes.

Shopping

Na!*
73, rue du Commerce, 75015 Paris
M° Commerce
Mon - Sat 10h00 - 19h00
01.48.42.37.65

Petits Petons*
20, rue Saint Placide, 75006 Paris
M° Sèvres-Babylone
Mon - Fri 10h30 - 14h00 and 14h30 - 19h00, Weds
and Sat 10h00 - 19h00
01.42.84.00.05

Six Pieds Trois Pouces*
85, rue de Longchamp, 75116 Paris
M° Rue de la Pompe, Trocadéro
Mon - Sat 10h30 - 18h00
01.45.53.64.21

Tavernier
99, rue Mouffetard, 75005 Paris
M° Censier Daubenton
Tues - Sat 10h00 - 13h00 and 14h30 - 19h15
01.47.07.21.90

Till*
51, rue de Sèvres, 75006 Paris
M° Sèvres-Babylone
Mon 12h00 - 19h00, Tues - Sat 09h30 - 19h00
01.42.22.25.25

Children's Hair Salons

Coup'Kid
3-5, boulevard des Italiens, 75002 Paris
M° Richelieu Drouot
Tues - Sat 10h00 - 19h00
01.40.15.00.66
💻 www.coup-kid.com

123 Ciseaux
10, boulevard de Courcelles, 75017 Paris
M° Villiers
01.42.12.03.60

Kid's Island
38, rue Falguière, 75015 Paris
M° Falguière, Pasteur
Mon - Sat 09h30 - 19h00
01.43.20.38.91

La Maison de Tif & Cut
73, rue des Vignes, 75016 Paris
M° La Muette, RER Boulainvilliers
01.42.88.66.80
Hairdressing salon downstairs and an upstairs
space for birthday parties.

Vert Tendre
58, avenue du Dr Arnold-Netter, 75012 Paris
M° Porte de Vincennes
Mon 13h30 - 18h30, Tues - Sat 09h30 - 18h30
01.46.28.05.55

Au pays d'Oscar
16, rue Vavin, 75006 Paris
M° Vavin, Notre-Dame des Champs
Mon, Tues, Fri 10h00 - 21h00, Weds and Sat
09h30 - 18h30, Thurs 10h00 - 19h00
0.826 000 616
💻 www.aupaysdoscar.com

Bookshops and Entertainment

English-language Bookshops

Abbey Bookshop
29, rue de la Parcheminerie, 75005 Paris
M° St Michel, Cluny-La Sorbonne or RER B or C St
Michel-Notre Dame
Mon - Sat 10h00 - 19h00, Sun 15h00 - 18h00
01.46.33.16.24
💻 www.abbeybookshop.net
Stocks about 13,000 titles (new and used).
Comprehensive women's studies section. Children's
book section with chairs. Also sells some Canadian
newspapers. Frequently holds literary events.

Attica
106, boulevard Richard Lenoir, 75011 Paris
M° Oberkampf
Mon 14h00 - 19h00, Tue - Sat 10h00 - 13h00 and
14h00 - 19h00
01.55.28.80.14
🖥 www.attica-langues.com
The language-learning bookshop in Paris. The children's section offers a vast selection of language-teaching books for use both at home and at school, including a good range of materials designed to help English-speaking children learn French. A catalogue is available on request. Has a *carte de fidélité*.

Brentano's
37, avenue de l'Opéra, 75002 Paris
M° Pyramides or Opéra, RER A Auber
Mon - Sat 10h00 - 19h30
01.42.61.52.50
🖥 www.brentanos.fr
English-language books in all categories, including children's titles. Particularly large creative skills section. Publishes various newsletters and runs a children's club with activity sessions (especially around Christmas and Halloween). Also stocks stationery, greeting cards, UK and USA press. Offers a *carte de fidélité* and various professional discounts. Children's books are in the basement down a spiral staircase and there is no lift.

Galignani
224, rue de Rivoli, 75001 Paris
M° Tuileries
Tue - Sat 10h00 - 19h00.
01.42.60.76.07
About 20,000 titles in English (including children's books) as well as a selection of French titles. Large fine arts section. Stocks UK and USA press.

Nouveau Quartier Latin
78, boulevard St Michel, 75006 Paris
RER B Luxembourg, Port-Royal
Mon - Sat 10h00 - 19h00
01.46.56.61.61

More than 30,000 titles in English (over 1,000 for children). Large dictionary and ELT sections. Also sells greeting cards in English. Has a *carte de fidélité*.

The Red Wheelbarrow Bookstore
22, rue St Paul, 75004 Paris
M° St Paul
Mon - Sat 10h00 - 19h00, Sun 14h00 - 18h00
01.48.04.75.08
Adult and children's books.

San Francisco Book Co.
17, rue Monsieur-le-Prince, 75006 Paris
M° Odéon
Mon - Sat 11h00 - 21h00, Sun 14h00 - 19h30
01.43.29.15.70
Second-hand bookshop, with around 10,000 titles in English. Usually has a few children's books in stock.

Shakespeare & Co
37, rue de la Bûcherie, 75005 Paris
M° St Michel
Daily 12h00 - 24h00
01.43.25.40.93
Large selection of new and used books in English, including children's. Popular notice board.

Tea and Tattered Pages
24, rue Mayet, 75006 Paris
M° Duroc, Falguière
Mon - Sat 11h00 - 19h00, Sun 12h00 - 18h00
01.40.65.94.35
More than 15,000 used books in English, including about 2,000 titles for children. Small tea shop.

Village Voice
6, rue Princesse, 75006 Paris
M° St Germain-des-Près, Mabillon
Tues - Sat 10h00 - 19h30
01.46.33.36.47
About 22,000 titles in English, small children's area, will order. Stocks USA press. Holds literary events and offers a *carte de fidélité*.

WH Smith
248, rue de Rivoli, 75001 Paris
M° Concorde
Mon - Sat 09h00 - 19h30, Sun 13h00 - 19h30
01.44.77.88.99
💻 www.whsmith.fr
Carries 50,000 titles on two floors. Children's room upstairs with wide range of books (including bilingual texts), games, videos and CD-ROMs. Reading sessions for children (especially around Christmas and Halloween). Good selection of greeting cards in English and English-language press. Accepts orders for UK or USA published books for shipment anywhere in the world. Free notice board upstairs. Has a *carte de fidélité*.

Toys, Craft Supplies and Children's Books

Le Bonhomme de Bois*
43, boulevard Malesherbes, 75008 Paris
M° St Augustin
Mon - Sat 10h00 - 19h30
01.40.17.03.33

Le ciel est à tout le monde*
7, avenue Trudaine, 75009 Paris
M° Anvers
Daily 10h30 - 19h00
01.49.27.93.03

Chantelivre
13, rue de Sèvres, 75006 Paris
M° Sèvres-Babylone
Mon 13h00 - 18h50, Tue - Sat 10h00 - 18h50.
01.45.48.87.90
Well-known shop with over 10,000 books (in French) for children. Also sells games, puzzles and craft materials.

Les Cousins d'Alice
36, rue Daguerre, 75014 Paris
M° Denfert Rochereau
Mon - Sat 10h00 - 13h30 and 14h30 - 19h15, Sun 11h00 - 13h00
01.43.20.24.86

Fnac Eveil et Jeux*
19, rue Vavin, 75006 Paris
M° Vavin
Mon - Sat 10h00 - 19h30
01.56.24.03.46
0 892 350 880
💻 www.eveiletjeux.com
Spacious, attractively decorated shops dedicated to children's books (very few in English), imaginative toys from around the world, CDs, software and videos. Children can try out most of the toys in the shop. A larger selection of items is sold through their popular catalogue and website which also offer baby and safety equipment, nursery furniture and books (in French). They also sell some clothes (swimsuits, sun hats, etc.).

La Grande Récré*
Centre commercial Passy Plaza
53, rue de Passy, 75016 Paris
M° Passy
Mon - Sat 10h00 - 19h30
01.42.30.52.02
💻 www.lagranderecre.fr
A toy supermarket.

Il était une fois
1, rue Cassette, 75006 Paris
M° St Sulpice
Mon - Sat 10h00 - 19h30
01.45.48.21.10

Joueclub
05.56.69.69.00
💻 www.joueclub.com
French website offering a good range of toys and children's entertainment.

Loisirs & Créations*
Centre commercial Passy Plaza
53, rue de Passy, 75016 Paris
M° Passy
Mon - Sat 10h00 - 19h30
01.42.15.13.43
A good selection of craft supplies and craft gifts.

La Maison du Cerf-Volant
7, rue de Prague, 75012 Paris
M° Ledru-Rollin
Tues - Sat 11h00 - 19h00
01.44.68.00.75
Kites of every description.

Multicubes
5, rue de Rivoli, 75004 Paris
M° Saint Paul
Tues - Sat 10h00 - 14h00 and 15h00 - 19h00
01.42.77.10.77
🖳 www.multicubes.fr

Au Nain Bleu
406/410, rue St Honoré, 75008 Paris
M° Concorde, Madeleine
Mon - Sat 10h00 - 18h30
01.42.60.39.01
🖳 www.au-nain-bleu.com
Traditional toy store dating from 1836.

Nature et Découvertes*
Le Carrousel du Louvre
99, rue de Rivoli, 75001 Paris
M° Palais Royal-Musée du Louvre
Daily 10h00 - 20h00
01.47.03.47.43
🖳 www.natureetdecouvertes.com
Educational toys and games ideal for children keen
to discover and appreciate more about their environment: the planets and stars, the sea and wildlife.
Many of the toys are made from environmentally-
friendly materials.

Pain d'Epices
29, passage Jouffroy, 75009 Paris
M° Grands Boulevards
Tues - Sat 10h00 - 19h00, Thurs open until 21h00
01.47.70.82.65

Panduro Hobby
0 820 000 224
🖳 www.panduro.fr
Offers a wide assortment of craft supplies, available
by catalogue or online.

Rougier et Plé
13-15, boulevard des Filles du Calvaire, 75003 Paris
M° Filles du Calvaire
Mon - Sat 9h30 - 19h00
0 825 160 560
🖳 www.crea.tm.fr
An abundance of craft supplies.

Si Tu Veux
68, Galerie Vivienne, 75002 Paris
01.42.60.59.97
M° Bourse
Mon - Sat 10h30 - 19h00
Accessories for birthday parties as well as toys and
dressing-up kits.

Toys"R"Us*
Centre commercial "Les Quatre Temps"
15, le Parvis de la Défense, 92092 Puteaux
Mon - Sat 10h00 - 20h00
01.47.76.29.78
🖳 www.toysrus.fr
The 11 warehouse-sized Toys"R"Us stores around
Paris offer a huge variety of toys, baby equipment
and sporting goods at very reasonable prices.

Letterbox
00 44 870 600 7878
🖥 www.letterbox.co.uk
Small, traditional collection of toys from the UK for all ages, including all-time favourites such as spinning tops and wooden horses. Toys can be personalised. Overseas delivery charged at cost. Order online or via their mail order catalogue.

FAO Schwarz
00 1 (800) 876 7867
🖥 www.faoschwarz.com
All the latest toys from the USA for children of all ages. Shipping is charged according to the weight of the parcel.

Websites selling English-language Books, Music and Films

Amazon
🖥   www.amazon.fr
🖥   www.amazon.co.uk
🖥   www.amazon.com
Popular and comprehensive sites based in France, the UK and the USA, offering a huge selection and good discounts on some books. Delivery is fast and efficient.

Mantralingua
00 44 208 445 5123
🖥 www.mantralingua.com
A UK company that specialises in bilingual resources for children, in particular books and CD-ROMs.

Play.com
00 44 153 487 7595
🖥 www.play.com
UK website offering books, DVDs and CDs. Free delivery.

The Red House
00 44 870 191 9980
🖥 www.redhouse.co.uk
A UK company that publishes a no-obligation monthly catalogue that is sent to members (subscriptions are free) featuring a range of children's books (toddlers to teenagers) often at greatly reduced prices. Delivery to Europe is charged at £25.00.

Tower Records
🖥   www.towerrecords.com
🖥   www.towereurope.com
Vast selection of CDs and DVDs from the USA or UK. Many available to be shipped from the UK site.

Home

IKEA*
Paris Nord 2
176, avenue de la plaine de France, 95970 Roissy
Mon - Fri 10h00 - 20h00, Thurs open until 22h00, Sat 09h00 - 20h00, Sun 10h00 - 20h00
0 825 826 826 (general information line)
🖥   www.ikea.fr
Also stores at Evry, Plaisir, Vélizy, Franconville, and Cergy. See website for maps and directions. Children (4 - 7 years old) can be left in the supervised play area while you shop. Pushchairs are available at the entrance. The restaurant provides a children's menu, high chairs and a play area. A carte de fidélité (IKEA family) is available. Baby changing facilities provided at all stores.

Habitat*
8, rue du Pont Neuf, 75001 Paris
M° Pont Neuf, Châtelet
Mon - Sat 10h00 - 19h30
01.53.00.99.88
Design-oriented home objects.

Pier Import*
1, rue de Rivoli, 75004 Paris
M° St Paul
Mon - Sat 10h00 - 19h30
01.40.29.04.99
Reasonably priced household objects from all over
the world.

The Great Little Trading Company
00 44 160 464 0106
www.gltc.co.uk
UK catalogue and website offering innovative products for children aged up to 10. Well-known for original safety and storage items, but also has a range of useful travel and bath accessories. Overseas delivery is charged at cost plus a handling charge.

Eco Family

Bambino Mio
00 44 160 488 3777
www.bambinomio.com
Reusable cotton nappies and accessories by
Internet.

Bébé au Naturel
0 820 825 487
www.bebe-au-naturel.com
A wide selection of natural baby products.

Fibris
40, boulevard St Michel, 75005 Paris
M° Gobelins, St Marcel
Tues - Sat 10h00 - 19h00
01.43.31.63.63
Clothes, underwear, tights, socks and baby clothes
made with organic wool, cotton, linen and silk.

Mots, Formes et Couleurs
03.88.40.00.95
www.monde-de-bebe.com
Mail order company managed by a mother of five
who chooses only natural products. Call for a catalogue. A range of toys, organic products, nappies,
some furniture and clothes. Good advice.

Food

Supermarket Chains

Auchan*
0 892 029 030
www.auchandirect.fr
A chain of supermarkets that also offers online grocery shopping and home delivery throughout Ile-de-France.

Carrefour*
0 826 826 500
www.ooshop.fr
One of the largest supermarket chains.
Comprehensive website for home deliveries.

Monoprix*
0 825 007 000
www.telemarket.fr
A good selection of food and basic household
items. It is also possible to order from the catalogue
(call the above number for a free copy). Deliveries
can often be made within a few hours of placing an
order.

International Food Stores

Kanae
11, rue Linois, 75015 Paris
M° Charles Michels, RER C Javel
Tues - Sun 10h30 - 20h00
01.40.59.98.03
A good source for Japanese products.

The Real McCoy
194, rue de Grenelle, 75007 Paris
M° La Tour Maubourg
Mon - Sun 11h00 - 19h00
01.45.56.98.82
An American grocery store carrying all kinds of
American products, from Oreos to plain Cheerios,
at a price.

Rose Bakery
46, rue des Martyrs, 75009 Paris
M° St Georges, Notre Dame
Tues - Sat 09h00 - 18h00, Sun 09h00 - 17h00
01.42.82.12.80
British-inspired bakery and restaurant (open for lunch only). They also sell a range of British goods.

Thanksgiving
20, rue St Paul, 75004 Paris
M° St Paul
Tues - Sat 11h00 - 19h00, Sun 11h00 - 18h00
01.42.77.68.28
Another American speciality store, also offering a catering service and restaurant.

Organic Markets

Canal Bio*
300, rue de Charenton, 75012 Paris
M° Dugommier
Tue - Fri 10h00 - 14h00 and 15h00 - 20h00, Sat 10h00 - 20h00
01.44.73.81.50
Also a store on the quai de Loire in the 19th *arrondissement*.

Côté Vert
332, rue Lecourbe, 75015 Paris
M° Lecourbe
Mon - Sat 10h00 - 20h00
01.40.60.60.66

L'Élan Nature
107 bis, avenue du Général Leclerc, 75014 Paris
M° Porte d'Orléans
Mon - Sat 09h30 - 20h00
01.45.42.35.00

Espace Bio Saint-Charles
2, rue Sainte-Lucie, 75015 Paris
M° Charles-Michel
Mon - Sat 09h30 - 20h00
01.75.75.79.45

Naturalia*
11/13, rue Montorgueil, 75001 Paris
01.55.80.77.81
🖳 www.naturalia.fr

Les nouveaux Robinsons*
49, rue Raspail, 93100 Montreuil
M° Robespierre
Tue - Fri 10h00 - 14h00 and 15h30 - 20h00,
Sat 10h00 - 20h00
01.49.88.77.44

Rayons Vert
9, place du Colonel-Fabien, 75010 Paris
M° Colonel Fabien
Mon 14h30 - 19h30, Tue - Sat 10h00 - 19h00
01.42.03.30.00

Shopping Centres / Malls

Phone the relevant contact number or look at the website for further information on access and for details of the stores that have outlets in each shopping centre.

Forum des Halles
101, Porte Berger, 75001 Paris
M° Les Halles, Châtelet
Mon - Sat 10h00 - 19h30
01.44.76.96.56
🖳 www.forum-des-halles.com

La Galerie du Carrousel du Louvre
99, rue de Rivoli, 75001 Paris
M° Palais Royal Musée du Louvre
Daily 09h00 - 20h00
01.43.16.47.10
🖳 www.lecarrouseldulouvre.com
Underground shopping centre in the heart of Paris. Open on Sundays.

Shopping

Parly 2
78158 Le Chesnay
Mon - Fri 10h00 - 21h00, Sat 10h00 - 21h00
01.39.54.30.45
www.parly2.com

Velizy 2
2, avenue de l'Europe, 78140 Vélizy-Villacoublay
Mon and Sat 10h00 - 20h00, Tues - Fri 10h00 -
22h00
01.39.46.24.96
www.velizy2.com

Quatre Temps
15, le Parvis de la Défense, 92092 Puteaux
Mon - Sat 10h00 - 20h00
01.47.73.54.44
www.les4temps.com

Bercy 2
4, place de l'Europe, 94220 Charenton-le-Pont
Mon - Fri 10h00 - 20h30, Sat 9h00 - 20h00
01.41.79.31.39
www.ccbercy2.com

Paris Nord 2
134, avenue de la Plaine de France, 95970 Roissy
01.48.63.20.72
Note that this is more a shopping area than a traditional shopping centre, offering a collection of large
chain stores in separate buildings (IKEA,
Castorama, Kiabi, La Halle aux Chaussures, Pier
Import) in addition to a *Usine Center*.

Factory Shopping Centres

Usine Center Villacoublay
route André Citroën, 78140 Vélizy-Villacoublay
Weds - Fri 11h00 - 20h00, Sat - Sun 10h00 - 20h00
01.39.46.45.00

Marques Avenue Ile-Saint-Denis
9, quai du Châtelier, 93450 L'Ile St Denis
M° Mairie de St Ouen
Mon - Fri 11h00 - 20h00, Sat 10h00 - 20h00
01.42.43.70.20
www.marquesavenue.com

Quai des Marques Franconville
395, avenue du Général Leclerc, 95130
Franconville
Mon - Fri 11h00 - 20h00, Sat 10h00 - 20h00
01.34.44.17.17
www.quaidesmarques.com

Usines Center Paris Nord 2
134, avenue de la plaine de la France
95970 Roissy
Mon - Fri 11h00 - 19h00, Sat - Sun 10h00 - 20h00
01.48.63.07.67

La Vallée Outlet Shopping Village
3, cours de la Garonne, 77700 Serris (Marne-la-
Vallée)
RER A, Val d'Europe Serris Montévrain
Mon - Sat 10h00 - 20h00, Sun 11h00 - 19h00
01.60.42.35.00
www.lavalleevillage.com

OTHER RESOURCES

Books

Le Guide des Magasins d'Usine
Marie-Paule Dousset
(Editions du Seuil)

Le Guide du Routard: Paris Exotique
(Hachette Tourisme)

Le Paris des Tout-Petits
(Mango Pratique)

Paris Pas Cher
Anne et Alain Riou
(Editions du Seuil)

Magazines

Aladin
monthly, €3.80
www.aladinmag.com
Antiques, *brocantes*, auctions, etc.

Fusac
(France USA contacts)
bi-monthly, free
www.fusac.fr
Classifieds

Que Choisir
monthly, €4.20
L'Union Fédérale des Consommateurs
Consumer Magazine

60 Millions de Consommateurs
monthly, annual subscription for 11 issues : €38
www.60millions-mag.com
Consumer Magazine

VOCABULARY

Baby Equipment

baby back pack	*un porte-bébé dorsal*
baby bath	*une baignoire*
baby bouncer	*un sautoir*
baby listener/monitor	*un moniteur* or *un écoute bébé*
baby scales (electronic or with weights)	*balance/pèse-bébé electronique ou mécanique*
baby walker	*un trotteur*
baby wipes	*des lingettes*
bath seat	*un siège de bain*
beaker/cup	*un gobelet / une tasse*
bed barrier	*une barrière de lit*
bib	*un bavoir*
bottle	*un biberon*
bottle warmer	*un chauffe-biberon*
bouncing cradle	*une transat*
breast pump	*un tire-lait*
car seat	*un siège auto*

Shopping

cot/crib	.un lit à barreaux
changing table	.une table à langer
cradle	.un berceau
double pushchair	.une poussette double
dummy/pacifier	.une sucette / une tétine
guarantee	.une garantie
high chair	.une chaise haute
kangaroo	.un porte-bébé ventral
Moses basket	.un couffin
nappy/diaper	.une couche
newborn baby	.un nouveau-né
playpen	.un parc d'enfant
potty	.un pot
pram	.un landau
pushchair/stroller	.une poussette
reins	.un harnais (de sécurité)
repairs	.une réparation
spouted drink cup	.une tasse inversable
steriliser	.un stérilisateur
teat	.une tétine
travel cot	.un lit parapluie / un lit de voyage

Safety Equipment

door gate	.une barrière
door stop	.un bloque-porte
electric socket cover	.un cache-prise
fire blanket	.une couverture anti-feu
first aid kit	.une trousse d'urgence
medicine cabinet (locking)	.une pharmacie (fermant à clef)
non-slip bathmat	.un tapis anti-dérapant
non-slip materials	.des matériaux anti-dérapant
protectors for table corners	.des coins de meubles protecteurs
small fire extinguisher	.un extincteur
smoke detector	.un détecteur/avertisseur de fumée
stair gate	.une barrière d'escalier
window lock	.une barrière de fenêtre

Clothes

back-to-school collection	.la collection de la rentrée
birth list	.une liste de naissance
bra	.un soutien-gorge
credit note	.un avoir
customer list	.un mailing/une liste clientèle
daytime support bra	.un soutien-gorge de maternité

discount card . . . . *une carte de fidélité*
discount . . . . *une remise*
factory shops . . . . *les magasins d'usine*
garage sale . . . . *un vide-grenier/une brocante*
maternity pants/briefs . . . . *des culottes de maternité*
maternity tights . . . . *un collant de maternité*
nursing bra . . . . *un soutien-gorge d'allaitement*
seconds/last season's collection shops . . . . *les stocks/magasins de dégriffe*
second-hand shop . . . . *un dépôt-vente*
Do you gift wrap? . . . . *Est-ce que vous faîtes des paquets-cadeaux?*
Is it big/small for size? . . . . *Est-ce que c'est une taille petite/grande?*
When is your sale on? . . . . *Quand est-ce que vous commencez les soldes?*
Will you exchange it? . . . . *Est-ce que vous pouvez l'échanger?*
Can I get a refund? . . . . *Peut-on se faire rembourser les articles?*

Children's Shoes

buckle . . . . *la boucle*
heel . . . . *le talon*
laces . . . . *les lacets*
leather . . . . *le cuir*
sandals . . . . *les sandales*
shoes . . . . *les chaussures*
slippers . . . . *les chaussons*
sole . . . . *la semelle*
trainers/sneakers . . . . *les baskets/les chaussures de sport*
wellies/rain boots . . . . *les bottes de marin (en caoutchouc)*
winter boots . . . . *les bottines/les bottillons*
it's too big . . . . *c'est trop grand*
it's too narrow . . . . *c'est trop serré*
it's too short . . . . *c'est trop court*
it's too wide . . . . *c'est trop large*

Hairdressers

children's rate . . . . *un forfait enfant*
clippers . . . . *une tondeuse*
cut/wash/blow-dry . . . . *un shampooing/coupe/brushing*
front . . . . *sur le front/devant*
home visit . . . . *une visite à domicile*
leave the back/top/sides . . . . *ne touchez pas derrière/dessus/les côtés*
trim . . . . *une petite coupe*
wash and set . . . . *un shampooing mise en pli*

Out and About with Baby

Balloon	*un ballon*
birthday party	*une fête/un goûter d'anniversaire*
booster seat	*un siège rehausseur*
bottle warmer	*un chauffe-biberon*
changing mat	*un matelas à langer*
changing table	*une table à langer*
children's menu	*un menu/une formule enfant*
children's show	*un spectacle pour enfants*
high chair	*une chaise haute*
non-smoking section	*une zone non-fumeur*
nursery/changing room	*une nurserie/ un change-bébé*
play area	*une aire de jeux*
straw	*une paille*
surprise gift	*un cadeau-surpise*
Do you have a breastfeeding area?	*Est-ce que il y'a un endroit où que je peux allaiter mon bébé?*
Where are the baby changing facilities?	*Où est-ce que je pourrais changer mon bébé?*

Toys

toy	*un jouet*
educational toy	*un jouet éducatif*
soft toy	*une peluche*
comfort/transitional object	*un doudou*
doll	*une poupée*
outdoor toy	*un jouet d'extérieur*
game	*un jeu*
jigsaw puzzle	*un puzzle*
art materials	*du matériel de dessin/peinture/coloriage*
craft materials	*du matériel pour les activités manuelles*
toy library	*une ludothèque*

Food

bakery	*une boulangerie*
butcher's	*une boucherie*
cheeseshop	*une fromagerie*
cobbler	*un cordonnier*
delivery charge	*frais de livraison*
grocer's	*une épicerie*
grocery trolley	*un chariot*
seafood platter	*plateau de fruits de mer*
supermarket	*un supermarché*

Travel

Compliled and edited by Jennifer Diamant Foulon

Regardless of whether you travel a little or a lot, the following chapter has information and practical advice for travelling with children in or away from France by car, train, ferry or plane. There is information ranging from how to find different kinds of child-friendly accommodation to updated information on the various transport options available to you. As anyone who has tried to soothe cranky and hungry 2 or 12 or 40 year olds can tell you, preparation and flexibility and a little bit of luck are key to family travel. The good news is that the culture of family holiday travel in France means that there are great resources available.

GENERAL PREPARATION

The following section includes information that will help you plan and prepare your trip so that everyone, including the planner, actually gets a holiday.

Dates to Consider

The travel calendar for many people living in France revolves around the public school holidays (*les vacances scolaires)*, and the national public and religious holiday dates. If you have just arrived in France from a country where most full-time working adults do not have the right to five weeks' holiday per year (as the French do), you might be surprised by these totally synchronized migrations of people living in urban areas to the beach or countryside whenever a holiday weekend or school holiday period hits.

All train stations, airports and the roads leading to popular holiday destinations are incredibly congested before, during and after the school and public holidays, especially during the beginning of the long summer break *(le grand depart)* and the return *(le retour des vacances)*. It can take two hours just to leave Paris heading in any direction, but especially going south. There are local traffic updates on TV (after the news) for potentially bad travel days – these are colour-coded, with red meaning the worst time to travel by car. You can also check the *calendrier du traffic* at www.bisonfute.equipement.gouv.fr, which will tell you more about which days are expected to be the worst, based on school and public holiday dates.

One place in France that is empty and calm in August is...Paris! It can be a pretty nice place to visit during these busy travel periods. Just do not forget that many Parisian butchers, bakers and babysitters may be taking their holidays as well, and this means you will find many of your local establishments closed for weeks at a time.

If you can travel outside the school holidays, you will find that transportation, and accommodation are less expensive and easier to book, and destinations are certainly less crowded. Taking a beach or warm weather trip in June or September, for example, can be half the cost of the same trip in July or August.

The French education website www.education.gouv.fr will give you the school holiday calendar for the current year (look under *calendrier scolaire)*. France is split into three zones for school holidays and each zone has different dates for the Winter and Spring breaks. Paris is in Zone C, which also includes Bordeaux, Créteil and Versailles. The All Saints' (*Toussant)*, Christmas and Summer holidays are usually the same for all three zones.

Health Planning

If you are planning to travel during your pregnancy, do check in with your obstetrician before leaving. It is also a good idea to ask your obstetrician when he or she will be on holiday and, if you communicate with your doctor in English, it is important to know if an English-speaking replacement will be available. A useful website for advice on travelling when pregnant is www.cdc.gov/travel/pregnant.htm.

If you have young children, it is a good idea to schedule a check up with the pædiatrician the week before you leave. There is no better way to put a wrench in a trip than to leave town with a child who has a budding ear infection or head lice. Again, keep in mind that the pædiatrician may also be going on holiday and, if you are planning to travel during the school holidays, the doctor could be very booked up. You might also want to stock-up on the usual over-the-counter medications to take with you. (☞Health and Medicine).

If you do not speak French and are travelling to a remote area, ask your doctor to write down the active chemicals in any medication you use regularly. That way any trained professional will be able to recommend a substitute if your preferred brand is not available.

If you are travelling abroad, information about the health situation in the country that you are travelling to is available on the Trip Prep website 🖳 www.trip-prep.com. For certain international destinations, specific vaccinations are required – ask your travel agent or doctor for information. It is advisable to find out well before the departure date as many of the vaccinations take at least a month before they are effective.

Centre de Vaccinations Internationales Air France
Aérogare des Invalides
2, rue Esnault Pelterie, 75007 Paris
M° RER C Invalides
Mon - Sat 09h00 - 16h45

Tips for Keeping the Family Comfortable During the Trip:

- Regardless of whether you are travelling by car, train, ferry or plane, it is a good idea to have snacks, bottled water and something that can be used as toilet paper with you at all times
- While most pharmacies carry some brands of milk formula and nappies (diapers), they may not carry the brand you need or prefer. It is a good idea to carry nappies, wipes, and enough formula to get you through a couple of days
- The Auchan and Carrefour stores or any other larger supermarket, as well as larger magazine and newspaper stands carry a selection of activity and colouring books, some complete with miniature crayons or pencils, for 3 - 10 year olds

---

01.43.17.22.00
This is a service provided by Air France. They will administer all vaccinations necessary for international travel and provide you with an International Vaccination Certificate. The administration is free, but there is a charge for the injections.

Institut Pasteur
Centre conseils aux voyageurs
211, rue Vaugirard, 75015 Paris
M° Pasteur, Volontaires
Mon - Fri 09h00 - 16h30, Sat 09h00 - 11h30
01.40.61.38.43
🖳 www.pasteur.fr
The Pasteur Institute will provide a list, by phone, of vaccinations and other medicine you may need for visiting a particular country. If you wish to have your vaccinations done there, you do not need to make an appointment – just turn up. Unlike most doctors in France, the Institute provides the vaccination for you.

Other Considerations
Keep in mind that many urban and rural areas in France still revolve around a long lunch break from Monday to Saturday. Shops and pharmacies are often not open over lunchtime and most places are closed on Sundays. Also be aware that many restaurants in France only serve meals between 12h00 and 14h00 and again from 19h00 to 22h00.

Do also remember that it is difficult to find "off season" clothing for children in France, so if you need a bathing suit for your 3 year old in January, or summer sandals for your 10 year old in November, you may need to borrow them or order them from an online store (☞ Shopping).

Passports and Documentation
France is part of a group of 15 countries in Europe who have agreed to end internal border checkpoints and controls. These countries are known as the "Schengen Zone" and the other 14 member countries are: Austria, Belgium, Denmark, Finland,

Germany, Iceland, Italy, Greece, Luxembourg, Netherlands, Norway, Portugal, Spain and Sweden (other countries are expected to implement the Schengen visa requirements in 2007, notably Switzerland and the eastern European countries) However, this does not alter the fact that you might be asked for proof of your identity at some point on your trip, particularly in view of ever increasing worldwide security regulations. If your passport is your only legitimate form of identification, you will still need to take it with you when you travel between these countries.

For information about exact documentation and visa requirements for travelling abroad, contact your consulate (☞Living for the relevant addresses). If you are a French citizen, contact your local *mairie*, or consult 💻www.service-public.fr. The consulate

of the country you are travelling to may also be able to give you an update on their security regulations, passport and official documentation guidelines as well as more information about travelling with children. Information about official documentation for all countries is also available on 💻www.abriggs.com.

Children Travelling without Parents

When children travel without their parents, and sometimes when they travel with one parent, but carry passports of differing nationality, a letter authorising the child to travel is required. You can get an authorisation letter from your local *mairie*. It is also a good idea to carry a photocopy of both parents' passports, with signatures and dates. For further information, consult your consulate or 💻www.vosdroits.service-public.fr.

Travel

Immigration and Customs

Here are some general guidelines for French residents going through immigration and customs when arriving in France or abroad:

• If even one member of your family is European, the entire family can be together in the EU line when passports or identification must be shown

• American citizens, even those with dual American/French nationality, are supposed to use their American passports when they travel internationally, and certainly when heading in and out of the USA

• Non-French citizens that have a French residence card would do well to show it with their foreign passport at the immigration and customs checkpoints when arriving back on French soil

• Travelling with photocopies of your identification documentation is highly advised and will facilitate identification and replacement in the event of a lost or stolen passport. Make sure that you photocopy the page of the passport with the photo, as well as the page of the passport where the signature is shown, for all members of the family keep these documents on your person but separated from the originals during travel

Travel

TRAVELLING BY CAR

Motorways and Main Roads

The quality of the motorways (autoroutes) and main roads (routes nationales/principales) all over France is generally excellent, making travelling by car relatively easy.

Autoroutes on maps and on road signs begin with a capital A, followed by a number, as in A10 or A13. Le Guide de l'Autoroute includes a directory of autoroutes and the services provided (see the Other Resources section at the end of this chapter for details). You can anticipate paying tolls (péages) along these roads, and you can pay with a credit card. The Telepeage Liber-T option is worth considering: this is a badge that allows the car to pass directly through the péage, with automatic billing to your bank account. The speed limit on autoroutes is 130 km per hour, enforced since 2003 by radar. If you are caught by the radar, you would not know it right away but your photo will accompany the ticket that will be waiting for you when you get home.

Routes nationales begin with a capital N, followed by a number, as in N110 or N45. You can anticipate occasional tolls along these roads, and you can pay with a credit card. The speed limit on routes nationales is lower than on the autoroutes, and many pass directly through towns and villages. They have the drawback of being more time-consuming but the potential benefit of being more scenic. For example, the nationales in the Dordogne afford wonderful views from the car.

Planning your Route

If you would like help planning your route, the following websites are useful:

🖳   www.mappy.fr
🖳   www.viamichelin.com

Services

There are numerous service stations (aires de service) with toilets, cafés, and restaurants catering to travellers with small children. These provide children's menus, recreation areas (terrains de jeux), and, occasionally, child-sized toilets and baby changing facilities. There are signs along the autoroutes (but not along the nationales) indicating the distances to aires de service. One of the benefits of the aires de service is that you can get basic supplies and a reasonably priced meal at any time of day.

Traffic

Since most school holidays and property rental periods begin on a Saturday in France, you can expect traffic congestion to begin as early as Thursday in Paris and major cities, and certainly all day Friday in all major French cities. Traffic is infamously bad around Paris and Lyon, Paris being where 20% of the French population lives, and Lyon being along the route everyone takes to the Alps and the Côte d'Azur. For up-to-date traffic information while you are on the road, tune to the radio on 107.7 FM.

If you are used to reading your speed dial in miles, this comparison table will help make sure you know how fast you are actually going!

Miles per hour	Kilometres per hour
50	80
60	96
70	112
80	128
90	144
100	160

In-car Accessories

You can buy in-car accessories (e.g., sunscreens which attach by suction to the window of the car) from specialist car accessory shops such as Feu Vert and Virage. Some hypermarkets also have a special car section.

As young children may spend some time asleep in the car, to avoid "head flop", you can buy child-sized inflatable head huggers from Prénatal and other baby stores, big supermarkets, and catalogues such as Graine d'éveil (☞Shopping).

Car Seats

French law requires that any child that is under 63 centimetres high when seated (approximately 6 years of age) must have a special child seat.

Newborn to 12 months

This car seat is called a *siège de nouveau né* and it is for babies up to 9 kilos or 20 pounds (roughly newborn to 12 months of age). This seat should be in the backseat of the car, facing backwards.

12 months and up

A *siège d'enfant* is for children from 9 to 18 kilos (20 to 40 pounds) or 66 to 102 centimetres (26 to 40 inches) tall. This seat should be in the back of the car facing forwards.

3 years to 6 years

A *siège d'appoint* (which come in different sizes) is appropriate for a child that weighs more than 18 kilos (40 pounds) and should be used up to the age of 6.
(☞Shopping for other information on car seats.)

Safety and Breakdowns

For detailed information and advice, consult *La Prévention Routière* on
⌨www.preventionroutiere.asso.fr. Their aim is to improve safety through education and information on cars, accessories and road safety.

French insurance companies offer roadside breakdown assistance insurance *(assistance routière)* and include services similar to that of the AA/RAC in the UK and AAA in the USA.

Should you break down on the motorway and main roads, the police *(Gendarmes)* advise that you get out of the car (especially at night) and away from the side of the road and behind the barriers. Use the orange emergency telephones located at regular intervals alongside the highway and you will be collected by the breakdown company authorised by the *autoroute* company that manages that particular motorway. You will have to pay for this service.

There are various highway code books *(Code de la Route)* available. The *Code Rousseau* is recommended as a good source of information (see Other Resources section at the end of the chapter).

Remember that in France, you must have your insurance details *(attestation d'assurance)* with a standardised accident form *(constat à l'amiable)*, a set of spare bulbs and a warning triangle *(triangle de détresse)* in your car. You should also ensure you take the car documents with you.

Car Hire

If you are considering hiring a car for your holiday, then here are a few of the options available to you in France:

- ⌨ www.hertz.fr
- ⌨ www.avis.fr
- ⌨ www.europcar.fr
- ⌨ www.rentacar.fr
- ⌨ www.renault-rent.com
- ⌨ www.easycar.com

TRAVELLING BY TRAIN

One of the benefits of living in France, especially if you are based in Paris, is the comfort and convenience of the train service and the discounted rates for family travel. The following section explains the different kinds of trains that are available, the facilities you can expect to find at Paris' main train stations, and advice on how to obtain discounts for travelling as a family.

Domestic Trains

There are two different rail networks in France – the *SNCF (la Société Nationale des Chemins de Fer)* and the *TGV (Train à Grande Vitesse)*:

SNCF
This is the extensive rail network covering the whole of France. Many *SNCF* stations in and around Paris link up with the *métro*, the *RER* and the buses (☞Living for more information on Public Transport).

TGV
This is the high speed service run by the *SNCF* and the speed it travels makes it a real alternative to domestic airline travel. The network covers much of France and some European countries such as Belgium, the Netherlands and Germany, the UK and Switzerland. You must have a reservation for the *TGV*.

For both regular and *TGV* trains, you must remember to validate *(composter)* your ticket before boarding the train. There are orange machines situated at the end of the platforms for this purpose. If you forget, be sure you find the conductor on board the train or you could be fined and/or possibly have to pay the full ticket price of the maximum length of travel on the route.

Some *SNCF* trains are designated as "family trains" with a number of family compartments (*compartiments familles*). For overnight journeys, there are sleeper compartments *(couchettes)* in which a conductor can install safety nets to prevent a child falling out of bed. In train carriages without compartments (including *TGV*) some seats are arranged in

pairs facing another pair across a table *(les places carrées)*. These seats, ideal for some families, can be requested when making reservations. Also look for the carriages equipped specially for young children with a play area and other games to entertain the little ones while aboard.

Family Discounts

There are three different kinds of discounts for families travelling on the *SNCF* and trains: *carte enfant+, carte 12 - 25, and carte famille nombreuse*. Once issued, these cards must be with you when you travel or you could be fined the difference between the discounted ticket that you purchased and the full price ticket.

The *carte enfant+* is for people travelling with a minimum of one child under the age of 12. It permits the child and up to 4 others (any combination of adults and children) to benefit from a 25% - 50% reduction, depending on the date and time of travel. If the child is under 4 years old, they are allocated a seat free of charge. The card costs €65, is valid for one year and can be used for an unlimited number of tickets. It will be issued in the child's name and the child must be travelling for others to benefit from the reduction.

The *carte 12 - 25* is for older children and offers the same types of reductions as the *carte enfant+*. It costs €49, is valid for one year and can be used for an unlimited number of tickets. The card is issued in the name of the child.

The *carte famille nombreuse* is for French families (or those of certain other nationalities) with 3 or more children under the age of 18. It costs €16 and entitles the family to reductions varying from 25% to 75%, depending on the number of children and the date of travel.

You can purchase any of these cards at mainline stations or *SNCF* ticket counters and boutiques located throughout Paris. You need to take your *livret de famille* or passports of all members of the family. You will also be asked to provide a photocopy of the documents, which the *SNCF* will keep. Make sure to bring small, wallet size photos of each person to be issued a card as these will be needed. Some *SNCF* boutiques will issue the card on the spot; other locations will deliver the card to you within 10 days.

Unaccompanied Children (Jeunes Voyageurs Service (JVS))

This is a paying service run by the SNCF, enabling parents to leave children aged 6 and over to travel under the supervision of accompanying staff, with activities organised during the journey. You leave your child with a qualified hostess at special check-in desks (*service d'accueil*), where you must provide identification. You must also provide details of the person collecting your child. For travel where a change of trains is necessary, you may want to try to book as early as possible in the day. That way, in the rare instance where a connection is missed, your child will have more options to get to his final destination without having to deal with an unplanned stopover in a strange town.

International Trains

Eurostar

The Eurostar is a *TGV* service running from *Gare du Nord* in Paris through a 31 mile tunnel under the English Channel to Waterloo Station in London. The journey takes 2 hours 40 minutes and there is also a London to Brussels service (which takes 2 hours 20 minutes). All the trains have nursery areas equipped with baby changing facilities and there are often activity packs for children under 7 available from Eurostar staff in the departure terminals in London, Paris and Brussels. For more information contact:

Eurostar
01.44.51.06.02
💻 www.eurostar.com

Thalys

The Thalys is a *TGV* service running from Gare du Nord to Brussels, taking 85 minutes. Thalys also runs direct trains to Bruges, Rotterdam, Amsterdam and Cologne. For more information contact:

Thalys
0 825 8425 97
💻 www.thalys.com.

Overnight Sleepers

You can get slower trains overnight to European destinations, such as Madrid, Barcelona, Rome, Florence, Milan, Venice and Zurich. Some of these offer motorail services, allowing you to transport your car on the train. A good source of information on these services is 💻 www.raileurope.co.uk.

Eurotunnel

Eurotunnel carries cars, buses and lorries with their passengers in drive-on trains through the Channel Tunnel between Calais and Folkestone. Transit time takes 35 minutes (making it the fastest Channel crossing) and there are up to 5 departures an hour. The departure terminal is located just outside Calais (junction 42 of the A16 motorway - the slip road takes you straight to the check-in booths) and you only need to arrive 30 minutes before your booked departure time. For more information contact:

Eurotunnel
01.42.66.31.31
💻 www.eurotunnel.com

Tickets and Reservations

You can buy tickets and make reservations directly from *SNCF* stations either over the counter *(guichet)* or in a boutique or using the ticket machines *(billeterie automatique)*. You can also book tickets through travel agents and on the Internet. It may be a good idea to make your first booking face to face so that you are fully informed of the latest deals for families and the pricing for seats for children of different ages.

More information about discounts, periods of travel, and reservations can be found on the *SNCF* website 💻www.sncf.fr. Again, keep in mind that tickets during the school holidays should be reserved well in advance, although there may be limits on how far in advance you can book.

Paris Train Stations and Family Facilities

Paris train stations are practically named so that you can quite easily figure out where you need to leave from, depending on your destination:

Gare de Lyon (TGV station)
Departures for southern France, the Alps, Switzerland, Italy and Greece.

Gare du Nord (Eurostar, Thalys and TGV station)
Departures for the UK, Belgium, Holland, northern Germany and Scandinavia.

Gare de l'Est
Departures for eastern France, Germany, Switzerland and Austria.

Gare Montparnasse (TGV station)
Departures for Brittany and western France.

Gare d'Austerlitz
Departures for the south-west of France, Spain and Portugal.

Gare Saint Lazare
Departures for Normandy and the UK, via Dieppe.

The *métro* and bus stops serving the train stations may be a long way from where the *SNCF* and *TGV* trains actually depart. You should allow time to transport your bags and your children through a crowded station. Do not count on there being convenient escalators or lifts and bear in mind that there are often long queues for the lift once you find it! Lifts at Montparnasse and Gare de Lyon are particularly hard to find, but are available if you ask an SNCF employee for assistance. Arriving by taxi usually gets you closer to where the trains actually depart.

Train stations in Paris are half indoors and half outdoors and the temperature in the waiting area usually feels the same as outdoors. Modest cafés with sandwiches and snacks, at least one pharmacy, and plenty of magazine shops are available at all *SNCF* and *TGV* stations.

Public toilets are usually not right next to the train departure area, and they do not always have baby-changing facilities. A good strategy is to board the train as early as possible since the facilities are actually better on the train itself.

SNCF Boutiques

The *SNCF* has *boutiques* all over Paris, in shopping centres, on local shopping streets and in some *RER* stations. The *boutiques* feel a bit like travel agents, where you can consult an *SNCF* advisor sitting across a desk from you. It is worth knowing about these because they are much more pleasant places to go and buy your tickets than standing in a long queue in a windy station. It is warm, there is space for the children to sit or play while you wait, and you can even hear what the advisor is telling you!

To find your local *boutique* look on 💻www.voyages-sncf.com, or check the *Pages Jaunes* 💻www.pagesjaunes.fr

AIR TRAVEL

Domestic Air Travel

Air France runs domestic flights to many French airports and has shuttle services *(navette)* to Nice and other major cities. It is also worth considering the budget airlines, which run very reasonably priced flights to French destinations out of Paris and Beauvais airports. For more information, consult:

- www.airfrance.com
- www.ryanair.com
- www.easyjet.com

International Air Travel

At time of printing, there are many websites specialising in discounted air, train, hotel and car rental rates. Among the most popular are:

- www.expedia.fr
- www.easyvols.fr
- www.ebookers.fr
- www.fr.lastminute.com
- www.farechase.com
- www.opodo.fr

It is also well worth the while checking the prices directly on the airlines' websites, since they now often have the lowest prices. If you have special requests such as bulkhead seats, infant cots, etc., then it is often best to go directly through the airline to avoid surprises at check-in. In any case, it is a good idea to check with the airline for their limits on baggage weight.

General Information

Getting to the Airport

Charles de Gaulle airport has *RER* stations for terminals one and two (line B). However, the *RER* stations are not very close to the terminal buildings and you will need to get a shuttle bus to drop you off. When travelling with children, it may be easier to get a bus which will drop you right outside the terminal buildings. Roissybus, run by the *RATP*, departs from Opéra (rue Scribe) every 15 minutes. There are also Les Car Air France bus services which run from the Arc de Triomphe (avenue Carnot) via Porte Maillot (every 15 minutes) and from Gare Montparnasse via Gare de Lyon (every 30 minutes). Details, schedules and prices can be found on www.cars.airfrance.fr. For further general information, consult www.paris-cdg.com.

Orly airport does not have a dedicated *RER* station, but you can take the Orlyval train from Antony RER station (line B) or go by Orlyrail from Port du Rungis *RER* station (line C). Again, you may find a bus from the centre of Paris easier. Orlybus, run by *RATP*, departs from Denfert Rochereau every 13 minutes and Air France runs a service from Les Invalides via Gare Montparnasse every 15 minutes. For further general information, consult www.paris-ory.com.

Beauvais airport is 100 kilometres north of Paris, and it is where many cheap flights to European destinations fly from. There is a bus transfer from Porte Maillot. The buses are scheduled to correspond with flight departures and you should board a bus three hours before your flight is due to leave. You may want to consider driving to Beauvais, as parking is cheap and it is fairly easy to get to from Paris on the *autoroute* A1. For further general information, consult www.aeroportbeauvais.com.

Travel

At the Airport

Increased airport security translates into lengthy check-in procedures and repetitive passport controls at both Charles de Gaulle and Orly airports. Procedures are slightly less lengthy at Beauvais, but assume that all international departures require that you arrive two hours prior to departure.

Baby-changing facilities at the airports are available, but do not assume that you can buy nappies, formula and baby food at the shops. There are sometimes play areas, but they can be hard to find. However, it is worth asking where they are as they are often pleasantly empty. You can expect to find very decent sandwich shops and cafes, as well as the usual fast food outlets.

FERRY TRAVEL

Travelling by ferry can be fantastic for family holidays. There is plenty of space for the children to run around in and you can take your car, so no need to travel light!

Most ferries have purpose-built baby changing and nursing facilities, often situated in, or close to, playrooms. Other facilities include: cots, bottle warming, children's menus and highchairs. Extra help with getting to and from the car deck is often available for lone parents, or parents travelling with several small children. Do request help when you book your ticket.

Ferries usually provide playrooms, but these are usually not supervised. Other entertainment varies from ship to ship, line to line, and season to season. However, all offer some sort of amusement, from specially trained entertainers to junior discos, cinemas, video rooms, and video games.

Destinations

The best known ferry destination from France is probably England. For an at-a-glance guide to crossing the Channel, see below:

Route	Crossing Time	Ferry Operator
Boulogne-Dover	50 minutes	Speed Ferries
Calais-Dover	55 minutes	P&O Ferries
		Sea France
Dunkerque-Dover	2 hours	Norfolk Line
Dieppe-Newhaven	4 hours	Transmanche
St Malo-Poole	5 1/4 hours	Condor Ferries
Cherbourg-Portsmouth	4 3/4 hours	Brittany Ferries
		Condor Ferries
St Malo-Weymouth	5 1/4 hours	Condor Ferries
Le Havre-Portsmouth	5 3/4 hours	LD Lines
Caen-Portsmouth	from 6 hours	Brittany Ferries
Roscoff-Plymout	from 7 hours	Brittany Ferries
St Malo-Portsmouth	from 9 hours	Brittany Ferries

You can also travel to Ireland by ferry: Irish Ferries run services to Rosslare from Cherbourg and Roscoff, and Brittany Ferries has a crossing from Roscoff to Cork. If you would like to travel by ferry from the south of France, there are services from Marseille and Nice to Corsica, Sardinia and Tunisia.

Contacts for Reservations and Information

Ferries to the UK:

- www.speedferries.com
- www.norfolklines.com
- www.seafrance.com
- www.poferries.com
- www.condorferries.com
- www.brittany-ferries.com
- www.transmancheferries.com
- www.ldlines.com

Ferries to Ireland:

- www.irishferries.com
- www.brittanyferries.com

Ferries to Corsica, Sardinia and Tunisia:

- www.sncm.fr
- www.cmn.fr
- www.corsicaferries.com

A very useful site about ferry travel from France is www.directferries.co.uk. This lists all current ferry routes from France, and compares the times and prices of different routes.

Travel

Travel

ACCOMODATION OPTIONS IN FRANCE

One of the reasons that France is so popular with tourists is the wide-range of family friendly options that are available for overnight, weekend and week-long breaks. The following section will explain the different kinds of accommodation in France, and where you can find further information for making your reservations.

General Information

Many French regions have an information office in Paris (often called the *Maison de...*) which can provide brochures and accommodation details. To find these, consult 💻www.lespagesjaune.fr. Alternatively, you can contact one of the following:

Maison de la France
20, avenue de l'Opera, 75001 Paris
01.42.96.70.00

Michelin Editions des Voyages
46, avenue de Breteuil, 75007 Paris
01.45.66.12.34

Office de Tourisme de Paris
127, avenue des Champs-Elysées, 75008 Paris
01.49.52.53.54

Another good source of information for accommodation options is 💻www.toursime.fr.

Many of the larger French companies negotiate special deals for the benefit of their employees with certain hotel chains, leisure parks and *villages vacances*. If you are employed by a French company, it is worth checking with the Human Resources department for details.

Gîtes

A *gîte* is a holiday home in the form of an apartment, attached cottage, farm or independent house. Accommodation can range from rustic (concrete floors and really basic bathroom facilities) to gorgeously renovated quarters in a *chateau*. *Gîtes* usually rent for a full week but are sometimes available for long weekends.

Everything you need for cooking (pots, pans, utensils) and sleeping (beds, and even sheets and towels for most) is there. While most *gîtes* are self-catering, you might find one attached to a property where there is also a bed and breakfast, which means you might be able to have breakfast provided for an extra fee.

If you decide to book a *gîte,* you will be expected to pay a deposit, either directly to the owner or through a central reservation service. You may also be expected to sign a formal rental contract. Bookings are usually confirmed in writing in French, by email or by letter, once you have sent your deposit cheque. Anticipate being asked to pay the balance in cash - credit cards are almost never accepted, although some places may accept a cheque from a French bank account.

How to Find a Gîte

The most comprehensive organisation is *Gîtes-de-France*, which lists over 56,000 properties for rental. All accommodation listed is inspected regularly and given a rating according to its setting, facilities, comfort and services. Ratings are updated at least once every five years and accommodation is inspected again in the event of a complaint. For more information (in French and English) consult their website, 💻www.gites-de-france.fr, where you can search for a property based on a number of criteria, from price to comfort, as well as by region.

Gîtes-de-France also publishes a wide range of national and regional guidebooks as well as specialty guides (such as Séjours à la Ferme, which lists farm accommodation). You can find the national guidebooks in bookshops, but all are available via their online shop and from their office in Paris (see the Other Resources section at the end of the chapter).

Regional and local tourist offices also have lists of properties available to rent, and there are plenty of other companies offering gîtes. The best place to find them is on the Internet - here are a few sites to get you started:

- www.pour-les-vacances.com
- www.les-vacances-en-france.com
- www.frenchholidayhomes.com
- www.best-of-perigord.tm.fr

Chambres d'Hôtes and Maisons d'Hôtes

The French equivalent to bed and breakfasts, chambres or maisons d'hôtes can be the ideal solution if you want to travel around while on holiday since, unlike gîtes, there is rarely a minimum number of nights that you must stay. Lodging ranges from just a room in the owners' home to an independent studio facility on the owner's property. Some have family-sized rooms and facilities for children of all ages, as well as en-suite bathrooms.

Breakfast is always provided, but be aware that it might not be included in the quoted accommodation price. It may be served in your room, but it is more often served in a common dining room and sometimes you eat with the owners.

Some chambres d'hôtes also run a table d'hôtes service, in which case dinner, (and sometimes lunch) can be provided. The price for this can be very reasonable, especially if the owners offer half-board (demi-pension) or full-board (pension complète) rates. Keep in mind that at many tables d'hôtes you will be eating with your hosts, and part of the charm of the experience is eating what your host chooses to serve, at the times that they choose to serve it.

How to Find Chambres, Maisons and Tables d'Hôtes

The Gîtes-de-France organisation includes details of chambres d'hôtes and publishes specific chambres d'hôtes guides (see the Other Resources section at the end of this chapter). There are also many other chambres d'hôtes services in France, and bookshops are well stocked with guides containing listings for the region you are planning to visit. It is also worth searching on the Internet. A good place to start is www.likhom.com.

Hotels

If you are planning to stay in a hotel, there are endless options open to you. This section aims to give you details of a few child-friendly hotels, although you are bound to find many more choices by conducting your own Internet search.

When planning to stay in a hotel, if travelling with a baby, it is advisable to book a cot (lit à barreaux) in advance. In any case, it is best to confirm in writing any special requirements you may have regarding double/twin beds or adjoining rooms.

Here are a few details of hotels in France to get you started:

Budget

Formule1 Hotels
- www.hotelformule1.com
Roadside hotels with 24 hour access

Campanile Hotels
- www.envergure.fr

Travel

Ibis Hotels
💻 www.ibishotel.com

Mid-budget
Novotel Hotels
💻 www.novotel.com

Mercure Hotels
💻 www.mercure.com

Luxury
Chateaux Hotels
💻 www.chateauxhotels.com

Relais et Chateaux
💻 www.relaischateaux.com

Lucien Barrière Hotels
💻 www.lucienbarriere.com

Other
Logis de France
💻 www.logis-de-france.fr
Accommodation ranging from fairly simple to very comfortable, often in beautiful surroundings. All are equipped to welcome babies and children. Most have a restaurant on site with good food at reasonable prices and some offer full or half-board rates.

Villages Vacances
The original holiday village system was designed in the 1950's to ensure that families of all economic means could afford a week or two in a modest, family-oriented environment during the summer school holidays. In France, holiday villages *(les villages vacances)* are still a popular option and they can be found all over the country. Accommodation is normally a studio, bungalow or apartment with access to a common pool, playground and often beach facilities. You can usually choose to go self-catering or opt for a full or half-board service. All villages have facilities to make life easier when holidaying

with children (washing machines, restaurants, shops, nurseries, etc.), and equipment hire is easy to arrange, e.g., cots, high chairs, playpens, etc.

Do note that in the *villages vacances*, the emphasis is on the convenience of the common facilities. This means that your studio or apartment might be tiny, but the swimming pool, where you spend the day, is likely to be huge and there may be water slides, fountains, play areas for children of all ages, and activities throughout the day. To avoid being disappointed with your accommodation, ask for sizes and details of the facilities before booking.

Villages vacances are very popular during the French school holidays, and it is advisable to book early. However, many offer special deals for weekend or out-of-season holidays and group rates are sometimes available - it is worth comparing the different chains to see what is on offer.

Club Med
Club Med is probably the most luxurious and best known chain of *villages vacances*. They run all-inclusive winter and summer holidays resorts with extensive sports facilities. Some Club Meds offer childcare, enabling you to spend a few hours a day without your children. For more information consult 💻www.clubmed.fr.

Pierre et Vacances
Pierre et Vacances run holiday residences (basic apartments) and holiday resorts. The holiday resorts are specifically aimed at families and offer on-site activities and entertainment. There is childcare available from age 3 months to 18 years old. Meals are free for children under 4 and special menus on offer for children aged 4 to 11. For more information consult 💻www.pierre-vacances.fr.

Maeva Holiday Residences
Maeva run holiday resorts by the sea and in the mountains with childcare from ages 3 to 18. Evening entertainment for adults is included in the price. They also run holiday residences (basic apartments) in costal town centres. For more infor-

MESSAGE Members' Top Holiday Destinations in France

"We really loved Provence (staying near but not too near Carpentras) but found that to hire a gîte you need to start around November to get the best deals, otherwise it gets very expensive. However, our two weeks were wonderful at "the house with a pool" as my daughter called it." Alexandra W., Australian mother of two.

"The Dordogne and Lot are great areas to visit with kids, with dramatic castles for the kids and great food/wine for the parents." Sallie C., American mother of two.

"The Cevennes region is gorgeous! We really prefer the Languedoc to Provence, as it is not (yet) overrun (sort of Umbria to Provence's Tuscany...). One thing to remember, though, if you are driving far into the Cevennes is that the roads are very winding and rough on children prone to carsickness." Sallie C., American mother of two.

"Les Cévennes. The best-kept secret great place for holidays in France. You are only about an hour from Montpellier, a lovely university town that is not overrun with tourists in the summer. You are not that far from the sea. You are in the most beautiful mountains. There are beautiful campgrounds and parks all over the mountains, with clear streams where you can bathe. It is cheap. And there are not too many other tourists." Meg C., American mother of one.

"The Alps are a good destination in summer; it makes a change from the beach." Zoe H., British mother of two.

*"We absolutely LOVE Barcelonnette, in the Alps on the border with Italy. You can rent fabulous chalets during peak season, there's an outdoor swimming pool in the village for the kids, a great jazz festival in July with music and dancing in the streets, and when our daughter was small we even managed to get a place in the garderie on some days so we could go rafting and canyoning. Not many tourists,quite far to drive, but a real gem!"*Joanne H., British mother of two.

"One of our best family holidays was the Savoie, in late July, which is less crowded than in August. The Alps are gorgeous at that time of year and so much to do, even with toddlers. The Auvergne is a good alternative to the Alps in winter for those who are snow/ ski beginners, once again less crowded too. Brittany for beaches, crêpes (my kids love eating in crêperies), cider, dolmens..." Cathy D., Australian mother of two.

"I have been enchanted on recent trips to Burgundy and Alsace... You know that feeling when you go to a new place and you think, "I've been hearing about it forever, but I cannot believe how amazing it is..." Renews that feeling that the planet is a wonderous place... " Ami S., American mother of three.

mation consult 🖳www.maeva.com.

Centerparcs

Centerparcs run holiday villages set in natural environments - there are two villages in France. Accommodation is available in independent cottages and also some apartment or hotel-style rooms. Childcare is provided for 3 to 12 year olds and, depending on the resort, there may be playgroups for babies and toddlers. For more information consult 🖳www.centerparcs.com.

Vacances Actives

Vacances Actives run 14 holiday villages in France for people who want full-on activity holidays. For more information consult 🖳www.vacances-actives.com.

Villages de Gîtes

Halfway between a *gîte* and a *village vacances,* this is a group of between 5 and 30 *gîtes* in the same area with a communal swimming pool and tennis court. Some entertainment is provided and housework and laundry services are available. There are currently 55 *villages de gîtes* in France. For more information consult 🖳www.villagesdegites.com.

Camping and Caravanning

Camping can be much cheaper then renting a *gîte* and there are many campsites in France, some privately run and others managed by the local town council. Some are open all year but most are closed between November and February and some are only open during the summer holidays. Many offer on-site caravan/tent or cabin accommodation that saves you towing your own caravan or pitching your own tent. Often sites are very close to beaches/lakes/mountains and there are usually lots of other children about for yours to make friends with! Most sites also provide laundry and shop facilities and some have restaurants and/or takeaway food. The main drawback is that you will have to set up camp close to your neighbours, although most sites have a 22h30 noise curfew.

The following websites and organisations offer further information on camping in France:

Camping France
🖳   www.campingfrance.com

Siblu
🖳   www.siblu.fr

Federation Française de Camping et de Caravaning
78, rue de Rivoli, 75004 Paris
01.42.72.84.08

Things to keep in mind when booking a gite:

• Ask questions about the availability of bedding, towels, size of bedrooms and the number and location of bathrooms. Is the gîte on one-level or multi-levelled and is there a cleaning service at the end of your stay

• If you have young children and are renting a property with a pool, ask about the security around the pool

• Consider that you may be in an apartment or cottage that is attached to the owners' home and you may be sharing the property and amenities with their family and friends

• If pictures are not available you should ask to see some

• Some gîtes are not available for rent for less than two consecutive weeks in July and August

• If you are arriving on a Saturday afternoon, ask about the opening times of local shops and restaurants. If you are in a rural area and things are closed on Sundays and Mondays, you would not want to be without supplies until Tuesday!

Camping and Caravaning Club de France
218, boulevard St. Germain, 75007 Paris
01.45.48.30.03

You can also consider booking through a UK holiday operator offering self-catering family camping holidays throughout France and Europe. Geared especially to families, these offer tents or mobile homes to rent on campgrounds that have extensive amenities, including pools, free children's activities, sports, restaurants, etc. And since most – but not all – of the other campers are from the UK, it's a great way to expose your children to English without leaving France.

Two well-known operators are Eurocamp www.eurocamp.co.uk and Keycamp www.keycamp.co.uk.

OTHER RESOURCES

Travel

Le Guide de l'autoroute
(Collectif)

Code de la route Rousseau
(Rousseau)

Gites de France Regional and National Guides
Broché publications available from
Maison des Gîtes de France
59, rue Saint-Lazare, 75009 Paris
01.49.70.75.75
www.gites-de-france.fr

Logis de France Guides
Broché Publications available from
Fédération Nationale des Logis de France
83, avenue d'Italie
75013 Paris
01.45.84.83.84
www.logis-de-france.fr.

Camping France 2006
(Michelin Guides)
Michelin Travel Publications

Eyewitness Guide to France
(Dorling Kindersley)

Rough Guide to France
(Rough Guide Publications)

Lonely Planet Guide to France
(Lonely Planet Publications)

Lonely Planet Guide to Travel with Children
(Lonely Planet Publications)

Alistar Sawday's Special Places to Stay
France – Hotels
France – Bed & Breakfasts
France – Holiday Homes
Paris – Hotels
(Alistar Sawday Publishing)

OTHER VOCABULARY

I would like to reserve a room	*Je voudrais réserver une chambre*
Do you provide cots?	*Avez-vous des lits d'enfants?*
Is breakfast included?	*Est-ce que le petit déjeuner est compris?*
Can we reserve for just the weekend?	*Serait-il possible de ne réserver que pour le week-end?*
Is there space for storing pushchairs?	*Y a-t-il un endroit pour les poussettes?*
How much is the deposit?	*La caution est de combien?*
To whom do I make cheque payable?	*Je fais le chèque à l'ordre de qui?*
What time can we arrive?	*A partir de quelle heure peut-on arriver?*
Are sheets and towels provided?	*Y aura-t-il des draps et des serviettes?*
Can you send me a map?	*Pourriez-vous m'envoyer un plan d'accès ?*
Can I put this car seat in (the taxi)?	*Puis-je installer le siège bébé?*
Can someone help me with my bags	*Y'a-t-il quelqu'un qui pourrait m'aider avec les bagages?*

Work

Compiled and edited by Stephanie M. Thom, with contributions from Lyndsay Peters Saussol, Sara Dupoux, Francesca Lahiguera, Caroline Peletengeas and Jennifer Diamant Foulon

Working in a foreign country is not straightforward at the best of times, with cultural differences, language barriers and different working practices. The extra dimensions of being a parent and desiring a suitable work/life balance do not make it any easier. Whether you are considering moving to France to work, accompanying your spouse who wants to enter the Parisian workforce, returning to work after being a stay-at-home mum or looking to set up your own business, this chapter endeavours to shed some light on some of the particularities of working in France.

EMPLOYMENT CONTRACTS

There are various types of contracts for foreign people working in France, and your employment rights and Social Security coverage will differ depending on your personal circumstances (☞Administration). This section summarises the main types of employment contracts and their particularities.

Letter of Mission/Secondment Agreement (lettre de mission)

This is most applicable to a short-term assignment. Issued in your home country, it details the terms and conditions relevant to your foreign placement: length of assignment, accommodation, pay etc. All other terms and conditions will remain as per your original contract.

Expatriation (contrat d'expatriation)

With this type of contract, your original work contract is suspended for a defined period and you sign a specific clause which details your new terms and conditions, as well as your pay in France. In this case, you are covered by the French Social Security system. (☞Administration)

Outside Assignment (détachement)

In this case, you are temporarily assigned to a foreign company or to a subsidiary office. Your employer in your home country may continue to contribute to your original Social Security regime. Many countries have international agreements with France, which would allow you in this case to benefit from the French Social Security and tax systems.

Local Contracts (contrat de travail de droit local)

In this case, you are employed directly (salarié) by a French company. Your ability to be so employed depends on your residential status (☞Administration). A local contract is governed by French law.

A job offer in France will be accompanied by a work contract (contrat de travail). The two main types of contract are CDI (Contrat de durée indeterminée), which is a permanent contract of unspecified duration and CDD (Contrat de durée determinée), which is a fixed term contract for a defined period of time up to a maximum 18 months, renewable once. The contract should specify the job description, the salary and benefits, the trial period, the place of work and the number of hours/days of work per week/year. There may be other clauses specific to the job in question, such as confidentiality, geographic mobility and exclusivity.

Working Mother Statistics

Based on 2004 data*, the following constitute the top 10 professions of Anglophone working mothers:

Education (excluding English Teacher)
Journalism / Writing
Law
Administration (Secretary; PA; Executive Assistant)
English Teacher
Consultant
Marketing & PR
Translator / Interpreter
Sales & Business Development (incl. Account management)
Artist

* Based on 2004 membership statistics from MESSAGE Mother Support Group, where some 49% of mothers have a current professional occupation.

Work

The minimum wage in France *(SMIC)* for a full-time 35 hour per week job is €1,154.18 before tax per month (July 2004 base). The value of the *SMIC* is revised every year. Your contract may include other types of income such as a thirteenth month of salary *(treizième mois)*, or a profit sharing scheme *(participation* and *intéressement)*.

Most contracts include a trial period *(période d'essai)* which varies from two weeks to three months, before the contract becomes binding for either party. During this period, you or your employer can decide to break the contract without any notice. After this period, if you wish to hand in your notice, you should write a letter to the human resources department and send it by certified mail with notice of receipt *(lettre recommandée avec accusé de réception)*. You will have to respect a period of notice *(préavis)* which may be up to three months. You should be aware that if you resign, you will general-ly not be entitled to unemployment benefits *(ASSEDIC)*, which is reserved for employees who have been made redundant. If your employer decides to make you redundant *(licenciement),* he has to give you three month's notice.

If you encounter difficulties with your employer regarding salary, harassment, health and safety issues or redundancy, you can seek advice and counselling from the members of the work council *(Comité d'entreprise* or *CE)* who can take up your case with management. The trade union members *(delegué syndical)* of the *CE* can also help you to work through a redundancy process by accompanying you to formal interviews with management and assisting you to negotiate a redundancy deal if necessary. If your company is too small to have a *CE*, you can contact the State Work Inspector *(Inspecteur de Travail)*, who will take up your case.

RELEVANT LEGISLATION

General Legislative Issues with Regards to Working in France

The basis of all employment rights in France is a set of legal texts called the *Code du Travail*. On top of this, each particular industry has a *convention collective*, an industry's collective bargaining agreement, which is generally more generous than the *Code du Travail* and includes issues that are specific to that industry.

Within an individual company, there is also the *accord collectif d'entreprise* and the *Réglement Intérieur* which govern the employees of that company. The *accord* applies to the company as a whole and covers subjects such as the 35-hour week law, extra leave other than the five week legal minimum, etc. The *Réglement Intérieur* applies to a site or office of more than 20 employees and includes rules and regulations such as opening and closing hours, eating and drinking, smoking, security, Internet and telephone use. The *Règlement*

Intérieur should be posted on-site and any other documents (i.e., *convention collective*) should be available from your human resources department unless they were given to you with your employment contract.

Companies that have more than 11 employees are obliged by law to have employee delegates *(délégués)*, who are elected every four years.

Companies that have more than 50 employees are obliged by law to have a *Comité d'entreprise* or *CE*. This committee receives a budget from management depending on the total salary costs of the company and is composed of a group of personnel that is elected every four years. These employees are either independent or union representatives, usually affiliated with one of the five major French trade unions *(syndicats)*: CFDT, CFE-CGC, CFTC, CGT and FO. The committee holds official meetings once a month to discuss matters relating to the day-to-day organisation of the company, and more major issues such as reorganisations, redundancy and the company's financial situation. The *CE* also has a social role and organises activities for employees and their families. Check out the notice board in your company to find out more.

The hygiene and safety of personnel is usually discussed by the *CHSCT* (Committee for Hygiene and Security). The *CHSCT* also gets involved when there are cases of sexual or moral harassment.

Leave

General Entitlement

Minimum legal paid leave *(congés payés)* in France is two and a half days per month (five weeks per year) earned over a reference period usually between 1st June and 31st May. Leave is calculated on a pro rata basis and entitlement to paid leave accrues monthly from the second month worked. In all companies, the 35-hour per week law has seen the introduction of extra days off, *JRTT (Journée de réduction de temps de Travail)*, to compensate for extra hours worked per week. Many companies have adopted this system, which can lead to the attribution of 10 *JRTT* days which may be taken weekly, monthly or yearly, depending on your applicable collective bargaining agreement.

Event	Number of days paid leave
Your marriage	4 days
Your child's marriage	1 day
Partner's or child's death	2 days
Death of a parent, parent-in-law or brother/sister	1 day
Birth/adoption for the father	3 days

Employees at management level who work with a certain autonomy *(cadres autonomes)* have their working time calculated in days per year rather than hours per week and may work no more than 218 days per year. In 2006, this meant obtaining 9 days of additional paid leave on top of the statutory holiday entitlement, national holidays and week-ends.

Legally, you are also entitled to family-related leave *(Congé d'évènements familiaux)* which covers births, deaths and marriages. Your company may have more generous benefits, including paid leave, for other events such as moving house. These benefits will be detailed in your particular work contract and/or in the applicable *convention collective*.

You are legally entitled to three days of unpaid leave per year to care for a sick child under the age of 16 years. This increases to five days if the child is one year old or less, or if there are at least three children in the household. Most *conventions collectives* allow for more generous time off for sick children. There is also the possibility of unpaid leave of up to one year to look after a seriously ill or handicapped child *(congé de présence parentale)*. The initial period of leave is for four months, which can be renewed twice, and the leave may be total or partial. You must advise your employer by certified mail with proof of receipt *(lettre recommandée avec accusé de reception)* at least 15 days beforehand and attach a medical certificate. In this case, you may be entitled to an allowance from Social Security.

Maternity Leave (congé de maternité)

When you find out that you are pregnant, one of your first questions may well be, how am I going to announce this to my boss? Legally, a pregnant woman is not required to tell her employer (or prospective employer) about her pregnancy until she wishes to exercise her protective legal rights and receive the benefits to which she is entitled. In order to do this, you must obtain a medical certificate from your doctor, both for your employer and for French Social Security indicating the beginning

Work

date of the pregnancy and the expected delivery date. Contact your local Social Security office for the necessary forms to fill out.

The amount of maternity leave that you are entitled to depends on how many children you already have and how many you are expecting.

	N° Weeks before birth	N° weeks after birth	Total
1st or 2nd child	6	10	16
3rd child and thereafter	8	18	26
Twins	12	22	34
Triplets or more	24	22	46

This leave may be longer if your doctor decides to stop you working for medical reasons. You may be granted up to two weeks extra before birth and four weeks after birth (congé pathologique). Of course if your medical situation necessitates otherwise, you may be given further leave, which will then be considered as sick leave and is in addition to maternity leave. You are also entitled to take your holiday entitlement after your maternity leave ends, even if this means you will not be taking it in the company's usual holiday period (for example, some companies oblige employees to take a certain amount of holiday in August).

In the event of birth after the due date, the amount of post-birth leave stays the same. Likewise, in the event of a premature birth, the total period of maternity leave stays the same.

If the baby has to stay in hospital, there are two possible solutions:

• if the baby is still in hospital six weeks after birth, the mother can go back to work and keep the remaining days of maternity leave for when the baby comes out of hospital

• if the baby is born premature by more than six weeks and has to be hospitalised, then there is an additional maternity leave, equivalent to the number of days difference between the due date and the actual birth date.

During your maternity leave, you will be paid an allowance by the Social Security (les indemnités journalières) on the condition that you have been registered with them for at least 10 months and that you have worked for at least 200 hours over the previous three months (or contributed on wages equivalent to 1,015 times the hourly SMIC during the last six months before the pregnancy or the parental leave). This allowance will be equivalent to your net salary, with a monthly maximum of €2,589 (based on the plafond de la sécurité sociale).

If your salary is superior to this amount, your employer may cover the difference, depending on the terms of your work contract. Also check with your human resources department regarding your industry's collective bargaining agreement (convention collective), as that may allow for more generous benefits. (☞Administration for more details on the medical benefits granted to pregnant women and families).

Your work contract may not be terminated once you have notified your employer of your pregnancy (except under exceptional circumstances, such as company closure or serious employee offence). Under no circumstances may your work contract be terminated during your maternity leave. Even in the case of a major restructuring, your contract cannot be terminated until four weeks after the end of your maternity leave. You are entitled, without loss of salary, paid leave or seniority, to the absences necessary in order to attend your required prenatal and postnatal medical appointments. Many conventions collectives also provide for small, incremental reductions in working hours during pregnancy.

If your health demands it, you may ask to be temporarily assigned to a less fatiguing position on presentation of a medical certificate. Your employer, in consultation with the employment doctor (médecin de travail), may also seek to assign you to a less taxing position. If you disagree that your health demands the change, you can refuse and request an inspection. As soon as your health permits, you must be returned to your original position unless the whole organisation has been restructured. In any case, you cannot lose salary. Some work is illegal for pregnant women, for example work outside at temperatures below freezing or work after 22h00.

At the end of your maternity leave, your employer has to take you back at the same or an equivalent position, with the same salary. You cannot be made redundant during your pregnancy or your maternity leave (and four weeks thereafter) provided that you have informed your employer of your pregnancy and your expected due date by way of a medical certificate.

Following the introduction of an Equal Pay law in March 2006, women on maternity leave are now entitled to benefit from the same general and individual pay increase granted to other employees in their department or, for small companies, in the company.

You have the right to resign during your pregnancy without giving the normal notice period (sans préavis) or paying any indemnification. To do this, you should send a letter by certified mail with proof of receipt. You have the right to resign during your maternity leave as well and, if you do so at least 15 days before the end of the leave, you will benefit from reemployment priority for one year from the time of your resignation. This means that if you wish to be reemployed, your former employer must offer you any open position for which you are qualified, in priority over other candidates and, once reemployed, you must receive the same benefits you had at the time you left.

What Makes a Woman a Good Manager?

At a recent talk given by the European Professional Women's Network's (EPWN) Veronique Bourez* (Responsible for the EPWN Women on Board initiative and ex. Director of Danone - LU) to MBA students of a Paris Grande Ecole, the following positive and negative characteristics of women in management positions were described:

Positive Characteristics:
Team Player: a woman has the ability to work as part of a team and make the team work for/with her

Empathy: a woman has the ability to understand where someone is coming from and see things from their point of view

Recognition of Differences: a woman can recognise personal differences and use them to the advantage of her team

Negative Characteristics:
Risk Averse: women are generally poor at taking risks

Too Nurturing: women can be too 'mothering' and they can lack ruthlessness

Angst: women tend to worry too much and take things personally

Too Conscientious: rather than 'doing the right thing', women have a tendency to 'do things right'

Not Accepting of Rejection: women fear rejection (resulting in risk aversion)

*(Many thanks to Veronique Bourez for agreeing to the use of her material)

Work

Work

Time Management for Working Parents

Always prepare school bags and clothes the night before to avoid morning rush.

Register at the beginning of the school year for any before-school, after-school, Wednesday or holiday-time care (e.g., the *centre de loisirs*) offered at your kids' school. Even if you do not use such care regularly, having the option available if you need it is a great back-up system to have in place, especially since there is generally no requirement to reserve for a particular day in advance.

Assign tasks to do routinely each morning and evening, so the weekend is not consumed with chores.

Declutter your - and your kids' - schedule. Rediscover the pleasure of being together, rather than running from one activity to the next. Save activities for during one of the many school vacations, when you can sign them up for an *atelier* or *colonie de vacances*, often offered by your local *mairie*.

Declutter your home and office space, and save hours picking up, cleaning and looking for items.

Have a designated spot for those documents that are requested over and over by French officials for e.g., your child's *carnet de santé,* vital records (birth certificates, *fiches d'état civil, livret de famille,* passports, etc.), recent proof of residence (utility bill, rent receipt), pay slips and work contracts, income tax filings and bank statements just to name a few.

Scan your vital records and print out a few copies to have on hand. Also keep an extra copy in the office, or email the scan to yourself - if you ever lose the originals, having a copy will save you time (and headaches!) in getting a replacement.

Turn off the screens (TV, computer, electronic games) during the week.

From doctors' appointments to expiration dates on your *carte de sejour* or passport to this year's *vacances scolaires* and *kermesse,* keep it all in one place and update immediately when a new item is scheduled. Try an Excel format to do list with pop up dates, or use Outlook, a PDA, or a plain old notebook. Whatever your system, keep it simple and make it a habit to review the list regularly.

Plan meals in advance, and try the Picard stores for quick meal ideas. (☞Shopping)

Since stores are not open on Sundays or 24h, most people do their shopping after work or on Saturdays. To avoid the crowds, try to shop at an alternative time - the hour after the store opens, and the hour before closing, are generally quieter, as is early afternoon (any day but a Saturday!).

Or consider shopping online - there is a delivery charge, but the time saved is often worth it. (☞Shopping)

Do not be a perfectionist - or a martyr - either at work or at home. Get the task at hand done "well enough", and move on, rather than wasting time being "perfect" when it is not called for. So finish the report, rather than agonizing over the wording of a footnote. And go ahead and bake some cookies with your kids, even if you have not found the perfect recipe. Both your boss and your kids will appreciate your increased productivity.

Paternity Leave (congé de paternité)

The European law introduced in 2002 makes paternity leave a legal entitlement for all fathers. The leave is 11 consecutive days (weekend included) for a single birth and 18 days for twins or more. This leave is additional to the three days family-related leave (see above). Paternity leave has to be taken within the four months following the birth, and the employer has to be notified of the dates of the leave at least one month in advance. Paternity leave is paid for by Social Security and the father receives *indemnités journalières* in the same way as the mother during her maternity leave. The benefit is equivalent to the net daily wage based on the last three pay slips within a maximum limit of €69.31 per day. Depending on the *accord collectif d'entreprise*, some companies may cover the difference.

Adoption Leave (congé d'adoption)

Adoption leave is equivalent to 10 weeks per family, 18 weeks if there are already two children in the household or 22 weeks if more than one child is being adopted at the same time. This leave is available to both the future mother and father and can either be used by one of the parents or be split and shared between the two. During the leave, the parents receive *indemnités journalières* from Social Security. At the end of the leave the same legal rights apply as for maternity leave.

Parental Leave (congé parental d'éducation)

If you have been employed at your company for at least one year prior to the birth of your baby, you are entitled to take a year's unpaid leave or switch to part-time employee status. The parental leave, which is available to the father as well as the mother, is renewable twice, ending on the child's third birthday. At the end of your leave, your company is required to return you to your original job or a similar one at an equivalent salary. You are also entitled to parental leave for any subsequent children. The leave works as described above, and ends on the youngest child's third birthday.

Part-time Status

You have the legal entitlement to work part time until your child's third birthday. Choosing part-time status requires that you reduce your working week by at least one-fifth but that you work at least 16 hours per week. The most common forms of part-time work during early motherhood are the three-day week *(le trois-cinquième)* and the four-day week *(le quatre-cinquième)*.

While on parental leave or part-time status, you may not have a second job except as a childcare worker. It is worth noting that finding part-time care for your child can be more difficult than full-time care in the regular *crèche* (nursery) system or from an official childminder *(assistante maternelle)*. Alternatives include private nursery centres, cooperative nurseries, or a mother's help (☞Childcare). As with parental leave, your absolute entitlement to work part-time ends on your child's third birthday, although most employers would not object to your continuing if the work relationship is good. Depending on your situation, you or your partner may be eligible for allowances from the *CAF (Caisse d'Allocations Familiales)* for childcare. These allowances and their restrictions can easily change so check at your local *CAF* for the latest information.

Breastfeeding at Work

Under French law, you have the right to reduce your working hours by one hour per day to breastfeed (or pump breastmilk) at work, for up to a year (half an hour in the morning and half an hour in the afternoon). If a specially equipped breastfeeding room is available, the time is reduced to 20 minutes in the morning and 20 minutes in the afternoon. The baby must be fed on the company's premises. Though the time is not required to be paid, it often is. Some *conventions collectives* provide for extended leave for breastfeeding *(congé d'allaitement)* paid by the employer at full or half salary.

For further information on your rights as a working mother consult the following sources:

Work

Code du Travail , found at
💻 www.legifrance.gouv.fr,
for basic employment laws
💻 www.caf.fr for information on family benefits
💻 www.service-public.fr for family law, including
maternity and employment law.
💻 www.ameli.fr

Service Info Emploi du Ministère de l'Emploi, du Travail et du Cohésion Sociale
0 825 347 347 (€0.15 per minute)
Mon - Fri 09h00 - 18h00

SETTING UP A BUSINESS IN FRANCE

If you have an idea for making money in France, you will need some type of business structure to cash in on your idea legally. Once you register your business, in whatever form, you will have to start paying contributions into many different organisations, including the *URSSAF* for family allowance contributions, a health insurance organisation, a retirement fund and, potentially, an additional health insurance organisation. The organisations you pay into will depend upon the legal structure you choose and the status you have in that structure. It is safe to say that approximately half of what you make will disappear in the form of regular Social Security contributions and basic overheads. What you earn will also be subject to income tax and you may also be subject to *TVA* (value added tax).

Depending on the activity you are hoping to carry out and the amount of capital investment involved, you will need to choose between setting up on your own (*entrepreneur individual*) and setting up a company.

If you set up a company, there is a distinction between your personal wealth and the company's wealth. A company will generally need more than one business associate and a minimum amount of capital. In 2003, the minimum legal capital for setting up a common form of limited company, the SARL (*société à responsabilité limitée*) was reduced from €7,500 to €1. However, if you are looking to take out a loan or want to have more credibility with suppliers, you would probably look to invest more initially.

If you set up as an individual entrepreneur, there is no distinction between your personal and your business wealth. This means that your personal belongings could be at risk if you have problems with creditors later on.

Setting Up as Entrepreneur Individuel

Setting up as an *entrepreneur individuel* is very easy to do, as it simply involves registering with your local *Centre de Formalités d'Entreprise (CFE)*. The relevant *CFE* depends on the type of professional activity: the local Chamber of Commerce and Industry *(CCI)* if your activity is a commercial one or the *URSSAF* if you have a *profession libérale* (any activity that is considered intellectual rather than commercial, from an architect to a chartered accountant or a lawyer, including the ubiquitous "consultant"). For further guidance (in French) refer to their websites at 💻www.cfe.ccip.fr or 💻www.parisrp.urssaf.fr.

You will be given a file to complete which you need to take back to the appropriate centre within eight days of beginning business. They will then ensure you are contacted by the health insurance organisation you opted for on your registration form and by the appropriate retirement fund.

Setting Up a Company

Setting up a company is more complex. You will need to decide what structure you want and what your role is to be in that structure. Your choice of company structure will determine the managerial function you can hold and the managerial function you hold will, in turn, determine your tax and Social Security regime. If you have been used to a more simple system like that in USA, the subtle differences between the different French functions and

French Company Structures - Useful Definitions

- *EURL (entreprise unique à responsabilité limitée)*: a single associate limited company
- *SARL (société à responsabilité limitée)*: a limited liability company
- *SAS (société par actions simplifié)*: a company limited by shares with a minimum capital requirement of €37,000 suitable for larger projects
- *SA (société anonyme)*: a corporation run by a Board of Directors, suitable for larger projects (only shares of an SA may be traded on the stock exchange)
- *gérant*: a manager - for Social Security purposes, a manager who owns more than 50% of the company is considered an independent worker, whilst a manager who owns less than 50% is considered a company employee.

See www.apce.com for more information regarding legal structures available in France.

their tax and Social Security implications can be daunting. The *Agence pour la Création d'Entreprise (APCE)* has a website (www.apce.com, English version available) which can help guide you through these difficulties and which offers a good amount of practical information for entrepreneurs in France.

Once you've decided on your company structure, the first stop is still your local *CFE*. Once you hand in your completed file, along with a cheque for certain formalities, it will ensure you are registered with organisations such as the INSEE *(L'Institut National de la Statistique et des Etudes Economiques)* which registers your company on a national list and attributes a special number and code to the company, the tax authorities, the *URSSAF* and the commercial court clerk *(greffe)*. Although the *CFE* does a lot of the work, you will still need to:

- where relevant, register with your professional body or obtain a licence
- draw up the bylaws or articles (*statuts*) of the company and register them with your local tax centre and commercial court
- draw up a list of acts carried out in the name of the company in the creation stage (e.g., taking out a lease or setting up a phone line) - this allows you to recover *TVA* on these expenses once the company actually exists
- open a bank account, in which you should deposit the initial capital of the company - this will remain blocked until the company is officially created
- find office space - note that the manager of certain types of company can elect for the company to be domiciled at his or her home for the first five years of existence as long as the company does not have inventory and does not receive clients
- publish notice of the creation of your company in an official newspaper such as the *Annonces de la Seine*

The file you obtain from the *CFE* explains all of this in more or less detail. You can ask for consulting time with a *CFE* adviser, but this is a paying service. Be careful about the order you do things in, as some things need to be done before others and you may then find yourself held up as you catch up on a lost step.

Your company is officially created once you have the registration paper *(Extrait Kbis)* back from the *INSEE*. You will then begin to receive regular correspondence from countless organisations, including the *URSSAF*, your health insurance organisation, your retirement fund and the tax authorities. Be careful to respond to all these official organisations by the due dates you are given to avoid penalties and complications.

Tax Concerns

The choice between individual entrepreneurship and a company may be guided by tax considerations. An individual entrepreneur is generally taxed at normal income tax rates, although special regimes can apply, depending on the type of activity. See table below.

A company is considered to have a separate legal existence to that of its owners and is taxed separately on any profit at company tax rates (around

Type of Activity	Tax Exemption
Provision of housing; purchase and sale of goods; provision of food	72% of turn-over, up to €76,300 in turn-over
Commercial (excluding above)	52% of turn-over, up to €27,000 in turn-over
Intellectual	37% of fees, up to €27,000 in fees

34%). Money is extracted from the company in the form of dividends or salary (or remuneration, in the case of managers who are also associates). The money that is extracted is taxed at your individual income tax rate and, in the case of salary and remuneration, is also subject to Social Security charges.

Monetary Aids

There are various forms of fiscal, financial and Social Security assistance for the creation of new businesses in France. The most notable one is an exemption from Social Security charges for twelve months, which can be granted in two specific cases:

Help for unemployed people setting up a business (ACCRE - aide aux chomeurs créateurs d'entreprise):
You are eligible under this exemption if you are registered as unemployed when you set up your own business. To qualify, you have to complete a detailed application form which can be obtained from your local *DDTEFP (Direction Départementale de Travail, de l'Emploi et de la Formation Professionnelle).*

Employee setting up a company:
You are eligible under this exemption if you set up a company but you also continue to work as an employee. You should check that your employment contract allows you to set up a company - it generally does, so long as the proposed activity does not compete with your current employer. To qualify you must be able to justify a minimum number of working hours in the twelve months prior to creation of your company and another minimum number in the following twelve months.

Additional information regarding monetary aids can be found on ⌨www.apce.com, which offers a database to help investors locate the kinds of assistance available.

There are many factors you need to take into account when you set up your own business and this guide is by no means exhaustive. Useful sources include the *APCE* (🖳www.apce.com), the *CFE* and any acquaintances who have set up their own business already. You should also seek legal advice on all aspects of your new venture (☞Administration for information on finding a lawyer or notary).

JOB-HUNTING

Job-hunting in Paris is easy and difficult at the same time: easy because the city has an enormous and varied job market, and difficult because there is a great deal of highly qualified competition and most non-French nationals do not speak fluent French.

Identifying Potential Employers

There are numerous places to look for a potential employer. Some of these are listed below:

- the general press, e.g., *Le Point, L'Express, Le Figaro* and *Le Monde*
- the specialised press, if you have experience in a particular skill or industry
- Chambers of Commerce, e.g., the Franco / British Chamber of Commerce, whose website 🖳www.francobritishchambers.com lists job offers.
- the Internet
- *ANPE* (French unemployment office for skilled workers)
- school or university associations
- professional associations
- job and industry salons
- your own network - it is said that 70% of jobs are found via personal networks, so make sure you build your own. Keep in touch with the people you know and put yourself in a position to meet new people.

Contacting Potential Employers

Spontaneous Applications

It is estimated that 20% to 25% of positions are filled in this way. In order to be successful some basic principals need to be respected:

- personalise your letters or e-mails, don't do impersonal mass mailings
- do your research to identify companies of interest
- be prepared for a very low response rate.

Recruitment Agencies

There are numerous recruitment agencies operating in the Paris area, some general and some specialised according to the industry or type of skill. It is possible to purchase a guide which lists them all and therefore allows more precise targeting.

A directory of a number of agencies can be found on the following web sites:
🖳 www.apr-job.com
🖳 www.netpage.tm.fr/emploi

Work

Writing Your Letter of Application

If you need to write the letter of application in French, then you need to make sure that the language is perfect. There are numerous books on the market which contain standard letters (see the Other Resources section at the end of this chapter). Though not ideal, these will help you avoid making glaring grammatical mistakes. Many French companies demand a handwritten cover letter *(lettre manuscript)*.

Writing Your CV

You will probably want to have a CV in both English and French. CVs should be adapted for the job you're applying for. Again, there are plenty of books on the marketplace which contain multiple CVs that you can copy and adapt (see the Other Resources section at the end of this chapter). An Internet service which can do this for you is www.100cv.com (paying service).

Be Realistic about Your Salary

Salaries in France are generally lower than in the UK and the USA. Try to research the salary appropriate for the job you are applying for and do not price yourself out of the market by asking for a salary based on what you were getting back home.

Patience and Perseverance

Do not expect rapid results. Most job searches take at least six months - and that without taking into account the difficulties of living in a foreign country. The whole interview process itself could take about three months.

Useful Websites

General job-hunting advice can be found at www.cyber-emploi-centre.com and practical information about the world of work in France can be found at www.pratique.fr. Both of these websites are in French.

Some basic advice in English about all sorts of issues relating to life in France can be found on www.expatica.com.

Some sites which have job offers include:
- www.cadremploi.fr
- www.cadresonline.com

Some Do's and Don'ts of French Business Etiquette

Do:

- Shake hands (optional) and say *Bonjour* (compulsory) the first time you see a work colleague during the day.
- In a meeting situation, it is expected to shake hands with everyone participating (unless you have already met them that day). Be prepared to exchange business cards.
- Use the *vous* form when addressing superiors and people you don't know, until they tell you otherwise or they use the *tu* form when addressing you.
- Try to speak a few words of French even if you're not fluent - it is always greatly appreciated.
- Call all lawyers and notaries *maître* - not Mr. or Ms. (or *maîtresse!*)

Don't:

- During the course of a business lunch, do not discuss business until dessert and coffee are served. Drinking alcohol - a glass of wine or beer - is not at all unusual over lunch.
- Do not ask work colleagues money-related questions such as their income, who they bank with, etc. These are considered highly personal questions.
- Don't expect to see any of your colleagues before 09h30 in the morning.
- Don't expect meetings to start on time.

- www.jobline.fr
- www.anpe.fr
- www.apec.asso.fr
- www.nouvelobs.com
- www.monster.fr
- www.cweb.com
- www.careerbuilder.com
- www.jobsearch.org

NETWORKING

In the Parisian professional world, networking or *cooptation* is important and job opportunities, particularly for skilled positions, are often reliant on who you know. This section aims to give you a taste of the networking opportunities which are available in the Paris area.

European Professional Women's Network (EPWN) - Paris

4, rue Galvani, 75838 Paris Cedex 17
01.39.21.94.1
- www.parispwn.net
- www.europeanpwn.net

This network of over 1,000 women is part of the European Professional Women's Network, and has sister organisations all over Europe. It offers its members workshops on professional development, potential contact with working women all over Europe via its website and an opportunity to meet peers. Activities include a series of speaker lunches, workshops on practical topics (time management, negotiation skills), an entrepreneurship training course in association with *ESCP* (a French business school), talks on management topics by *INSEAD* faculty (a graduate business school based in Fontainebleau, near Paris) and other networking opportunities. The web site is very comprehensive and much of it is open to the public. There is a members-only section featuring chat rooms, bulletin boards and a searchable directory of all members Europe-wide.

To join, you must be in a business-related position of responsibility, or looking for such a position. Members come from all over the world, and are about 50% French, 50% "other nationality". Events

are held in either French or English so in order to get the most out of your membership, it is best to have a working knowledge of French.

EPWN - Paris holds a networking evening once a month which is open to non-members. It is usually held on the last Thursday of the month at the *Nicolas* bar in place de la Madeleine and is open to all, with no reservations needed, 18h00 - 20h00. For more information on this event, and on how to join EPWN - Paris, go to their website.

LinkedIn

- www.linkedin.com

LinkedIn is a very rich and useful web tool, available to all with an Internet connection. It is a network of over a million people all over the world linked to each other by acquaintance. Once you have signed up for membership, you can invite other people you know to connect to you, which then connects you to all their contacts. In this way, you can build an online network of thousands of people very quickly.

LinkedIn provides a way to find business contacts in industries that you might not otherwise have found, which can be useful, both for job hunting and for finding new clients.

While people in all industries and business sectors

are featured, there is an especially strong USA and high technology contingent.

American University Club in France

www.aucfrance.org

The American University Club (AUC) groups dozens of USA university alumni clubs in France and gives them a platform upon which to hold events together. There are approximately 4,000 graduates of USA universities in the Ile de France area, so events draw upon a wide number of schools and nationalities. Check their website to see if your school is represented. You can sign up for activities with your own school alumni, or for AUC events including the famous American Embassy cocktail held every spring.

Business Development Network International

Parc Croix-Marie
4, avenue des Jonchères, 78121 Crespières
01.30.54.94.67
This network is made up of around 400 small busi-

nesses, consultants and entrepreneurs. Both French and English are spoken.

For other, non-professional organisations which may lead to networking opportunities ☞Organisations and Charities. For instance, MESSAGE has a Working Mothers' Group for its members that organises meetings, such as regular networking lunches, all over the Paris area.

OTHER RESOURCES

Vital Issues - How to Survive Officialdom While Living in France

(Association of American Wives of Europeans (AAWE))

www.aaweparis.org (order forms can be downloaded)

Living & Working in Franc - Chez vous en France

Geneviève Brame (Kogan Page)

Culture Shock! Living & Working in Paris

Frances Gendlin (Kuperard (London))

Welcome to France

Claude Michel (Relocation Net)

Droits des Femmes

Françoise Dekeuwer-Defossez (Dalloz)

J'attends un enfant

Laurence Pernoud, Agnès Grison (Horay)

Le Guide du CV et de la Recherche d'emploi, 2005

Nicolas Barrier (First)

100 modèles de lettres de motivation

Elodie Thivard, Camille Fontaine (Studyrama, 3rd Ed.)

OTHER VOCABULARY

advance notice. . . . . *un préavis*
advertisements. . . . . *les annonces*
application letter. . . . . *une lettre d'accompagnement*
availability (e.g. to work) . . . . *la disponibilité*
bonus . . . . *une prime*
childcare. . . . . *la garde d'enfants*
civil servant . . . . *un/e fonctionnaire*
classifieds . . . . *les petites annonces*
collective bargaining agreement . . . . *la convention collective*
computer science. . . . . *l'informatique*
continuing education . . . . *la formation continue*
contributions to social security. . . . . *les cotisations*
cv/resume . . . . *un résumé*
declaration of employment. . . . . *une attestation de travail*
employee benefits . . . . *les avantages sociaux*
employment agency (public) . . . . *ANPE (agence nationale pour l'emploi)*
employment agency (for managers, public) . . . . *APEC (association pour l'emploi des cadres)*
executive . . . . *un cadre*
full-time work . . . . *le travail à plein temps*
gross/net salary . . . . *le salaire brut/net*
headhunter. . . . . *un chasseur de têtes*
human resources director . . . . *le directeur des ressources humaines (DRH)*
human resources. . . . . *les ressources humaines*
independent consultant . . . . *un travailleur indépendant*
internship . . . . *un stage*
interview. . . . . *un entretien*
personal skills inventory. . . . . *un bilan personnel*
professional skills inventory . . . . *un bilan des compétences*
job application . . . . *le dossier de candidature*
job offer . . . . *un offre d'emploi*
job transfer. . . . . *une mutation*
management . . . . *la gestion*
maternity leave. . . . . *le congé de maternité*
meeting . . . . *un rendez-vous*
merchants/retailers . . . . *les commerçants*
minimum wage. . . . . *SMIC (salaire minimum interprofessionnel de croissance)*
non-profit organisation . . . . *organisation à but non lucratif*
overtime. . . . . *les heures supplémentaires*
paid leave. . . . . *les congés payés*
parental leave . . . . *le congé parentale*
part-time work . . . . *le travail à temps partiel*
paternity leave . . . . *le congé de paternité*

Work

pay slip	un bulletin de paie (or une fiche de paie)
payment (for work)	la rémunération
profession (i.e. line of work)	un métier
profession (such as medicine, law,...)	une profession libérale
professional experience	l'expérience professionnelle
professional objective	objectif professionnel
receptionist	une réceptionniste
references	les références
registered mail, return receipt requested	courrier recommandé avec accusé de réception
retirement / pension	la retraite
salaried employee	un salarié
salary expectation	les prétentions
sales representative	un agent commercial
secretary	un/e secrétaire
seniority	l'ancienneté
shareholder	un associé
sick leave	arrêt de travail
social charges (withholdings)	les charges sociales
supplemental health insurance	une mutuelle
temporary work	l'intérim
to dismiss, fire	licencier
to hire	embaucher
to resign	donner sa démission
trade show	un salon professionnel
training / education	la formation
translator (court sworn)	un traducteur (assermenté or juré)
trial period	période d'essai
unemployment insurance agency	ASSEDIC
unemployment payments	l'allocation de chômage
unemployment	le chômage
union	le syndicat
unsolicited job application	une candidature spontanée
work contract (long-term, permanent)	CDI (le contrat à durée indéterminée)
work contract (short-term, temporary)	CDD (le contrat à durée déterminée)
work contract	le contrat d'emploi (or contrat de travail)
work hours	les horaires
work permit	permis de travail

At the office

adding machine	une machine à calculer
binder	un classeur
briefcase	un porte-documents
calculator	une calculatrice
computer	un ordinateur
copy machine	une machine à photocopier
desk, office	un bureau

diary	*un agenda*
electronic mail (email)	*le courrier électronique (l'e-mail)*
fax machine	*un télécopieur*
file folder	*une chemise*
file	*un dossier*
filing cabinet	*un classeur*
highlighter	*un surligneur*
inbox	*le courrier arrivé*
outbox	*le courrier départ*
paper	*le papier*
paperclip	*un trombone*
pen	*un stylo*
pencil	*un crayon*
piece of paper	*une feuille de papier*
printer (ink jet)	*une imprimante à jet d'encre*
printer (laser)	*une imprimante laser*
software	*un logiciel*
staple	*une agrafe*
stapler	*une agrafeuse*
telephone	*une téléphone*
to email	*adresser un e-mail*
typewriter	*une machine à écrire*
voicemail	*la boite vocale*

Work

Notes

Index

Index

Advertiser:	See Ad Under:
A Good Start in France	Relocation Services
Alain Azambuja, Family Portraits Photography	Special Occasions
American Hospital of Paris	Health Services
American Library in Paris	Activities
Association Suryoma	Fitness/Well-Being
Avenue des Anges	Shopping
Bébé Au Lait	Shopping
The Book Fountain	Shopping
Brentano's	Shopping
Centre de Yoga du Marais	Fitness/Well-Being
CoreBody Centre Pilates	Fitness/Well-Being
Delahaye Movers	Relocation Services
L'École Aujourd'hui	Education
École Everest	Education
Ecole Internationale Malherbe	Education
Emily McKoane Borel, Certified Shiatsu Practitioner	Fitness/Well-Being
First Steps	Activities
Forest International School	Education
French Property Managers	Relocation Services
Gymboree	Activities
The Hertford British Hospital/Hôpital Franco-Brittanique	Health Services
ICS International Counseling Service	Health Services
Inspiration Air Purifiers	Shopping
International Montessori School	Education
Kaplan Test Prep and Admissions	Education
Ludimax	Activities
MamaNANA	Shopping
Margaret Lanzenberg, Education Consultant	Education
Marymount School	Eduaction
MESSAGE Mother Support Group	Associations; Family Orgs.
MyBoulangerie.com	Shopping
La Petite École Montessori	Education
Sections Internationales de Sèvres	Education
Sing and Play	Activities
SOS Helpline	Health Services
St. George's Anglican Church	Places of Worship
St. Louis/Notre Dame du Bel Air	Education
Stuart Boreham, Natural Portraits Photography	Special Occasions
Tracy's Treats	Special Occasions
Unitarian Universalist Fellowship of Paris	Places of Worship
WHSmith	Activities

Helpful Services

Helpful Services

Zac du Trianon
rue de la Pépinière
78450 VILLEPREUX
Tel: 01 72 33 90 90 www.ludimax.fr

Ouvert tous les jours de 10h00 à 18h00
Fermé les mardis scolaires.
Entrée: € 7.00 par enfant 2 ans et plus
€ 2.50 en dessous de 2 ans,
Bébés et parents GRATUITS

SING AND PLAY

- Playgroups for children from 18 months and up (in English or in French)
- Music, musical movement, art or drama workshops for children (in English)
- English, French, Spanish, Italian (etc…) classes for children or adults (all levels)
- Special French courses for children with 1 or 2 parents
- Drama or art classes for adults (in French or in English) etc.

Small groups in several cultural centres in Paris, in schools and at your home

WE CREATE WORKSHOPS ACCORDING TO YOUR NEEDS

Please phone: Eliane Delage, Phd: 01 45 56 96 09
Or email sing21st@aol.com www.geocities.com/singandplay_21st

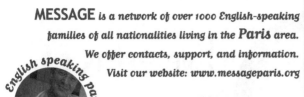

Everest is :

A school for your child !

➤ A bilingual school based on the principle "one person, one language ", the English teacher speaks only in English to her students and the French teacher speaks only in French.

➤ The timetable is equally distributed: half-time in one language and half-time in the other language

➤ Stimulating activities in well-equipped facilities (gym and playing court)

➤ Catholic - oriented education

➤ small groups which enable the teachers to give personal attention to each child.

Tuition: 300€ per month
Canteen and after-school child care program

Métro : Porte de Saint Cloud
20 rue Henri Martin 92100 Boulogne Billancourt
01 46 08 54 91
info@ecoleeverest.com   www.ecoleeverest.com

Marymount School
72, bd de la Saussaye
92200 Neuilly-sur-Seine
Tel: 01 46 24 93 25
Fax: 01 46 24 93 26

Email: admissions@marymount.fr
Website: www.marymount.fr
Headmistress: Sr. Anne Marie Hill

Marymount is a Catholic school which accepts children of all nationalities and faiths. Marymount follows an American curriculum and is open to boys and girls, from Pre-kindergarten (age 4) through Grade 8 (age 14).

Students benefit from a nurturing environment, an international school community, small class sizes, state-of-the-art facilities, and a rigorous, modern curriculum.

Special aid is offered to students through the Learning Support Services department.

Marymount School is accredited by the Middle States Association of Schools and Colleges and by the Council of International Schools (CIS).

The school is part of a worldwide network of Marymount schools in Fatima, Lisbon, London, Los Angeles, Medellin, New York, Porto, and Rome.

International Montessori School

- Versailles
- Bilingual Montessori class for 2 ½ to 6 years old.
- Full-time qualified Montessori teachers in both English and French.
- Extra activities: pony lessons (Haras de jardy), music, art and cooking.
- For more information contact Rachael Olanié Tel. 06 86 17 63 80

imschool@numericable.fr

Helpful Services

Helpful Services

Helpful Services

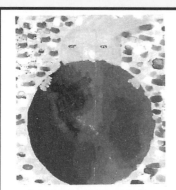
Helpful Services

Helpful Services

Helpful Services

Helpful Services

The Maternity Unit
of the American Hospital of Paris

Safety

Rigorously selected and accredited obstetricians-gynecologists, pediatric physicians specialized in neonatology, pediatric nurses and nurse midwives work together to make sure that you and your baby receive the safest, best care possible.

Pain Management

Highly trained anesthesiologists are mobilized to fight against pain during childbirth (epidural or spinal anesthesia) and postnatal, especially after a Caesarean section.

Personalized Care

Our 18-bed Maternity Unit (rooms or suites) with private bathrooms, television, WIFI, room service, beauticians, estheticians, air conditioning, valets and more are available for you, ensuring a comfortable stay.

We care about you.
American Hospital of Paris

63, Bd Victor Hugo • 92200 Neuilly sur Seine • Tel. : 01 46 41 25 25
www.american-hospital.org

Helpful Services

Helpful Services

Helpful Services

Helpful Services

Helpful Services

Helpful Services

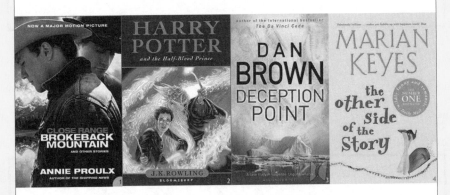

Family Portraits with an Artist's Touch...

"If you're looking for something different, whether portraits by a monument or shots in a favourite garden, I can help!"

Paris is such a beautiful city to shoot in - there are fabulous shots to be had everywhere you look, from the famous landmarks to Parisian corners.

Our business in London shoots exclusively for the ex-pat community - we are well known for natural relaxed pictures that show the character of families and the life of the kids in their environment.

Pictures can be taken at your home or on location. The session is fun, stress free and the shots will reflect that. The family can be themselves and I'll work with them to ensure everyone gets the most from the shoot - sometimes even Dads enjoy it!

I travel over for weekend and evening sessions, so to get a better feel for my work check out our website - **www.NaturalPortraits.net**, e-mail me or call my Paris agent to find out more. Meanwhile, enjoy France!

01.47.66.49.09 / +44 1932 563318
stuart@boreham.co.uk   www.NaturalPortraits.net

Helpful Services

My Important Numbers

Notes

ABC's of Parenting in Paris

5th edition

A mother support group publication

The essential guide to survive and thrive with children in the French capital

Researched and written by a team of MESSAGE members and reviewed by professionals, the ABCs of Parenting in Paris has been completely revised and updated.

With dozens of contributions from parents living and working in the great French capital, the ABCs of Parenting in Paris is your essential guide for navigating the ins and outs of raising a family in Paris.

Filled with insiders' tips, practical information and detailed descriptions on parenting topics such as :

- child-friendly establishments
- schooling
- rainy-day activities
- employment in France
- pre-natal services
- and a variety of legal and administrative matters,

The 5th Edition ABC's of Parenting in Paris is a complete, up-to-date manual that puts the answers you need at your fingertips.

The ABC's of Parenting in Paris is an absolute "must" for anyone living – or contemplating life in Paris with a family. Even if you've been in Paris for years – with or without children – you're sure to learn something new.

ABCs of Parenting
in Paris

To order an additional copy, fill in the order form on the right side and send it, with your cheque, to :

ABCs Orders, 20, Ave. Leonard de Vinci, 92400 Courbevoie

Contact treasurer@messageparis.org for shipping costs outside France and/or the option of paying by PayPal.
Send any other queries, including regarding bulk orders, to : abcsales@messageparis.org.
Your comments and feedback on the 5th Edition ABCs of Parenting in Paris are welcome, and should go to abc@messageparis.org.

ABC's of Parenting in Paris

5th edition

Order Form – MESSAGE members / individuals
Shipping to France

I'd like to order _____ (quantity) copy (ies) of

ABCs of Parenting in Paris
A MESSAGE Mother Support Group publication

I enclose my cheque in euros, drawn from my French bank account and made out to :

MESSAGE Mother Support Group

for the following amount :

(tick box)

☐ MESSAGE
Members : 20 euros x _____ n° of copies = _____ euros TOTAL
16 euros + 4 euros p&p = vingt euros

☐ Non-Members : 25 euros x _____ n° of copies = _____ euros TOTAL
21 euros + 4 euros p&p = vingt-cinq euros

Please send my copy (ies) to me as follows :

NAME : _____

ADDRESS : _____

Telephone Number : _____

E-mail : _____

I heard about the ABCs of Parenting in Paris through :

☐ www.messageparis.org   ☐ The MESSAGE Magazine   ☐ Poster/Brochure
☐ Advertisement   ☐ Word of Mouth   ☐ A Book Seller/Store
☐ Other (please specify) _____

Send this form with your cheque to :

**ABCs Orders
20, Ave. Leonard de Vinci
92400 Courbevoie**

ABCs of Parenting
in Paris